GIVING ONE'S WORD

GIVING ONE'S WORD

*Psychological Analogy
as Social Analogy in
Aquinas's Trinitarian Theology*

MICHAEL JOSEPH HIGGINS

The Catholic University of America Press
Washington, D.C.

Copyright © 2025
The Catholic University of America Press

Portions of chapters 4 and 7 are revised from
"The Family as an Image of the Trinity in Aquinas."
Communio: International Catholic Review 49, no. 2 (Summer 2022): 99–330.
Portions of chapter 5 are revised from "Aquinas on the Role of Another
in Perfect Self-Knowledge." *Modern Theology* 38, no. 1 (2022): 19–35.
Used with permission.

All rights reserved

The paper used in this publication meets the minimum requirements
of American National Standards for Information Science—
Permanence of Paper for Printed Library Materials, ANSI Z39.48-1992.

Cataloging-in-Publication Data available from the Library of Congress

ISBN: 978-0-8132-3948-4
eISBN: 978-0-8132-3949-1

Text is set in Academy Engraved LET, Adobe Garamond Pro, and Goudy Oldstyle.
Book design by Burt&Burt

To Michael:

The word of my heart,

the splendor of the Father

CONTENTS

Acknowledgments IX
Abbreviations XI

INTRODUCTION 1
Social or Psychological? 4
Social and Psychological 11
What We'll Do 14
How We'll Do It 16
What We Won't Do 19

PART I

1   A GOING-FORTH THAT REMAINS WITHIN 31
Word and Love 34
A Going-Forth That Remains Within 39
"The Word Goes Forth from the Heart and Remains Therein" 47
The History of the Word 50
Whence the Word? 57

2   A STANDING-OUTSIDE THAT REMAINS WITHIN 67
Immanently Proceeding, Distinctly Subsisting 71
"Not in Another" 75
Inside as Outside 86
"This Distinction Excels All Distinctions" 96

3   OUTSIDE BECAUSE INSIDE 103
One, Therefore Many 104
SCG IV, Ch. 11 108
"He Was in the Beginning with God" 126

PART II

4 IMMANENT PROCESSION AS TOTAL SELF-GIVING ... 135
  The Principles 141
  The Passages 148
  A Family Trinity and Self-Diffusive Goodness 163

5 SELF-KNOWLEDGE AS INTERPERSONAL KNOWLEDGE AS INTERPERSONAL SELF-GIVING 183
  In the Beginning Was the Word 188
  In the Word Was Understanding 194
  Understanding Oneself in Another 203
  Understanding Another in Oneself 211
  As Other 216
  Understanding Another, Understanding Oneself, Giving Oneself 218

6 SELF-LOVE AS INTERPERSONAL LOVE AS INTERPERSONAL COMMUNION AS INTERPERSONAL SELF-GIVING AS INTERPERSONAL BEING-GIVEN 223
  Self-Love as Interpersonal Love 228
  Self-Love as Mutual Love 236
  Self-Love as Interpersonal Love as Interpersonal Communion as Interpersonal Self-Giving 243
  Self-Love as Interpersonal Love as Interpersonal Communion as Interpersonal Self-Giving as Interpersonal Being-Given 249
  Essential Love 252

7 THE IMAGE OF GOD 263
  Knowing and Loving Another in Knowing and Loving Oneself 265
  Intimate Indwelling, Infinite Distance, Interpersonal Giving 267
  Self-Giving 269
  "Given to Us by the Father and the Son" 271
  "All Fellow Men" 273

  Conclusion 275
  Bibliography 277
  Index 295

ACKNOWLEDGMENTS

Almost all of the insights in this book emerged while I was a student at the John Paul II Institute for Studies on Marriage and Family, and it is unlikely that I would have seen any of them had I not been nourished by the vision of the Institute and by the example of my teachers there. Equally important were friendships with fellow students. Thanks especially to Michael Camacho, James Stanley, and Erik van Versendaal for hours upon hours of lifegiving conversation that have borne endless fruit, and to which this book owes a great deal.

Much of the actual writing of this book has happened since I began my time at the St. Jerome Institute. I am grateful every day to belong to a community where all things are centered in and shaped by Christ, where the intellectual life is nurtured and celebrated, and where the tradition is handed down with so much joy, integrity, and creativity. My own writing and thinking have benefited immensely from my being immersed in such an environment. Thanks to my colleagues and students for making it a reality. Special thanks to Peter Crawford and Andrew Shivone for encouraging my scholarly pursuits, for captaining the Good Ship SJI through its crucial early years, and for bringing us deeper into the embrace of Christ Who takes all thought captive to Himself.

Finally, the greatest debt of gratitude is owed to my family. Thanks to my parents for supporting me every step of the way. Thanks to my children for showing me the face of God every day. Thanks most of all to Amanda, in whom all my words find their center: nothing could be written without you, and, if it were, it would be empty and vain.

ABBREVIATIONS

See the bibliography for English translations of Aquinas I have used. I have, however, modified those translations where appropriate. Emphasis is added in all passages from Thomas throughout this study.

Works by Thomas Aquinas

Cat. Aur. in Matt.	*Catena aurea in quatuor Evangelia Expositio in Matthaeum*
Comp. Theo.	*Compendium theologiae seu Brevis compilatio theologiae ad fratrem Raynaldum*
contra impugnantes	*Liber contra impugnantes Dei cultum et religionem*
de 108 art.	*Responsio ad magistrum Ioannem de Vercellis de 108 articulis*
de decem praeceptis	*Collationes in decem praeceptis*
De Malo	*Quaestiones disputatae de malo*
de perfectione	*De perfectione spiritualis vitae*
De Pot.	*Quaestiones disputatae de potentia*
de rationibus fidei	*De rationibus fidei ad Cantorem Antiochenum*
de sensu et sensato	*Sentencia libri De sensu et sensato cuius secundus tractatus est De memoria et reminiscencia*
De Ver.	*Quaestiones disputatae de veritate*
de virtutibus	*Quaestiones disputatae de virtutibus*
in psalmos	*In psalmos Davidis expositio*

in Boeth. de Trin.	*Super Boetium De Trinitate*
in Col.	*Super Epistolam B. Pauli ad Colossenses lectura*
in I Cor.	*Super I Epistolam B. Pauli ad Corinthios lectura*
in II Cor.	*Super II Epistolam B. Pauli ad Corinthios lectura*
in de anima	*Sententia Libri de anima*
in Eph.	*Super Epistolam B. Pauli ad Ephesios lectura*
in div. nom.	*In librum Beati Dionysii De divinis nominibus expositio*
in Gal.	*Super Epistolam B. Pauli ad Galatas lectura*
in Heb.	*Super Epistolam B. Pauli ad Hebraeos lectura*
in Ioan.	*Super Evangelium S. Ioannis lectura*
in Iob.	*Expositio super Iob ad litteram*
in Matt.	*Super Evangelium S. Matthaei lectura*
in Metap.	*In duodecim libros Metaphysicorum Aristotelis expositio*
in Rom.	*Super Epistolam B. Pauli ad Romanos lectura*
in Symb. Apost.	*In Symbolum Apostolorum, scilicet "Credo in Deum" expositio*
LR	*Lectura Romana in primum Sententiarum Petri Lombardi*
Quodl. V	*Quaestiones de quolibet*
SCG	*Summa contra Gentiles*
Sent.	*Scriptum super libros Sententiarum*
ST	*Summa theologiae*
Super Decretalem	*Expositio super primam et secundam Decretalem ad Archdiaconum Tudertinum*

Works by Gilles Emery, OP

TA	*Trinity in Aquinas.* Ypsilanti, MI: Sapientia Press of Ave Maria University, 2003.
TCHP	*Trinity, Church, and the Human Person: Thomistic Essays.* Naples, FL: Sapientia Press of Ave Maria University, 2007.
TTTA	*The Trinitarian Theology of St. Thomas Aquinas.* Translated by Francesca Murphy. Oxford: Oxford University Press, 2007.

INTRODUCTION

God is Love.

God is three Persons, each of Whom loves the others, each of Whom knows the others, and each of Whom shares all He has with the others. God is the superabundant fullness of interpersonal intimacy and of interpersonal communion, of interpersonal distinction and interpersonal encounter, and of interpersonal knowledge and interpersonal love: God is the eternal act of giving the whole of oneself to another and of welcoming the whole of another into the depths of one's heart. God is not an impersonal force or presence. God is not an unknowable apophatic question mark. God is not a single person delighting in Himself in splendid—or not so splendid—isolation. God is Love.

That's what it means that God is Trinity: it means that God is Love.

Or at least that's what a lot of Trinitarian theologians have said recently. Such thinkers are often labelled "social Trinitarians," and they are generally associated with the "Trinitarian Revivals" that swept through the second half of the twentieth century.[1] These thinkers varied

---

1 For background information on social Trinitarians, see Thomas McCall and Michael C. Rea, introduction to *Philosophical and Theological Essays on the Trinity*, ed. Thomas McCall and Michael C. Rea, 1–18 (Oxford: Oxford University Press, 2009); and Gijsbert van den Brink, "Social Trinitarianism: A Discussion of Some Recently Theological Criticisms," *The International Journal of Systematic Theology* 16, no. 3 (2014): 331–50. For a critical assessment, see Karen Kilby, "Perichoresis and Projection," *New Blackfriars* 81 (2000): 432–45; and Kathryn Tanner, "Social Trinitarianism and Its Critics," in *Rethinking*

greatly. Yet they almost all argued that the best way to approach the Trinity is by reflecting on human community. For social Trinitarians, when we say that the Father, the Son, and the Holy Spirit are "three Persons in one nature," we mean that each is a distinct Person—much like you are one person and I am a second person—Who are seamlessly united by perfect love. The best window we have into the Trinity, therefore, is human love and intimacy. If you want to understand the Trinity, then look to the intimacy of human friendships; look to the love of a human family; look to the communion of believers in the Church.

Do not, however, look to an individual human mind. And, whatever you do, do not look to an individual mind as it reflects on itself. Do not look to self-knowledge, self-love, or self-possession. And so, do not look too closely at the Trinitarian theology of St. Thomas Aquinas.

Social Trinitarianism, after all, is not the only theological framework on offer. Instead, before the recent surge of the social, the "psychological analogy" for the Trinity had long carried the day in Western theology.[2] According to social Trinitarians, Western theologians had long eschewed talk of interpersonal relationships and reciprocity: fearing that such language would put asunder the unity of the divine essence, they narrowed their sights to the confines of their own minds. They argued that just as I remain a single substance in my three acts of remembering myself, knowing myself, and loving myself, so God remains a single substance in the three Persons of Father, Son, and Holy Spirit; or, just as my concept of myself and my love for myself remain within me as I know myself and love myself, so the Son and the Holy

---

Trinitarian Theology, ed. Giulio Maspero and Robert J. Wozniak, 368–86 (New York: Continuum, 2012). For background information on the Trinitarian Revivals, see *Les sources du renouveau de la théologie trinitarie au XXe siècle,* ed. Emmanuel Durand and Vincent Holzer (Paris: Cerf, 2008); *Les realizations du renouveau de la théologie trinitarie au XXe siècle,* ed. Emmanuel Durand and Vincent Holzer (Paris: Cerf, 2010); and Sarah Coakley, "Afterword: 'Relational Ontology,' Trinity, and Science," in *The Trinity and an Entangled World,* ed. John Polkinghorne, 184–99 (Grand Rapids, MI: Eerdmans, 2010). Again, for a critical assessment, see Stephen R. Holmes, *The Quest for the Trinity* (Downers Grove, IL: InterVarsity Press, 2012). For some prominent Revivalist voices who were skeptical of social Trinitarianism, see Coakley, "Afterword," 188.

[2] For the role that talk of the "Latin West" played in the Trinitarian Revivals, see Glenn D. Butner, "For and Against de Régnon: Trinitarianism East and West," *International Journal of Systematic Theology* 17, no. 4 (2015): 399–412.

Spirit remain within the divine essence as the Father knows Himself and loves Himself. Human community and interpersonal love have nothing to do with it.

The first to propose such a psychological Trinity was Augustine.[3] And, accordingly, a great deal of blame for the psychological turn was laid at Augustine's feet.[4] Yet Augustine was not alone. He had a whole Latin Tradition's worth of colluders—chief among whom was Aquinas. Indeed, talk of an "Augustinian-Thomistic" model sometimes became shorthand for the tradition social Trinitarians were trying to overcome.[5] At times, Aquinas even came in for the harshest treatment. For Augustine may have given the West its psychological framework, yet he also offered at least periodic nods towards the social. The *De Trinitate* itself contains such gems as, "[if we want to see the Trinity,] the only thing we really have to see is what true love is," for "love means someone loving and something loved with love. There you are with three, the lover, what is being loved, and love."[6] Not so Aquinas. His *Summa Theologiae* is psychological through and through. If Augustine invented the psychological analogy, then Aquinas perfected it—and he thereby cemented its hold on the West, closing off any stray avenues towards the interpersonal that Augustine may have left open.[7]

---

3 Even here, the regnant narrative missed some important nuances. For the presence of "psychological" language in thinkers from the "Greek East" (some of whom preceded Augustine), see John T. Slotemaker, "Peter Lombard and the *imago Trinitatis*," in *A Companion to Medieval Christian Humanism*, ed. John P. Bequette, 169–70 (Leiden: Brill, 2016). For some basic background on the psychological analogy in Augustine, see Cheuk Yin Yam and Anthony Dupont, "A Mind-Centered Approach of the '*Imago Dei*': A Dynamic Construction in Augustine's '*De Trinitate*' XIV," *Augustiniana* 62 (2012): 7–43.

4 See, for example, Joshua McNall, *A Free Corrector: Colin Gunton and the Legacy of Augustine* (Minneapolis: Fortress Press, 2015). For an overview of the criticisms levelled at the psychological analogy more generally, see Neil Ormerod, "The Psychological Analogy for the Trinity: At Odds with Modernity," *Pacifica* 14, no. 3 (2001): 281–94.

5 See, for example, Anne Hunt, "Psychological Analogy and Paschal Mystery in Trinitarian Theology," *Theological Studies* 59, no. 2 (1998): 200.

6 *De Trinitate*, trans. Edmund Hill (Hyde Park, NY: New City Press, 1991), 253–55.

7 Joseph Ratzinger offers this judgement in "Concerning the Notion of Person in Theology," *Communio: International Catholic Review* 17, no. 3 (1990): 454n12. See also William Hasker, *Metaphysics and the Tri-Personal God* (Oxford: Oxford University Press, 2013), 40–49 (where he argues that Augustine, despite his psychological analogy, is "pro-Social"), and 36–39, 52–53, 109–10 (where he is less nuanced towards Aquinas).

SOCIAL OR PSYCHOLOGICAL?

Most social Trinitarians bought into this social-versus-psychological scheme. Some even believed that if a social Trinity is to hold sway, then the psychological analogy must be swept into the dust heap of history. So away they swept. Peter C. Phan, in his outline of contemporary Trinitarian theology, writes that "Leonardo Boff, John Zizioulas, and Catherine M. LaCugna among others . . . would jettison the whole psychological conceptual apparatus and adopt a social model which favors interpersonal relationships."[8] Among such "others," we might mention Colin Gunton, for whom the psychological analogy ends in divine "individualism."[9] Particularly bellicose was Jürgen Moltmann, who links the psychological analogy to the baleful "development of individualism, and especially 'possessive individualism,' in the Western world."[10] For Gunton and Moltmann, a psychological God is not a community; He is a mere individual. And so much the worse for a psychological God.

More diplomatic, but no less decisive in his judgment, was Wolfhart Pannenberg. He wrote that,

> a psychological interpretation ultimately involves a reduction to nontrinitarian monotheism. For all the differentiation in the self-consciousness, the God of this understanding is a single subject. The moments in this self-consciousness have no subjectivity of their own. From the very outset, then, those who take this line have difficulty with the dogma that there are three persons or hypostases in the one God. . . . Attempts to find self-subsistent relations for the Son and

---

[8] "Systematic Issues in Trinitarian Theology," in *The Cambridge Companion to the Trinity*, ed. Peter C. Phan (Cambridge: Cambridge University Press, 2011), 18 and 27n22.

[9] See Gunton, *The Promise of Trinitarian Theology* (Edinburgh: T&T Clark, 1997), 42–48. For more on Gunton, see McNall, *A Free Corrector*, 87; and Travis Ables, *Incarnational Realism: Trinity and the Spirit in Augustine and Barth* (London: Bloomsbury T&T Clark, 2013), 19–21.

[10] *The Trinity and the Kingdom of God*, trans. Margaret Kohl (Minneapolis: Fortress, 1993), 198–99.

Spirit rather than relations merely in the Father remained artificial in the context of the psychological model.[11]

Zeroing in on Thomas, Pannenberg writes that in Aquinas's "psychological model," "[r]elations or persons in God can only be conceptually distinct."[12] In Aquinas's God, real distinction is not merely reduced to different elements within a single Person's mind. Instead, there is no *real* distinction in Aquinas's God at all.

These social Trinitarians held sway through the end of the twentieth century. Yet even in their heyday, they did not go unchallenged. Indeed, some of the godfathers of the Trinitarian Revivals distanced themselves from what they saw as the tritheistic tendency in social Trinitarianism.[13] Most important for us is Karl Rahner, who was convinced that "within the Trinity, there is no reciprocal 'Thou,'"[14] and who held that there is "properly no mutual love between the Father and Son."[15] Rahner was certainly not above criticizing Aquinas.[16] He was even critical of Aquinas's psychological analogy.[17] Yet, when he went about constructing his own Trinitarian theology, he sometimes did so along psychological lines.[18] Rahner's psychological analogy is

---

[11] *Systematic Theology*, trans. Geoffrey W. Bromiley (Grand Rapids, MI: Eerdmans, 1991), 1:295.

[12] *Systematic Theology*, 295n122.

[13] See Angel Cordovilla Pérez, "The Trinitarian Concept of Person," in *Rethinking Trinitarian Theology*, 124–25.

[14] *The Trinity*, trans. Joseph Doncell (New York: Herder and Herder, 2010), 76n130.

[15] *The Trinity*, 106.

[16] See Timothy L. Smith, *Thomas Aquinas's Trinitarian Theology: A Study in Theological Method* (Washington, DC: The Catholic University of America Press, 2003), 1–11.

[17] See Jeremy Daniel Wilkins, "Method, Order, and Analogy in Trinitarian Theology: Karl Rahner's Critique of the 'Psychological' Approach," *The Thomist* 74, no. 4 (2010): 563–92.

[18] In *The Trinity*, Rahner argues that we can "connect, in a special and specific way, the intra-divine procession of the Logos from the Father with God's knowledge, and the procession of the Spirit from the Father through the Son with God's love" (116). He also "affirm[s] this mutual ordination of 'generation' and knowledge on the one hand, of 'spiration' of the Spirit and love on the other hand" (*The Trinity*, 117). On page 119, he writes that "we may build a psychological theology of the Trinity," but he distances himself from the "classic" psychological analogy. For a nuanced assessment of the place of psychological language in Rahner, see Travis Ables, "A Pneumatology of Christian

neither Augustine's psychological analogy nor Aquinas's psychological analogy. Yet, over against the dominant social tenor of the time, Rahner was willing at least sometimes to frame his Trinity in some sort of psychological terms.

For all his differences with social Trinitarians, however, Rahner seems to share a key assumption with the most strident of them: he seems to assume that a psychological Trinity has no room for interpersonal love, intimacy, or reciprocity. Based on this assumption, social Trinitarians eschewed the psychological and embraced the social. Based on the same assumption, Rahner took the opposite path: he kept his distance from the social and he carved out space for the psychological. Yet, like social Trinitarians, Rahner assumed that to opt for a psychological Trinity is to reject a social Trinity.

Other thinkers were more subtle. Indeed, some contemporary figures who might be grouped—at least loosely—with social Trinitarians extended an olive branch to the psychological analogy. Hans Urs von Balthasar, for example, writes of "two Trinitarian models whose common feature is to point upward toward an integration that cannot be achieved from within the horizon of the world. The interpersonal model cannot attain the substantial unity of God, whereas the intrapersonal model cannot give an adequate picture of the real and abiding face-to-face encounter of the hypostases."[19] For Balthasar, the "interpersonal" approach of a social analogy and the "intrapersonal" approach of a psychological analogy are not incompatible; they are complementary. Each has its place, and each can supply for the failings of the other. Indeed, each must be held in tension with the other if either would do justice to the paradox of the Trinity.

This second group of thinkers went a good deal further than most of their peers. Indeed, by refusing to pit the social against the psychological,

---

Knowledge: The Holy Spirit and the Performance of the Mystery of God in Augustine and Barth" (PhD diss., Vanderbilt University, 2010), 24–29 and 38.

19 *Theo-logic II*, trans. Adrian J. Walker (San Francisco: Ignatius, 2004), 38. See also Balthasar, *Theo-Drama III*, trans. Graham Harrison (San Francisco: Ignatius, 1992), 526–27; Maurice Nedoncelle, "L'intersubjectivité humaine est-elle pour saint Augustin une image de la Trinité?," in *Augustinus Magister* I (Paris, 1954), 595–602; and Marc Ouellet, *Divine Likeness: Toward a Trinitarian Anthropology of the Family* (Grand Rapids, MI: Eerdmans, 2006), 20–25.

they helped prepare the way for this study. We can therefore receive their work with gratitude. Yet, even here, a certain opposition—or, perhaps better, a juxtaposition—of the social to the psychological remains. Balthasar may propose a certain complementarity. Yet it is the complementarity of fragments: Balthasar gives us two pieces that fit together at their outermost edges but remain extrinsic to each other. Each begins where the other ends. Turning to Aquinas, these thinkers tended to be more open to his Trinitarian theology. Yet, after assuming a basic divide between the psychological and the social, they located him squarely on the side of the psychological: they assumed that because he emphasizes the intrapersonal in God, he leaves the interpersonal undeveloped.[20]

A handful of contemporary Thomists, however, have complicated the regnant reading of Aquinas. They have shown that, for all Thomas's psychological language, he is willing to speak of the Trinity in strikingly social terms. Michael Waldstein led the way here by calling attention to a number of passages where Thomas speaks of interpersonal love and self-giving within the eternal Trinity.[21] Yet, even as Waldstein highlights these passages, he admits that "the only unfolded theological account of the Trinity which [Thomas] gives is that first elaborated by St. Augustine, which makes use of [the] processions [of word and love] within one human person to approach the mystery of the Trinity."[22] Waldstein does not deny that Thomas's Trinity is first of all psychological. He merely points out that, alongside his fully developed psychological analogy, there are also "a number of passages in his work" where Thomas offers "an alternate account of the Trinity in terms of *interpersonal* relations."[23] This alternate approach, however, is limited to

---

[20] As Balthasar puts it, "A Thomistic system ... suffers from the same difficulty that the whole psychological starting point of the Augustinian school does of not being able to make the relations in the innermost core of the divine substance meaningful in terms of the relations between the Persons." *Explorations in Theology IV*, trans. Edward T. Oakes, SJ (San Francisco: Ignatius, 1995), 210. See also Ouellet, *Divine Likeness*, 23.

[21] See "John Paul II and St. Thomas on Love and the Trinity," *Anthropotes* 18 (2002): 113–38, 269–86.

[22] "John Paul II and St. Thomas," 278.

[23] "John Paul II and St. Thomas," 278.

"certain scattered considerations of St. Thomas," which are not "fully developed."[24] Indeed, these passages are only present at all insofar as Thomas's psychological model "does not make claims to an encompassing completeness. It is a partial illumination of the mysteries of our faith," and it therefore "leaves room for" an interpersonal approach.[25]

In what follows, we will build on the social dimensions of Thomas's thought that Waldstein has highlighted. In this way, we owe even more to him than to Balthasar. Yet we will also differ from him. For Waldstein finds within Thomas himself the same fault line between the interpersonal and the psychological that Balthasar had identified within the tradition as a whole: Thomas's psychological Trinity may be compatible with the interpersonal, but it does not in any way include the interpersonal. They are "alternate" approaches. Indeed, in this sense, the two are *not* compatible: Thomas's psychological analogy *would* entirely crowd out an interpersonal Trinity if it filled up the whole of Thomas's Trinitarian theology. It only "leaves room for" an interpersonal approach because there are corners of that theology that it does not occupy. There is no room for the interpersonal *within* the psychological.[26]

Matthew Levering offers a subtler version of a similar scheme. Like Waldstein, he highlights several powerful passages where Thomas speaks of eternal self-giving in the Trinity. He even argues that "Aquinas holds that the Trinity is constituted by absolute self-giving."[27] Yet he concludes his treatment of self-giving as follows: "As ways of instilling within believers greater contemplative understanding of the mystery

---

24 "John Paul II and St. Thomas," 238.

25 "John Paul II and St. Thomas," 285.

26 Waldstein has returned to this question more recently in *The Glory of the Logos in the Flesh: St. John Paul II's Theology of the Body* (Ave Maria, FL: Sapientia Press of Ave Maria University, 2021), 594–671. He again highlights the presence of the interpersonal in Aquinas's Trinity (see especially p. 613). Yet he sees the need once more to make room for the interpersonal by downplaying the psychological; see pp. 619–50, which conclude with the judgement that "the analogy of the word cannot be the heart of Trinitarian theology" (650). Finally, citing Balthasar and Nedoncelle, he proposes that the "two analogies complement each other" and "strengthen each other by their opposite directions" (652). They are complementary, but they are opposites.

27 *Scripture and Metaphysics* (Oxford: Blackwell, 2004), 141. See also 137–38.

of the Trinity, reflection upon the Paschal mystery [or on God as a mystery of self-giving] and the psychological analogy, as developed metaphysically by Aquinas, complement each other."[28] In the very next chapter, Levering focuses on Thomas's psychological analogy. Yet, when he does so, talk of self-giving all but disappears.[29] Levering, that is, goes *from* Thomas's talk of self-giving *to* his psychological analogy. He stresses that the two are not incompatible, and he sees a certain complementarity between them—and, in so doing, he lays out important groundwork for our study. Yet, as with Balthasar, he gives us a complementarity of the edges: the social and the psychological are not mutually exclusive, yet they are mutually extrinsic. Interpersonal self-giving is present within Thomas's Trinitarian theology, but not within his psychological analogy.

Summing up, the bulk of recent thinkers have assumed that we must choose between a psychological Trinity and an interpersonal Trinity. Most have opted for the social and swept aside the psychological; some have balked at the social and have taken up the psychological; but all choose one and reject the other. A smaller group allows a place for the psychological alongside the social: Trinitarian theology has room for both models, but neither model has any room for the other. Finally, two of Thomas's ablest contemporary acolytes have shown that the social has a place within Thomas's Trinitarian theology; yet they suggest that it has no place within his psychological analogy.

A final group of thinkers take a further—and decisive—step. They recognize that the social and the psychological represent distinct approaches to Trinitarian theology. Yet they argue that, in Thomas's Trinitarian theology, the social does not only have a place alongside the psychological. It is at home *within* the psychological. Some of these thinkers make this point while speaking to questions we will address in particular chapters. We will therefore review those insights as we begin those chapters. Yet others have spoken more broadly. With reference to Thomas's teaching that "the trinitarian persons are relations within a

---

28 *Scripture and Metaphysics*, 143.

29 It reemerges that the very end of the chapter. Yet such language is entirely absent as Levering works through the details of Thomas's psychological approach.

single intellectual substance," Adrian J. Walker writes that, on "a careful examination of Thomas'—and Augustine's—trinitarian theology . . . the divine being is a coincidence of ecstasy and enstasy, of substance and relation, in which all the values of the inter-personal and the intra-personal are combined."[30] Also important is Bernard Lonergan, who has perhaps been the most influential contemporary defender of the psychological analogy.[31] Lonergan is especially relevant insofar as he uses psychological language right on the cusp of arguing that for Thomas, the divine Persons are "three conscious divine subjects" Who "are conscious of one another through one consciousness."[32]

The most developed articulation of this claim comes from Thomas Joseph White. First, he writes, "because the relations in God are subsistent, the immaterial generation of the Son as Word . . . and the spiration of the Spirit . . . must entail the plenary communication of divine nature to the Son and Spirit respectively. . . . Consequently, the first analogy from psychological actions is qualified by a substantial account of personal distinction."[33] Personal distinction and total self-communication are not merely added to Thomas's psychological analogy from the outside. Instead, they arise from within Thomas's psychological analogy: this analogy itself demands that distinct Persons communicate all They have to each other. White continues, "just as the use of relation sends us from the psychological analogy to the interpersonal analogy (by way of the consideration of *subsistent* relation: the communication of the whole godhead), the use of relation also sends us from the interpersonal

---

[30] "Personal Singularity and the *Communio Personarum*: A Creative Development of Thomas Aquinas' Doctrine of *Esse Commune*," *Communio: International Catholic Review* 31, no. 3 (2004): 461n7.

[31] For more on Lonergan and the psychological analogy, see Peter Drilling, "The Psychological Analogy of the Trinity: Augustine, Aquinas, and Lonergan," *The Irish Theological Quarterly* 71, no. 3–4 (2006): 320–37.

[32] *The Collected Works of Bernard Lonergan*, vol. 12, *The Triune God: Systematics*, ed. Robert M. Doran and H. Daniel Monsour (Toronto: University of Toronto Press, 2009), 389–91.

[33] *The Trinity: On the Nature and Mystery of the One God* (Washington, DC: The Catholic University of America Press, 2022), 440.

analogy back to the psychological analogy (by way of consideration of subsistent *relation*: each person is wholly relational in all he is)."[34]

An interpersonal lens is not merely present alongside Thomas's psychological lens. Instead, the interpersonal and the psychological point towards each other. To think all the way through the psychological is to arrive at the interpersonal; to think all the way through the interpersonal is to arrive at the psychological. On White's reading, the two approaches are not only "mutually compatible." They are "mutually convergent."[35]

I will spend this study expanding on this insight: I will argue that Thomas's psychological analogy itself, on its own terms, is already a fully interpersonal analogy for the Trinity. For Thomas, the immanent processions of a divine Word and Love are themselves a matter of interpersonal love, interpersonal knowledge, and interpersonal self-giving. The psychological, in other words, is not opposed to the interpersonal. Nor is the psychological juxtaposed to the interpersonal. Instead, the psychological itself is already interpersonal, even as the interpersonal is always psychological.

SOCIAL AND PSYCHOLOGICAL

In showing as much, I hope first of all to suggest that those who are interested in a social Trinity need not regard Thomas with suspicion. Instead, they should see him as a friend, and they should look to him for resources towards the sort of interpersonal God Whom they are set on worshipping. Most basically, I hope to show that they can find in Thomas a basic affirmation of their fundamental intuition: that a Triune God is a social God.

Yet they might also find in him a challenge—hopefully a fruitful one. For, in opposing the social to the psychological, many social Trinitarians assumed—and reinforced—a deeper opposition: they assumed that the Trinity must be a matter *either* of self-knowledge and self-love *or* of interpersonal knowledge and interpersonal love; *either* of self-possession *or* of self-gift; *either* of turning inwards towards oneself

---

[34] White, *The Trinity*, 441.
[35] White, *The Trinity*, 439.

or of turning outwards towards another. These oppositions were rarely expressed so baldly. Yet they often lurked beneath the surface, and they sometimes set the terms for the discussion. Indeed, even to insist that one must choose between the psychological and the social is already to assume some version of this opposition. Closer to the surface, however, was another great either-or. For many social Trinitarians opposed their project not only to the psychological analogy, but also to a "strong" reading of consubstantiality: they rejected traditional claims that all three Persons are really identical to a single divine essence.[36] The interpersonal distinction they are after, in other words, is compatible with only a certain degree of unity: it can only survive if each divine Person enjoys His own distinct instance of the divine nature.

For many social Trinitarians, then, it is unity *or* distinction; it is the intrapersonal *or* the interpersonal. They take up the banner of distinction and of the interpersonal, and they see in Thomas the specter of unity and of the intrapersonal. One of the great achievements of Thomas's psychological analogy, however, is that it liberates us from any such false alternative. It synthesizes strands that are often put at odds: it marries the interpersonal to the intrapersonal, unity to distinction, self-knowledge and self-love to reciprocal knowledge and reciprocal love, and self-possession to self-gift. It even arranges a marriage of equals: it ensures that each set of terms is just as basic as the other. And it can therefore help us to get beneath a number of sterile oppositions that have beset Trinitarian theology for some time.

Even more deeply, it can therefore secure the interpersonal intimacy that social Trinitarians are so bent on securing. For if I were to cease knowing and loving myself in knowing and loving my wife, I would not be in communion with her. I would be colonized by her. If a lover merely lost himself in giving himself, then he would destroy the very "self" he had hoped to give—and he would therefore grieve his beloved, who had presumably loved the self that is now lost. The paradox of

---

36 As Thomas McCall and Michael C. Rea report, the first of "the core tenets" of social Trinitarianism is that "the Father, the Son, and the Holy Spirit are 'of one essence,' but are not numerically the same substance. . . . Furthermore, this sharing of a common nature can be understood in a fairly straightforward sense via the 'social analogy' in which Peter, James, and John share human nature" (*Philosophical and Theological Essays on the Trinity*, 3).

communion is that we really do *find* ourselves in giving ourselves; we really do *gain* ourselves in losing ourselves; we really do—and we perhaps *only*—come to know and love ourselves in knowing and loving another.[37] Just so, one of the paradoxes of love is that the more I am made one with my beloved, the more we are each able to stand on our own feet.[38] Real unity does not swallow up distinction; it rejoices in distinction.[39] Social Trinitarians often recognize at least some version of these points.[40] Yet, to the extent that they insist on a conflict between the psychological and the social, and to the extent that they oppose personal distinction to a strong reading of consubstantial unity, they undermine the very marriage of self-to-other and unity-to-distinction that they would place at the center of the divine life.

Thomas, for his part, may not be able to do everything. Yet I will argue that his psychological analogy for the Trinity can offer a rich marriage of these seemingly opposed elements, and I hope that it

---

[37] If we did not find ourselves in giving ourselves, then Christ's words in Luke 9:24 would lose their force. For a deep reflection here, see John Paul II, *Man and Woman He Created Them: A Theology of the Body*, trans. Michael Waldstein (Boston: Pauline Books and Media, 2006), 195–97. For self-knowledge and self-love as a fruit—and an indispensable fruit—of interpersonal knowledge and love, see Hans Urs von Balthasar, *Explorations in Theology III*, trans. Brian McNeil (San Francisco, Ignatius: 1993), 15. For more, see D. C. Schindler, *Hans Urs von Balthasar and the Dramatic Structure of Truth* (New York: Fordham University Press, 2004), 96–162.

[38] See D. C. Schindler, "The Word as the Center of Man's Onto-Dramatic Task," *Communio: International Catholic Review* 46, no. 1 (2019): 76–77.

[39] Joseph Ratzinger applies this point to consubstantial unity in *Introduction to Christianity*, trans. J. R. Foster (San Francisco: Ignatius, 2004), 179. Adrienne von Speyr does the same in *The World of Prayer*, trans. Graham Harrison (San Francisco: Ignatius Press, 1985), 65–66, 73–74.

[40] They often celebrate the interpersonal through seizing on the language of "perichoresis"—which they sometimes oppose to consubstantial unity. For Moltmann on perichoresis, see Thomas H. McCall, *Which Trinity? Whose Monotheism? Philosophical and Systematic Theologians on the Metaphysics of Trinitarian Theology* (Grand Rapids, MI: Eerdmans, 2010), 156–74. See also Cornelius Plantinga, "Social Trinity and Tritheism," in *Trinity, Incarnation, and Atonement: Philosophical and Theological Essays*, ed. Ronald J. Feenstra and Cornelius Plantinga (Notre Dame, IN: University of Notre Dame Press, 1989), 28. Others, however, are more resolute and deliberate in opposing distinction-in-oneself to intimacy-with-another. William Lane Craig, for example, denies the possibility of interpersonal indwelling: he writes that "persons are not the sort of entity that exists in another person" ("Towards a Tenable Social Trinitarianism," in *Philosophical and Theological Essays on the Trinity*, 92).

will therefore be able to begin healing needless and fruitless rifts that underlie many contemporary discussions.[41]

WHAT WE'LL DO

To see as much, I will proceed in two parts. We just saw that, in the telling of many, the psychological analogy secures the unity of the divine essence at the expense of the distinction of the Persons, whereas a social analogy highlights distinction but gives short shrift to unity. Part one will be devoted to challenging this scheme. To do so, we will dive into two paradoxes that go to the center of Thomas's psychological analogy for the Trinity. In chapter one, we will focus on the paradox of an "immanent procession"—which literally means a "going-forth that remains within." We will see that by appealing to the logic of an immanent procession, Thomas is able to hold *both* that Word and Love remain within the Father in a unity of essence *and* that They go forth from the Father as really distinct from Him. Indeed, he is even able to hold that Their going-forth is just as logically basic as Their

---

[41] While my main hope is to contribute to questions around the social and the psychological, I will also speak—at least indirectly—to other questions in contemporary Trinitarian theology. First, this study finds itself amidst a wave of recent studies on Thomas's Trinitarian theology, many of which have already responded to the Revivalist misreading of Aquinas. Gilles Emery has been at the forefront of this movement, but he has been joined by many others (such as Matthew Levering, Jean-Pierre Torrell, and Dominic Legge). These thinkers largely agree with each other, and their reading of Thomas has become the dominant one. For my part, I am hugely indebted to them, especially to Emery. I will cite him at almost every turn, and some of my conclusions (in, for example, the section "Whence the Word?" in chapter one) could not have been drawn without the work he has already done. I will, however, push back on Emery at certain points (see, for example, the very beginning of chapter one and the section "Self-Love as Interpersonal Love" in chapter six), and this study ought not to be read as one more step down the path Emery has blazed. Instead, it ought to be read as indebted to Emery, but also as gratefully and charitably challenging certain dimensions of his reading—and so the now-dominant reading—of Aquinas.

Finally, I hope to address a recent spate of criticism to which the Trinitarian Revivals, along with social Trinitarians in particular, have been subjected. These critical voices are certainly right to call out social Trinitarianism for its excesses. Yet they are sometimes prone to excesses of their own, and they too easily join social Trinitarians in assuming that Thomas is a natural ally to the social-skeptic. I will address them directly only on rare occasions. Yet this study as a whole might be read as a challenge to their assumption that Thomas stands as a counterweight to an interpersonal Trinity.

remaining-within—which means that their distinction is just as basic as Their unity. That said, even if this distinction is real and basic, if it is limited to the mind of a single person, then it will have little to do with anything interpersonal. In order to meet this objection, we will spend chapter two drawing out the character of this distinction. To do so, we will dig into an even starker paradox: a standing-outside that remains within. For we will see that, because the divine Word and Love are a subsistent Word and Love, They stand in a certain way "outside" of the Father—even as They remain perfectly within the Father. Finally, in chapter three, we will see that the poles of these two paradoxes are not in conflict. In Thomas's Trinity, remaining-within—or consubstantial unity—is at odds neither with interpersonal going-forth nor with interpersonal standing-outside. Instead, the remaining-within of Word and Love requires Their going-forth and Their standing-outside. In Thomas's psychological analogy, consubstantial unity and radical distinction stand or fall together.

In part two, we will enter into the meat of our argument. Having seen that Thomas's psychological analogy marries unity to distinction, we will see that it also marries the intrapersonal to the interpersonal: it marries self-knowledge and self-love to interpersonal knowledge, interpersonal love, and interpersonal self-giving. In chapter four, we will focus on self-giving. We will see that, in Thomas's Trinitarian theology, to conceive a Word within one's mind or to breathe forth Love within one's affections is to give the whole of oneself to a distinct Person: immanent procession is already interpersonal self-giving. In chapter five, we will turn to the Word. We will also see that, as almost everyone recognizes, the divine Word proceeds in the Father's act of understanding Himself. Yet we will see that, in this procession, the Father knows His Word just as basically as He knows Himself, and He gives Himself to His Word just as basically as He knows anything. Even insofar as interpersonal knowledge, self-knowledge, and self-giving are logically distinct, they are equally basic in the procession of the divine Word. Similarly, we will see in chapter six that the procession of divine Love is a matter of self-love; yet it is just as basically a matter of interpersonal love, interpersonal communion, interpersonal self-giving, and even one Person's giving a third Person to a second Person. Finally, we will end in chapter seven by asking what all of this might have to do with us. Having seen that the interpersonal goes to the foundation of Thomas's psychological Trinity, we will ask whether it might go to the foundation of his *imago Trinitatis*.

Summing up, there are two ways in which the overarching goal of this study might be expressed, and our two parts might be organized according to either of these goals. First of all, and most basically, I hope to show that Thomas's psychological analogy both marries unity to distinction and marries the intrapersonal to the interpersonal. In part one, I will focus on the marriage of unity to distinction: I will argue that the immanence and consubstantiality of the divine Persons demands Their radical distinction. In part two, I will focus on the marriage of the intrapersonal to the interpersonal: I will argue that, for Thomas, divine self-knowledge and divine self-love are *themselves* a matter of interpersonal love, interpersonal knowledge, and interpersonal self-giving. Second, and a bit more specifically, my governing aim will be to show that Thomas's psychological Trinity is already an interpersonal Trinity. In part one, I will argue that it is an *inter*personal Trinity: the distinction *between* Father, Word, and Love is a radical one. In part two, I will argue that it is an inter*personal* Trinity. For, on Thomas's terms, part of what makes a person a person is the ability to understand and to will. In showing, therefore, that the Word and Love understand and love Themselves and the Father, and in showing that the Father understands and loves Himself and each of Them, I hope to show that Thomas's psychological Trinity is a matter of inter*personal* relationships.

HOW WE'LL DO IT

To see as much, I will often range over the whole of Thomas's corpus. Sometimes I will devote the better part of a chapter to the close reading of just one text. At other times, I will simply work through an argument as Thomas articulates it in the *Summa*. Elsewhere, I will attend directly to major developments in Thomas's thought over time. Yet, most of the time, I will focus on the text or texts where Thomas most strongly and clearly articulates the point we are considering, and I will often use the footnotes to indicate other texts where this same point is present, but where it is developed less fully. This method has certain limits.

First, we will jump freely—some might say haphazardly—from text to text. Second, although we will spend time early on with the historical development of Thomas's thought, and although the conclusions we draw there will be in the background throughout the whole of this study, I generally will not devote much attention directly to the context of the texts we are studying. Instead, I will give the background needed to appreciate the specific point we will draw out of it, and then I will focus chiefly on the logic of Thomas's claim itself. Again, these limits are real. Yet this approach also has its advantages. First, by pulling from a wide range of texts, I hope to show that many of the points we will explore are present throughout Thomas's mature corpus, and that they emerge across genres that are sometimes put in tension with each other.[42] Second, and more basically, I hope that, by focusing on the texts where Thomas articulates these points most strongly, we will be best able to appreciate just how present these points are in his thought.

On a related note, my way of approaching Thomas will vary from chapter to chapter. It will often vary even within chapters. At some points, I will simply exposit Thomas: I will draw to the surface claims that he explicitly registers, but which have received little attention. At other points, I will highlight principles that are basic to his thought, I will explore those principles in light of questions he does not directly ask, and I will develop those principles in order to draw conclusions he does not explicitly draw. Every chapter will have elements of both approaches. Chapters one, three, and four, however, will be mostly expository, whereas chapters two, five, and six will be more creative.

---

[42] Most importantly, Thomas's dogmatic treatises and his Biblical commentaries are sometimes put at odds, and it is sometimes assumed that Thomas is more open to the interpersonal in Biblical settings (where he is forced to deal with the concrete demands of Scripture), while he is more resolutely intrapersonal in the "dogmatic" (where those details make fewer demands on him). For a subtle version of this scheme, see Anne Hunt, "The Trinity Through Paschal Eyes," in *Rethinking Trinitarian Theology*, 474. Indeed, this scheme may even be present under the surface in Levering. In his chapter on self-giving, Levering cites exclusively from Thomas's commentary on John; in the chapter on Thomas's psychological analogy, he works methodically through q. 27 (and part of q. 29) of the *Summa*. Emery has already pointed out the limits of the crasser versions of this Scripture-versus-systematics scheme in *TA*, 271–319. I hope to deepen this point by showing that many of our central points appear both in dogmatic settings and in Biblical commentaries. Indeed, as rich as Thomas's biblical commentaries are, we will see that he is sometimes most interpersonal where he is most "dogmatic."

During these more creative chapters, I will sometimes insist very strongly that Thomas's principles demand a certain conclusion. At other points, I will more gingerly suggest that those principles open up towards, or even just allow space for, a conclusion that may not follow unavoidably on them. In either case, however, this study will always be a study of *Thomas's* Trinitarian theology. Even when I go beyond the letter of Thomas, I will remain bound by the letter: any implications I draw out from Thomas's principles should be judged by whether or not they really are demanded by—or, in some cases, suggested by—principles that Thomas really does lay out explicitly.

One might object, however, that if Thomas had wanted to draw the conclusions we will draw from him, then he would have drawn them himself. This point is fair enough. Yet if Thomas refrained from drawing certain conclusions, then he may have done so because he refrained from asking certain questions in certain terms; and, if he refrained from asking certain questions in certain terms, then he may have done so not because he had nothing to say to those questions, but because those were not the questions his inheritance—which differs from ours—prompted him to ask. For example, we will ask in chapter five whether self-knowledge is more basic than interpersonal knowledge. Thomas, for his part, speaks both of self-knowledge in God and of reciprocal knowledge in God. He even gives some indication as to how they might relate. Yet he also leaves a great deal of questions open. If we are prompted to ask these questions, it might be because we live in the wake of Descartes's seismic shift towards a new kind of self-knowledge. It might also be because we live in the wake of Buber's reemphasis on interpersonal knowledge as a source of self-knowledge. And so on. If Thomas is not prompted to ask these questions, it might be because he wrote before these shifts took place.[43] Be that as it may, I hope to suggest that Thomas's thought is fruitful enough to offer insights into questions that he himself did not ask, and I hope to show that it is rich enough to contain conclusions that he himself did not draw. I hope, in other words, to show that Thomas's thought did not

---

43 For another reflection on the importance of Thomas's not answering every question, see Josef Pieper, *The Silence of St. Thomas*, trans. John Murray and Daniel O'Connor (South Bend, IN: St. Augustine's Press, 1999).

die with Thomas. Instead, it remains alive, and it is therefore able to give life beyond that specific range of questions with which Thomas, in his finitude, was able to engage.[44]

WHAT WE WON'T DO

That said, I will by no means ask every question Thomas's principles might allow one to ask. Indeed, I will need to leave untouched a number of questions that bear directly on my main concern. First of all, I am interested in the presence of the interpersonal in Thomas's psychological analogy. To speak of the "interpersonal," however, is to speak implicitly of personhood. Yet I will not be able to focus much on the meaning of personhood in Thomas's Trinitarian theology. This omission is particularly glaring given the amount of attention "personhood"—both in general and in God—has received in recent decades. We cannot address these developments here.[45] Yet we should at least note that, in recent years, some have proposed that to be a person is, by definition, to be a unique center of consciousness and freedom.[46] Others have rethought personhood in terms of self-giving: to be a person is to give oneself.[47] Still others hold that to be a person is to be an "I" in relation to a "Thou," and that there can be no personhood of

---

[44] In this sense, I will build on a number of recent thinkers who have creatively developed Thomas's thought. See Norris Clarke, *Person and Being* (Milwaukee: Marquette University Press, 1993); Walker, "Personal Singularity and the *Communio Personarum*"; and Ferdinand Ulrich, *Homo Abyssus: The Drama of the Question of Being*, trans. D. C. Schindler (Washington, DC: Humanum Academic Press, 2018). Indeed, I will build on these particular thinkers in another respect: they have all found a marriage of the intrapersonal and the interpersonal (or of being-in-oneself and being-from-and-with-and-for-others) within Thomas's metaphysics and anthropology. We will find a similar (though very different) marriage in his Trinity.

[45] For divine personhood in recent decades, see Pérez, "The Trinitarian Concept of Person," 105–45. For Thomas specifically, see Emery, *TTTA*, 103–27.

[46] This move is basic to many versions of social Trinitarianism: see McCall and Rea, *Philosophical and Theological Essays on the Trinity*, 2.

[47] See Norris Clarke, "Person, Being, and St. Thomas," *Communio: International Catholic Review* 19 (1992): 610.

any kind apart from such a "Thou."[48] Some have argued that Thomas's Trinitarian theology has room for these more recent renderings of personhood.[49] Others—both among Thomas's critics and among his defenders—have disagreed.[50] We cannot, however, enter into any of these questions. Instead, we must content ourselves with the surface of Thomas's teaching: for Thomas, whatever else personhood might mean, a person is an individual substance of a rational nature, and to be a distinct person is to subsist distinctly in a rational nature.[51] And, because a rational nature, by definition, carries with it intellect and will, to be a person is to be able to understand and to will. Therefore, when I refer here to a "person," I will generally mean a distinctly subsistent thing that is able to understand and to will or love.[52]

We will speak a great deal of subsistence and of personhood in what follows, especially in chapter two. There are other questions, however, that we will not touch at all. Most importantly, our interest is in Thomas's psychological analogy for the Trinity. Yet even to speak of

---

[48] See Martin Buber, *I and Thou*, trans. Ronald Gregor Smith (New York: Scribner, 1958). With reference to the Trinity, see Walter Kasper, *The God of Jesus Christ* (New York: Continuum, 2012), 243; and John Zizioulas, *Communion and Otherness: Further Studies in Personhood and the Church*, ed. Paul McPartlan (New York: Continuum, 2009), 9.

[49] For distinct centers of consciousness, see Lonergan, *The Triune God*, 389–91; Cirilo Folch Gomes, "La Réciprocité psychologique des personnes divines selon la théologie de St. Thomas d'Aquin," *Studi tomistici* 13 (1981): 153–71; and François Bourassa, "Personne et conscience en théologie trinitaire," pts. 1 and 2, *Gregorianum* 55, no. 3 (1974): 471–93; 55, no. 4 (1974): 677–720. For self-giving, see Clarke, "Person, Being, and St. Thomas," 610.

[50] For centers of consciousness and freedom, see Herbert McCabe, "Aquinas on the Trinity," *New Blackfriars* 80 (1999): 292; Rudi Te Velde, "The Divine Person(s): Trinity, Person, and Analogous Naming," in *The Oxford Handbook of the Trinity*, ed. Gilles Emery and Matthew Levering (Oxford: Oxford University Press, 2012), 360; Matthew Levering, *Scripture and Metaphysics*, 232n108; and *Engaging the Doctrine of the Holy Spirit: Love and Gift in the Trinity and the Church* (Grand Rapids, MI: Baker Publishing Group, 2016), 34. For "I-Thou" relations, see Christopher J. Malloy, "The 'I-Thou' Argument for the Trinity: Wherefore Art Thou?" *Nova et Vetera* English edition 15, no. 1 (2016): 113–59.

[51] See Emery, *TTTA*, 104–11; and "On the Dignity of Being a Substance: Person, Subsistence, Nature," *Nova et Vetera*, 9, no. 4 (2011): 991–1001.

[52] In God, things are complicated insofar as that which subsists distinctly are relations. This point touches on Thomas's famous definition of a divine Person as a "subsistent relation." We will touch briefly on this teaching several times (especially in the section "Inside as Outside" in chapter two), but we will not be able to dive into it (others have done so at great length. For a helpful introduction, see Emery, *TTTA*, 114–20).

"the psychological analogy" is already to wade into a number of controversies. First of all, there is no such thing as *the* psychological analogy. There is a whole constellation of Trinitarian theologies that vary among themselves and that are spread all through the tradition—East as well as West, contemporary as well as patristic and medieval—which center on spiritual acts of intellect and will.[53] I will not enter into the relationship between Thomas's particular articulation of the psychological analogy and other—sometimes very different—articulations. We can note, however, that Thomas's version of the psychological analogy is unique to Thomas, that it is different from other versions that pop up throughout the tradition, and that Thomas is willing to distance himself from other versions because those versions cannot secure the sort of interpersonal distinction that goes to the heart of his own psychological analogy.[54] More to the point, I have no hopes of defending "the" psychological analogy "in general." Instead, I hope to dive deeply into Thomas's particular interpretation of the psychological analogy, and I hope to argue that his particular interpretation is shot through with the interpersonal. Other articulations might ultimately fall prey to the criticisms social Trinitarians have raised: some Words and Loves might not be "Persons" in anything but an equivocal way.[55] Other psychological analogies

---

[53] For "psychological" language in Origen and Gregory of Nyssa (the latter of whom was often invoked as a counterweight to the psychological theologies of the "Latin West"), see Slotemaker, "Peter Lombard and the *imago Trinitatis*," 169. See also Drilling, "The Psychological Analogy of the Trinity," 321–22.

[54] See *ST* I q. 34, a. 1, ad 3, where Thomas distances himself from Anselm because Anselm cannot account for the distinction of the Word from the Father. For more on this point, see Emery, *TTTA*, 186–87. For differences in the psychological analogies of Thomas, Augustine, Scotus, and Henry of Ghent, see Scott M. Williams, "Augustine, Thomas Aquinas, Henry of Ghent and John Duns Scotus: On the Theology of the Father's Intellectual Generation of the Word," *Recherches de Théologie et Philosophie médiévales* 77 (2010): 35–81. As we will see in the section "Whence the Word?" in chapter one, Scotus and Henry reject the dimension of Thomas's psychological analogy that will ground many of our conclusions.

[55] Augustine is sometimes read on these terms, largely in light of *De Trinitate* VII.7–11 (see Pérez, "The Trinitarian Concept of Person," 108). Elsewhere, however, Augustine perhaps points to something richer: see Ayres, *Augustine and the Trinity* (Cambridge: Cambridge University Press, 2010), 161.

might lead to divine individualism.[56] Finally, a good deal of Thomists have read—and have championed—Thomas's psychological analogy in terms of such individualism.[57] When social Trinitarians complain that Thomas's psychological analogy is insufficiently interpersonal, therefore, their reading may pick up on a tradition that long precedes them. This tradition understands itself to be faithful to Thomas. Yet, in fact, it may have been obscuring Thomas well before Trinitarian theology had been revived or renewed. Be that as it may, the most basic point is that, in defending Thomas's psychological analogy, I am not defending those who have spoken in the name of that analogy. Nor am I defending every psychological analogy. Instead, I am focusing exclusively on Thomas's very specific version of the psychological analogy.[58]

If to speak of *the* psychological analogy for the Trinity is to invite controversy, then so too is to speak of the *psychological* analogy for the Trinity. This phrase is of relatively recent coinage: it was never used by Aquinas, and it may not be the term most apt to convey exactly what he means by the eternal processions of Word and of Love.[59] Still, while these limits are real, they are not grave enough to require that we break from the discourse of the last century by inventing some new term that better gets at the heart of Thomas's Trinitarian thought. Instead, we will use the now-standard term, yet we will do so while recognizing its limits.

---

56 While Anselm's Trinitarian theology is certainly too rich to be dismissed with a single footnote, we just saw Thomas suggest that Anselm might tend in this direction.

57 M. T. L. Penido, for example, opposes the psychological to the social in the harshest of terms: we have here "two irreducible types of Trinitarian theology. . . . Aiming at the mystery from opposed points, these two conceptions cannot be reconciled." "Gloses sur la procession d'amour dans la Trinité," *Ephemerides theologicae lovanienses* 14 (1937): 48. See also 62.

58 That said, my reading of Thomas will sometimes resonate with parallel attempts to defend Augustine from similar charges. I will gesture towards these points of contact in the footnotes when relevant.

59 Slotemaker is particularly critical of the term in "Peter Lombard and the *imago Trinitatis*," 169n5. For more measured reflections, see White, *The Trinity*, 13n4. The phrase "psychological analogy" first appeared in It first appeared in Michael Schmaus, *De Psychologische Trinitätslehre des Heiligen Auginstinus* (Munster: Aschendorffsche Verlagsbuchhandlung, 1927).

Finally, and most daunting of all, while talk of *the* psychological analogy or of the *psychological* analogy might involve us in a controversy or two, talk of the psychological *analogy* plants us in whole thicket of hotly contested questions.[60] The question of analogy in Aquinas's theology is a world unto itself: it can already claim a shelf's worth of books that stretch back decades, and it promises to continue raising hackles for years to come.[61] Without hoping to resolve any of these questions, we can make one very brief point. There seems to be general agreement that Thomas uses the word "analogy" differently in different contexts.[62] To select just some of these differences, analogy sometimes concerns our use of language: a word is used analogously if it is "located between two other linguistic phenomena, univocation and equivocation," and if there is "some degree of difference, but also some degree of sameness" between the things of which it is predicated.[63] At other times, "analogy" points to a proportional relationship: A is analogous to B if A is to X as B is to Y.[64] Finally, analogy can spring from causal participation: A is analogous to B if A is caused by and participates in B.[65]

---

60 For a catalogue of the most salient questions around analogy in Aquinas, see Joshua P. Hochschild, "Aquinas's Two Concepts of Analogy and a Complex Semantics for Naming the Simple God," *The Thomist* 83, no. 2 (2019): 159.

61 For a sampling of monographs written from 1952 to 2004, see Hochschild, "Aquinas's Two Concepts of Analogy," 160n7. More recently, see Domenic D'Ettore, *Analogy after Aquinas: Logical Problems, Thomistic Answers* (Washington, DC: The Catholic University of America Press, 2018). In fact, discussion around analogy in Aquinas stretches back not decades but centuries, at least to Cajetan's *"De nominum analogia"*—which is *itself* controversial. For controversy around Cajetan, see Hochschild, *The Semantics of Analogy: Reading Cajetan's* De Nominum Analogia (Notre Dame, IN: University of Notre Dame Press, 2010); and D'Ettore, *Analogy after Aquinas*.

62 For a quick summary of the overlap and differences between six texts where Thomas gives a lengthy treatment of analogy, see Hochschild, "Proportionality and Divine Naming: Did St. Thomas Change His Mind about Analogy?" *The Thomist* 77, no. 4 (2013): 534–36. Hochschild mentions differences (for example, the difference between many-to-one and one-to-another in *ST* I q. 13, a. 5) on which we will not touch here.

63 Hochschild, "Aquinas's Two Concepts of Analogy," 160. For the differences between this "logical" or "semantic" version of analogy and more "metaphysical" versions, see Alan Philip Darley, "Predication or Participation? What is the Nature of Aquinas's Doctrine of Analogy?," *The Heythrop Journal* 57, no. 2 (2016): 312–24.

64 See Hochschild, "Aquinas's Two Concepts of Analogy," 163–65.

65 See Hochschild, "Proportionality and Divine Naming," 541–42. Stephen A. Long focuses on the differences between the last two sorts of analogy in "Thoughts on Analogy

Without doing more than skimming these very choppy surfaces, we can at least note that Thomas's psychological analogy is analogous in all three of these senses. First, Thomas is clear that "Word" is said of God not merely metaphorically or equivocally or figuratively, but properly.[66] Yet it is not said univocally.[67] It steers between the extremes of univocity and equivocity. Yet this analogy is not merely linguistic: there is also a proportional likeness at work. My relations to my words and to my loves are proportional to the Father's relation to His Word and to His Love: my words and loves proceed from me, and His Word and Love proceed from Him—though in a very different way. Similarly, my words' relations to me are proportional to the divine Word's relation to the Father, and my loves' relations to me and to my words are proportional to the divine Love's relation to the Father and to the divine Word. Finally, Thomas teaches both that the divine Word causes all created words and that all created words participate in the divine Word.[68] An analogy of causal participation is therefore also in play.

These three meanings of analogy often interpenetrate, and, in what follows, we will sometimes move fairly fluidly between them. Because my interest is not directly in this question, I will not always pause to specify which exact sort—or sorts—of analogy are in play in a given moment. Most of the time, however, the first sense of analogy—analogy as a mean between equivocity and univocity—will be front and center. Other meanings of analogy will often be in the background of our arguments, and sometimes in the foreground. Yet many of our conclusions will hinge on the particular marriage of similarity and difference that Thomas identifies between human words and loves and the divine Word and Love, and, when we call direct attention to analogy, it will often be because a conclusion we are drawing would cease to make sense if we were to lose sight either of those similarities

---

and Relation," *Quaestiones Disputatae* 6, no. 1 (2015): 73–89. He discusses these points in more depth in *Analogia Entis: On the Analogy of Being, Metaphysics, and the Act of Faith* (Notre Dame, IN: University of Notre Dame Press, 2011).

66 See *ST* I q. 34, a. 1.

67 See *in Ioan.*, ##26–28.

68 For the divine Word as the cause of all created words, see *in Heb.*, #217. For all created words as participations in the divine Word, see *in Ioan.*, #33.

or of those differences. Neither an equivocal Word and Love nor a univocal Word and Love can bear the weight of our conclusions. Only an analogous Word and Love can yield an interpersonal Trinity.

Taking a step back from analogy, we can return to our narrower question: the place of the interpersonal in Thomas's psychological analogy for the Trinity. First of all, I should emphasize that my aim is not to fend off every criticism to which this particular analogy has been subjected. Some charged that it constructs a Trinitarian theology in abstraction from the economy of salvation.[69] Others held that it subordinates faith to reason and projects uncritically into God details from our human acts of intellect and will.[70] Others found other shortcomings.[71] I will at times speak to some of these points. Yet I will speak to them only insofar as doing so will allow me to respond more deeply to the one criticism with which I am ultimately concerned: that Thomas's psychological analogy shuts down the possibility of anything social in God.

Most deeply, my goal is not to show that Thomas's psychological analogy—or his Trinitarian theology as a whole—is above every criticism. I do not hope to suggest that it is the best of all possible Trinitarian theologies, or even that it is the best of all actual Trinitarian theologies currently on offer. It cannot give us everything. Indeed, it may not even be able to give us everything social: there may be interpersonal realities that Revelation shows to be present in God, which social Trinitarians have seized on but Thomas cannot recognize. Social Trinitarians, therefore, may be able to give us something—and something important—that Thomas cannot.

To elaborate, there are at least two levels on which Thomas might be enriched by more recent social approaches. First, some recent thinkers have proposed dimensions of the interpersonal that are not even implicitly present in Thomas's psychological analogy, and that Thomas might have flatly rejected had they been proposed in his time.[72] Some of

---

69 See Rahner, *The Trinity*, 119; and Ormerod, "At Odds with Modernity," 287.
70 See Moltmann, *The Trinity and the Kingdom*, 17
71 See Ormerod, "At Odds with Modernity," 284–87.
72 See, for example, Adrienne von Speyr, *The World of Prayer*, 28–74.

these new dimensions may be problematic. Others, however, may well be valid, beautiful, and important. Thomas might therefore learn from them. Second, the recent swell of the social has placed front and center a host of conclusions that I will argue *are* present in Thomas's psychological analogy. Yet many of these conclusions remain undeveloped in Thomas, and some never even come to the surface: they are buried in Thomas's thought, and we will need to do a good deal of digging to unearth them. I hope this digging will reveal quite a bit. For now, however, we can admit that even if these interpersonal dimensions are present beneath the surface of Thomas's Trinity, it remains that, on a cursory read, Thomas seems to foreground self-knowledge and self-love far more than he foregrounds anything social. One could walk away from a surface reading of the *Summa* thinking that, for Thomas, God merely knows and loves Himself. One could not walk away from a Balthasar or a Gunton with the same impression, no matter how quickly one were to skim them. Surfaces, of course, are not everything. They are not even the most important thing. In going deeper than a cursory reading, therefore, I hope to uncover depths that matter more than these surfaces. But surfaces matter too. And, on its surface, Thomas's psychological analogy takes its fundamental bearings from a mind knowing and loving itself. Other Trinitarian theologies that take their bearings more immediately and obviously from the social can therefore offer something that Thomas cannot.

In this sense, Thomas's psychological analogy might be complemented by other more obviously social Trinities. The most important point for us to stress, however, is that this complementarity is not that of a jigsaw puzzle: it is not the complementarity of two alien realties that exist independently of each other, which are then pieced together from the outside and might just as easily be taken apart. Instead, it is a complementarity in which each pole is inseparable from the other, and in which each pole bears the other wholly within itself, but in which each pole does so differently. It is, we might say, a perichoretic complementarity.[73] Be that as it may, the point is that Thomas's psychological

---

[73] For a development, in very different contexts, of something like this richer "complementarity" of indwelling, see Pierre Rousselot, *The Eyes of Faith*, trans. Avery Dulles (New York: Fordham University Press, 1990), 45; Prudence Allen, "Integral Sex Complementarity

analogy is not at odds with the interpersonal, and that it therefore need not be reconciled with the interpersonal from the outside. Instead, it already contains the interpersonal. It can certainly be enriched if it is read together with more obviously interpersonal approaches. Yet this enrichment will first of all bring to the surface elements it bears within itself. Those elements can perhaps be deepened and developed—and sometimes challenged—by insights that have been unearthed by other approaches. Yet they are not simply imported from the outside.

I do not hope, then, to show that Thomas can do everything. I hope, instead, to argue that criticisms of his psychological analogy, especially those motivated by "social" concerns, have been largely misguided; that contemporary Trinitarian theology has gone astray to the extent that it has not merely developed or played with or pushed back on figures like Aquinas, but has openly rejected and abandoned them; that, while Thomas's Trinity cannot give us everything, or even everything interpersonal, it can give us something a good deal more interpersonal than has been acknowledged; that Thomas's psychological analogy for the Trinity, even if it does not already contain every conceivable answer to every serious question, can make a deep contribution to contemporary Trinitarian theology; and that one of its deepest contributions lies in its ability to marry unity to distinction, interiority to encounter, self-love to interpersonal love, self-knowledge to interpersonal knowledge, and self-regard to self-gift.

---

and the Theology of Communion," *Communio: International Catholic Review* 17, no. 4 (1990): 523–44; and D. C. Schindler, *The Catholicity of Reason* (Grand Rapids, MI: Eerdmans, 2013), 305–33.

PART I

1

A GOING-FORTH THAT REMAINS WITHIN

As we noted in our introduction, almost everyone agrees that Thomas's psychological approach privileges the unity of the divine Persons over Their distinction. Gilles Emery is certainly more subtle than most. He has shown in detail that, for Thomas, the divine Word and Love are distinct "Persons" in the proper and analogous sense of the term.[1] Indeed, he has taken the lead in showing that Thomas's psychological analogy has little to do with the ham-fisted "essentialism" of which it has often been accused.[2] Yet even Emery seems to endorse some version of this scheme. In the course of discussing Thomas's treatment of the Son, Emery writes that "Thomas does not place the notion of 'generation' (as the communication of nature to the engendered) at the beginning of his exposition, but starts with the intellectual procession of the Word instead, because this enables one clearly to grasp an *immanent* action whose issue is *consubstantial* with its principle, both being a *unity*."[3] Talk of a divine "generation" secures the Father's communication of His nature to a Son Who subsists

---

[1] See *TTTA*, 104–11; and "On the Dignity of Being a Substance."

[2] See *TA*, 165–208, especially 184–92.

[3] *TTTA*, 60. In chapter six, we will see something similar in Emery's reading of the Holy Spirit as Love.

distinctly from Him; talk of a divine "Word" secures the immanence, the consubstantiality, and the unity of the Son with the Father. And Thomas privileges the language of "Word" because, in his Trinity, immanence and unity come first.

Before saying more, I should clarify that there is certainly some sense in which, for Thomas, the essential unity of the Persons comes "before" Their personal distinction. Most importantly, Thomas consistently structures his doctrine of God by beginning with that which belongs to the one divine essence, and by turning next to that which concerns the distinction of the divine Persons.[4] Thomas has come under heavy fire for this move, and defenses have been mounted on his behalf.[5] The charge I am interested in, however, is different. For many hold that, even *after* Thomas has begun considering that which concerns the distinction of the divine Persons—in, say, q. 27 of the *Prima Pars* or book IV of the *SCG*—he *continues* privileging unity over distinction. Gunton and Moltmann aggressively advance a crass version of this scheme, whereas Emery is more nuanced. Yet they all hold that, *within* Thomas's Trinitarian theology, unity comes first. And they all hold that Thomas's psychological analogy allows him to cement this priority of unity.

In this chapter, I hope to begin pushing back on this scheme. Specifically, I hope to lay groundwork for seeing that Thomas's psychological analogy does not secure the unity of the divine Persons instead of, or at the expense of, securing Their distinction. Nor does it secure Their unity before securing Their distinction. Instead, it secures Their distinction just as basically as it secures Their unity.

---

4 See, most famously, *ST* I q. 2, prol. See also Emery, *TTTA*, 44–48.

5 For a survey of criticisms, see Emery, *TA*, 166–69. For a defense of Thomas (which distinguishes his method from the Neo-Scholastic division of a *De Deo Trino* from a *De Deo Uno*) see Emery, *TTTA*, 39–40. See also Christopher R. J. Holmes, "Architectonics Matter: Some Advantages of Treating the Unicity of God in Advance of the Trinity of Persons, in Dialogue with Thomas Aquinas," *International Journal of Systematic Theology* 19, no. 2 (2017): 130–43. At stake here is also our order of coming to know God, which begins with the knowledge of His essence available through our encounter with creation: see Smith, *Thomas Aquinas's Trinitarian Theology*, 48–70. For more on the *ordo disciplinae* in Aquinas's Trinitarian theology, see R. L. Richard, *The Problem of an Apologetical Perspective in the Trinitarian Theology of St. Thomas Aquinas* (Rome: Gregorian University Press, 1963).

To see as much, I will spend this chapter focusing on a category that stands at the foundation of Thomas's psychological analogy for the Trinity: an "immanent procession."[6] My main aim will be to show that the very notion of an "immanent procession" is paradoxical: it means that the Son and the Holy Spirit go forth from the Father even as They remain within the Father. Half of this claim, of course, is hardly news: almost everyone recognizes that, for Thomas, a word and love remain within the one who understands and loves, and that the divine Word and Love therefore remain within the Father. And almost everyone recognizes that this remaining-within allows Thomas to secure the essential unity of the divine Persons. Less often recognized—and sometimes actively denied—is Thomas's claim that a word and love really *proceed*, or go forth, from the one who understands and loves, and that this procession demands that the divine Word and Love be really distinct from the Father.[7] In later chapters, I will argue that this procession also demands that Word and Love know and love the Father, and that the Father give the whole of Himself to Them. In this chapter, I will argue that this procession goes to the heart of Thomas's psychological categories.

I will begin by offering a brief sketch of Thomas's two most important psychological terms: "word" and "love." Next, I will take a broader look at the paradox of an "immanent procession" in Thomas's Trinitarian theology. Most importantly, I will argue that this paradox really is a paradox: I will argue that, for Thomas, the Son and the Holy Spirit *both* remain within the Father *and* go forth from the Father, and that Their remaining-within is no threat to Their going-forth. From there, I will return more directly to word and love, and I will argue that Thomas

---

[6] If a psychological approach to the Trinity has had a rough go of it lately, then the language of "procession"—immanent or otherwise—has fared little better. See Elizabeth Johnson, *She Who Is: The Mystery of God in Feminist Theological Discourse* (New York: Crossroad, 1992), 194–97; and Leonardo Boff, *Trinity and Society*, trans. Paul Burns (Maryknoll, NY: Orbis Books, 1988), 142. While we cannot answer every objection leveled by the likes of Johnson and Boff, we will see in later chapters that, for Thomas, "procession" is bound up with things like relationality, total self-giving, and interpersonal love—all of which both Boff and Johnson would greet with enthusiasm (though they might read those terms very differently than Aquinas does).

[7] Pannenberg, for example, effectively denies this point in *Systematic Theology*, 295n122.

frames his Trinitarian theology in psychological terms not only in order to safeguard the unity demanded by an *immanent* procession but just as basically in order to safeguard the distinction demanded by an immanent *procession*. I will then dive into the historical development of Thomas's doctrine of the word in order to reinforce this point. For, by reviewing this history, we will unearth strong suggestions that if the logic of a word and love secured only unity of the divine Persons, and if they did not just as basically secure Their distinction, then Thomas would not have placed the word and love at the center of his Trinitarian theology. Finally, I will end by underscoring this point by looking to a cluster of related questions around faith, reason, and the origin of Thomas's psychological categories.[8]

WORD AND LOVE
"There Proceeds Something within Him"

Before doing anything else, we should define—or at least begin to sketch—our two most basic terms: "word" and "love." Beginning with the word, Thomas writes that

> the intellect, having been informed by the species of the thing, by an act of understanding forms within itself a certain intention of the thing understood. . . . Now, since this intention understood is a quasi-terminus of intelligible operation, it is distinct from the intelligible species which actualizes the intellect and which we must consider as the

---

[8] In this chapter, we will see the first instance of a pattern that will emerge through this study: while at some points we will discuss both Word and Love, at others we will focus on the Word alone. Love will recede into the background. Thomas's Trinitarian theology has been accused of being inadequately pneumatological; see Jean-Pierre Torrell, *St. Thomas Aquinas: Spiritual Master*, trans. Robert Royal (Washington, DC: The Catholic University of America Press, 2003), 153–54. Torrell responds to this charge more broadly, as does Levering in *Engaging the Doctrine of the Holy Spirit*. We cannot deal with this question here. Yet we should at least note that, so far as this chapter goes, some (though not all) of the texts we will study speak directly of Love. Even more, we will see that some of the conclusions Thomas draws with reference to the Word would hold for Love as well.

principle of intellectual operation; though both the species and the intention are a likeness of the thing understood.[9]

We will dive into all of these points in great detail as we go along. For now, we can note that this "intention," which Thomas goes on to identify as an inner word, is like the intelligible species, insofar as each is a "likeness of the thing understood." Yet, whereas the species is a principle of understanding that informs and actualizes the intellect, the word is a "quasi-terminus" of understanding that is formed by the intellect.[10] The word, then, is distinct both from the intelligible species and from the act of understanding. It is distinct, moreover, because it is formed in—and hence proceeds in[11]—the act of understanding. It is a sort of "fruit" of understanding that proceeds from the one who understands as he understands.[12]

We can offer a similarly brief overview of love. For Thomas, "from the fact that anyone loves anything, there comes forth a certain impression, so to speak, of the beloved thing in the affection of the lover, by reason of which the beloved thing is said to be in the lover."[13] As a word proceeds from the one who understands, so a love-impression proceeds—or "comes forth"—from the one who loves. In the case of intellect, however, we have language to distinguish the word from the act of understanding; no such language exists with regard to love. Instead, we use the term "love" to refer both to the act of love and to the impression that proceeds in the affection of the lover. For our purposes, in what follows, I will generally speak of the impression that proceeds in love as a "love-impression." For now, the point to stress is that this love-impression is distinct from the act of love because it,

---

[9] *SCG* I 53§§3–4.

[10] See Emery, *TTTA*, 182–85 for more on this point.

[11] For the link between formation and procession, see *SCG* IV 11§13.

[12] For this language of "fruit," see Emery, *TA*, 139. To be sure, actions also, in a certain sense, proceed from an agent; and so the act of understanding proceeds, in a certain sense, from the one who understands. Yet Thomas clarifies that action only *rationally* proceeds from the agent (see *De Ver.*, q. 4, a. 2)—which is why divine action can be really identical to the divine Persons Who act. A word, in contrast, *really* proceeds from its speaker.

[13] *ST* I q. 37, a. 1.

unlike the act of love, really proceeds from the lover. Like a word, it is a sort of fruit that proceeds in the act of love.[14]

Again, we will say a great deal more about word and love as we continue. Yet we have already seen enough to establish our first major point: a word and love-impression—unlike other elements of intellect and will—proceed from the person who understands and loves.

Word and love, however, not only proceed *from* another; they also proceed *within* another. Their processions are *immanent* processions. This last point comes to the fore in the opening of the *Summa*'s Trinitarian questions. After citing Scripture in order to establish that the Son proceeds from the Father, Thomas argues that both Arius and Sabellius erred insofar as they assumed that, because the Son proceeds from the Father, He cannot remain within the divine nature. According to Thomas, however, fidelity to Scripture demands something more: it demands that we recognize a procession *within* God. And it is in order to account for such an immanent procession that Thomas introduces his psychological categories. He writes that immanent procession

> applies most conspicuously to intellect, the action of which remains in the intelligent agent. For whoever understands, from the very fact that he understands, there *proceeds* something *within* him, which is a conception of the object understood, a conception coming forth from the intellectual power and proceeding from the knowledge of the object. This conception is signified by the spoken word; and it is called the word of the heart signified by the word of the voice.[15]

In the immanent act of understanding, we find the immanent procession of a word. And it is precisely the *immanence* of this procession that secures its place at the center of the *Summa*'s Trinitarian theology.

We see the same pattern with the Holy Spirit. Later in the same question, Thomas clarifies that there are not one, but two—and only two—acts that remain within an intellectual nature: "the act of intellect

---

14 For more on the impression of love, see Emery, *TTTA*, 62–69.

15 *ST* I q. 27, a. 1.

and the act of will."[16] He continues: "The procession of the Word is by way of an intelligible act. The operation of the will in us involves also another procession, that of love, whereby the object loved is *in* the lover, just as, by the conception of the word, the object spoken of or understood is *in* the one understanding." Just as the word, this love-impression takes center stage in Thomas's Trinitarian theology because it remains within the lover from whom it proceeds.

"The Central Feature Which a Word Bears in Itself"

The immanence of these processions will be central to all of our conclusions here. Yet it can also be misleading. Indeed, if we were to say nothing further, then we might risk reinforcing the very sorts of readings we are trying to overcome. For, again, it is because a word and love remain within a speaker and a lover that they can account for the consubstantial unity of the Persons. Yet the foregoing might have given the impression that *the* central feature of a word and love-impression is that they remain within a speaker and a lover—which, in turn, might suggest that Thomas allows "word" and "love" to govern his mature Trinitarian theology because they secure the unity of the divine Persons, even if they leave the distinction between those Persons underdeveloped.

To begin pushing back on such a reading, we can highlight a basic point: procession is not merely a marginal feature that is present in some words and loves but might be absent from others. Instead, to focus on the word, Thomas affirms several times that procession belongs to the *ratio* of a word.[17] If a word, therefore, were somehow to cease proceeding from another, then it would cease to be a word.

This procession, moreover, is not merely a feature that attends on created words, but which Thomas, given his insistence on apophaticism and analogy, is hesitant to ascribe to the divine Word. Instead, all of his claims regarding procession and the *ratio* of a word come from the thick of his Trinitarian theology. It seems all but certain, therefore, that he

---

16 *ST* I q. 27, a. 3.

17 See *SCG* IV 11§13; *de rationibus fidei*, ch. 3; *ST* I q. 34, a. 1.

stakes these claims with the divine Word specifically in mind. And so it therefore seems safe to say that, if the divine Word did not proceed from the Father, then He would cease to be a word. Put differently, if the divine Word did not proceed, then Thomas's "psychological analogy" for the Trinity would cease to be an *analogy*. It would become a sort of psychological equivocity. Thomas, however, is clear that when he speaks of the divine Word, he is not speaking equivocally or metaphorically or improperly; he is speaking analogously. Given the *ratio* of a word, therefore, the divine Word must somehow proceed from the Father.[18]

The next point is even more important. Indeed, it is among the most important points of this chapter. In brief, a word does not, even logically speaking, first remain within its speaker and only *then* proceed from its speaker. Instead, its going-forth is just as logically basic as its remaining-within. Indeed, there is nothing more logically basic in a word than its procession. As Emery puts it, "*the* central feature which a word bears in itself is the fact of proceeding from an active intellect."[19] Procession is not just *a* feature of a word; it is *the* central feature of a word.[20] Hyacinthe Paissac suggests something similar when he argues that, for Thomas, "the whole of [a word's] essence is to be relative to its principle":[21] a word "is a pure relation"[22] and "pure relativity."[23] A word is not a "thing" that first exists and is then *in* relation. Nor is it a thing that exists in itself but that also, in addition to existing in itself, is related to its speaker. It *is* relation and it *is* relativity.[24] This relation, in turn, is

---

[18] Although he does not develop this point as fully, Thomas suggests that procession goes to the foundation of a love-impression as well: see *SCG* IV 19§8; and *ST* I q. 27, a. 3, ad 3.

[19] *TTTA*, 184; emphasis added.

[20] See also Emery, *TCHP*, 78–79.

[21] *Théologie du Verbe. Saint Augustin et saint Thomas* (Paris: Cerf, 1951), 190.

[22] *Théologie du Verbe*, 190.

[23] *Théologie du Verbe*, 195.

[24] For Paissac, this "pure relativity" is not opposed to word's remaining-within its speaker; it is vouchsafed by this remaining-within:

> The function of a concept, even to the point of being its very nature and its reason for being, is precisely coming from me, remaining turned towards me, being in relation to me, facing me, before me. The word is not, to any degree, exterior to me or strange to me; it is with me, no longer something simply placed exterior to me, but a being which interests me, because it exists only for me.

founded on a word's *procession* from its speaker.[25] If a word's relation, therefore, goes to its logical foundation, then its procession goes even deeper. Indeed, elsewhere in his Trinitarian theology, Thomas suggests that, in *anything* that takes its origin from another, its procession from its source logically precedes even its existence in itself.[26] Returning more directly to the word, Thomas suggests our point here when he writes that the divine Word has "the *ratio* of proceeding from another: for without this a word cannot be understood."[27] It is not merely that a word cannot exist without proceeding from another. It is even that, logically speaking, a word cannot be *understood* apart from its procession from another. If we were, in our minds, to bracket a word from its procession, then whatever remained in our understanding would not be a word.

That said, it is also of course true that an inner word would cease to be an inner word if it ceased to remain within its speaker. My claim, however, is not that the word's going-forth is somehow more logically basic than its remaining-within. My claim is simply that its going-forth is no *less* basic than its remaining-within. A word both goes forth and remains within, and a word can only be a word if its going-forth is just as logically basic as its remaining-within.

A GOING-FORTH THAT REMAINS WITHIN

THE PARADOX

With these features of a word and love-impression in the background, we can turn for a moment from Thomas's psychological categories in order to attend to the logic of an "immanent procession" more broadly. We can begin with a point that is very basic but has received almost no direct attention: the very notion of an "immanent procession"

Théologie du Verbe, 190. The fact that a word is not "exterior to me" means that its relation to me must go to its foundation.

25 See *ST* I q. 28, a. 4; and Emery, *TTTA*, 53–55.
26 See *ST* I q. 40, a. 4, c. and ad 3.
27 *De rationibus fidei*, ch. 3.

is paradoxical. First, to "proceed," or *pro-cedere*, means literally to "go-forth."[28] Yet to be "immanent," or *in-manens*, means literally to "remain-within."[29] An "immanent procession," therefore, is literally a going-forth that remains within. It would be difficult to think up a flatter-sounding paradox.[30]

We can get a better sense for this paradox if we survey the additional language Thomas uses for it. In various contexts, he describes the processions of the Son and the Holy Spirit as a "going-out,"[31] a "flowing-out,"[32] a "stepping-out,"[33] a "streaming-forth,"[34] a "bringing-forth,"[35] a "drawing-out,"[36] a "sending,"[37] and a "sending-out."[38] The Son and the Holy Spirit, then, eternally go out from the Father, flow out from the Father, step out from the Father, stream forth from the Father, are brought forth from the Father, are drawn out from the Father, and are sent out from the Father—all while remaining within the Father. Each term adds a different hue to the paradox. Yet none of the terms softens the paradox. Instead, each reinforces and refines the paradox: because

---

28 *Pro* means "forward"; *cedere* means "to go." For this point and those to follow, see Roy J. Deferrari, *A Latin-English Dictionary of St. Thomas Aquinas* (Boston: St. Paul Editions, 1960).

29 *In* means "within"; *manens* means "remaining."

30 I know of only one scholar who has recognized the presence of this paradox in Thomas's Trinitarian theology: see Karen Kilby, "Aquinas, the Trinity and the Limits of Understanding," *The International Journal of Systematic Theology* 7, no. 4 (2005): 414–27. I will speak to Kilby's reading of Thomas below.

31 Thomas has the Son say, "*exivi* a Patre, ut verbum ab aeterno" (*in Ioan.*, #1236). See also I *Sent.*, d. 14, q. 3, a. 1; *ST* I q. 42, a. 5, ad 2; *in Ioan.*, #2161.

32 See *De Pot.*, q. 10, a. 1, which we will study in some detail in a moment.

33 Thomas applies the Psalmist's words "a summa caelo *egressio* ejus" to the eternal Son, "through the eternal generation" (*in psalmos*, 18§4).

34 He writes that "idem est in divinis personis *profluere* a patre quod procedure" (*Contra Errores Graecorum* II, ch. 27).

35 Thomas speaks of "aeternam Dei locutionem, qua Deus pater verbum unicum *protulit* sibi coaeternum" (*ST* III q. 45, a. 4, ad 1).

36 See I *Sent.*, d. 13, q. 1, a. 1, which we will give below.

37 Speaking of the Holy Spirit, Thomas writes, "a patre et filio dicitur *missus*. Quod non minorationem in ipso, sed processionem ostendit" (*SCG* IV 27§4).

38 The Father and the Son "send-out," or "e-mit" the Holy Spirit as love in *De Pot.*, q. 10, a. 4, ad 11.

the Son proceeds immanently from the Father, He both eternally goes out from the Father and eternally remains within the Father.

"The Emanation of One Thing from Another"

Again, virtually all of Thomas's readers recognize that the Son and the Holy Spirit, because They proceed as Word and Love, remain within the Father in a unity of nature. It has been less widely acknowledged, however—indeed, it has been actively denied—that the Son and the Holy Spirit, *precisely because They proceed as Word and Love*, really do go forth from the Father as really distinct Persons. And not without reason. For remaining-within and going-forth appear to be mutually exclusive. And given how emphatic Thomas is that the Son and Holy Spirit remain within the Father, it is tempting to reason that They cannot *really* go forth from the Father: for, if They did, how could They remain within Him? The first point to establish, then, is that this paradox really is a paradox: the Son and the Holy Spirit really do remain within the Father, yet They also really do go forth from the Father, and Their really going-forth is in no way threatened by Their remaining-within.[39]

---

[39] This paradox has been ignored by many who read Thomas's psychological analogy as "individualistic": they recognize that his Word and Love remain within the Father, but they assume that his Word and Love cannot go forth from the Father as distinct Persons. Indeed, on Pannenberg's reading, his Word and Love do not *really* go forth at all: see *Systematic Theology*, 295n122.

More interesting is Karen Kilby, who is the only reader of Thomas to have noticed any sort of tension here. Citing Thomas's claim in *ST* I q. 27, a. 1, ad 2 that "the divine Word is of necessity perfectly one with the source whence He proceeds, without any kind of diversity," she writes, "In God we precisely *cannot* think of difference between that which proceeds and that from which it proceeds: divine simplicity requires the denial of this. Thomas is presenting us with a procession that is so perfect that we in fact have no idea why it could not also be called 'not a procession.'" ("Aquinas," 420). For Kilby, the idea of an immanent procession is an "intellectual dead end" (p. 423; see also 414, 418, 424) that yields "not the least bit of understanding" (423) and that stands as an apophatic check on our impulse to exceed the limits of our understanding and to forget that the Trinity is an ungraspable mystery.

The first—and more superficial—response to Kilby is that when Thomas is being most careful about his Trinitarian language, he affirms Kilby's central point: we cannot speak of "diversity" or "difference" between the divine Persons; yet he also clarifies that we *can* speak of a "distinction" between Them (see *ST* I q. 31, a. 2; and *De Pot.*, q. 9, a. 8, c., and ad 2). Thus, when Thomas denies that there is "any kind of *diversity*" between the

To see as much, we can turn to a text where Thomas dives into what exactly "procession" in God means. He writes that

> in us, intellectual knowledge originates in the imagination and senses, which do not go beyond continuous matter. For this reason, we take terms that apply to continuous matter and transfer them to whatever we grasp with the intellect. . . . [In this way,] the term "procession" was first used to signify local motion . . . and from there it was used to signify anything in which there is any order of one thing from another, or of one thing after another. Hence . . . we use the word procession to indicate the *emanation* of one thing from another. In this way, we say that a ray proceeds from the sun, and that the operation or even the thing produced proceeds from the operator.[40]

"Procession" was first employed to designate local motion. Indeed, it is still used to this purpose. Yet it also admits other uses: it can designate "the emanation of one thing from another." And, as Thomas goes on to explain, it is only in this latter sense that "procession" is used properly of the divine Persons. When Thomas speaks of an intra-divine "procession," what he really means, therefore, is an intra-divine "emanation" of one thing from another.

We saw above that to speak of an "immanent procession" is to speak paradoxically. We might expect, however, that Thomas would be

---

Father and His Word, he is not shutting down the room needed for a *distinction* between Them. Procession, for its part, requires neither difference nor diversity; it requires only distinction (see I *Sent.*, d. 15, q. 1, a. 1). Thus, in virtue of the distinction between Word and Speaker, the procession of the divine Word can be a *procession* in the strictest sense of the term—and *not* "not a procession"—even as the Word is neither "diverse" nor "different" from His Speaker.

The deeper point is that, for Kilby, because the Word remains perfectly within His Speaker, He cannot *actually* proceed from His Speaker. She assumes that our paradox is a mere contradiction: she assumes that one pole of it must crowd the other out and that it therefore ends in sheer unintelligibility. We will see presently, however, that Thomas seems to assume otherwise (in the section "One, Therefore Many" in chapter three, we will also speak to Kilby's claim regarding simplicity). Be that as it may, Kilby is unique, and she is uniquely helpful, in that she recognizes—and refuses to gloss over—the tensions entailed in the very idea of an "immanent procession."

40 *De Pot.*, q. 10, a. 1.

more sober and straightforward when he is most carefully identifying the precise meaning of "procession" in God. We might expect him to make the requisite distinctions and clarifications: we might expect him to explain that, for example, procession in God need not *really* entail anything *actually* going forth from anything else. Yet he does no such thing. Instead, he explains that, in God, what "procession" *really* means is "emanation." Yet, if *pro-cedere* means to "go-forth," then *e-manare* means to "flow-out."[41] An immanent emanation, therefore, is no less paradoxical than an immanent procession: a flowing-out that remains within is no less paradoxical than a going-forth that remains within. In explaining the paradox, Thomas merely restates the paradox. He leaves us with the same paradox in slightly different words.

Of course, all of the rules governing and limiting our proper speech of God apply here as well. First, our knowledge of "procession," like our knowledge of every term we predicate properly of God, comes through our "senses, which do not go beyond continuous matter." "Procession," therefore, must be separated from all the imperfections with which we encounter it among material creatures.[42] The main imperfection Thomas identifies here is local motion. The point we can stress, however, is that *going-out is no such imperfection*. As Thomas writes later in the same article, "The procession attributed to the divine Persons is *not* a local motion, *but* one that implies an order of emanation."[43] Emanation—or flowing-out—is not an imperfection that must be carefully removed from "procession" if we would attribute "procession" to the divine Persons; flowing-out is an *alternative* to the imperfection of motion, and emanation therefore *can* be "attributed to the divine Persons." Indeed, flowing-out is *all that remains* of procession when all creaturely imperfections have been removed.[44]

---

41 See Deferrari, *A Latin-English Dictionary*, 627.

42 For Thomas's teaching on *separatio*, see *in Boeth. de Trin.*, q. 5, a. 3. For some helpful background, see John F. Wippel, *Metaphysical Themes in Thomas Aquinas* (Washington, DC: The Catholic University of America Press, 1984), 69–104.

43 *De Pot.*, q. 10, a. 1, ad 2.

44 Thomas makes this move consistently when he asks whether there is procession in God. In I *Sent.*, d. 13, q. 1, a. 1, he separates procession from "local motion," and he clarifies that in God, procession "designates the *drawing out [educatio]* of a principled

The most basic point is that we cannot invoke the fact that the Son and the Holy Spirit remain within the Father in order to deny that They really go forth from the Father. If we were to do so, then we would be left, at best, with procession in an equivocal or metaphorical sense. Thomas, however, is clear that he is speaking properly—and therefore analogously—when he speaks of procession in God,[45] and if such procession does not mean that the Son and the Spirit really go forth from the Father, then it does not mean anything. We cannot, therefore, treat the remaining-within of the divine Persons as a threat to Their going-forth. Instead, we must hold both prongs of the paradox: the divine Persons go forth even as They remain within, and They remain within even as They go forth.[46]

"Always in the Father and Always Going out from the Father"

We will see shortly that Thomas does not merely assert this paradox. Nor does he demand that we blindly accept it despite its irrationality. Instead, he shows this paradox to be reasonable. Before seeing as much, however, we should make clear just how starkly and strongly he presents us with this paradox. To do so, we can turn to Thomas's commentary on John 16:28, "I went forth from the Father." He writes that Christ

---

thing from its principle"—which leaves us with a drawing-out that remains within. In *ST* I q. 27, a. 1, Thomas separates procession from "local motion" and from "the act of a cause on an exterior effect." He then writes that "procession in God" is "an intelligible *emanation*"—which leaves us once again with a flowing-out that remains within. As Thomas clarifies here, this emanation does not flow out *to* "an exterior effect"; yet it must somehow flow out *from* its source. Otherwise, it would cease to be an emanation. In these two briefer texts, then, when all imperfections are removed from an immanent "procession," what remains is a drawing-out that remains within and a flowing-out that remains within—neither of which is any less paradoxical than a going-forth that remains within.

45 Thomas makes this point particularly clear in I *Sent.*, d. 13, q. 1, a. 1: insofar as "procession" points to a "drawing-out," "procession is properly in God."

46 There are other points where Thomas explains that in the immaterial God, the spatial language of "going-forth" simply means that the Son and the Father are really distinct Persons (see *in Ioan.*, #2161). This move might seem to explain away the reality of procession in God, and hence to collapse our paradox. In our next chapter, however, we will see that it actually radicalizes our paradox.

> refers to the eternal procession when He says, "I went out [*exivi*] from the Father," eternally generated by Him. . . . In material things, what goes out from another is no longer in it, since it goes out from it by a separation from it in place or in essence. This is not the kind of going out we have here, for the Son went out from the Father from all eternity in such a way that the Son is nevertheless in the Father from all eternity. And so when the Son is in the Father, He goes out; and when the Son goes out, He is in the Father: so the Son is always in the Father and always going out from the Father.[47]

Thomas gives a clue here as to why going-out and remaining-within seem to be incompatible: among material things, they *are* incompatible. A baseball cannot go forth from my hand while remaining within my hand. Among spiritual things, however, going-out and remaining-within are not incompatible—and they therefore are not incompatible among the divine Persons. Because the divine Persons are removed from matter, They are removed from any opposition between going-out and remaining-within. More specifically, because the Son is removed from matter, He does not merely go out from the Father after He has stopped remaining within the Father. Nor does He merely remain within after He has stopped going out. Instead, the Son goes out "*when*" He is in, and the Son remains within "*when*" He goes out. He does both at once, eternally.[48]

This passage is also helpful because it closes a door through which we might otherwise have tried to wiggle out of our paradox. For we might be tempted to smooth things over by clarifying that the Son goes out from one thing but remains within another: that, for example, He goes out from the person of the Father, but that He remains within the divine essence—an essence that is at least rationally distinct from

---

[47] *In Ioan.*, #2161.

[48] Thomas continues by writing that "there is scarcely any other place in Sacred Scripture where the origin of Christ is so openly expressed as here" (*in Ioan.*, #2165). Thus, on Thomas's reckoning, we have here one of Scripture's plainest articulations of the Son's eternal procession. Thomas's exposition of these words, therefore, might represent a privileged window into his understanding of this procession.

the person of the Father. Thomas, however, writes that "the Son is always in *the Father* and always going out from *the Father*." The Son both eternally goes out from and eternally remains within one and the same thing: the person of the Father.[49]

Most basically, this passage strongly suggests that Thomas is aware that his proposal here is paradoxical. Yet he proposes it all the same. He even proposes it with full knowledge that, even in spiritual things, there is a tension at work here: "the Son went out from the Father from all eternity in such a way that the Son is *nevertheless* in the Father from all eternity." Yet the fact that Thomas acknowledges this tension—and the fact that he thereby brings it to our attention—only makes it more remarkable when he ends by embracing it. To domesticate or deflate this paradox—or to assume that the immanence of these processions leaves no room for any real going-forth—would therefore be to deny that an immanent procession is an immanent *procession*. And it would therefore be to take leave of Thomas.[50]

---

49 The same holds for a word. For Thomas sometimes gives the impression that a word goes forth from the *knowledge* of its speaker (for example, see *ST* I q. 27, a. 1, and q. 34, a. 1). Were it so, we might have room to say that a word remains within one thing and goes forth from another: we might be able to say that it remains within its speaker *himself* without going forth from him, and that it goes forth from its speaker's *knowledge* without remaining within it (for created speakers are really distinct from their knowledge of things). When Thomas puts things more precisely, however, he clarifies that a word goes forth from its speaker himself—the speaker within whom it remains. He writes, "that is properly called an inner word which *the one understanding* forms by understanding" (*in Ioan.*, #25). Indeed, if a word proceeded not from its speaker but from its speaker's knowledge, then the divine Word would proceed from, and hence be really distinct from, the divine knowledge. Because, however, He is really identical to this knowledge, He cannot proceed from it. Indeed, because He is distinct only from His Speaker, He must proceed only from His Speaker—which means that words must proceed from their speakers and remain within their speakers.

50 This passage can also allow for a deeper response to Kilby. For it opens up a way in which, despite all her insistence on apophaticism, she may ultimately slip into a strange univocity. Specifically, Thomas suggests here that if we were to insist that the Son cannot both go forth from the Father and remain perfectly one with the Father, then we would imply that the laws governing material things hold sway among the divine Persons. In insisting on the radical otherness and unknowability of God, therefore, Kilby may ultimately collapse the difference between God and the material things that we know so readily. For ways in which univocity and equivocity always melt into each other, see Ulrich, *Homo Abyssus*, 206–8.

"THE WORD GOES FORTH FROM THE HEART AND REMAINS THEREIN"

We mentioned above that Thomas does not merely assert this paradox. Instead, he attempts to make sense of it. And, importantly for us, he appeals to the logic of a word and love in order to do so. Specifically, he reminds us that it is not only the divine Persons Who both go forth from and remain within the same thing. Human words and loves do the same. Limiting ourselves to the *Summa*'s Trinitarian questions, he writes that "the interior word proceeds from the one speaking so as to remain within him"; he tells us that "the word goes forth from the heart and remains therein"; and he speaks of "the intelligible word which proceeds from the speaker, yet remains in him."[51] Thomas is not speaking here of a divine Person or of the divine Word, and so he is not gesturing feebly towards some mystery veiled in light inaccessible. Instead, he is speaking of the human words with which we are intimately familiar.

This point comes out more fully when Thomas puts in the mouth of his objector the sorts of objections one cannot but raise when confronted with the paradox of an immanent procession. These passages are important for us for two reasons. First, they underscore just how deliberate Thomas is in presenting us with this paradox: he knows that the very idea of an immanent procession sounds contradictory, and he has his objector take issue with this apparent contradiction. Yet he proposes it all the same. Second, and more deeply, when Thomas defends his proposal in the face of these objections, he does so with recourse to his psychological categories. He explains that it is reasonable to believe that an immanent procession exists in God, for we already know that immanent processions exist in us.

Within the *Summa*, this point first comes out when Thomas is asking whether the divine Persons are within each other, and when he faces the objection that "nothing that has gone out of another is within it. But the Son from eternity went out from the Father. . . . Therefore the

---

[51] The first passage comes from *ST* I q. 34, a. 1, ad 1, the second from *ST* I q. 42, a. 5, ad 2, and the third from *ST* I q. 27, a. 1.

Son is not in the Father."[52] Again, Thomas recognizes that his proposal is paradoxical: he sees that going-out and remaining-within appear to be incompatible. Yet he appeals to our experience with our inner words in order to argue that, in fact, they are not: "The Son's going out from the Father is according to the mode of interior procession, whereby the word goes forth from the heart and remains therein."[53] Thomas's aim here is to show that his position is more than mere contradiction. And he does so by reminding us that our own inner words are marked by the very paradox on which the objector has put his finger: they remain within the heart from which they go forth. Such remaining-within, therefore, cannot actually be incompatible with going-forth. If it were, then our own inner words could not exist.

Thus, in this passage, Thomas justifies a paradox with which we have no direct experience—the procession of the Son—with a reference to *another* paradox with which we *do* have experience: the processions of our inner words. The logic of an inner word allows him to maintain, and to begin to render intelligible, the paradox of procession in God. Yet it allows him to do so without making the paradox any less paradoxical.

We see a similar dynamic in Thomas's response to an objection around the procession of the Holy Spirit: "Nothing proceeds from that wherein it rests; but the Holy Spirit rests in the Son. . . . Therefore the Holy Spirit does not proceed from the Son."[54] Again, Thomas acknowledges that resting-in and proceeding-from appear to be mutually exclusive. Yet he responds, "when the Holy Spirit is said to rest or remain in the Son, it does not mean that He does not proceed from Him; for the Son is also said to remain in the Father, although He proceeds from the Father. The Holy Spirit is also said to rest in the Son as the love of the lover rests in the beloved."[55] Thomas begins by reasoning that because the Son proceeds from the Father in Whom He remains, it must be possible for the Holy Spirit to proceed from the Son in Whom He rests. Once again, he justifies this current paradox by referring his

---

52 *ST* I q. 42, a. 5, arg. 2.
53 *ST* I q. 42, a. 5, ad 2.
54 *ST* I q. 36, a. 2, arg. 4.
55 *ST* I q. 36, a. 2, ad 4.

readers to another paradox that they have already accepted. Perhaps even more important for us, however, is Thomas's final claim. For he ends by invoking his psychological categories: "The Holy Spirit is also said to rest in the Son as *the love of the lover* rests in the beloved."[56] We will return at great length in chapter six to the procession of divine Love, and to the relationship between His status as an immanent Love-impression and His role in the love of the Father for the Son. For now, we can limit ourselves to a single modest point: Thomas reasons that, *because the Holy Spirit proceeds as Love*, we can coherently affirm both that He rests in the Son and that He proceeds from the Son. It is by referring to the Holy Spirit's status as a Love-impression—and so it is by appealing to his psychological analogy—that Thomas shows the paradox of an immanent procession to be reasonable.

Again, a going-out that remains within might initially sound like nonsense. Yet Thomas suggests that we can know, based on our experience in this life, that there is no real contradiction here: for we can know that our words and our loves remain within us even as they proceed from us. And he suggests that we can therefore begin to see that it is not impossible—even if it is paradoxical, and even if we cannot come close to grasping the mystery in this life—that we should find a radically different coincidence of going-forth and remaining-within in God.[57]

The most important point for us, then, is that Thomas introduces his psychological language in order to secure *both* sides of this paradox. When he meets the objection that the Son cannot go forth from and

---

[56] Thomas offers the same response to the same objection in *De Pot.*, q. 10, a. 4, ad 18.

[57] We should offer a final response to Kilby in light of these points. For Kilby argues that Thomas proposes a contradictory and nonsensical (and not merely paradoxical) procession-that-is-not-a-procession in order to show that we cannot gain "the least bit of understanding" into the Trinity ("Aquinas," 423). For Kilby, talk of an "immanent procession" is a matter of mere apophasis. The passages we have given, however, suggest that Thomas's psychological analogy—that is, his appeal to our experience with our words and loves—*can* give us at least a bit of understanding into the Trinity. Indeed, Thomas affirms elsewhere that his Trinitarian theology can offer us a "foretaste" of beatific vision. See Emery, "Trinitarian Theology as Spiritual Exercise in Augustine and Aquinas," in *Aquinas the Augustinian*, ed. Michael Dauphinais, Barry David, and Matthew Levering, 1–40 (Washington, DC: The Catholic University of America Press, 2007). It seems, moreover, that it can only convey this foretaste if an "immanent procession" is not a contradiction bereft of meaning but a paradox rich in intelligibility.

remain within the same thing, he does not respond by reminding us that, because the Son proceeds as a Word, He merely remains within the Father instead of going forth from the Father. Instead, he responds by reminding us that, because the Son proceeds as a Word, He remains within the Father even as He really does go forth from the Father. And, given that, as we saw above, the going-forth of a word is just as logically basic as its remaining-within, Thomas's claim here suggests that the Son, because He is a Word, goes forth from the Father just as basically as He remains within the Father. Again, "*the* central feature which a word bears in itself is the fact of proceeding from an active intellect."[58] Thomas's psychological analogy does not merely secure going-forth *and* remaining-within, distinction *and* unity. It secures going-forth and distinction *just as basically* as it secures remaining-within and unity.

The most basic point, however, is that Thomas's psychological categories do not give him a way to unilaterally privilege remaining-within over going-forth; they give him a way to hold remaining-within together with going-forth. They allow our paradox to remain paradoxical but to begin to become coherent.

Again, we will spend later chapters drawing out the interpersonal implications of this going-forth. First, however, we will spend the rest of this chapter reinforcing our current point. For it is not only that, in fact, Thomas's psychological terms secure both remaining-within and going-forth. It is also that, in principle, Thomas would not have chosen to cast the Trinity in psychological terms unless they secured both this remaining-within and this going-forth.

THE HISTORY OF THE WORD

To see as much, we can turn to the historical development of Thomas's theology of the Word. This history has been the subject of several illuminating studies, and we need not enter into all its detail here.[59] By surveying a few key junctures along this development, however, we

---

58 *TTTA*, 184; emphasis added.

59 See Paissac, *Théologie du Verbe*, 117–236; Emery, *TTTA*, 180–85; A. F. von Gunton, "*In principio erat verbum*. Une evolution de saint Thomas en théologie trinitaire," in *Ordo Sapienta et Amoris* (Fribourg: Éditions Universitaires Fribourg Suisse, 1993), 119–41; and

will be able to unearth the strongest evidence for our claim here: that Thomas only chooses to place the word at the center of his Trinitarian theology because it can account both for a going-forth and for a remaining-within.

THE *RATIO* OF A WORD

We saw at the opening of this chapter that Thomas, in his mature thought, distinguishes the inner word both from the act of understanding and from the intelligible species. He did not, however, always draw this distinction. In his *Commentary on the Sentences*, Thomas devotes an article to asking whether "word" is an essential or a personal name in God.[60] After writing that the inner word must be "the concept of the intellect," he continues

> The conception of the intellect is *either the operation itself,* which is to understand, *or the species understood.* Hence "word" must refer either to *the operation itself* of understanding, or to *the species itself* which is the likeness of the thing understood. . . . And therefore it is *impossible* that, in understanding [an inner] word, anyone should understand anything but the word of his intellect, which is *its operation,* or . . . the *species* of the thing understood.

Thomas makes the same point thrice over: to speak of an "inner word" is to speak either of the intelligible species or of the act of understanding. It is "impossible" that our talk of an inner "word" should refer to anything else.

This account of what a word is goes on to drive Thomas's account of how "word" functions in our talk of God. Thomas first recalls that personal names in God imply a real distinction, and that they therefore refer to a distinct divine Person; essential names, in contrast, imply no

---

Harm Goris, "Theology and Theory of the Word in Aquinas: Understanding Augustine by Innovating Aristotle," in *Aquinas the Augustinian*, 62–78.

60 See I *Sent.*, d. 27, q. 2, a. 2, qc. 1, from which all of the following quotes will come. For some background on this text, along with its redaction history, see Goris, "Theology and Theory of the Word," 65–68.

such real distinction, and they therefore refer to all three divine Persons in common. Thomas then writes that "the name 'word,' by virtue of the meaning of the term itself [*ex virtu vocabuli*], can be understood both personally and essentially." He elaborates,

> If the relationship implied in this name "word" is only a rational relation, then nothing prevents it from being said essentially. And *this seems to suffice for the ratio of a word*, according as we transfer it from us to God; because in us, as we said in the previous article, the word is nothing but the *species understood*, or perhaps the very *operation of intellect*: and neither of these are really distinct from the divine essence. But if it implies a relation that demands a real distinction, it must be said personally, for there is no real distinction in God except that of the Persons. . . . In the use of the saints and in common speech, however, the name "word" does imply a real relation and real distinction, as when Augustine says that the word is generated wisdom.

Thomas reminds us that an inner word, based on "the *ratio* of a word," can ultimately be "*nothing but* the species understood, or perhaps the very operation of intellect." Yet he also goes further: he applies these claims directly to questions of Trinitarian theology. Specifically, he reasons that neither the divine species nor the divine act of understanding are "really distinct" from anything else in God. There is certainly a "rational relation," and hence a rational distinction, between the divine species, the divine act of understanding, and the divine Persons Who understand. But there is no real relation or real distinction between them. Both the divine species and the divine act of understanding, therefore, are said essentially of God. And, because "word" can ultimately refer only to this species or to this act, "word" can be said essentially of God. So far as "the *ratio* of a word" goes, "word" is an essential term.

Of course, Thomas goes on to acknowledge a sense in which "word" "does imply a real relation and real distinction," which means that "word" can be used personally of God. Yet he holds that, because nothing in the meaning or nature of a word can secure a real distinction, *nothing in the meaning or nature of a word* can ground the personal use of "word" in God. Its being used "personally" springs not from the meaning of the term itself, but from "the use of the saints." Thomas, in other words, is well aware that both Scripture and tradition use "Word" as a personal name for the Son. Thomas is not willing to gainsay this tradition; yet nor is he able to justify this tradition with recourse to the intrinsic suitability of the term "word" for Trinitarian theology. Indeed, he makes quite clear that a word, based on its *ratio* or intrinsic meaning, is *not* suitable for Trinitarian theology.[61]

Things change dramatically in Thomas's mature Trinitarian thought. First of all, from the *SCG* onward, Thomas distinguishes the word both from the act of understanding and from the intelligible species: the word is not the species that informs the intellect but a fruit that is formed by intellect; the word is not the act of understanding but the terminus of understanding that proceeds in this act.[62] This note of procession comes to the fore when, in the *Summa*, Thomas distinguishes the word from the act of understanding, and when he explains why the former is said personally of God and the latter is not, "Nothing belonging to intellect can be said personally of God, except 'word' alone, for only 'word' signifies something which *emanates* from another," whereas "the act of understanding does *not* signify an act going out from the intelligent agent, *but* an act remaining in the agent."[63] The act of understanding remains within *instead of* going out; a word remains within *and* goes out. And it is for this reason that "word" is a personal name in God and "understanding" is not.[64] As Thomas writes in the same article, "Word" in God is "a personal name,

---

[61] Things develop a bit, but they stop well short of Thomas's mature thought, in the *De Ver.*, q. 4. See Emery, *TTTA*, 182; Goris, "Theology and Theory of the Word," 69–73.

[62] For developed articulations of these points, see *SCG* I 53§§3–4; *De Pot.*, q. 8, a. 1; *ST* I q. 34, a. 1; and *in Ioan.*, #25.

[63] *ST* I q. 34, a. 1, ad 2. See *in Ioan.*, #25 for very similar language.

[64] This point has been lost even on some of Thomas's more sympathetic and insightful readers. A. N. Williams, for example, writes that, for Thomas, "the *actions* of knowing and loving take the form of Persons" (*The Ground of Union* [Oxford: Oxford University Press, 1999], 57; emphasis added), and "the Word is the Father's self-understanding" (p. 59). Bourassa too refers to the Son as the "thought" of the Father in "Personne et conscience" (689). For a more on the distinctions between "word," "intellect," "speaking," and "understanding," see Emery, *TTTA*, 185–87.

and in no way an essential name," for a word "has from its *ratio* that it proceed from another."[65] Unlike the word of Thomas's early career, this "Word" is not a personal name in some respects and an essential name in other respects; it is only personal, and it is in no way essential. And it is exclusively essential because, by virtue of its *ratio* as a word, it is inseparable from procession.[66]

FROM THE MARGINS TO THE CENTER

To sum up, Thomas in his mature thought *insists* that "Word" *must* be a personal name in God *because of* the definition of a word: for this definition includes procession. In his *Sentences* commentary, he *allows* that "Word" *might* be a personal name in God *despite* the definition of a word: for this definition has nothing to do with procession. Again, this early word can only be a cipher either for the intelligible species or for the act of understanding. And, in God, both this species and this act are identical to the Father; yet neither of them go forth from the Father. This early word, therefore, can give us only a remaining-within; it cannot give a remaining-within that goes forth. These points become important for us when we note that, in Thomas's early career, this procession-less word is *all but irrelevant to Thomas's Trinitarian theology*. Out of deference to tradition and to "the use of the saints," Thomas acknowledges "word" as a valid name for the Son. Yet, when he goes about building up his own Trinitarian theology, he makes virtually no use of it. When the word does not really proceed, and so when a word can offer only a remaining-within that does not really go forth, Thomas leaves the word on the margins of his Trinitarian theology.[67]

---

[65] *ST* I q. 34, a. 1.

[66] For something of the intensity with which Thomas eventually distanced himself from—or, as Paissac puts it, "solemnly excommunicated"—his early teaching that "Word" can be said essentially, see Paissac, *Théologie du Verbe*, 202n1.

[67] Paissac offers a helpful contrast between Thomas's *Sentences* commentary and the *Summa* on this score in *Théologie du Verbe*, 117–22. In addition to the texts Paissac offers from the *Sentences*, see *in Boeth. de Trin.*, Prol. and q. 3, a. 4; and *Contra Errores Greacorum* I, ch. 1–2, and II, chs. 8–11. Both were written before book IV of the *SCG*; see Torrell, *St. Thomas Aquinas: The Person and His Work*, trans. Robert Royal (Washington, DC: The Catholic University of America Press, 2023), 390 and 410; and, in both, the Son's status

From the other direction, as soon as Thomas recognizes that a word both goes forth and remains within, he enthrones the word at the center of his theology of the Son. It is in the *SCG* that procession first enters the *ratio* of a word, and so it is in the *SCG* that a word begins both to go out from its speaker and to remain within its speaker.[68] And, accordingly, it is in the *SCG* that the word first stands at the governing center of Thomas's Trinitarian theology. Just so, as Thomas's career continues beyond the *SCG*, the word continues to hold both sides of this paradox together, and it continues to set the frame for his Trinitarian thought.[69]

Summing up, when a word merely remains within its speaker without going forth from its speaker, it is relegated to the margins of Thomas's Trinitarian theology; once it begins both to go forth and to remain within, it stands at the center of Thomas's Trinitarian theology; and, so long as it continues both to go forth and to remain within, it remains at the center of Thomas's Trinitarian theology. It therefore seems safe to say that it is *because* a word both goes forth and remains within—and so it is because a word does justice to both sides of our paradox—that it enjoys its privileged status at the center of Thomas's Trinitarian theology.

A similar pattern can be drawn out with love, though we will have to tread a bit more tentatively here, for the history of Thomas's development on this point has been less amply documented.[70] First, in

---

as Word figures only marginally. *De Ver.*, q. 4 (which comes from the same period as *in Boeth. de Trin.* and *Contra Errores Greacorum*) might seem to be an exception. For after spending q. 1 on truth, q. 2 on God's knowledge, and q. 3 on the divine ideas, Thomas devotes all of q. 4 to the divine Word, and he speaks of the Son as a Word all through q. 4. Yet he seems to do so not because "Word" stands at the center of his Trinitarian theology but because "Word" is relevant to his larger concern with the divine intellect—a concern that is evident throughout the *De Ver.*'s opening questions. It seems, that is, that he treats of the Son as Word not because "Word" is the most fitting name for the Son, but because "Word" is the point at which the Trinity intersects with the divine intellect, and because he is interested here first and foremost with the divine intellect.

68 See IV 11§13. See also Emery, *TTTA*, 182; Goris, 73–77.

69 Again, see Paissac, 117–22.

70 It has, however, received some attention. In what follows, I will draw chiefly from Emery, *TTTA*, 67–69; and H. D. Simonin, "Autour de la solution Thomiste de problème de l'amour," *Archives d'histoire et littéraire de Moyen Age* 6 (1931): 174–276.

his early thought, Thomas does not recognize anything that proceeds within the will of a lover: "the will does not have anything proceeding from it except in the manner of an operation."[71] It is once more with the *SCG* that Thomas first teaches that the will produces an immanent fruit: as he writes, "when the mind loves itself, it *produces* its own self as loved in the will."[72] It should perhaps come as no surprise, therefore, that it is in the *SCG* that Thomas first casts the Holy Spirit primarily in terms of the love that proceeds within the lover.[73] In his *Sentences* commentary, when he had yet to land on such an immanent term produced within the will, he had framed the procession of the Holy Spirit more explicitly and frequently in terms of the mutual love between the Father and the Son. Indeed, the shift is so evident that some scholars have argued that Thomas, as his teaching matures, deliberately shies away from casting the Holy Spirit as mutual or interpersonal love in favor of self-love.[74] We will return to this point in chapter six. For now, we can stress that Thomas only begins to cast the Holy Spirit in terms of the immanent act of love when that act begins to entail the *procession* of an immanent *fruit* that is really distinct from the lover himself. When love entails only an immanent action that does not go out from the lover, it remains marginal to Thomas's theology of the Holy Spirit. The immanent act of love only takes center stage when Thomas discovers the love-*impression* that goes forth from the lover within whom it remains.

Historically speaking, then, Thomas only seizes on the language of "word" and "love" once the logic of a word and love-impression require that they go beyond mere immanence: he only embraces them once they can secure a going-forth that remains within. Immanence without procession is not Trinitarian immanence; a remaining-within that does not go forth is useless for Trinitarian theology. And it therefore remains unused. In the beginning, then, was the Word. And this Word was in

---

[71] *De Ver.*, q. 4, a. 2, ad 7. The whole of this passage is relevant for our question. See also Emery, *TTTA*, 68.

[72] *SCG* IV 26§6. See also Emery, *TTTA*, 68.

[73] See *SCG* IV, ch. 19.

[74] See Emery, *TTTA*, 233–34; Penido, "Gloses sur la procession d'amour," and "A Propos de la procession d'amour en Dieu," *Ephemerides theologicae lovanienses* 15 (1938): 338–44.

God, and this Word was God. But this Word did not go forth from God. And, because it secured only one side of our paradox, it remained on the sidelines of Thomas's Trinitarian theology. This historical fact, moreover, helps to unveil a theological truth: when Thomas ultimately decides to cast his Trinitarian theology in psychological terms, it is not because he is interested in unity or immanence over distinction or procession. Instead, it is because he is interested in unity *and* in distinction. He would have continued ignoring his psychological terms had they continued to secure only unity, and he only ends up embracing his psychological terms because they become able to secure the going-forth of the divine Persons just as fundamentally as they secure the remaining-within of the divine Persons—which means that he only embraces them because they become able to secure personal distinction just as basically as they secure essential unity.[75]

WHENCE THE WORD?

This study is devoted to arguing that Thomas's psychological Trinity is already an interpersonal Trinity. Yet, as we mentioned in the introduction, Thomas's psychological analogy was not only criticized for

---

[75] These points can allow us to address another objection. For one might acknowledge that Thomas, through his psychological analogy, allows for *some* sort of intra-divine distinction. Yet one might object that he was obliged to do so in order to remain within the parameters of orthodox Christianity, and that he chooses a psychological approach in order to technically account for that distinction while minimizing it as far as possible. I will turn to part of this objection (regarding the distinction of the divine Persons as "minimal") in the section "This Distinction Excels all Distinctions" in chapter two. For now, it bears noting that the tradition to which Thomas was bound contained voices that, like the early Thomas, identified the "Word" of John 1:1 with the act of understanding (or with knowledge). And, like the early Thomas, these voices held that such a word-as-knowledge does not really proceed from anything else in God. Yet, unlike the early Thomas, those voices made this procession-less word central to their Trinitarian theology (especially important here is Anselm: see Emery, *TTTA*, 186). If Thomas, therefore, had been interested merely in securing the unity of the divine Persons, but if he had felt himself extrinsically beholden to the letter of a tradition that demanded at least a nominal recognition of distinction, then he could have remained within the bounds of that tradition through a word that *did* secure a bare level of distinction but was merely a cipher for the act of understanding, and which therefore privileged essential unity over distinction. Yet he declines to do so (see especially *ST* I q. 34, a. 1, ad 3)—which suggests further that his psychological categories are not, in fact, a means of minimizing the distinction of the divine Persons, but of holding Their distinction together with Their unity.

privileging unity over distinction. It was also criticized for privileging reason and philosophy over faith and Revelation: it was charged with reducing the Gospel to Aristotle and for stuffing Revelation into a set of a prepackaged, pre-Christian, and a-Trinitarian philosophical commitments.[76] These two criticisms were far from unrelated. For if it was commonly alleged that Thomas's psychological analogy allowed him to swallow up the distinction of the divine Persons into Their unity, then it was also alleged that his pre-Christian philosophical commitments—the commitments that *really* govern his Trinitarian thought—obliged him to do so.[77] At the foundation of his Trinitarian theology, in other words, was allegedly an a priori commitment to divine unity over against any properly interpersonal distinction: for Thomas's philosophical priors allegedly demanded this emphasis on unity. Also at the foundation of Trinitarian theology, therefore, was allegedly an a priori commitment to a psychological Trinity: for his psychological analogy allegedly gave him a path towards securing unity and minimizing distinction.[78]

We just saw, however, that Thomas's commitment to a psychological Trinity is neither a priori nor unconditional. Instead, constant through his career is an a priori and unconditional commitment both to the distinction of the divine Persons and to Their unity, and his commitment to a psychological Trinity is conditioned on its being able to secure both. When his psychological categories became able to accommodate both this distinction and this unity, he embraced them; when they could accommodate only unity but not distinction, he largely ignored them. We can probe this point further if we attend briefly to the role that

---

[76] For more subtle versions of this criticism, see John Zizioulas, *Being as Communion* (New York: St. Vladimir's Seminary Press, 1985), 104; and Balthasar, *Theo-Logic II*, 161–62 and 164. Less subtle is Moltmann: see *The Trinity and the Kingdom*, 17.

[77] Moltmann again offers a particularly clear link between a philosophical commitment to "classical theism" and a non-Trinitarian monotheism (this point emerges throughout *The Trinity and the Kingdom*).

[78] It might also be alleged that Thomas's governing commitment was not merely to philosophical reason, but also to an Augustinian heritage that demanded a psychological approach to the Trinity (and that was *itself* philosophical before it was theological). In fact, however, Augustine (along with his heritage) straightforwardly privileges neither unity over distinction nor philosophy over theology; see Bourassa, "Le Saint-Esprit unite d'amour du Père et du Fils," *Science et Esprit* 14 (1962): 375–415.

Revelation played in Thomas's ultimate embrace of the psychological analogy. We cannot, of course, pursue these questions of faith, reason, and the Trinity at any great length here. Yet, because these questions are bound up with our main concern, and because the points we just uncovered regarding the history of the word can shed some new light on them, we can end this chapter by speaking at least briefly to them.[79]

BEYOND ARISTOTLE

It is no secret that Thomas's account of intellect owes a great deal to Aristotle. It is also well known that Aristotle's intellect figures prominently in Thomas's Trinitarian theology.[80] Yet, as others have already established, Thomas does not merely copy and paste Aristotle into his Trinitarian theology. As Emery puts it, Thomas holds that

> intellection and willing are fruitful acts that "produce" something in the one who knows and loves. Thomas must work here a *profound modification* of Aristotle's anthropology. For Aristotle, the immanent operations of the intellect and the will, strictly speaking, "produce" nothing. In the two cases, St. Thomas *rereads Aristotle* in light of the Augustinian heritage in order to recognize the production of a "fruit" of the intelligence and of the will of God, that is, an immanent "term": such are the Word and Love.[81]

---

[79] The question of Scripture, Revelation, and the Trinity is, of course, vast. For some general reflections on the role of Scripture in Thomas's Trinitarian theology, see Emery, *TTTA*, 18–22 and *TA*, 271–319. These larger questions were also central to the Trinitarian "Revivals" of the twentieth century (see Holmes, *The Quest for the Trinity*, 9–12). I certainly cannot enter directly into any of these questions here. Nor do I hope to deny that in this respect, the Revivals might go beyond Thomas. Instead, I hope only to shed some new light on the much narrower question on the role of Revelation in the development of Thomas's doctrine of the Word.

[80] See Emery, "Central Aristotelian Themes in Aquinas's Trinitarian Theology," in *Aristotle in Aquinas's Theology*, ed. Gilles Emery and Matthew Levering (Oxford: Oxford University Press, 2015), 6–8.

[81] *TA*, 139; emphasis added. Emery makes a similar point in *TA*, 149; *TTTA*, 58; and "Central Aristotelian Themes," 22–23. See also Harm Goris, "Theology of the Word," 63 and 74–78. Also, while I will focus here once more on the intellect and its word, Emery suggests that similar points might be made regarding the will and love.

Thomas's account of intellect certainly draws heavily on Aristotle. Yet Thomas also goes beyond Aristotle: he discovers the procession of a word of which Aristotle knew nothing.

This immanent procession, moreover, is not merely layered atop an otherwise intact Aristotelian framework. Instead, in introducing this the procession of a word, Thomas ends up reworking some of Aristotle's basic categories. This point was already recognized, at least in seed, by Scotus and by Henry of Ghent. As Scott M. Williams reports,

> on Aquinas's view, an intellectual operation (an act of understanding) is productive of something, that is, a mental word. Indeed, as Henry and Duns Scotus will point out, this is a category mistake. An operation does not have an end term distinct from itself but a production does have an end term distinct from itself. How then it is possible that an act of understanding something—an intellectual operation—is also the production of a mental word?[82]

To be sure, Thomas does not dismiss the distinction between two kinds of action: on the one hand, there is a "making," which "passes over into an external thing, and is a perfection of the thing made as a result of that operation, as the acts of heating, cutting, and building"; on the other, there is an "operation," which "remains in the agent and is a perfection of it, as the act of sensing, understanding, and willing."[83] This distinction comes from Aristotle, and it figures prominently in Thomas's Trinitarian theology.[84] For Aristotle, however, makings produce something other than themselves, whereas operations do not. For Thomas, in contrast, *both* makings *and* operations are fruitful—but differently. Makings bear fruit outside of the agent; operations bear fruit within the agent. Yet both bear fruit. In claiming as much, however, Thomas ends up reworking Aristotle so thoroughly that, judged by a Scotus

---

[82] "Augustine, Thomas Aquinas, Henry of Ghent and John Duns Scotus," 44–45. See 66n64 for the relevant texts from Scotus. For more on "production" and "operation" in Scotus, see Richard Cross, *Duns Scotus on God* (London: Routledge, 2005), 20–21; see 21n11 for his "denial that thinking itself is productive of some further product" and his "criticism of Aquinas's theory of the mental word."

[83] *SCG* II 1§§2 and 4.

[84] See Emery, "Central Aristotelian Themes," 2–3.

or a Henry—who, at least in this respect, adhere to a more pristine Aristotelianism—his position is incoherent. Thomas's proposal sounds like a "category mistake" to those who have not allowed Revelation to reshape their categories. And Thomas can only propose it because, prompted by Revelation, he opens Aristotle up and shifts around some of the basic building blocks of Aristotle's framework.[85]

THE REVEALED WORD

This last claim might seem a bit much. For to establish that Thomas reworks Aristotle is not yet to establish that he does so at the prompting of Revelation. If we return to the historical development of Thomas's teaching on the Word, however, we can begin to discern the role that Revelation played in this reworking.

First of all, we just saw that, in his *Sentences* commentary, Thomas holds that it is "impossible" that "word" should refer to anything other than the act of understanding or the intelligible species.[86] Aristotle, for his part, had been familiar both with this act and with this species. At this point in his career, therefore, Thomas assumes that "word" could only possibly refer to one of those elements of intellect that Aristotle had discovered: he does not allow for the possibility that Revelation might open up a dimension of the word that had evaded Aristotle. He works with Aristotle, but he does not rework Aristotle.

As we noted above, it is in the *SCG* that Thomas first puts his finger on a word that proceeds as a term of understanding—and which,

---

85 Without developing or insisting on this point, we can more gingerly offer at least some indication of just how fundamental these building blocks might be. For Aristotle, God is purely actual, and His pure actuality is an operation instead of a production: God's eternal act of thinking is an activity enjoyed in itself and for its own sake. Thomas, of course, agrees: the divine act of understanding is enjoyed for its own sake; it is not instrumentalized for the sake of any end beyond itself. Yet Thomas would not hold that this purely actual activity is enjoyed for its own sake *instead of* being fruitful. Instead, by way of this act, the Father produces a subsistent "fruit": He produces the Son-Word. Thomas's pure actuality, therefore, might not merely be the same thing as Aristotle's pure actuality: it might go beyond Aristotle. Indeed, it might even seem to overturn Aristotle. It marries the intransitive to the transitive, or goodness-for-its-own-sake to fruitfulness-beyond-oneself—and this shift in the meaning of pure actuality might carry any number of metaphysical implications.

86 I *Sent.*, d. 27, q. 2, a. 2, qc. 1.

therefore, goes beyond anything Aristotle had discovered. This point, however, might seem to provide ammunition for Thomas's critics. For Thomas first presents this extra-Aristotelian word in *SCG* I, ch. 53. Book I of the *SCG*, however, falls within the ambit of natural reason.[87] The word Thomas introduces here, therefore, may not have been discovered by *the* Philosopher; yet it seems that it could have been discovered by *a* philosopher. Revelation seems to have nothing to do with it. If, therefore, Thomas places this word at the center of his Trinitarian theology, then it seems that he allows a philosophical term to set the terms for his Trinity.

Things, however, are more complicated. For it is true that the *SCG*'s first mention of the inner word comes in book I, ch. 53. And it is true that, in book I, Thomas is investigating the divine intellect in terms accessible to reason. Yet the *SCG*'s most developed treatment of the inner word comes as Thomas is operating not according to reason, but according to faith: it comes in book IV, ch. 11, where Thomas is contemplating the Trinity, and where he is taking his bearings from Revelation in order to do so.[88] Most importantly for us, book I's discussion of the word certainly comes before book IV's in the final arrangement of the text. Yet historians agree that, chronologically speaking, book IV, ch. 11 was written *before* the final redaction of book I, ch. 53. Historians, moreover, agree that Thomas *first* discovered and articulated his mature account of the word as he was composing the "manifestation" of the Trinity in book IV, ch. 11, and that he *subsequently* went back to book I and inserted this mature account into his earlier reflections on the word.[89] Finally, Thomas did not compose book IV, ch. 11's manifestation of the Trinity and then later, at some unrelated time, return to book I's "philosophical" account of the word. Instead, historians agree that Thomas composed the final redaction of book I, ch.

---

[87] See *SCG* I, ch. 9. For some complications here, see Torrell, *Person and Work*, 124–27. For more on the context of book I, ch. 53, see Goris, "Theology and Theory of the Word," 73–77.

[88] See *SCG* IV 1§9.

[89] L.-B. Geiger speaks of Thomas's "discovery" of his mature teaching on the word in *SCG* IV, ch. 11. See "Les Rédactions Successives de *Contra Gentiles* I, 53 d'après l'Autographe," in *Saint Thomas d'Aquin Aujourd'hui* (Paris: Desclée de Brouwer, 1963), 240n1.

53 *as he was in the thick of working through book IV, ch. 11*.⁹⁰ Historians, that is, agree that Thomas first saw what an inner word *is*—at least according to his mature doctrine of the word—as he was engaging directly with Revelation and as he was contemplating the Trinity; and they agree that, in light of this discovery, he went back and revised book I's "philosophical" account of the word. Put differently, it seems that Thomas's mature account of the word, or his insight into the word as an immanent fruit of understanding, is *itself* a fruit of Revelation. It seems that the nature of a word was made manifest to Thomas as he was attempting to manifest the Trinity.

Thomas, moreover, not only discovered the inner word as he was reflecting directly on the Trinity. He also continued developing his teaching on the word in almost exclusively Trinitarian contexts. For, within his Trinitarian theology, he not only reflects on the divine Word; he also reflects at length on inner words more broadly.⁹¹ Indeed, in his Trinitarian theology, Thomas registers any number of developed claims concerning specifically *human* words, and he offers lengthy discussions on the role that human words play in human understanding.⁹² Yet, in non-Trinitarian contexts, when Thomas turns directly to our human intellect, he *never* reflects at any length on the inner word. Indeed, he rarely so much as mentions the inner word. As John O'Callaghan has pointed out, the inner word is all but absent from all three of "St. Thomas's last, most detailed and developed philosophical discussions of the substance and faculties of the human person."⁹³ In none of these

---

90 Thus R. A. Gauthier writes, "There is every reason to believe that it was at the moment when he had written chapter 11 of Book IV of the *Summa Contra Gentiles* that St. Thomas, reengaging the depths of the problem, dictated the third redaction of chapter 53 of Book I." Introduction to Saint Thomas d'Aquin, *Somme contre les gentils*, ed. Henri Hude (Paris: Vrin, 1993), 105. This same thesis is endorsed by Torrell in *Person and Work*, 123. For more detail and background, see Geiger, "Les Rédactions Successives." In a somewhat different vein, see Paissac, *Théologie du Verbe*, 172n1.

91 See, most importantly, *SCG* IV 11§§9–13; *De Pot.*, q. 8, a. 1, and q. 9, a. 5, and q. 9, a. 9; *ST* I qq. 27 and 34; *in Ioan.*, ##25–28.

92 Most of the texts just cited contain such claims.

93 See O'Callaghan, "*Verbum Mentis*: Philosophical or Theological Doctrine in Aquinas?" *ACPA Proceedings* 74 (2000): 103–19; quoted on 110. O'Callaghan mentions the *Disputed Questions on the Soul*, Thomas's commentary on *De Anima*, and *ST* I qq. 75–89. O'Callaghan is right that neither of the first two works contain any reference to the inner

contexts does Thomas take his bearings directly from Revelation, in none is his thinking directly at the service of manifesting the Trinity—and in none does he pay any attention to the inner word, despite its relevance to the discussions at hand.

It seems safe to say, therefore, that the word is not a pre-Trinitarian datum that Thomas—let alone a pre-Christian thinker—had already discovered and developed in a merely philosophical context, and which Thomas then projects up to the Trinity. Instead, Thomas's mature account of the word is discovered and developed within, and as a fruit of, his contemplation of the revealed Trinity. His mature account of the word is not extrinsically imposed *onto* his encounter with Revelation; it is born *out of*, and it is developed inside of, his encounter with Revelation.[94]

---

word. In *ST* I qq. 75–89, however, Thomas at least alludes to the inner word (see *ST* I q. 85, a. 2, ad 3 and a. 5, s.c.). Yet he does so only twice, only in passing, and he never even explicitly names it a "word." Even if the word is not entirely absent here, therefore, it is not discussed with any of the detail or directness it receives within Thomas's Trinitarian theology.

94 That said, we would miss some of the subtleties here if we concluded that Thomas's doctrine of the Word is theological *instead of* philosophical (O'Callaghan seems to argue as much, and thus to overstate matters). Such a thesis seems unsustainable given that Thomas discusses the word in philosophical contexts. These philosophical treatments of the word are certainly dwarfed by what we find within his Trinitarian theology; yet they still exist. In addition to *SCG* I, ch. 53 and the texts from *ST* I q. 85 just given, see *in Metap.*, #2539. This last text is especially important, for Thomas may ultimately be doing theology in *ST* I q. 85, and book I of the *SCG* may be "philosophical" only in a qualified way (see Torrell, *Person and Work*, 124–27). Yet, in his commentary on the *Metaphysics*, Thomas is operating unambiguously within the bounds of natural reason. Indeed, in this passage, he is first of all reporting what he takes *Aristotle* to have seen through the use of reason—which seems to make clear that the necessity of a word for understanding cannot be *simply* inaccessible to natural reason. O'Callaghan, however, never deals with any of these texts.

From the other direction, because Thomas seems to present the inner word as accessible to natural reason in *SCG* I, ch. 53 (and, even more, in *in Metap.*, #2539), we might suspect that his doctrine of the word is *essentially* philosophical, and that it represents one of those truths that are accessible to reason, yet which, without Revelation, "would only be known by a few, and that after a long time, and with the admixture of many errors" (*ST* I q. 1, a. 1). Such a reading would fit well with James C. Doig's response to O'Callaghan in "O'Callaghan on *Verbum Mentis* in Aquinas," *American Catholic Philosophical Quarterly* 77, no. 2 (2003): 233–55.

If, however, the word were straightforwardly accessible to reason, then one would expect Thomas, once he had discovered it, to discuss it readily and at length in philosophical contexts. The fact that he reserves almost all such discussions for theological contexts may suggest that we are dealing with something a bit more complicated—something that might nudge us beyond conventional accounts of "faith" and "reason," or "philosophy"

To say more about faith and reason would bring us well beyond our scope here. Instead, we can focus on a single point. We just saw that, in his *Sentences* commentary, Thomas assumes that a "word" can refer only to an aspect of understanding that Aristotle had already discovered: he assumes that Revelation can tell us nothing new about the inner word. Yet we saw earlier that, in his *Sentences* commentary, this non-revealed word remains largely irrelevant to his Trinitarian theology. A merely Aristotelian word is not a Trinitarian word; a prepackaged word cannot unpack Revelation. It is all but useless for Trinitarian theology, and it therefore goes all but unused in Thomas's Trinitarian theology. It is only in the *SCG*, when Thomas's contemplation of the revealed Trinity first brings him beyond Aristotle, that the word first takes center stage in his Trinitarian theology. Thomas only centers his Trinitarian theology around a word once his contemplation of the Trinity prompts him to reconsider what a word *is*. Thomas, then, certainly offers a psychological reading of the Trinity—but only after effecting a Trinitarian reading of the psyche: he only allows an inner word to tell us about the Trinity once he has allowed the Trinity to tell him about the inner word.[95]

CONCLUSION

Again, these revealed dimensions of the Trinity are anything but irrelevant to the interpersonal dimensions in which I am interested here. For when Thomas discovers new dimensions of the word in the light of Revelation, what he discovers is that a word *really proceeds* within the one who understands. A merely Aristotelian word—which can only be

---

and "theology." For a helpful starting point towards a deeper approach to these questions, see D. C. Schindler, *The Catholicity of Reason*, 305–33.

[95] Which is not to say that Thomas ceases to draw on Aristotle as he works through his mature doctrine of the word (see, for example, *Comp. Theo.* I, 37 and *in Ioan.*, #25). Instead, his mature account of the word seems to be a fruit of the interplay between Revelation and Aristotle. Be that as it may, Lewis Ayres has found an echo of our main claim here in Augustine's articulation of the psychological analogy: Ayres writes that Augustine's "analysis of the analogical site in question [i.e., memory, intellect, and will] is conducted not only in order to discover the Trinity therein reflected, but also with the analytical tools of, and in light of, a faith commitment to the language of the Nicene Creed" (*Augustine and the Trinity*, 317). Ayres reiterates this point frequently: see 281, 283, 287, 288, 289, 305, and 315.

a cipher for the act of understanding or the intelligible species—merely remains within. It is only when his contemplation of the Trinity urges him beyond Aristotle that Thomas discovers a word that both goes forth and remains within. When Thomas allows Revelation to open up new insights into the meaning of a word, what he finds is the paradox that has been at the center of this chapter as a whole.

And so we return to our major burden in this chapter: for Thomas, an inner word and love-impression really do go forth from the one who understands and loves, and Thomas only chooses to cast the Trinity in psychological terms once—and because—this going-forth becomes just as foundational as this remaining-within.

That said, to establish that a word and love really go forth from another, or even to establish that their going-forth is just as foundational as their remaining-within, is still to establish very little. For my human words and loves proceed from me as well. They might even proceed from me just as basically as they remain within me. Yet they do not subsist as distinct persons alongside me; I do not give my whole self to them; they do not know me or love me in return. The fact that the Son and the Spirit proceed as a Word and Love within the mind of the Father, therefore, may still seem to suggest that Their processions are less than fully interpersonal. We will see in later chapters, however, that *because* the Son and the Spirit proceed as a Word and Love within the mind of the Father, it follows that each must be a Person Who subsists distinctly from the Father, it follows that the Father must give the whole of Himself to each, and it follows that each must know and love the Father in return. We will, however, only be able to establish that these interpersonal elements go to the center of Thomas's psychological Trinity because we first spent this chapter establishing our main burden: that procession goes to the foundation of Thomas's psychological terms—to the point that, if those psychological terms had failed to secure this procession, then Thomas would have abandoned them, unused, on the margins of his Trinitarian thought.

Having seen as much, we can now begin towards the more obviously interpersonal categories in which I am directly interested.

2

A STANDING-OUTSIDE THAT REMAINS WITHIN

Again, it is no secret that my words and loves are not persons alongside me. Just this point, however, has led to a good deal of the ire directed at Thomas—and at his psychological analogy—by theologians of a social bent. Colin Gunton, for example, holds that the "problem" with casting the divine Persons as Word and Love is that "such inward faculties (whatever they are) are not persons."[1] Pannenberg ends with the same judgement: according to "a psychological interpretation" of the Trinity, God is but "a single subject"; the Word and Love "have no subjectivity of their own. From the very outset, then, those who take this line have difficulty with the dogma that there are three persons or hypostases in the one God."[2] Gunton and Pannenberg might admit that Thomas speaks often of three divine "Persons," for even a cursory glance through his Trinitarian theology can establish this point beyond any real doubt. But they seem to suggest that, because two of these "Persons" are a Word and Love, Their "personhood"—whatever it might mean—can have nothing to do with personhood as we encounter it among creatures. To use Thomas's language, the divine Persons would be called "Persons" not

---

[1] Josh McNall, *A Free Corrector*, 87.

[2] *Systematic Theology*, 295.

analogously, but equivocally. Nothing "interpersonal" between Them, therefore, would have much to do with things like my love for my wife or my intimacy with my friends.[3]

Such critics might be surprised to learn that Thomas had anticipated their objections, at least in part. For he recognizes that Trinitarian theology must secure personal distinction in God. He also insists that our talk of divine "Persons" must be analogous; it cannot be equivocal.[4] Yet he sees that our words and loves are not persons alongside us, and he admits that a psychological approach to the Trinity might therefore seem ill-advised. As he puts it, "the Son is a subsisting Person in God. But 'word' does not signify a subsisting thing, as is clear in us. Therefore, 'Word' cannot be the proper name of the Person of the Son."[5] Just so, "the Holy Spirit is a subsisting person, but 'love' is not used to signify a subsisting person, but rather an action passing from the lover to the beloved."[6] "Word" and "Love" do not refer to subsisting persons, and they therefore seem ill-suited to Trinitarian theology.

These passages, however, come in objections. In them, Thomas acknowledges that the non-subsistence of our non-personal words and loves could stand as a stumbling block to our rightly understanding his account of the Trinity. Yet he does not respond to this difficulty by pivoting away from his psychological approach. Instead, he responds by underlining a point that stands at the center of his psychological approach: the divine Word and Love may be like human words and loves in some respects. Yet They are radically unlike them in others. And one point of radical unlikeness is that the divine Word and Love *subsist* in the divine nature, which means that They are distinct Persons in the divine nature. If, therefore, we were to get overly hung up on the non-subsistence of our non-personal words and loves, or if we were to project this non-subsistence into God, then we would misunderstand Thomas's psychological analogy. We would forget that his psychological

---

[3] This objection might have more teeth insofar as Augustine sometimes gives the impression of such an equivocal use of "personhood" in God: see Pérez, "The Trinitarian Concept of Person," 108.

[4] See Emery, *TTTA*, 115.

[5] *ST* I q. 34, a. 2, arg. 1. See also I *Sent* d. 27, q. 2, a. 1, arg. 2.

[6] *ST* I q. 37, a. 1, arg. 2. See also I *Sent* d. 10, q. 1, a. 1, arg. 1; and *LR*, d. 10, q. 1, arg. 3.

analogy is an analogy. We would collapse it into a sort of psychological univocity.

In chapters five and six, we will dig deeper into the personhood of Word and Love: we will see that, because each is a Person, each knows and loves Himself and the others.[7] We will spend this chapter, however, on more modest ground. For Thomas's account of divine personhood may include these more obviously interpersonal notes. Yet, when he goes about directly defining personhood in his Trinitarian theology, Thomas almost always zeroes in on one point: to be a person is to subsist in a rational nature. Thomas also consistently argues that because the divine Persons subsist in the supremely intelligent divine nature, each is a "Person" in the strictest sense. "Person," that is, is said of Them not equivocally, but analogously.[8]

Like the language of "procession," the language of "subsistence" has failed to set aflutter the hearts of many socially inclined theologians.[9] Yet we will see in this chapter that, at least in Thomas's hands, to claim merely that Word and Love subsist distinctly in God is already to open the door towards a set of surprisingly social conclusions.

To see as much, we will begin where we left off: with the immanent processions of Word and Love. We saw in our last chapter that these processions go to the foundation of Thomas's psychological analogy. We will begin here by seeing that distinct subsistence goes to the foundation of these processions: because of the logic of an immanent procession, whatever proceeds in God necessarily subsists distinctly in God. From

---

[7] Throughout this study, I will refer to Word and Love as "He" and "Him"—not as "it." Thomas, of course, uses neither set of pronouns. Yet a number of his readers have referred to his Word as "it"—sometimes in the course of arguing that there is no room for anything interpersonal in his Trinity; see Steven A. Long, "Divine and Creaturely 'Receptivity': The Search for a Middle Term," *Communio: International Catholic Review* 21, no. 1 (1994): 158. I hope to suggest that this choice of pronoun is misleading.

[8] For more background here, see Emery, "On the Dignity of Being a Substance" and *TTTA*, 104–11. Emery speaks of personhood and analogy in *TTTA*, 107–11.

[9] See Dominic Holtz, "Divine Personhood and the Critique of Substance Metaphysics," *Nova et Vetera* English edition 12, no. 4 (2014): 1191–213. That said, the language of "subsistence" found at least one prominent contemporary champion: Karl Rahner. Rahner defines the divine Persons as "ways of subsistence" (*The Trinity*, 109–13). Ironically, however, Rahner casts the divine Persons in these terms precisely to avoid the sort of "face-to-face" encounter that, as we will argue, is implicit in Thomas's account of distinct subsistence.

there, we will attend more directly to the logic of subsistence. Specifically, we will drill into a claim Thomas registers again and again when discussing the subsistence of the divine Persons: to subsist is to exist in oneself and not in another. Taking this language seriously will lead us to a conclusion more paradoxical than anything we saw in our last chapter. For we will see that, because the divine Word and Love subsist, They must stand somehow "outside" of the Father, even as They remain within the Father.[10] That claim may sound excessively paradoxical. Our next step will therefore be to spend some time defending it. For we will see that this marriage of remaining-within and standing-outside is not limited to Thomas's rendering of subsistence. It is also suggestive of his teaching on relation—which stands at the center of his Trinitarian theology. We will then end by turning to a series of passages where Thomas speaks more directly to the distinction between the divine Persons, and where he highlights a respect in which this distinction is greater than any distinction found among creatures.

Throughout this chapter, my main goal will be to draw out something of the character of the distinction secured by Thomas's psychological analogy. We just mentioned that even Thomas's most strident critics must admit that he speaks of three divine "Persons." Just so, it would be hard to deny that, insofar as Thomas officially rejects Seballianism, he at least pays lip service to some sort of real distinction in God.[11] Again, even a cursory glance through his Trinitarian theology bears this point out.[12] The question, however, is the character of this distinction. A good deal of contemporary thinkers have assumed that the distinction Thomas's psychological analogy entails is too minimal,

---

10 Seeing as much will allow for a particularly deep response to Pannenberg's charge: "Attempts to find self-subsistent relations for the Son and Spirit rather than relations *merely in* the Father remained artificial in the context of the psychological model" (*Systematic Theology*, 295; emphasis added).

11 Though some deny even this: some have accused Thomas of "modalism" (see, for example, William Lane Craig, "Toward a Tenable Social Trinitarianism," 91). In a bit more depth, Pannenberg writes that in Thomas's Trinity, "persons in God can only be conceptually distinct" (*Systematic Theology*, 295n122).

12 See *ST* I q. 28, a. 3.

or too lopsidedly intrapersonal, to be robustly interpersonal.[13] We will see throughout part two that, for Thomas, this distinction really is inter*personal*: it is shot through with reciprocal knowledge, reciprocal love, and total self-giving. Our claim now is that this distinction really is *inter*personal. Thomas's psychological analogy, in other words, opens up the "space" in God needed for a *between*-Persons.[14] We will continue unfolding this point in chapter three, but we will attend to it most directly here.

IMMANENTLY PROCEEDING, DISTINCTLY SUBSISTING

We can begin by building a bridge from our previous chapter to this chapter: for Thomas, nothing can proceed immanently in God without subsisting distinctly in God. Elsewhere, I have argued in detail that the logic of an immanent divine procession unavoidably leads to distinct divine subsistence.[15] For our current purposes, I will remain with the bare outlines of this path, and I will limit myself to Thomas's articulation of these points in the *Summa*.

This path begins from what might seem an unlikely place: God's simplicity.

> The act of human understanding in ourselves is not the substance itself of the intellect; hence the word which proceeds within us by intelligible operation is not of the same nature as the source whence it proceeds. . . . But the divine act of intelligence is the very substance itself of the

---

[13] As we saw in our introduction, Balthasar may admit that this distinction is real, but he argues that a psychological Trinity "cannot give an adequate picture of the real and abiding face-to-face encounter of the hypostases" (*Theo-Logic II*, 38). We will return to this language of "face-to-face" both later in this chapter and in chapter three.

[14] I use this language of "space" with reservations, given that Thomas could—at best—use it only metaphorically. Yet I hope that it can allow us to put Thomas in dialogue with someone like Barth or Balthasar: see Balthasar, *Theo-Drama II*, trans. Graham Harrison (San Francisco: Ignatius, 1990), 257; and Barth, *Church Dogmatics* II/1, trans. G. W. Bromiley (Edinburgh: T&T Clark, 1964), 475–76.

[15] See my "Perfection and the Necessity of the Trinity in Aquinas," *New Blackfriars* 102 (2021): 75–95.

one who understands." The Word proceeding therefore proceeds *as subsisting in the same nature* as His source.[16]

We are not perfectly simple. Our act of understanding, therefore, is not identical to our intellect, and our words do not share our nature. God, however, is simple. His act of understanding, therefore, is identical to His substance. And because of this identity, the divine Word and His Speaker must share "the same nature."[17]

Thomas continues,

> when something proceeds from a principle *of the same nature*, it is necessary that both the one proceeding and the source of procession agree in the same order. In this way it must be that they have real relations to each other. Therefore, because the divine processions are in the identity of the same nature, as above explained, it is *necessary* that these relations, according to the divine processions, are *real relations*.[18]

Because of simplicity, the Word Who proceeds from the Father must "share the same nature" as the Father, and, because of the consequences of procession within a shared nature, there must be reciprocally real relations between the Father and His Word.[19]

The logic of real relation leads to the next step: "Belonging to the *ratio* of relation is the regard of one to another, according as one is relatively opposed to another. Therefore, because there is in God real relation, there must also be real opposition. And relative opposition, in its *ratio*, includes distinction. Hence, *there must be real distinction*

---

16 *ST* I q. 27, a. 2, ad 2. Thomas already here sounds the note on which we will end: the Word proceeds "as subsisting." To appreciate this point fully, however, we will first have to work through a few more passages.

17 See also *SCG* IV 11§11; *Comp. Theo.* I, 42; *de rationibus fidei*, ch. 3; *De Pot.*, q. 8, a. 1, and q. 9, a. 5; and *in Ioan.*, #28.

18 *ST* I q. 28, a. 1.

19 Thomas reiterates this point in *De Pot.*, q. 8, a. 1, and q. 7, a. 10, arg. 3 and ad 3. He also suggests that real relation follows on any procession of any word in any intellect in *ST* I q. 28, a. 1, ad 4, and q. 28, a. 4, ad 1.

in God . . . according to what is relative."[20] Opposition belongs to the *ratio* of relation, and distinction belongs to the *ratio* of opposition. Because the Word is really related to the Father, He must be really distinct from the Father.[21]

This note of real distinction takes on real heft when Thomas writes that "in God, existence and understanding are the same: hence the Word of God is not an accident in Him, or an effect of His, but belongs to His very nature. And *therefore* He must be something *subsistent*, for all that is in the divine nature subsists; and therefore Damascene says that 'the Word of God is substantial and has *hypostatic* being.' "[22] We began with simplicity, and we end with simplicity: because existence and understanding are "the same" in God, the divine Word must be "subsistent" and enjoy "hypostatic being." If He did not subsist, then He would be an accident, and the divine nature would no longer be simple.

Summing up, divine simplicity demands that any Word that proceeds in God must share the nature of His Speaker. The logic of procession within a single nature further demands that this Word must be really related to His Speaker. The logic of real relation demands that He must be really distinct from the Speaker to Whom He is really related. Finally, the logic of simplicity again demands that anything that *exists* as really distinct in God must *subsist* as really distinct in God.

The same principles hold with divine Love. Because of simplicity, Love must likewise share the nature of both the Speaker and the Word from Whom He proceeds.[23] Yet, for the reasons just discussed, such procession within a shared nature must again yield real relation, real relation must again yield real distinction, and real distinction

---

[20] *ST* I q. 28, a. 3.

[21] See also *De Pot.*, q. 8, a. 2, ad 3. From a different route, Thomas again teaches that real relation entails real distinction in I *Sent.*, d. 31, q. 1, a. 1; *De Ver.*, q. 2, a. 2, ad 1; and *ST* I q. 42, a. 1, ad 2. See also Emery, "*Ad aliquid*: Relation in the Thought of St. Thomas Aquinas," in *Theology Needs Philosophy: Acting against Reason is Contrary to the Nature of God*, ed. Matthew L. Lamb (Washington, DC: The Catholic University of America Press, 2016), 185. Thomas also suggests that real distinction necessarily follows directly on any procession of any sort: see I *Sent.*, d. 15, q. 1, a. 1; and *Comp. Theo.* I, 51.

[22] *ST* I q. 34, a. 2, ad 1. See also *ST* I q. 29, a. 4; *SCG* IV 26§7; *De Pot.*, q. 9, a. 9, and q. 10, a. 1, ad 5; and *in Ioan.*, #28.

[23] See *SCG* IV 19§7; *Comp. Theo.* I, 48.

must again yield subsistent distinction. As Thomas puts it, because "existence, intelligence *and will* are one and the same in God, it follows of necessity that Word *and Love* in God are not accidents but subsist distinctly in the divine nature."[24] Not only a Word but Love as well must subsist distinctly in the divine nature. The logic of an immanent divine procession demands it.

The final point comes from Thomas's definition of a Person as "a subsisting thing in a rational nature."[25] For, given that the divine nature is supremely intellectual, any Word or Love that subsist distinctly in the divine nature must subsist distinctly in a rational nature—and they must therefore subsist as distinct Persons. As Thomas puts it, "there are multiple realities subsisting in the divine nature, which means that there are multiple Persons in God."[26]

We will return to the language of personhood throughout this study. For now, we can focus on subsistence. Most importantly, the main burden of our first chapter was that immanent procession goes to the foundation of Thomas's psychological analogy for the Trinity. We see now that the subsistence of Word and Love follows organically from the logic of such an immanent divine procession. This subsistence—and any consequence it carries—is no marginal quirk on the periphery of Thomas's psychological analogy. Instead, because it is intrinsic to the logic of an immanent procession, it goes to the heart of Thomas's psychological analogy.

We can also note very briefly that this subsistence follows not only on the logic of an immanent procession but also on an even less likely source: it follows on Thomas's strong reading of consubstantiality. We will explore this point at length in chapter three. For now, we can simply note that it is only because Speaker and Word "are in the identity of the

---

24 *De Pot.*, q. 9, a. 9. See also q. 10, a. 1, ad 5; *ST* I q. 37, a. 1, ad 2. See also *LR* d. 10, q. 1, ad 3.

25 *ST* I q. 29, a. 3.

26 *ST* I q. 30, a. 1. See also *SCG* IV 26§7. All that said, it is of course true that, for Thomas, natural reason cannot conclude that there are multiple Persons in God merely by reflecting on the nature of a word and love (see *ST* I q. 32, a. 1, ad 2; and *De Pot.*, q. 8, a. 1, ad 12). The principles we have discussed here might stand in a certain tension with these limits on natural reason; yet they cannot contradict those limits. We will return to this point in chapter three.

same nature" that the relations between Them are reciprocally real.[27] Just so, the Word only subsists because He *is* the one self-subsistent divine nature, in which there can be no accidents. Consubstantial unity yields subsistent distinction. Again, we will come back to these points in chapter three. For now, we can focus on our most basic claim: because Word and Love proceed within the one divine essence, each must subsist in that essence. Having seen as much, we will now see something of how radical a thing it is to say that Word and Love subsist distinctly in God.

"NOT IN ANOTHER"
"In Itself and Not in Another"

We can begin with an article from the *Summa*'s Trinitarian questions where Thomas is identifying the exact meanings of "person," "essence," "subsistence," and "hypostasis." Thomas, that is, is inquiring directly into the meaning of "subsistence," and he is searching for the precise point that distinguishes it from a range of closely related terms. And, in this context, he tells us one—and only one—thing about the meaning of subsistence: "as it exists in itself and *not in another*, [a substance] is called a 'subsistence'; as we say that those things subsist which exist in themselves, and *not in another*."[28] The most basic point here—which Thomas reiterates twice in a single sentence—is so commonplace that we might pass right over it: to subsist is to exist in oneself and not in another. Accidents inhere in subjects distinct from themselves; subsisting things exist in themselves. They do not exist in another.[29]

This same language, used to the same purpose, surfaces elsewhere in Thomas's Trinitarian theology. In his *Sentences* commentary, he writes that "to subsist indicates a determined mode of existing: namely, insofar as something exists through itself and *not in another*, as an accident

---

[27] *ST* I q. 28, a. 1.

[28] *ST* I q. 29, a. 2.

[29] White, following Thomas, defines subsistence in just these terms in *The Trinity*, 443.

does."[30] Just so, in the *De Potentia*, he writes that a substance "does not need an extrinsic foundation in which it is sustained. Instead, it is sustained in itself, and it is therefore said to *subsist*, as existing *not in another* but in itself."[31] And again, "a hypostasis . . . is said to *subsist* as *not* existing *in another*."[32] As was the case in our *Summa* passage, all of these claims come as Thomas is identifying the precise meaning of "subsistence" as distinct from "person," "hypostasis," "substance," and "essence." All of these claims, therefore, come as Thomas is being most careful to nail down the exact meaning of subsistence. Even more importantly, all of these passages, like our *Summa* passage, come from the thick of Thomas's Trinitarian theology: the *Summa* and *De Potentia* passages come from questions devoted to the divine Persons, and the passage from the *Sentences* comes from an article that asks, in its title, "Whether 'substance,' 'subsistence,' 'essence,' and 'person' are said synonymously *of God*."[33] It seems plain enough, therefore, that Thomas is not highlighting this meaning of subsistence merely to better understand subsistence in general; he is doing so to better understand the subsistence of the divine Persons. And, in all three texts, Thomas is consistent and clear: to subsist is to exist in oneself and not in another. Indeed, in the *Summa* and the *De Potentia*, this note of not-being-in-another is the *only* thing Thomas tells us about the meaning of subsistence.

A Standing-Outside that Remains Within

We saw above that, because the Word and Love proceed within the divine nature, They must subsist distinctly in that nature. We see now that if this distinct subsistence means anything, it means that Word and Love must each exist in Himself, and that neither can exist in another. Yet to say that neither Word nor Love can exist in another

---

30 I *Sent.*, d. 23, q. 1, a. 1.

31 *De Pot.*, q. 9, a. 1.

32 *De Pot.*, q. 9, a. 1, ad 4.

33 The *Summa* passage comes from *ST* I q. 29, the *De Potentia* from q. 9, and the *Sentences* text from I *Sent.*, d. 23, q. 1, a. 1.

is to suggest something somewhat startling: there is some respect in which *neither the divine Word nor the divine Love exists in the Father*. It is to suggest that each must stand, as it were, "outside" of the Father and "outside" of each other.

To be sure, subsistence alone is not enough to ensure that a subsisting thing stands "outside" of something else. Divine simplicity demands that God's goodness and actuality, for example, be self-subsistent. And, because each is self-subsistent, each exists in itself, and neither can exist in anything other than itself. Yet, again because of simplicity, neither God's goodness nor God's actuality is really distinct from anything else in God. Instead, God's goodness is identical to His actuality, and both of these are identical to His power and to His wisdom—and all of these are identical to all three divine Persons. Neither divine goodness nor divine actuality, therefore, exists outside of anything other than itself: for, in God, there *is* nothing other than goodness and actuality. Put differently, a subsistent thing need not necessarily stand outside of anything else: if that one subsistent thing were the only thing that existed, then it would exist in itself, but it would not stand outside of anything else, for there would not *be* anything else for it to stand outside of. *Two* subsistent things, however, necessarily stand outside of *each other*. Unlike goodness or actuality, however, the divine Word and Love proceed. They therefore *are* really distinct from each other and from the Father—and They therefore stand outside of each other and the Father. Yet it is only because They subsist distinctly *from* each other and the Father that They do not exist *in* each other or the Father.

That said, to deny that Word and Love exist *merely* within the Father is not to deny that They exist *entirely* within the Father. We saw all throughout chapter one that They remain within the Father even as They go forth from the Father: there is no ultimate conflict between Their going-forth and Their remaining-within. Just so, one of our most important claims here is that Word and Love remain within the Father even as They stand somehow "outside" of the Father: there is no ultimate conflict between Their standing-outside and Their remaining-within. Indeed, *because* there is no conflict between Their going-forth and Their remaining-within, there *cannot* be any conflict between Their standing-outside and Their remaining-within. For we saw above that Their standing-outside—that is, Their distinct subsistence—follows necessarily on Their going-forth. The paradox of a standing-outside that remains within, then, is but a final unfolding of the paradox of a going-forth that remains within. To deny that Word and Love stand outside of the Father is to deny that They go forth from the Father—and thus to gut Thomas's psychological analogy for the Trinity.

Indeed, it is here that our conclusions from chapter one yield their most striking fruit. For we saw all through chapter one that going forth from another goes to the foundation of a word and love. Indeed, we saw that, if a word and love were not marked by this procession, then Thomas would not have chosen to cast his Trinity in psychological terms. Yet we see now that because Word and Love go forth from the Father, They necessarily stand somehow outside of the Father. Therefore, because Their going-forth from the Father goes to the foundation of Thomas's psychological analogy, Their standing-somehow-outside of the Father must *itself* go to the foundation of Thomas's psychological analogy. This subsistent standing-outside is no negligible anomaly at the fringes of Thomas's Trinitarian thought. Nor is it secured despite a psychological approach that recognizes only immanence and unity. Instead, it goes down to the foundation of Thomas's psychological analogy.[34]

---

[34] At least in one passage, Thomas seems to suggest that a similar paradox holds not only in intra-divine subsistence, but in subsistence simply. He writes that "the return to one's own essence is called the very subsistence of a thing in itself. For non-subsistent forms are, as it were, poured out upon something other than themselves, and are not in possession of themselves. But subsistent forms reach out to other things, perfecting them and flowing into [*influendo*] them—in such a way, however, that they still remain within themselves through themselves [*in seipsis per se manet*]" (De Ver., q. 2, a. 2, ad 2). Even in creatures, subsistence means *both* remaining within oneself *and* flowing-forth into others: it is a flowing-out that remains within. Even more, subsisting things do not merely flow into others *and also* remain within themselves. Instead, their "very subsistence" *is* "the return to [their] own essence." The stable, in other words, *is* the fluid; remaining-within-oneself *is* returning-to-oneself after having flowed into others. For more on this passage, see Schindler, "The Word as the Center of Man's Onto-Dramatic Task," 76–78. In the section "Intimate Indwelling, Infinite Distance, Interpersonal Giving" in chapter seven, we will see another way in which the paradox of a standing-outside that remains within ripples all through creation.

Three Objections

Of course, any number of objections might be raised here. First, one might object that we are making too much of a very simple point. For when Thomas says that to subsist is to exist in oneself and not in another, he seems merely to be saying that to subsist is not to be an accident. Accidents, by definition, exist in subsisting substances; subsisting substances, in contrast, exist in themselves. To affirm that the divine Word and Love do not exist in another, therefore, is merely to clarify that They are not accidents.

This argument may be solid enough. Yet it in no way makes our paradox any less paradoxical. For to claim that the divine Word and Love do not exist in the Father might amount to nothing more than claiming that They are not accidents. Yet to claim that They are distinct from the Father, but to insist that They are not accidents, already entails *nothing less* than claiming that They do not exist merely within the Father. To exist merely within something, and not to exist in any way outside of that thing, is, by definition, to be an accident of that thing.[35] And because neither the divine Word nor the divine Love are accidents, neither can exist merely within the Father. Simply because They are not accidents, Word and Love must exist in some way "outside" of the Father.[36]

---

[35] As Thomas puts it, *"accidentis enim esse est inesse"*: see I *Sent.*, d. 8, q. 4, a. 3, and d. 46, q. 1, a. 2; *SCG* IV 62§6; and *ST* I q. 28, a. 2.

[36] Thomas perhaps points in this direction in a dense passage from his commentary on John. He begins by arguing that when the Evangelist writes "In the beginning was the Word," "beginning" can stand for the person of the Father (see *in Ioan.*, #36). He continues by facing objections against such a reading:
> You say that "In the beginning was the Word," that is, the Son was in the Father. But *that which is in something does not seem to be subsistent*, as a hypostasis; just as the whiteness in a body does not subsist. This objection is solved by the statement, "the Word was with God," taking "with" in its first condition, as implying the *subsistence* of its grammatical antecedent. So according to Chrysostom, the meaning is this: "In the beginning was the Word," *not as an accident*, but he was "with God," *as subsisting*, and a divine hypostasis.

In Ioan., #49. The Word, then, is not only *in* the Father: merely being-in is not enough. Indeed, to merely be-in-another is to cease to subsist. If we were to say *only* that the Word is in the Father, then we would reduce the Word to "an accident." And, in order to avoid such an error, Thomas—without in any way denying that the Word is also in

Second, one might object that we are saying too much. For one might admit that this note of "not being in another" holds in creaturely subsistence. But one might draw a line and clarify that we cannot know whether it holds analogously in the subsistence of the divine Persons.[37] In response, we should begin with a point we already mentioned: in all of the passages where Thomas defines subsistence in terms of not-being-in-another, he is neck-deep in his Trinitarian theology. This language, therefore, comes as he is preparing to consider the subsistence of the divine Persons. Indeed, the only reason Thomas registers this point at all—and the only reason he so much as raises the question of the meaning of subsistence in this context—is to discuss the subsistence of the divine Persons. It seems something of a stretch, therefore, to claim that the dimension of subsistence he highlights here is limited to creatures.

Even more, when Thomas discusses subsistence in non-Trinitarian contexts, he sometimes refrains from defining it explicitly in terms of not-being-in-another. In his commentary on the *Metaphysics*, for example, he writes that first substance "subsists through itself and is separable because it is distinct from everything else and cannot be common to many."[38] There would be much to say about this text, but we can limit ourselves to two points. First, what Thomas says here is certainly related to the claim that to subsist is to exist in oneself and not in another. Yet Thomas stops short of using this language explicitly. Second, and more importantly, this passage suggests that if Thomas had deemed talk of not-being-in-another unfit for Trinitarian theology, then he could have discussed the subsistence of the divine Persons without mentioning it. He could, for example, have picked up on the dimension of subsistence highlighted here in his commentary on the *Metaphysics*: he could have explained that, while the divine essence is common to the three Persons, the Persons, as subsistent, are not common. Instead,

---

the Father—introduces the Word's subsistence as a sort of counterweight to the Word's being "in" the Father.

37 Such a tack would be in keeping with the upsurge of "apophatic" readings of Thomas that we saw last chapter with Kilby and that also appears in Holmes, *The Quest for the Trinity*, 154–59 and Levering, *Engaging the Doctrine of the Holy Spirit*, 35–36.

38 *In Metap.*, #903.

they are incommunicable. Thomas makes a similar point elsewhere in his Trinitarian theology.[39] Yet he refrains from mentioning it when he is speaking directly to the meaning of subsistence. Instead, he fastens consistently onto the language of not-being-in-another.

Most basically, Thomas could have explained that, like all terms, "subsistence" must be purified before it is used of God, and he could have clarified that this dimension of not-being-in-another is limited to creaturely subsistence. Yet he does no such thing. Instead, he consistently brings this dimension of not-being-in-another front and center precisely as he is preparing to discuss the subsistence of the divine Persons, and he does so despite having access to other accounts of subsistence that would have yielded less paradoxical results.[40]

A third objection touches on a number of very deep theological questions. For the divine Word and Love certainly subsist, yet They do so insofar as They are identical to the one self-subsistent divine essence. It might seem, therefore, as though Their subsistence concerns only Their unity, and not Their distinction.[41] Two points bear noting here. First, and more superficially, Thomas tells us that "there are several subsisting things [*plures res subsistentes*] in the divine nature."[42] He also

---

[39] See *ST* I q. 29, a. 4, ad 3, and q. 30, a. 4, c. and ad 2.

[40] To be clear, Thomas does not merely invent this note of not-being-in-another for his Trinitarian theology: it really does belong to the logic of subsistence, on its own terms. It is no surprise, therefore, that it appears in non-Trinitarian contexts as well (see II *Sent.*, d. 3 q. 1 a. 5; and *SCG* I 25§10). The point is simply that if Thomas were convinced that there was no sense at all in which the divine Persons are "outside" of each other, then he could have avoided highlighting this particular dimension or formulation of subsistence within his Trinitarian theology. He could, for example, have fastened onto the point he makes in *in Metap.*, #903: he could have explained that the divine Persons subsist insofar as Their personhood is incommunicable.

[41] For a crasser version of this charge, which is bound up with an "essentialist" reading of Thomas, see Sergei Bulgakov, *The Comforter*, trans. Boris Jakim (Grand Rapids, MI: Eerdmans, 2004), 44. A more subtle version might look to Thomas's teaching on relation. For Thomas teaches that the divine relations subsist by virtue of their *esse*, which is identical to the one divine essence; they are distinct by virtue of their *ratio* as relations. They are only *subsistent* relations, that is, insofar as They are all identical to the one divine essence. We will return to this particular objection in note 75 below, once we have said a bit more about relation.

[42] *ST* I q. 30, a. 1.

speaks of the three Persons as "three subsistences."[43] Elsewhere, he writes that "the three Persons are three subsisting things."[44] He is also clear that, as subsistent, the Persons are distinct from each other: "this is common in idea to the divine Persons, that each of Them *subsists* in the divine nature, *distinct* from the others";[45] " a divine Person must signify a *distinct subsistent* thing in the divine nature";[46] "in God there must be some *distinction* . . . in respect of that which *subsists* in the divine nature";[47] and, most plainly, "Word and Love in God are not accidents but *subsist distinctly* in the divine nature."[48] Even without diving into the context of these claims, the basic point should be clear: the three divine Persons might subsist *by* a single essence. Yet *those three Persons Themselves* really do subsist by that one essence, and They subsist as distinct from each other.[49]

The second point is deeper. In brief, the one divine essence is not in any way sealed off from the distinction of the divine Persons. Instead, the one divine essence exists according to the relations by which those Persons are distinguished from each other. As Thomas puts it, "the same essence is fatherhood in the Father and sonship in the Son," and "in the Father fatherhood is the divine essence or the divine goodness, and the numerically same essence or goodness is sonship in the Son."[50] We will return to these principles at greater length in chapters five and six. For now, one point will suffice: it is true that Word and Love only subsist because each is identical to a single self-subsistent essence, yet it is just as true that this single self-subsistent essence only ever exists according to the three distinct "ways of existing" proper to the three

---

43 *ST* I q. 29, a. 2, ad 2. See also *De Pot.*, q. 9, a. 2, ad 8.

44 *Comp. Theo.* I, 60.

45 *ST* I q. 30, a. 4.

46 *De Pot.*, q. 9, a. 4.

47 *De Pot.*, q. 8, a. 1.

48 *De Pot.*, q. 9, a. 9.

49 For a nuanced and balanced—and fuller—treatment of this first point, see Emery, *TA*, 198–206.

50 *ST* I q. 42, a. 6, ad 3; I *Sent.*, d. 9, q. 2, a. 1, ad 4.

divine Persons.⁵¹ The distinct subsistence of the divine Word and Love, therefore, does not bleed into the single subsistence of the Father. Nor does it bleed into any single essential subsistence: the one divine essence does not in any way swallow up or lurk beneath the *distinct* subsistence of Word and Love. Instead, the distinct subsistence of the divine Persons governs the way in which the divine essence exists. Even logically speaking, distinct subsistence goes all the way down.

"A Certain Quasi-Extrinsic Union"

Before we move on, we should face a final, and more straightforward, objection: whatever implications might be buried in his definition of subsistence, Thomas seems to rule out language of the Persons as "outside" of each other. First, Thomas claims that "in God, nothing is properly said to be inside or outside."⁵² Yet he seems especially wary of "outside": "the Son Himself is not outside of the Father Who generates Him, but in Him."⁵³ Thomas enters into more detail when commenting on John 1:1, "the Word was with God":

> the preposition "in" signifies a certain intrinsic union, whereas the preposition "with" [*apud*] signifies in a certain way an *extrinsic union* [*quodammodo extrinsecam coniunctionem*]. And we state both in divine matters, namely, that the Son is in the Father and with the Father. Here the intrinsic union pertains to consubstantiality, but the extrinsic union (if we may use such an expression, since "extrinsic" is improperly employed in divine matters) refers only to a personal distinction.⁵⁴

---

51 For this language of "*modus existendi*," see Emery, *TCHP*, 134–38.

52 *De 108 art.*, q. 55.

53 *SCG* IV 11§8. This may be Thomas's strongest denial of the Son's being "outside" of the Father. Yet it comes at the beginning of a "manifestation" of the Trinity that, in *SCG* IV 11§18, culminates in one of Thomas's most vivid suggestions that the Son *is* somehow "outside" of the Father. We will treat this passage in detail in the section "*SCG* IV, Ch. 11" in chapter three.

54 *In Ioan.*, #45.

We cannot properly speak of the divine Persons as "extrinsic" to each other, and Thomas only introduces this language with careful qualification. Yet he does not reject it entirely. Instead, he only inserts these qualifications after he has chosen to introduce this language of "extrinsic" in the first place. He treats this language carefully, but he does not merely banish it.[55]

Indeed, with these qualifications in place, Thomas chooses to use this language again two sentences later: "The proposition 'with' principally signifies a personal distinction, but also consubstantiality inasmuch as it signifies a certain *quasi-extrinsic* union."[56] We cannot speak of the Persons as extrinsic to each other; yet we can speak of Them as "quasi-extrinsic" to each other. Indeed, we can even speak of Their *union* as quasi-extrinsic—which suggests that there is no conflict between Their being united to each other and Their being somehow outside of each other.

This language of "extrinsic," then, is inexact, and it can only be used "improperly" of God. Left unqualified, it would be misleading. Yet, once it is qualified, the distinct subsistence of the divine Persons is grounds enough for Thomas to speak of Their "quasi-extrinsic union." The Persons are not, strictly speaking, extrinsic to each other. Yet the distinction between subsistent created things, which *are* extrinsic to each other, is at least somehow dimly *like* the distinction between the Persons, and this likeness is strong enough for Thomas to speak of a "quasi-extrinsic union" between those Persons.

In the end, then, we may not be able to speak straightforwardly of the divine Word and Love as "outside" of the Father. Yet, for our purposes, it is enough to say that we also cannot speak of Them as *merely* inside of the Father. Again, if Their distinct subsistence means anything, it means that neither Word nor Love can exist merely in

---

[55] So far as I know, Thomas nowhere else teaches that "*apud*" signifies an "extrinsic union." Indeed, he even seems to contrast "*apud*" and "*extra*" in *De Ver.*, q. 2, a. 12, arg. 11 and in *Cat. Aur. in Matt.*, c. 22, l. 4 (in the quote he attributes to Chrysostom). When Thomas brings this dimension of *apud* to the fore here as he is speaking of the relation of the Son to the Father, therefore, he does not do so because he is boxed in by the meaning of the term. Instead, it seems that he *chooses* to highlight this dimension of the term with direct reference to the distinction of the divine Persons.

[56] *In Ioan.*, #45.

another. And, insofar as to be outside of something means not to be inside of it, the logic of subsistence seems to introduce a respect in which the divine Word and Love are "outside" of each other and the Father.[57]

Radical Distinction

We can remain, then, with the most basic point: because the divine Word and Love subsist, neither the divine Word nor the divine Love exists merely within the Father. To use Thomas's language, neither stands on any "foundation" other than Himself.[58] Because each is subsistent, each is founded in Himself and on Himself. In this sense, distinction in God is a *radical* distinction. It goes to the root and foundation of each divine Person. Even logically speaking, it goes all the way down.

Again, our main aim in part two will be to draw out the inter*personal* dimensions of Thomas's psychological approach to the Trinity. We will see that, because of the details of Thomas's psychological analogy, his divine Persons know each other, love each other, and give or receive Themselves to or from each other. Our main aim in part one is to see that, because of the details of Thomas's psychological analogy, this interpersonal knowledge, love, and self-giving really is *inter*personal: it plays out *between* distinct Persons. When the divine Speaker, Word, and Love know each other, love each other, or give Themselves to each other, They do so from within each other; yet They also do so from "outside" of each other. And it is this note of subsistence that first and foremost guarantees the sort of reciprocal "outside" required by the "between" entailed by the "*inter*personal."[59]

---

[57] I will, therefore, speak of the Word and Love as "outside" of each other and the Father going forward, yet I will generally do so in scare quotes in order to recall these qualifications.

[58] *De Pot.*, q. 9, a. 1.

[59] This reciprocal "outside" of distinct subsistence is also where Thomas opens up most to the sort of intra-divine "face-to-face" encounter that we saw Balthasar speak of above.

INSIDE AS OUTSIDE

In our next chapter, we will dive into passages where Thomas points evocatively towards this "outside." First, however, we can shift gears a bit. As we saw in our last chapter, Thomas acknowledges that his talk of a divine going-forth that remains within seems contradictory. Yet he responds to this objection by reminding us that we are already familiar with a created echo of this paradox. We see it in the human words and love-impressions that go forth from us even while they remain within us.

We are confronted now with an even starker paradox: a standing-outside that remains within. Thomas himself never draws any attention to this paradox, and so he never attempts to show its reasonableness with reference to any created realities with which we might already be familiar. Within his Trinitarian theology, however, he offers hints that some sort of standing-outside that remains within might be discernable in the logic of a category that stands at the center of his Trinitarian theology: relation.

In showing as much, I hope first to lend support to my claim that the paradox of a standing-outside that remains within is, in fact, present at the foundation of Thomas's psychological analogy. For, if we can show that it is present elsewhere in his Trinitarian thought, then we will have stronger grounds for concluding that it is present in his rendering of the distinct subsistence of Word and Love. Yet I also hope to suggest that the paradox we have uncovered can provide insight into Thomas's Trinitarian thought as a whole. It is not only implicit in his rendering of subsistence; it is also suggested in his rendering of relation. And, given how central the categories of "subsistence" and "relation" are to Thomas's Trinitarian theology, any pattern that is present in the logic of both terms might run deep in his Trinitarian theology as a whole.[60]

Before going on, I should acknowledge that we will touch here on one of the deepest and richest—and most difficult—dimensions of Thomas's Trinitarian thought: the divine Persons as subsistent relations.

---

60 For the importance of "relation" in Thomas's Trinitarian theology, see Emery, *TTTA*, 120–27: relation is the "heart" (p. 120) and the "soul" (127) of that theology.

We cannot, of course, do justice to this theme here.[61] Yet we should at least note that this is not our first time encountering relation. For we saw earlier in this chapter that if the divine Word and Love are really distinct from each other and from the Father, then it is because They are really related to each other and to the Father. Immanent procession in God, that is, only yields real distinction in God because it yields real relation in God. Thomas's psychological analogy for the Trinity, then, can only do justice to the basic givens of Trinitarian orthodoxy—three really distinct Persons—because it includes relation within itself. Put differently, it is not merely the case that Thomas presents us with a psychological Trinity and *also* with a relational Trinity, as though these two approaches were merely juxtaposed. Still less are they in conflict. Instead, his psychological Trinity is *itself* a relational Trinity, and his relational Trinity is *itself* a psychological Trinity.[62] It should perhaps not greatly surprise us, therefore, that the paradox we have been drawing out of his psychological categories should also be present in his rendering of relation.

INSIDE AND OUTSIDE

We can begin with a distinction that, according to Thomas, runs through every real relation:

> in each of the nine genera of accidents, there are two points for remark. One is the existence belonging to each one of them considered as an accident, which commonly applies to each of them as *inherent in a subject*, for the existence

---

[61] As usual, Emery offers a thorough and lucid presentation of Thomas's thought here: see *TTTA*, 78–102. For relation more generally, see Emery, "*Ad aliquid*: Relation in the Thought of St. Thomas Aquinas."

[62] A "relational" Trinity is sometimes set against a "classical" Trinity: see, for example, *Two Views on the Doctrine of the Trinity*, ed. Jason S. Sexton (Grand Rapids, MI: Zondervan, 2014). More relevant to us, social Trinitarians who are critical of Thomas's psychological approach are sometimes gentler—or even positive—on his doctrine of subsistent relations. See Johnson, *She Who Is*, 216; Gisbert Greshake, *Der dreieine Gott: Eine trinitarische Theologie* (Basel: Herder, 1997), 337. Thomas means something very different—and something far more "psychological"—by "subsistent relations" than do most social Trinitarians who appreciate this language. Yet one of my main burdens here is that he does not necessarily mean anything less social.

> of an accident is existence in another. The other point of remark is the proper *ratio* of each one of these genera. In the genera, apart from that of "relation," as in quantity and quality, even the proper *ratio* of the genus itself is derived from a respect to the subject. . . . But the proper *ratio* of relation is not taken from its respect to that in which it is, but from its respect to *something outside*.[63]

As we saw above, an accident can only exist at all if it exists in a subject. As Thomas puts it here, "the existence of an accident is existence in another." According to its *esse* as an accident, therefore, relation exists inside of the substance that is related.

Relation, however, is unlike other accidents. The blackness of my hair, for example, exists in my hair not only insofar as it is an accident but also insofar as it is a quality or a color. There is no straightforward respect in which that blackness either exists outside of me or refers to anything outside of me. My relation to my wife, however, exists within me according to its *esse* as an accident. Yet, according to its *ratio* as a relation, it does not point towards me; it points to "something outside" of me. It points towards my wife.

Thomas puts the matter even more strongly: "So, even in creatures, if we consider relations according as they are relations, in that aspect they are said to be 'assistant,' and *not intrinsically affixed*. . . . Whereas, if relation is considered as an accident, it inheres in a subject, and it has an accidental existence in it."[64] Relations, according to their *ratio* as relations, do not inhere in their subjects: they are "not intrinsically affixed." They are located, as it were, outside of their subjects. As Thomas puts it elsewhere, relations are "a certain medium *between* the related substance and that to which it is related."[65] Considered according to their *esse*, relations remain within their substance; considered according to their *ratio*, relations stretch out between substances. Emery sums up the

---

[63] *ST* I q. 28, a. 2. Thomas discusses the *esse* and *ratio* of relation with some frequency, and often in great detail, through his Trinitarian theology. For especially rich treatments, see I *Sent.*, d. 26, q. 2, a. 1, and d. 33, q. 1, a. 1; and *De Pot.*, q. 8, a. 2. See also Emery, *TTTA*, 89–96.

[64] *ST* I q. 28, a. 2.

[65] *De Pot.*, q. 8, a. 2.

matter: relation in its *ratio* "is an ec-stasis, a pure outside-referring": it is a "mode of exteriority," and it "can indeed be considered as 'positioned from outside.'"⁶⁶ Thomas himself writes that a relation, as a relation, does not name "anything in the thing of which it is said; instead, it places something outside of it [*ponit aliquid extra*]."⁶⁷

Of course, it is also true that the same relation, according to its existence as an accident, exists within the substance that is related. Indeed, a relation that is merely apprehended between two things, but that exists within neither of them, is a rational relation.⁶⁸ If a relation, in its *esse*, does not inhere in a subject, then it does not *really* exist at all.

Even this brief sketch of relation is enough to bring us to our first conclusion: considered according to its *esse* as an accident, a relation is inside of its subject; considered according to its *ratio* as a relation, a relation is outside of its subject. Considered according to its *esse* and its *ratio* together, therefore, a relation is *both* inside of its subject *and* outside of its subject. For Thomas, therefore, there seems to be no conflict between being-inside of something in one respect and being-outside of that same thing in another respect. Every real relation we ever encounter, even among creatures, is able to be both at once.

INSIDE AS OUTSIDE

Our next step will take us further than Thomas ever explicitly goes. We will therefore take it more tentatively. Yet, given some of Thomas's most fundamental metaphysical commitments, this step seems all but unavoidable.

Beginning with those fundamental principles, Thomas first of all makes clear that the existence and essence of any created thing are really distinct. Yet they are also intimately united. The existence of a thing, that is, can never be a naked preessential act of existence: it does not hover in any way above or behind or before the specific thing that exists. Instead, it is only ever the existence *of the thing* that exists,

---

66 *TTTA*, 92–93.
67 I *Sent.*, d. 26, q. 2, a. 1, ad 1.
68 See *ST* I q. 28, a. 1; and Emery, *TTTA*, 86.

and this existing thing never exists except as already determined by its essence. Just so, an essence never enjoys any shadowy proto-existence or pseudo-existence apart from or before its *esse*: apart from its *esse*, it does not exist at all.[69]

If these points hold with *esse* and essence more generally, then they should hold no less with the *esse* and *ratio* of relation.[70] Beginning with *esse*, there is no pre-relational or a-relational act of existence buried beneath the relation itself. Instead, a relation's act of existence is only ever the existence *of a relation*. A relation's existence, therefore, can never exist apart from the relation itself or from its *ratio* as relation. Yet this relation, according to its *ratio* as a relation, is *outside* of its subject—which seems to suggest that this existence *itself* must be somehow outside of the subject. Otherwise, it would exist apart from the relation whose existence it is. Thomas perhaps gestures in this direction when he writes that "the *existence* of a relative thing is towards another [*relativi esse est ad aliud se habere*]."[71] It is not merely that the *ratio* of a

---

[69] Ferdinand Ulrich meditates on these principles in great detail. See Rachel M. Coleman, "Thinking the 'Nothing' of Being: Ferdinand Ulrich on Transnihilation," *Communio: International Catholic Review* 46, no. 1 (2019): 182–98.

[70] *Ratio* and *essentia* are, of course, not merely synonymous, and very subtle qualifications could perhaps be introduced here. Yet they are very closely related. Indeed, Ghislain Lafont argues that, "in practice, '*inesse*' and '*ratio*' correspond, when one speaks of an accident, to *esse* and *essentia* at the level of substance." *Peut-on Connaitre Dieu Jesus-Christ?* (Paris: Cerf, 1969), 119. For our purposes, therefore, I will treat the "*ratio*" of a relation and the "essence" of a relation as interchangeable.

[71] See IV *Sent.*, d. 8, q. 1, a. 1, qc. 1, ad 1; *De Ver.*, q. 4, a. 5, arg. 8; *De Pot.*, q. 8, a. 2, ad 12; *in Metap.*, #1028; and *ST* I q. 40, a. 2, ad 4. Thomas ascribes these words to Aristotle in *ST* I q. 28, a. 2, arg. 3. On its face, the Latin here might be rendered differently: if "*relativi*" is nominative plural instead of genitive singular, then this passage might perhaps be read as making a claim not about the *esse* of a relative thing, but about the relative thing itself. In *in Metap.*, #1028, however, Thomas is very clear that at stake here is the *esse* of a relative thing—and that this *esse itself* is towards another. This point also comes out, though it is qualified a bit, in *De Pot.*, q. 8, a. 2, ad 12. In response to an objection that centers around the words just quoted, Thomas writes, "Because, in creatures, relation is an accident, its *esse* is existence in another; its *esse*, therefore, is not towards another. But its *esse*, insofar as it is a relation, *is* towards another [*sed esse huius secundum quod ad aliquid, est ad aliud se habere*]." Insofar as it is considered as an accident (or in the abstract), the *esse* of a relation is in another and not towards another. Yet, insofar as the relation in question is considered as a relation, *its existence itself* is towards another. In reality, moreover, the existence of a relation is never merely an "abstract" or merely accidental act of existence; it is only ever the existence of a relation. Even in this passage,

relation is towards another. Instead, because the existence of a relation is the existence *of a relation*, this existence *itself* is "towards another."[72]

The same point holds from the other direction. For, in its *ratio*, a real relation is outside of its subject. Yet, if this relation really exists, then it cannot exist apart from its own act of existence. This act of existence, however, is inside a subject. A relation, even according to its *ratio* as a relation, can only *be* outside of its subject if it *is* inside of its subject.[73]

Taking a step back, Thomas is certainly careful to distinguish the *esse* and *ratio* of a relation: considered according to its *esse*, a relation exists within its subject; considered according to its *ratio*, it "places something outside" of its subject.[74] A surface reading of these principles, however, might be misleading. On the one hand, one might get the impression that, within a given subject, there is a sort of floating core of relation-in-its-*esse*: an *esse* that somehow belongs to the relation but is itself a-relational or pre-relational and exists merely within the subject. On the other hand, one might get the impression that, somewhere outside of the subject, there is a floating relation-in-its-*ratio*: a *ratio* that is somehow tethered to the existence that is within the subject, but which itself stretches out merely outside of its subject. One might envision the *esse* as a point within the subject and the *ratio* as a vector arching out from the subject: that vector might be rooted in the *esse*-point, but it is extrinsic to the *esse*-point. In reality, these two distinct

---

then, it seems that the *existence itself* of a relation only exists towards another—even as that existence, considered as existence or as an accident, is in its subject.

72 Paissac discerns something similar in the logic of a word. He not only describes a word as a "pure relation" (*Théologie du Verbe*, 190); he also writes that the *existence* of a word is "relative existence" (p. 197). He even writes that "the essence of a word is *esse ad*" (197n1). In a move that parallels our current discussion, he also clarifies that insofar as a word is an accident, it exists "in an intellectual substance . . . and this is its *esse in*" (197n1). Still, he draws out a respect in which a word's very *esse* is towards another. Emery seems to follow Paissac here, at least loosely: he writes that the word's "existence is intrinsically relative" (*TTTA*, 182). White perhaps gestures in a similar direction, though in a different vein, in *The Trinity*, 445–46.

73 Of course, the *esse* and *ratio* of a relation are not "things" that exist in "places." Instead, the only thing that exists is the relation itself, which is inside the subject by its *esse* and outside by its *ratio*—an *esse* and *ratio* that are inextricably united.

74 I *Sent.*, d. 26, q. 2, a. 1, ad 1.

aspects of a relation are mutually inherent. Neither can be collapsed into the other; yet neither exists anywhere but in and through the other.

There are not, in other words, two halves of relation. Instead, there are two aspects under which the whole of a relation can be considered. According to its *esse*, the *whole* of a relation is within its subject: to say anything else would be to say that a relation's relation-ness exists somewhere apart from its existence. According to its *ratio*, the *whole* of a relation is outside of its subject: to say anything else would be to say that a relation's existence exists somewhere apart from its relation-ness. Relation is not half inside and half outside. It is fully inside and fully outside. Indeed, relation is inside *as* outside and outside *as* inside: it is outside by an existence that is inside, and it is inside as a relation that is outside.[75]

Again, drawing this conclusion takes us beyond anything Thomas tells us explicitly. I therefore propose it tentatively. Yet the most basic point is already secured by what Thomas *does* tell us explicitly: a relation is inside of its subject insofar as it is considered as an accident, and it is outside of its subject insofar as it is considered as a relation. Whatever the ultimate relation of *esse* and *ratio*, therefore, Thomas is clear that some marriage of being-inside and being-outside is written into the most basic structure of relation. When we claim that a similar marriage of remaining-within and standing-outside goes to the foundation of his psychological analogy, therefore, we might not be positing some strange and inscrutable paradox that stands at odds with the otherwise sober austerity of Thomas's Trinitarian theology. Instead, we may be identifying a paradox that helps to structure Thomas's Trinitarian theology as a whole.[76]

---

[75] These points can allow us to respond to the objection mentioned in note 41 above. For it is true that the three divine relations only subsist in virtue of their one *esse*. Yet it is the *three relations* that subsist, and to locate their subsistence in their existence *instead of* in their *ratio* as relations would be to compartmentalize the *esse* and *ratio* of the divine relations—an *esse* and *ratio* that, even as logically distinct, are mutually inherent.

[76] Indeed, this paradox may stretch beyond subsistence and relation into other categories at the heart of Thomas's Trinitarian theology. First, when Thomas asks why the Greek *logos* is translated as *verbum* rather than as *ratio*, he writes that " '*ratio*,' properly speaking, names a conception of the mind *according as it is in the mind*, even if through it nothing exterior comes to be; but '*verbum*' signifies *a reference to something exterior*" (*in Ioan.*, #32. See also *De Ver.*, q. 4, a. 5, s.c.). An inner word not only proceeds within its speaker's

"Fatherhood Is Not in the Son"

As similar paradox comes closer to the surface when Thomas turns to a related category: relative opposition.[77] For the divine Persons are not merely related; Their respective relations are mutually opposed. And opposed relations, by definition, cannot each be in the same subject. If I am a father, for example, then my fatherhood—that is, my relation to my son as his father—must exist in me. Otherwise, I would not be a father. Yet this same fatherhood-in-relation-to-my-son cannot exist in my son. If it did, then he would be his own father, which is

---

mind. Instead, like a relation, it bears a reference to something outside of its speaker: it refers to the external word that is spoken by the lips. An inner word is therefore inside the soul as tending outside of the soul (*in Ioan.*, #25 is more complicated, yet it seems to suggest that the inner word remains "within our soul," even as it "proceed[s] to the exterior of the one understanding").

Things are stronger with love. As Thomas is preparing to speak of the Holy Spirit as Love, he writes that in any act of love, the beloved "is in the will of the lover as the term of a movement is in its proportioned motive principle by reason of the suitability and proportion which the term has for that principle. Just so, in a certain way, there is in fire the heavens by reason of that lightness which gives it proportion and suitability to such a place" (*SCG* IV 19§4). Thomas's example of fire is helpful. Fire only rises up to the heavens because the heavens are already *in* the fire: they are in it through the fire's "proportion and suitability" to be drawn heavenward. The heavens are *in* the fire as a place *outside* of the fire, towards which the fire tends and in which the fire rests. Thomas, moreover, uses this example to illustrate what happens every time anyone loves anything: the beloved both dwells within the lover and stands outside of the lover. In a different vein, Thomas writes elsewhere that love causes both the indwelling of the beloved in the lover and the ecstasy of the lover into the beloved (see *ST* I-II q. 28, aa. 2–3). In love, the lover is carried ecstatically *outside* of himself into a beloved who, as beloved, is already *within* him. To love is to be both outside of oneself and inside of oneself.

Finally, Thomas teaches that the divine Persons are distinct not only by Their relations, but also by Their notional actions (See *ST* I q. 40, a. 2; *De Pot.*, q. 10, a. 3). Yet he writes, "Some categories, such as quality and quantity, are signified as inherent according to their *ratio* . . . But others, as is most clear in action, are signified in their *ratio* as being *from* another, and *not* as *in* another. For an action, according as it is an action, is signified as being *from* an agent; insofar as it is an accident, it is *in* the agent" (I *Sent.*, d. 32, q. 1, a. 1. See also I *Sent.*, d. 8, q. 4, a. 3, ad 3; *De Pot.*, q. 7, a. 8, and q. 7, a. 9, ad 7, and q. 8, a. 2). The parallels to Thomas's teaching on relation are evident: as an accident, action exists in its agent; as an action, it is *not* in its agent, but from its agent. It is both in the agent and not in the agent.

The paradox at the center of this chapter, then, may be present in the logic not only of subsistence and relation but also of a word, love, and action. It may be present, that is, in virtually all of the building blocks of Thomas's Trinitarian theology.

77 See Emery, *TTTA*, 96–99 for basic background on relative opposition and for its importance in Thomas's Trinitarian thought.

impossible. Shifting to the Trinity, the Father's relation of fatherhood to the Son cannot be in the Son; it must be in the Father. As Thomas puts it, "fatherhood is not in the Son, because fatherhood is opposed to sonship."[78] Thomas repeats this point with some frequency, and his reasoning makes clear that, for the same reason, sonship cannot be in the Father.[79]

This point is straightforward enough. Yet it yields some surprising conclusions. For fatherhood—the fatherhood that is not in the Son—is not just something the Father *has*. Fatherhood is what the Father *is*. Because of simplicity, the Person of the Father is identical to His relation of fatherhood.[80] Yet, if the Father is His fatherhood, and if fatherhood is not in the Son, then the Father *Himself* cannot be in the Son. Just so, if the Son is His sonship, and if this sonship is not in the Father, then the Son *Himself* cannot be in the Father. The divine Persons, of course, *are* perfectly within each other. Yet Thomas's teaching on relative opposition seems to recall his teaching on subsistence: it seems to introduce another respect in which the divine Persons cannot be within each other. Because each *is* an opposed relation, each must stand "outside" of the others, even as each remains perfectly within the others.[81]

Indeed, it is not merely that the divine Persons are within each other *and also*, because of Their opposed relations, outside of each other. Instead, the logic of opposed relations *itself* demands that each Person must be in the others. When Thomas asks directly whether the divine Persons are within each other, he argues that They are within each other "according to Their relations," for "it is manifest that each of two relative opposites is in the notion of the other."[82] A father, by definition, is the father of a son: because sonship is opposed to fatherhood, sonship enters into the definition of fatherhood. The

---

[78] *De Pot.*, q. 2, a. 5.

[79] See *De Pot.*, q. 8, a. 2, ad 10; *SCG* IV 14§7; I *Sent.*, d. 7, q. 2, a. 1, arg. 1, and d. 26, q. 1, a. 2, arg. 4; and *ST* I q. 40, a. 3, arg. 2. In the last three texts, this claim appears in an objection, but Thomas accepts it in his response.

[80] See *ST* I q. 40, a. 1.

[81] Similarly, the Holy Spirit is His relation of proceeding, which cannot be in the principle from which He proceeds.

[82] *ST* I q. 42, a. 5.

idea of fatherhood, that is, includes the idea of sonship within it. Yet Thomas goes further. For, in the passage we just cited, Thomas does not merely argue that because fatherhood and sonship are relatively opposed, the *idea* of the Son's sonship is somehow contained within the *idea* of the Father's fatherhood. Instead, he concludes that because sonship and fatherhood are relative opposites, the Father *Himself* must be in the Son.[83] Because the Persons are opposed relations, the Persons Themselves dwell in each other.

Thomas, then, says both: on the one hand, "fatherhood is *not* in the Son, because fatherhood is opposed to sonship";[84] on the other, fatherhood *is* in the Son, because "one relative opposite is in the notion of the other."[85] Two opposed relations cannot possibly be in each other, yet two opposed relations must necessarily be in each other. One and the same logic of relative opposition demands that they both dwell inside of each other and stand outside of each other.

Again, my main claim in this chapter is that even as Thomas's psychological analogy centers around immanent processions, it does not give us a Trinity of mere immanence. Instead, the very logic of an immanent procession demands that neither Word nor Love can be merely inside of the Father. I hope to have shown now that Thomas's rendering of relation and of relative opposition reinforces this point: both because Word and Love subsist distinctly, and because They subsist as distinct relations, They must somehow stand outside of the Father, even as They remain within the Father. The logic of distinct subsistence and the logic of relation—both of which are central to Thomas's psychological analogy—both open up to this conclusion.

---

[83] As Thomas puts it elsewhere, "a relative cannot exist without its correlate" (*De Pot.*, q. 8, a. 1, arg. 10; Thomas accepts this point in his response). With reference to this passage, Emery writes, "It is not just that a relative reality cannot be *thought* without its correlative. It cannot *exist* as such without it" (*TTTA*, 304).

[84] *De Pot.*, q. 2, a. 5.

[85] *ST* I q. 42, a. 5.

"THIS DISTINCTION EXCELS ALL DISTINCTIONS"

This talk of relation, however, brings us to a final objection. In the definitions of subsistence that appear in his Trinitarian theology, Thomas may suggest that the divine Persons are not merely within each other. Similarly, he may tell us both that the Father is His fatherhood and that fatherhood is not in the Son. He may therefore sow seeds for the conclusion that the divine Persons stand somehow outside of each other, and that the distinction between Them is radical. Yet, by and large, when Thomas speaks directly to this distinction, he takes pains not to emphasize it, but to minimize it. Even more, he appeals to the logic of relation in order to do so. As he puts it, "relation of all the genera is the least stable in point of reality," and "the distinction of the Persons must be by that which distinguishes the least possible; and this is by relation."[86]

Again, I am interested in Thomas's psychological approach to the Trinity, and not in his teaching on relation or on the divine Persons as subsistent relations. Yet we saw above that, according to Thomas's psychological analogy, the divine Word is only really distinct from His Speaker because He is really related to His Speaker. If relation, therefore, cannot give us anything more than the least possible distinction, then Thomas's psychological analogy cannot give us anything more than the least possible distinction. We ought, therefore, to deal with this objection.

In order to respond to it, we should note first that Thomas not only teaches that the relative distinction of the divine Persons is the least of all possible distinctions. He also, in a series of passages from his *Sentences* commentary, points to ways in which this distinction is greater than all creaturely distinctions. Even more, he sometimes does so within the same breath as he affirms that this distinction is the least of all distinctions. The passages we will survey now, therefore, do not contradict those passages where Thomas downplays the distinction

---

[86] *De Pot.*, q. 9, a. 5, ad 14; *ST* I q. 40, a. 2, ad 3.

between the divine Persons. Instead, they complement them and fill them out.

In the first passage, Thomas takes on the question of relation most directly: he writes that

> the order of distinction can be considered in two ways: either according to the quantity of distinction, or according to its dignity and causality. If according to the quantity of distinction, in this way the distinction of the divine hypostases is the least real distinction that can exist.... And therefore to distinction of this kind belongs the least being, namely relation. But, according to the order of dignity and causality, *this distinction excels all distinctions*; and similarly the relation which is the principle of this distinction excels in dignity all that distinguishes in creatures: not, indeed, from the fact that it is relation, but from the fact that it is a divine relation. It also excels in causality, for out of the procession of the distinct divine Persons is caused all creaturely procession and multiplication.[87]

Thomas affirms the point with which we began: if the quantity of the distinction is considered, then the distinction of the divine Persons by relation is less "real" than is the distinction between any two creatures. In this respect, the distinction of the divine Persons is the least of all distinctions.

Thomas, however, continues by arguing that, so far as dignity and causality go, the distinction of the divine Persons "excels all distinctions."[88] Of course, neither dignity nor causality speak directly to the degree of distinction, and when Thomas speaks to the "quantity" of distinction, he minimizes the distinction of the divine Persons. Yet, even as he identifies one respect in which the distinction between the divine Persons is less than the distinction between any two creatures,

---

[87] I *Sent.*, d. 26, q. 2, a. 2, ad 2.

[88] Though he does not use this same language outside of his *Sentences* commentary, Thomas reaffirms through the end of his career one of the principles that underlies this claim: the processions of the divine Persons are the cause of all creaturely processions from God (see *ST* I q. 45, a. 6, ad 1. For more, see Emery, *TCHP*, 115–53).

he identifies two respects in which it excels any distinction between any two creatures.[89]

The next passage speaks more directly to our reflections on subsistence earlier in this chapter. It comes two distinctions earlier in the same commentary, as Thomas is asking whether there is number in God:

> If we compare the number of Persons to the number of absolute properties which are in creatures, they exceed in some respects and are exceeded in others. For if the reason of the distinction [*ratio distinctionis*] is considered, a greater distinction is found in the absolute properties of creatures than in the divine Persons; because color and flavor are distinguished according to one and another accidental act of existence, but in the divine Persons there is one and the same act of existence. But if the perfection of the distinctions is considered, in this way the number of the Persons *exceeds*, because relation in God are *subsistent Persons*. Hence, in God, the number of Persons corresponds to the number of relations; in creatures, distinct Persons do not correspond to distinct properties in creatures, because properties in creatures *are not subsistent*, but only inherent.[90]

As in our first passage, Thomas begins by identifying a respect in which the distinction between Father and Son is less than the distinction between any two accidents within a single creature: the divine Persons, unlike the color and flavor of an apple, share a single act of existence. Yet he continues by clarifying that the divine Persons, unlike any accidents in any creature, subsist. And, because They subsist, the distinction

---

[89] Its greatness in "causality" is especially important for us. For Thomas teaches here that the distinction of the divine Persons causes all of the distinctions entailed in the "multiplication" of creatures. Elsewhere, moreover, he teaches that nothing can be more present in the thing caused than it is in the cause: a fire cannot make anything hotter than the fire itself is, the supremely good and intelligent divine nature cannot make a goodness better or an intelligence more intelligent than it itself is, and so on (see *ST* I q. 4, a. 2, and q. 6, a. 2). We can tentatively suggest that if this logic holds here, then it may be that the distinction of the divine Persons cannot cause any distinction more distinct than itself. Thomas might suggest a way, that is, in which distinction in God is a distinction more distinct than any distinction between any two creatures.

[90] I *Sent.*, d. 24, q. 2, a. 1.

between Them is more perfect than is the distinction between any two created accidents.[91]

The final passage is perhaps the strongest, though it is also the least developed. It comes several distinctions earlier, as Thomas is arguing that there is more than one procession in God: "because the Persons are distinguished according to procession, which are really many, it cannot be said that the processions are not different in reality but only in reason. *For nothing causes a greater distinction*, formally speaking, than the distinction whereby the Persons are distinguished from each other."[92] Thomas does not enter any detail here. He does not, for example, tell us why, "formally speaking," there is no distinction greater than the distinction between the divine Persons. Yet he affirms the central point plainly: formally speaking, the distinction between the Father and the Son is a distinction greater than which no distinction has been wrought.

Of course, none of these passages make any mention of the divine Word or Love. Even more, they all come from Thomas's *Commentary on the Sentences*, where his psychological terms remain marginal.[93] At the same time, however, the subsistence of the divine Persons is the foundation for Thomas's conclusions in the second passage, and Their processions are the foundation for his conclusions in the third—and subsistence and procession both stand at the center of Thomas's psychological analogy. Be that as it may, there are certainly points where Thomas downplays the distinction between the divine Persons. And, even in our passages, he often identifies some respect in which this distinction is less than any distinction between any two created things. Yet he also points towards other respects in which this distinction "excels" any distinction between any two creatures.

---

[91] Thomas does not explain what the "perfection" of a distinction might mean (it might have to do with the perfection of subsistence as compared to accidental being). For our purposes, the only point worth emphasizing is that, because the divine Persons subsist, there is some respect in which the distinction between Them exceeds the distinction between non-subsistent accidents.

[92] I *Sent.*, d. 13, q. 1, a. 2, ad 4.

[93] That said, we spend most of our next chapter looking closely at passages from later in Thomas's career that are more obviously psychological and that point in a similar direction.

CONCLUSION

We should conclude by reiterating a more basic point. Our reflections so far have revolved around two paradoxes: in chapter one, a going-forth that remains within; in chapter two, a standing-outside that remains within. In both chapters, I have spent most of my time emphasizing only one pole of those paradoxes. I have stressed that the divine Word and Love really do go forth from the Father, and I have highlighted a respect in which They stand "outside" of the Father. My claim, however, is not that Their going-forth or Their standing-outside is any more important than Their remaining-within. Instead, it is that Their going-forth and Their standing-outside is *no less* important than Their remaining-within. If I have emphasized one side, it is only because that side has so often been underemphasized or ignored—or even flat out denied.

I do not, however, hope to replace a lopsided emphasis on interiority with a lopsided emphasis on distinction. I should close, therefore, by restating the other side of our paradox: there is no part of the Word or Love that is not entirely swaddled and embraced by the Father; Word and Love are nestled in and welcomed into the heart of the Father, the womb of the Father, and "the most secret" recesses of the Father.[94] Indeed, we mentioned in the introduction that if They were not, then the very interpersonal communion that social Trinitarians prize would be undone. For Moltmann might be right that belief in a monopersonal God—along with certain articulations of the psychological analogy—could lead to "possessive individualism."[95] Yet so too could belief in a God of three isolated and mutually extrinsic individuals. If the divine Persons *merely* met each other from the outside, and if each did not also bear the others intimately within Himself, then Their communion would be imperfect. Indeed, three mutually extrinsic divine Persons might ultimately be no less individualistic than a single divine Person. They might even be three times as individualistic. Only a divine life

---

94 *In Ioan.*, #218.
95 *The Trinity and the Kingdom*, 198–99.

of face-to-face encounter *within* interpersonal indwelling can lead us beyond mere individualism to intimacy and communion.

Again, many social Trinitarians recognize this point.[96] My claim is not that Thomas succeeds where they fail. Nor is my claim that Thomas's synthesis is richer or fuller or more beautiful or more truly interpersonal than theirs is. My claim is, first, that Thomas *does* offer a synthesis of unity and distinction; second, that distinction goes just as deep in this synthesis as unity does; and third, that Thomas can therefore bring us beyond at least some of the oppositions that have plagued at least some versions of social Trinitrianism in recent decades.

Most basically, however, my claim is that Thomas's insistence on the immanence of the divine processions does not shut down the room needed for radical distinction in God. Yet it is only now, as we move on to chapter three, that we will see just how deeply immanence is bound up with radical distinction. We will also begin to see in detail a point to which we alluded in this chapter: Thomas's strong reading of consubstantiality is equally bound up with radical distinction. We have already seen, in other words, that immanence and consubstantial unity are not incompatible with radical distinction. We will see now that they are not juxtaposed to radical distinction. Thomas's psychological analogy, that is, does not merely secure radical distinction *and* perfect unity; it secures radical distinction *in* securing perfect unity. It secures standing-outside *in* securing remaining-within.

---

96 We mentioned in the introduction that Moltmann and Plantinga both do so; though we also saw that Craig misses this point entirely.

3

OUTSIDE BECAUSE INSIDE

I have mentioned several times now that my deepest interest in Thomas's psychological analogy does not lie in its ability to sustain a genuine—or even a radical—interpersonal distinction. Many other Trinitarian theologies can do that. My main interest lies in its ability to integrate elements that, in contemporary discourse, are often set at odds: unity and distinction, immanence and outsideness, the interpersonal and the intrapersonal. In this chapter, we will take a step further into this integration. For we have seen that, in Thomas's psychological analogy, it is not *either* remaining-within *or* standing-outside. We will see now that it is not merely *both* remaining-within *and also* standing-outside. Instead, it is remaining-within and *therefore* standing-outside. It is because Word and Love remain perfectly within the Father—and it is because of Thomas's rendering of consubstantial unity—that Word and Love stand somehow outside of the Father.

To see as much, I will begin with a bird's-eye view: I will explore principles that are basic to Thomas's Trinitarian theology, and which demand that the divine Word cannot be consubstantial with the Father unless He subsists distinctly from the Father. From there, I will descend into particulars: I will give a close reading of two texts where Thomas enters more deeply into this dynamic. First, I will work at length through

SCG IV, ch. 11; next, I will walk more briefly through some details from Thomas's commentary on the opening verses of John's Gospel.[1]

There are, of course, other passages that might be studied, and the points we will draw out from these two texts could be complemented by others that are fleshed out more fully elsewhere. In these two texts, however, Thomas enters with unique depth into our theme. Moreover, our *SCG* text is the first articulation of Thomas's mature theology of the Word; our text from his John commentary is the last. In fastening onto these two texts, therefore, we will cover the whole temporal sweep of Thomas's mature theology of the Word. Finally, while Thomas is certainly guided by Scripture in our *SCG* passage, he ultimately grounds his arguments in the nature of a word. In the John text, in contrast, his conclusions are built on small details—down to grammatical minutiae—of Scripture. In choosing these texts, then, I hope to show that the pattern we are tracing out here is grounded both in Thomas's "dogmatic" treatments of the divine Word and in his "exegetical" attention to the details of the Gospel text.[2]

ONE, THEREFORE MANY

We can begin by underlining a point we have mentioned only briefly, which might seem to give social Trinitarians further reason to regard Thomas with suspicion: it is not merely that the divine Word and Love, like created words and love-impressions, remain within the mind of the one Who speaks and breathes Them. Instead, They *are* the mind of the one Who speaks and breathes Them. They are consubstantial

---

[1] Even more than in chapter one, most of the texts we will study here focus on the Word and make little mention of Love. That said, all of the most basic conclusions we will draw here (especially in the first two sections of this chapter) will follow ultimately on the procession and subsistence of the divine Word. And given that the divine Love proceeds no less (and is no less subsistent) than the Word, all of these conclusions would seem to hold for Love as much as for the Word. Indeed, although Thomas articulates these conclusions most fully as he is reflecting on the Word, we will provide texts in note 10 of this chapter where he extends some of them to Love.

[2] As we mentioned in our introduction, Thomas's "dogmatic" treatises are often opposed to his "exegetical" or "Biblical" works. It is in this chapter that we will most clearly see the differences between these two genres as well as the harmony that underlies these differences.

with the Father. We have here, that is, not just one more instance of intra-mental interiority. Instead, we have a unity and an interiority that infinitely outstrips anything I might find between myself and my words or love-impressions.

Again, this point would seem to add fuel to social Trinitarians' ire. For it seems to suggest that there is even less room for anything interpersonal in God than there is between me and my words and love-impressions. We saw briefly in our last chapter, however, that things are more complicated. We will see this same point in detail now, that is, we will see that, in Thomas's Trinitarian theology, it is precisely consubstantial unity that demands the radical distinction—and the interpersonal standing-outside—on which we focused in our last chapter.

This point comes out with particular clarity in two shorter passages. First, in the *Summa*, Thomas writes,

> Being and speaking are not the same in us. Hence that which in us has intellectual being, does not belong to our nature. But in God being and understanding are one and the same: hence the Word in God is not an accident in Him, or an effect of His; instead, the Word belongs to His very nature. And *therefore* it must be something *subsistent*, because whatever is in the nature of God subsists; and so Damascene says that "the Word of God is substantial and has a *hypostatic* being."[3]

We see almost the same language and logic in his John commentary:

> our word is not of the same nature as we; but the divine Word is of the same nature as God. And *therefore* He is something that *subsists* in the divine nature. For . . . in God, understanding and existence are the same; and therefore the Word of the divine intellect is not an accident but belongs to its nature: because whatever is in the nature of God is God.

---

3 *ST* I q. 34, a. 2, ad 1.

Therefore Damascene says that God is a substantial Word, and a *hypostasis*, but our words are concepts in our mind.[4]

Several points bear noting here. First of all, if traditional accounts of consubstantiality have come under fire from social Trinitarians, then traditional accounts of simplicity have fared little better.[5] In response, some of Thomas's defenders have argued that his account of simplicity is not incompatible with the real distinction of the divine Persons.[6] Here, however, we see something deeper: the subsistence of the divine Word—along with all of the radical consequences that follow from distinct subsistence—is not only compatible with divine simplicity. Instead, it is *demanded by* simplicity and it *depends on* simplicity. If the divine nature were not simple, then the divine Word would be a non-subsistent accident. It is only because there can be no accidents in God that the Word must subsist—and it is only because He subsists that He is in any way "outside" of the Father or "quasi-extrinsic" to the Father.[7]

For our immediate purposes, however, there is a more important point. Thomas's argument does not run directly from simplicity to subsistence. Instead, it passes through consubstantiality. Thomas writes that "the divine Word is of the same nature as God. And *therefore* He is something that *subsists* in the divine nature." The *reason* that the Word subsists is His unity of nature with the Father. The Father's nature, of course, is simple. If, therefore, the Word shares the Father's nature, then the Word's nature must be simple as well. Yet, because the Word's nature must be simple, there can be no accidents in it—which means that the Word must subsist. The subsistence of the divine Word, therefore, is *demanded by* the consubstantiality of Word and Father. From the other direction, this subsistence *depends on* this consubstantiality. For the Word can only subsist if He exists in a simple nature. Yet there is only one simple nature: the divine nature, which also belongs to the

---

4 *In Ioan.*, #28.

5 See James E. Dolezal, "Trinity, Simplicity and the Status of God's Personal Relations," *International Journal of Systematic Theology* 16, no. 1 (2014): 79–81.

6 Dolezal offers a nice example of such an argument in the article just cited.

7 Recall *in Ioan.*, #45 for this language of "quasi-extrinsic."

Father.[8] The Word can only subsist, therefore, if He shares the nature of the Father.

The most basic point is that Thomas does not need to hold back the logic of consubstantiality in order to make room for distinct subsistence in God. Instead, it is *by following the logic of consubstantiality all the way out* that he arrives at distinct subsistence.

We come, then, to the first articulation of a claim that will run all through this chapter: there is no conflict between the radical unity of Word and Father and the radical distinction of Word from Father. Instead, Their subsistent distinction both depends on and follows from Their consubstantial unity. If we dismissed this unity, we would not open up room for a more robust or radical distinction in God. Instead, we would lose the radical distinction between two subsistent Persons. We would be left with a merely intra-personal distinction between a single person and his accidental word. So far as Thomas's psychological analogy goes, anything less than consubstantial unity would yield something less than interpersonal distinction.[9]

---

[8] For the impossibility of there being more than one instance of the divine nature, see *SCG* I, ch. 42. This is, of course, a point on which Thomas differs from most social Trinitarians.

[9] That said, one might raise an objection here. For one might admit that unity and distinction are bound together in Thomas's Trinity. Yet one might complain that unity still has the upper hand. The divine Persons, that is, are only distinct because They are perfectly one, yet Thomas seems unable to allow that the divine essence is only perfectly one because the Persons are distinct. Their unity grounds Their distinction, but Their distinction seems not to ground Their unity (some contemporaries affirm strongly that divine distinction does indeed ground divine unity: see Ratzinger, *Introduction to Christianity*, 179). To respond, we can note first that, for Thomas, perfect unity can only be *perfectly* one if it is purely actual (see *ST* I q. 11, a. 4); second, pure actuality can only be purely actual if it is simple and intelligent: for the interdependence of the essential divine attributes, see D. Stephen Long, *The Perfectly Simple Triune God: Aquinas and His Legacy* (Minneapolis: Fortress, 2016), 21. Some scholars, however, have argued that, for Thomas, there can be no simple act of intellect apart from the procession of a subsistent Word—which means that there can be no simple intelligence without interpersonal distinction: see John Milbank, "Truth and Vision," in *The Radical Orthodoxy Reader*, ed. John Milbank and Simon Oliver, 101–3 (New York: Routledge, 2009); Wayne Hankey, *God in Himself* (Oxford: Oxford University Press, 1987), 134 and 147; Pannenberg, *Systematic Theology*, 287–88; and Lydia Schumacher, "The Trinity and Christian Life: A Broadly Thomistic Account of Participation," *New Blackfriars* 96 (2015): 651. In a different vein, see Cyprian Vagaggini, "La hantise des *rationes necessariae* de saint Anselme dans la théologie des processions trinitaires de saint Thomas," in *Specilegium Beccense. Congrès International de ixe centenaire de l'arrivée d'Anselm au Bec* (Paris: Vrin, 1959), 103–39. If this reading of Thomas turns out to be sustainable, then God could not be perfectly one

All through his Trinitarian theology, Thomas lays out similar arguments from simplicity and consubstantiality to subsistence.[10] The principles that demand this conclusion, therefore, not only go to the foundation of his Trinitarian theology; they also come regularly to the surface. In order to go deeper into these principles, we can turn now to a text where they are elaborated with particular fullness: *SCG* IV, ch. 11.

SCG IV, CH. 11

SCG IV, ch. 11 is especially notable for our purposes. For the chapter as a whole seems to be organized around the assumption that unity and inwardness are matters of perfection, whereas distinction and outwardness are matters of imperfection.[11] Even here, however, where Thomas seems to privilege unity and interiority most, he actually makes a marriage of unity to distinction and of inwardness to outwardness. Indeed, it is here that he offers one of his strongest and most evocative suggestions that the divine Word stands somehow "outside" of His Speaker.

He begins the chapter, however, as follows: "Following a diversity of natures, one finds a diverse manner of emanation in things; and, the

---

unless He were Triune: divine distinction would ground divine unity just as much as unity grounds distinction. For more on these readings of Aquinas, see my "Perfection and the Necessity of the Trinity." For some of the very difficult questions around faith and reason that this claim raises, see my " 'The More We Wonder': Union with God, Distance from God, and the Vexing Question of 'Necessary Reasons' in Aquinas's Trinitarian Theology," *Irish Theological Quarterly* 86, no. 2 (2021): 147–63; and "The Reach of Reason and The Eyes of Faith: Pierre Rousselot and the Question of «Necessary Reasons» in Aquinas's Trinitarian Theology," *Gregorianum* 100, no. 3 (2019): 559–83. See also my "On the Open Question of «Necessary Reasons» in Aquinas's Trinitarian Theology," *Angelicum* 97, no. 2 (2020): 177–212.

10 See *ST* I q. 29, a. 4; *SCG* IV 26§7; *De Pot.*, q. 9, a. 9, and q. 10, a. 1, ad 5. For similar arguments regarding the Holy Spirit as Love, see *SCG* IV 19§7 and *Comp. Theo.* I, 48.

11 Reading this chapter simply in such terms is far from uncommon. See, for example, Susan Waldstein, "Reading Natural Hierarchy in a Trinitarian Key," *Communio: International Catholic Review* 42, no. 4 (2015): 652–92. Especially relevant is her claim that Thomas's reflections here need to be "filled out" by attention to "the personal relations between Father, Son, and Holy Spirit" that one finds in Richard of St. Victor (p. 689). The implication, then, is that these "personal relations" are not fully present in Thomas's text itself. Such a reading might appear plausible if one were to read §§1–7 in isolation. It becomes difficult to sustain, however, in light of the chapter as a whole.

higher the nature is, the more intimate to the nature is that which flows from it."[12] The higher a given nature ranks, the more interiority—and the less outwardness—is associated with it.

Thomas begins at the bottom: he begins with "inanimate bodies," in which emanation takes place "by the action of one thing upon another," and in which agent and patient are "extraneous" to each other.[13] He uses the example of "the way in which fire is generated by fire, when an extraneous body is changed by the fire and brought to the quality and species of fire." At the lowest rung of the hierarchy stands pure exteriority: two extrinsic bodies acting on each other from the outside.

Thomas turns next to plants, whose seeds emanate from within themselves. Yet these seeds end up being "entirely extrinsic" to the plant: "when the fruit is perfected, it is separated from the tree altogether."[14] Two inanimate things operate on each other from the outside; a plant bears its seed from within. Plants, then, are capable of an emanation more interior than anything found among inanimate bodies—plants are therefore more perfect than inanimate bodies. Yet plants remain near the bottom of the scale insofar as this interiority is still fairly limited.

Thomas identifies a greater interiority in the sensitive soul. A sensory emanation "may have an external beginning, but it has an internal termination."[15] That which is perceived sensibly begins outside the sense organ. Yet, through the sense organ, its image enters into the one perceiving: it "proceeds to the imagination, and, further, to the storehouse of memory." In plants, a seed emanates outward from the plant; in the senses, an image of the perceived object emanates inward into the soul. And it is because the emanation proper to the sensitive soul is more inward that the sensitive soul ranks higher than the vegetative. Again, greater interiority corresponds to greater perfection.

Thomas continues, however, that "no sensory power reflects on itself," and that the life of the senses is therefore "not an entirely perfect

---

12 *SCG* IV 11§1.
13 IV 11§2.
14 IV 11§3.
15 IV 11§4.

life, since [its] emanation is always from one thing into another."¹⁶ The senses can only be actualized by a sensible thing outside of the sense organ, and this outward orientation bars the senses from the highest perfection.

From there, Thomas moves on to intellect, which is entirely perfect—and which is entirely perfect because it can reflect on *itself*. As Thomas puts it, "The supreme and perfect grade of life is in the intellect, for the intellect reflects upon itself and the intellect can understand itself."¹⁷ Yet he continues that "even in intellectual life one finds diverse grades. For the human intellect, although it can know itself, does indeed take the first beginning of its knowledge from something outside of itself. . . . There is, therefore, a more perfect intellectual life in the angels. In them the intellect does not proceed to self-knowledge from anything exterior, but knows itself through itself."¹⁸ Human intellect is higher than the senses because it can reflect on itself. Yet human intellect remains imperfect because it begins with something outside of itself.¹⁹ Angelic intellect, in contrast, is more perfect than human intellect because it is not bound up with anything outside of itself. It is perfect because it can know itself through itself. Perfection seems to consist in self-sufficient self-directedness.

Thomas pushes further down this same path as he continues: "Nonetheless, angels' life does not reach the highest perfection. The reason is this: although the intention understood is entirely intrinsic to them, the very intention understood is not their substance, for in them understanding is not identified with existence."²⁰ The slimmest remnant of otherness—indeed, the mere intra-mental distinction between angelic word and angelic essence—is enough to disqualify angels from absolute perfection. The more perfect a given being is, the less it is necessarily involved with others; and, in the most perfect

---

16 IV 11§4.

17 IV 11§5.

18 IV 11§5.

19 For more here, see Therese Scarpelli Cory, *Aquinas on Human Self-Knowledge* (Cambridge: Cambridge University Press, 2014), 63.

20 *SCG* IV 11§5.

creatures, even a distinction within one's own immanent activity brings imperfection in its wake.

This pattern culminates in God. Thomas writes that "the ultimate perfection of life belongs to God, in Whom understanding is not other than being, as has been shown. Accordingly, the intention understood in God must be the divine essence itself."[21] Angels are less than supremely perfect because their inner words are other than their essence; God is supremely perfect because His Word is identical to His essence. In God, the last hint of distinction that had lingered in angelic self-understanding is closed down. And it is for this reason that "the ultimate perfection of life" is found in God alone.

THE GENERATION OF THE WORD

To this point, perfection seems to be entirely a matter of interiority, and any outwardness or otherness seems to be a source of imperfection.[22] Thomas, however, has yet to conclude his reflections. Indeed, he has scarcely begun them. For his aim in this chapter as a whole is to defend the "truth" of "the divine generation" from those who would "attack" it, and he only lays out this hierarchy of emanations in the first place so that they might serve as a backdrop to this larger goal.[23] With this

---

21 IV 11§5. Thomas goes on to identify "the intention understood" with "the inner word" in IV 11§6.

22 Even here, however, things may be more complicated than Thomas lets on. First, returning to inanimate bodies, Thomas teaches elsewhere that *all* causality is a matter of intimacy: in any instance of any causality—even in the example of fire heating, which Thomas invokes in 11§2—the cause is imaged by, and is interior to, its effect (see *ST* I q. 4, a. 3, and q. 8, a. 1; both texts are studded with examples drawn from inanimate things). From the other direction, angelic self-reflection cannot ultimately be self-sufficient in every sense: for angelic *existence* is not self-sufficient. As created, angels' existence depends on God. Indeed, Thomas teaches elsewhere that angelic intellects can only remain angelic if they turn towards God: a created intellect that sunk into mere self-direction would become a demonic intellect; for this last point, see my "Aquinas on the Role of Another in Perfect Self-Knowledge," *Modern Theology* 38, no. 1 (2022): 19–35. Thomas has reasons not to introduce these points in this context, and it is certainly true that even if we account for these points, his hierarchy here progresses from a greater degree of outwardness at the bottom to a greater degree of inwardness at the top. Yet we will see soon that Thomas brings about a marriage of inwardness and outwardness when he comes to the Trinity, and we can suggest now that this marriage might find certain echoes in creation.

23 *SCG* IV 10§15.

backdrop in mind, he concludes that "we are left to understand the divine generation according to an intellectual emanation."[24] Thomas's hierarchy of emanations, in other words, allows him to draw a Trinitarian conclusion: it allows him to establish that the divine generation is the "intellectual emanation" of a Word. Yet even though Thomas has reached this conclusion, he is not finished. Instead, having established *that* generation in God is a matter of intellectual emanation, he spends the rest of this chapter attempting to "manifest" *how* generation in God could be a matter of intellectual emanation.

Thomas adopts new methods as he takes on this new goal. Before this point in book IV, ch. 11, Thomas had not so much as alluded to Scripture or to the faith. Now, he conspicuously regrounds his reflections in "what the faith sets down," and he begins citing Scripture prominently—to the point that some scholars have read the passages to follow as a commentary on Scripture.[25] And once Thomas embarks on this faith-founded and Scripture-soaked "manifestation" of the Trinity, he begins to register some surprising claims. For he ultimately suggests that perfection may not be a matter of interiority instead of exteriority. Instead, perfection might make a marriage of interiority and exteriority.[26]

Thomas begins this manifestation of the Trinity where he left off: with the intellectual emanation of the divine Word. After offering a new argument for the presence of this Word,[27] he goes on to reason that

> the existence of the divine Word is identical with the existence of the divine intellect; and, consequently, it is identical with the existence of God, Who is His own intellect. The

---

[24] IV 11§8. All quotes to follow are from the same passage.

[25] Paissac writes that *SCG* IV 11§§9–13 "should be understood as a commentary on the opening verses of St. John" (*Théologie du Verbe*, 170n1). Emery agrees: this section of the *SCG* "reads like a sort of commentary on the opening verses of St. John's Gospel. . . . This is very close to being a doctrinal commentary on Scripture" (*TA*, 101). See also Cesar Izquierdo, "La teología del Verbo en la 'Summa Contra Gentiles,' " *Scripta Theologica* 14, no. 2 (1982): 555.

[26] In what follows, I will walk through almost the whole of book IV, ch. 11. I will not, however, give the final paragraph (§19). This final paragraph reinforces the conclusions I will draw here, but it is more relevant to my argument in the section "The Passages" in chapter four. I will therefore save my engagement with it for then.

[27] *SCG* IV 11§9.

> existence of God, of course, is His essence or nature, which is the same as God Himself, as was shown in Book I. The Word of God, therefore, is the divine existence and His essence, and is true God Himself.[28]

This point is already familiar to us: because of simplicity, the divine Word cannot be an accident in God. Instead, He must be "true God Himself."

Thomas takes the next step with reference to Scripture. At the end of the same paragraph, he writes, "When, therefore, it is said in John 1:1 that 'God was the Word,' this is shown: the divine Word is not merely an intention understood, as our word is, but it is also a thing existing and *subsisting* in nature. For God is a true subsistent thing, since His is substantial being in the highest degree."[29] The subsistence of the Word is suggested by Scripture. Yet Thomas does not merely posit this subsistence in a fideistic way: he does not rely on the authority of Scripture alone. Instead, he had just shown that, because of simplicity, the divine Word is the divine essence. Yet he had shown earlier in the *SCG*—and he recalls now—that the divine essence is "a true subsistent thing."[30] If, therefore, the divine Word is identical to the self-subsistent divine essence, then the Word *Himself* must be subsistent.

The next step follows from the nature of a word: "it belongs to the *ratio* of the interior word, which is the intention understood, that it proceeds from the one understanding in accord with his act of understanding.... From God, therefore, in His very act of understanding, His Word must proceed."[31] As we saw in chapter one, procession is not affixed to a word from the outside. Nor is it a marginal feature that might hold in some words but not in others. Instead, it belongs to the *ratio* of a word. The divine Word, therefore, must proceed in the divine nature.

---

28 IV 11§11.
29 IV 11§11.
30 See *SCG* I 26§12.
31 IV 11§13.

Word, Image, Son

All of our conclusions here will hinge on the subsistence of the divine Word and on His procession from His Speaker. Before coming to those conclusions, however, we can continue moving step-by-step through Thomas's argument. Thomas next digs a bit deeper into the nature of a word. First, he writes that "the word interiorly conceived is a kind of account and likeness of the thing understood."[32] A word, by definition, bears a likeness to the thing understood in it. Because, therefore, the divine Speaker understands Himself in His Word, the divine Word must be like His Speaker.[33] Thomas continues that "one thing which is like another has the *ratio* of an exemplar if it is the principle of that other thing, or it has the *ratio* of an *image* if that thing is its principle." Thomas then concludes that because the divine Word proceeds from His Speaker, and because He is like His Speaker, the divine Word must be the "image" of His Speaker.

Taking a step back, Thomas's manifestation of the Trinity had, to this point, been straightforwardly psychological. All talk has been of intellect, word, simplicity, and immanent procession. Now, however, Thomas introduces different language: that of "image." Elsewhere in his Trinitarian theology, Thomas follows Scripture and Tradition in affirming that "Word" is one name for the Son, and that "Image" is another. Thomas might seem, therefore, to be taking a step away from his psychological categories: he might seem to be shifting from the-Son-as-Word to the-Son-as-Image. In fact, however, Thomas introduces this talk of "image" by taking a step further *into* his psychological categories. After having established that a word proceeds from another, he begins this passage by writing that a word, by definition, is a "likeness of the thing understood." And he continues that, merely because of the "*ratio* of an image," to proceed as such a likeness is to be an image. Given the definitions of "word" and "image," then, the divine Word is necessarily

---

[32] IV 11§14.

[33] We will spend much of chapter five unpacking—and complicating—the claim that the divine Speaker understands Himself in His Word.

a divine Image. This talk of "image" is not an alternative to Thomas's psychological approach; it is intrinsic to his psychological approach.[34]

Thomas's next step comes from thinking more deeply into the meaning of an image. First, he clarifies that "things have images of two kinds. For there is an image which does not share the nature with that whose image it is."[35] Thomas gives two examples: a statue of a man, and an inner word that a man might have of himself. Both are images of that man, but neither is itself a man. Yet Thomas continues,

> When the image of a thing has the same nature with that whose image it is, it is like the son of a king: in him the image of his father appears and he is the same in nature as his father. Now, it was shown that the Word of God is the image of His Speaker . . . and that the Word shares the nature of His Speaker. The conclusion, therefore, is that the Word of God is not only an image, but also a Son. For so to be one's image as to be of the same nature with him *is not discovered in one who cannot be called a son*, so long as we are speaking of living things. For *that which proceeds from a living thing in the likeness of species is called a son.* Hence, we read in a Psalm (2:7): "The Lord said to Me: You are My Son."[36]

For Thomas, an image within a common living nature is, by definition, a son. Indeed, he claims that there is no such thing as a living image who shares the nature of his exemplar but "who cannot be called a son." And, because Thomas had already established that the divine Word is the Image of His Speaker, that He shares a single nature with His Speaker, and that this nature is living, the conclusion draws itself: the divine Word must be the Son of His Speaker.[37]

---

[34] Thomas reiterates these points in the *ST*: "a true image proceeds from another like to it in species" (I q. 35, a. 1), and the divine Word is therefore an Image because "it belongs to the *ratio* of a word to proceed from another in likeness of species" (a. 2).

[35] *SCG* IV 11§16.

[36] IV 11§16.

[37] For the divine nature as living, see *SCG* I, ch. 97. Returning to the larger point, Thomas makes a similar argument—from the meaning of a word and sonship to the

Thomas makes the same point even more strongly as he continues: "it belongs to the *ratio* of true generation in living things that the generated proceeds from the generator as his likeness and within the same nature. Therefore, the Word of God is truly generated by His Speaker, and His procession can be called 'generation' or 'birth.'"[38] Thomas had already established—again, because of the nature of a word and the demands of simplicity—that the divine Word proceeds from His Speaker, that He proceeds as the likeness of His Speaker, and that he shares His Speaker's nature. Here, he need only invoke "the *ratio* of true generation" in order to conclude that the divine Word's procession is therefore a "generation" or "birth." The meaning of a word, of simplicity, and of generation demand it.[39]

We saw above that Thomas did not need to take leave of his psychological categories in order to introduce talk of a divine Image. We see now that the same point holds with sonship and generation. It is not merely that the divine Word is *also* a divine Son; instead, the meaning of a word, of an image, of simplicity, and of sonship demand that the divine Word *could not be a divine Word* if He were not *therefore* a divine Son. Sonship and generation are not juxtaposed to Thomas's psychological approach. Nor are they airlifted into that approach from the outside. Still less are they in competition with that approach. Instead, they are intrinsic to, and they are required by, Thomas's psychological approach. Therefore, all of the conclusions to follow, which emerge as Thomas thinks more deeply through the logic of sonship and of generation, are themselves part of his psychological approach to the Trinity.

This point is reflected concretely in Thomas's language. For he does not abandon the language of "Word" as he introduces the language of "Son." Instead, the language of "Word" remains front and center throughout: it is because "the *Word* shares the nature of His *Speaker*"

---

conclusion that the divine Word is a generated Son—with some frequency: see *ST* I q. 29, a. 2; *Comp. Theo.* I, 38–40; *in Ioan.*, #29; and, more briefly, *De Pot.*, q. 9, a. 5.

38 *SCG* IV 11§17.

39 As Emery notes, the authenticity of *SCG* 11§17 has been questioned (see *TA* 101n94). The conclusion we have drawn from it, however, merely reinforces a point Thomas had already established in 11§16: because of the meaning of a word, of sonship, and of simplicity, the divine Word is necessarily a divine Son.

that "the *Word* of God is not only the image, but also the Son."[40] Just so, "the *Word* of God is truly generated by His *Speaker*, and His procession can be called 'generation' or 'birth.' "[41] If there is generation and birth in God, then it is the generation and birth of a Word from a Speaker. Thomas's theology remains Word-centered—and it therefore remains psychological—even as he introduces the language of "generation," "birth," and "sonship."

Conceived-in, Born-from, Present-to

Having established that the speaking of a divine Word is the generation of a divine Son, Thomas continues by reasoning that

> what is generated, so long as it remains within the generator, is said to be "conceived." But the Word is God is generated by God in such a way that He does not withdraw from God, but remains in God, as is clear from the above. Rightly, therefore, the Word of God can be called "conceived" by God. . . . But there is a difference between the conception of the Word of God and the material conception discovered by us in animals. For the offspring, so long as it is conceived and is enclosed in the womb, does not have its final perfection so as to subsist of itself in a place distinct from the one generating. . . . Now, the Word of God, Who exists in God Speaking, is perfect, subsisting in Himself and distinct from God Speaking: for one does not look for a local distinction there; instead, They are really distinguished only by a relation as was said. Therefore, in the generation of the Word of God, conception and birth are identical.[42]

As above, Thomas is thinking through the logic of birth. Yet his psychological language takes center stage throughout. He does not write that the Son of God both exists in the Father and subsists distinctly from the Father; he writes that "the *Word* of God, Who exists in God

---

40 *SCG* 11§16.

41 11§17.

42 11§18.

Speaking, is perfect, subsisting in Himself and distinct from God *Speaking*."

More importantly, Thomas here draws out new a dimension from the logic of sonship: a child is only fully perfect once it is able "to subsist of itself in a place distinct from the one generating." When a created child has been conceived, but before she is ready to be born, she remains in her mother's womb. And, because she has not yet been completely formed, she is not yet perfect. Once she is fully formed and perfect, she is born: she begins subsisting in a place distinct from her mother's womb. The divine Word, however, "is perfect": He is not still being formed.[43] And the suggestion is that, because He is perfect, He "subsist[s] in Himself and distinct from God Speaking."

In the divine generation, of course, there is no "local distinction" between Word and Speaker. They subsist distinctly, but They do not subsist in distinct places. And, because there is no local distinction, the Word can be simultaneously "enclosed in the womb" of His Speaker and born from His Speaker. Thomas presents us here with the paradox of an immanent procession, expressed now in the register of generation. Indeed, the remaining-within of the Word's conception does not merely *coincide* with the going-forth of His birth. Instead, His remaining-within *is* His going-forth: "in the generation of the Word of God, conception and birth are identical."

Thomas remains with this point as he continues:

> in corporeal things . . . the term of conception is the being of the conceived in the one conceiving, and the term of birth is the being of the one born distinct from the parent. . . . But the conception and birth of an intelligible word involves neither motion nor succession. Hence, at once it is conceived and it is; and at once it is born and it is distinct. Since one discovers this situation *in our intelligible word*, by so much the more is it proper to God's Word.[44]

---

[43] For the divine Word as already formed from eternity, see *in Ioan.*, #26.

[44] *SCG* IV 11§18.

A material offspring ceases existing "in the one conceiving" once it begins to be born, and it ceases being born once it begins to exist outside of its parent.[45] The divine Word does no such thing: all at once, He remains within His Speaker as conceived, He goes forth from His Speaker as being-born, and He exists distinctly from His Speaker as having-been-born. Yet these elements coincide not only because the divine generation is eternal and immutable; they coincide also because it is the generation *of a word*: "the conception and birth of an intelligible word involves neither motion nor succession." Even in human words, remaining-within, going-forth, and having-gone-forth all coincide. Once again, Thomas's reflection on sonship and generation is *itself* psychological: it concerns the conception, birth, and distinct existence of "God's *Word*," and Thomas illustrates this particular point with a reference to "*our* intelligible word."

As Thomas continues, he lays out the claim that will be the most important for us:

> Accordingly, after the saying of Wisdom, "Before the hills I was being-born [*parturiebar*]," to keep us from thinking that while He was being-born He did not yet exist, this is added, "While He was preparing the heavens I was present [*aderam*]" (Prov. 8:27).[46] In this way—although in the fleshly generation of animals first a thing is conceived, then it is being-born, and finally it acquires a presence [*adesse*] to the parent, in fellowship with the parent as distinct from him—we can understand that in divine generation these are all simultaneous. For the Word of God is at once conceived, being-born, and present [*adest*].[47]

This passage largely reiterates points we have already seen, though with a new wrinkle: when fleshy offspring cease being-born, they acquire a

---

45 Again, going-out and remaining-within *are* incompatible in material things: see *in Ioan.*, #2161.

46 With *parturiebar*, Thomas seems not to mean merely that the Word had *been* born, but that He was *being*-born: that He was "still" going out of the Father. For more here, see *in Heb.*, #49.

47 *SCG* IV 11§18.

"presence" to their parents. Unlike fleshy offspring, the divine Word never ceases being-born. Yet, like fleshy offspring, He is "present" to His Speaker.

Thomas, of course, introduces this "presence" as he is considering the Word under the aspect of sonship and of birth. Yet he does so as he is considering *the Word* under the aspect of sonship and of birth. Indeed, at the crucial moment, he speaks of the Word as a Word: he does not write that the Son of God is at once conceived, being-born, and present; he writes that "the *Word* of God is at once conceived, being-born, and present." Thomas casts this interpersonal presence in psychological terms, and his psychological approach includes this interpersonal presence: to proceed as a divine Word is to stand present towards one's Speaker.[48]

Thomas draws this language of "present" from Proverbs, and he does not discuss its meaning in any detail. The only direct guidance he offers here is that, when a fleshy child is present to her parent, she is "in fellowship with the parent as distinct from him." A few sentences earlier, however, we saw Thomas claim that a fleshy child only has "its final perfection" once it can "subsist of itself in a place distinct from the one generating." The language of "presence" seems to be a further elaboration of this distinct subsistence outside of the womb.

Indeed, it might seem reasonable to conclude that the language of "presence" is *merely* a way of speaking about distinct subsistence. Thomas, after all, had just reminded us that there is no "local distinction" between Word and Speaker, and subsistence may be all that remains of presence once physical space has been removed. It might seem, therefore, that all Thomas *really* means to convey by this language of "presence" is the distinct subsistence of the Word. The main burden of our last chapter, however, was that distinct subsistence itself *really* means quite a bit more than has often been acknowledged: it means

---

[48] Through much of what follows, I will continue speaking of "interpersonal" presence in God. One might object, however, that Thomas never develops the theme of the Word's personhood in *SCG* IV, ch. 11 (see Izquierdo, "*La teología de verbo*," 564). Thomas does, however, affirm repeatedly that the divine Word subsists in the divine nature—which, of course, is supremely intelligent. And, given that in the previous chapter of the *SCG*, he had defined a person as "a subsistent thing in intellectual natures" (IV 10§6), it seems plain enough that this presence of Word to Speaker is the presence of one Person to another.

that the Word does not merely remain within the Father, but instead stands somehow outside of the Father. With this language of "presence," Thomas offers one of his richest gestures towards this standing-outside. First of all, even when a child is "enclosed in the womb" or is "being-born," she is not a mere accident of the mother. Instead, she is already a distinctly subsisting substance.[49] A child does not begin subsisting *distinctly* once she is no longer conceived and no longer being-born; she begins subsisting *outside* of the mother. The language of *adest*, then, does not go beyond *concipitur* and *parturitur* insofar as it adds distinct subsistence. It goes beyond other language insofar as it adds the stable standing-in-oneself of a child who has already been born, who now exists outside of her parents, and who can encounter her parents face-to-face. And, in using this language, Thomas therefore draws out a dimension of the Word's subsistence that might otherwise have escaped our notice. The divine Word, of course, is present to His Speaker without any "local distinction" or physical space between them. Yet the nature of this presence is most aptly captured by the image of a fleshy offspring's standing on her own ground and on her own feet, of her standing outside of her parents, and of her meeting her parents face-to-face.[50]

We saw in chapter one that a word not only remains within its speaker. Instead, all words go forth from their speakers, and their going-forth is just as basic as their remaining-within. We saw in chapter two

---

[49] Thomas teaches that, so far as human beings go, our rational soul is self-subsistent, and it is created while we are still in the womb (see *ST* I q. 75, a. 2, and q. 118, a. 2). Thomas suggests something similar with nonrational animals, whose souls are not self-subsistent, but who, in the womb, are already themselves subsistent composites of body and soul: see *SCG* II 89§2. Children in the womb may not be able to exist independently of their mother, but they are not therefore non-subsistent. Indeed, within his Trinitarian theology, Thomas suggests that all sons everywhere—and not merely those who have been born—subsist distinctly from their parents (see *ST* I q. 33, a. 2, ad 3).

[50] It is in this passage that we find the richest opening in Thomas to an eternal "face-to-face encounter" between the divine Persons. Indeed, the language of *adest* might also draw out a further dimension, which further reinforces the radical "between" of the divine Persons: it might suggest that the Word, in going forth from His Speaker, also "turns back" towards His Speaker. Durand, with reference to this passage, speaks of the Son's "manifest, personal presence" to the Father, and he sees in the language of *adest* a suggestion of the Son's "'returning' to the Father" ("The Theology of God the Father," in *The Oxford Handbook of Trinitarian Theology*, 376).

that the divine Word goes beyond this paradox: because He proceeds as subsistent, He must, all at once, remain within the Father, go forth from the Father, and stand somehow "outside" of the Father. Yet we also saw that while Thomas's rendering of subsistence seems to demand this conclusion, he never draws it explicitly. We see now that when Thomas is reflecting on the birth of the divine Word, he uses the language of "presence" to describe the relationship of Word to Speaker. The Word in no way ceases to remain within His Speaker, He in no way ceases to go forth from His Speaker, and His relationship to His Speaker is removed from any "local distinction." Yet He still stands somehow present to His Speaker.[51]

In claiming as much, Thomas offers one of his most evocative suggestions that the Word in some way meets His Speaker from the "outside." For if the Word were merely within His Speaker, and even if He were merely *going* forth from His Speaker, then He might be conceived within His Speaker, and He might be being-born from His Speaker. Yet it is difficult to see how He could be meaningfully said to be present towards His Speaker. Insofar as this "presence" refers to a distinct moment in the birth of a child, and insofar as this moment adds something that is not already accounted for either in the conception or in the being-born of the child, it seems that the language of *adest* can only be used properly of God—and not equivocally—if the Word somehow placelessly meets His Speaker from something like an "outside." If "presence" were to be removed from anything at all like a face-to-face encounter, then it is difficult to see how it could

---

[51] As we will see in chapter seven, Thomas is willing to speak elsewhere of God as "infinitely distant" from the blessed angels (see *ST* I q. 56, a. 3, ad 2, and II-II q. 19, a. 11, ad 3). There is no physical space between God and the angels (or, as Thomas puts it in our current passage, "one does not look for a local distinction there"). Yet there *is* what we might call an "ontological space"—and even an *infinite* ontological space—between them. Again, they are "infinitely distant." The relationship between God and the angels is, of course, radically different from the relationship between the Father and His Word. Yet the language Thomas uses for the angels at least suggests that he is comfortable speaking of a sort of "distance" where there is no physical space. In our passage, his language of "presence" might suggest a similar—though very different—sort of "ontological space" between the Father and His Word (it might also therefore open up a point of contact between Thomas and Barth or Balthasar, both of whom find a sort of ground for physical space in the Trinity: see Balthasar, *Theo-Drama II*, 257; and Barth, *Church Dogmatics* II/1, 475–76.).

remain presence: it is difficult to see how it could avoid melting back into conception or being-born.

Perfect Unity, Radical Distinction

Be that as it may, the most important point is that this passage speaks directly to our larger burden in part one. For, in this language of *adest*, Thomas offers one of his richest suggestions that even though God is removed from all "local distinction," there is still somehow room in God for the sort of "between" required by the *inter*personal. Yet this passage also speaks to the specific burden of this chapter. As we saw above, Thomas seems to open—and to organize—*SCG* IV, ch. 11 around a priority of unity and inwardness over distinction and outwardness. Throughout §§1–7, he seems to associate unity and interiority with perfection, and he seems to associate distinction and outwardness with imperfection. Yet we also saw that, once he reaches the apex of perfection and of unity in the divine nature in §8, both the tenor and the goal of his reflections shift: he grounds his conclusions conspicuously in Scripture and in the faith, and he sets about making manifest the Trinity and the divine generation. And we saw that, once his reflections shift in §§9–18, everything changes—even as everything remains the same. For, just before the shift, Thomas had shown that there is no room for any distinction between the divine Word and the divine essence. After the shift, he upholds this identity of Word and essence. Indeed, he emphatically reaffirms it.[52] Yet *within* this identity, he finds an explosion of outwardness—an explosion that both confirms and overturns the association of perfection and unity that had governed things to this point.

Specifically, Thomas argues that because the Word proceeds from His Speaker, because He is like His Speaker, and because He shares the nature of His Speaker, He must be the Son of His Speaker and His procession must be a birth; and he continues that because to be fully born is to attain a presence to one's parents, this Word is eternally present to His Speaker. Yet this conclusion only follows because *the*

---

[52] Recall IV 11§§11–12.

Word shares the nature of His Speaker. When I know myself, my human words proceed from me and they are like me; but they are not identical to my human essence, and they therefore do not share that essence—and they therefore are not my sons. And, because they are not my sons, they are not present to me. It is only because the divine Word is identical to His Speaker's nature, and because He therefore shares that nature, that He is a divine Son—and it is only because He is a divine Son that He stands present to the Father. It is *because* there is no space in God for the intrapersonal distinction of an essence and its non-subsistent word that there *is* space in God for the interpersonal distinction of a Speaker and His subsistent Word; it is *because* the distinction between Word and essence is only rational that the distinction between Word and Speaker is not only real, but interpersonal; it is *because* the unity of Word and essence goes all the way to identity that the distinction of Word and Speaker goes all the way to interpersonal presence.

Perhaps surprisingly, then, it is not that my human words are impersonal and non-subsistent because they are somehow too closely identified with me, or because they are not adequately distinct from my own inmost interiority. Instead, they are not subsistent because there is *too much* distinction between their being and mine; they are impersonal because they are not adequately *identified* with my essence. If one allows for the slimmest of distinctions within a single person—the distinction of angelic word from angelic intellect—then one is left with but a single person. It is only by pushing beyond any such distinction, and by pressing into an identity of Word and essence, that one finds a Word Who is personally present to His Speaker.

Thus, it might seem as though, in the first half of this chapter, Thomas moves away from distinction and outwardness and moves towards unity and interiority; and it might seem that, in the second half, he abandons this path and takes a different path back down to distinction. In fact, however, he never strays from the path inward. Instead, he faithfully follows it all the way through—and, in following it all the way through, he shows that *this path itself* doubles back on itself. Once the path inward leads all the way inward, this path itself leads outward; yet it only becomes a path outward once it has led all the way in.[53]

We saw in our introduction that, according to many social Trinitarians, there cannot be a truly interpersonal distinction in God if the divine Persons are all identical to a single essence. We see now that, for Thomas, there *cannot but* be a truly interpersonal distinction in God—and there even cannot but be interpersonal presence in God—*because* the divine Speaker and the divine Word are identical to a single essence. In Thomas's psychological analogy, consubstantiality is not an obstacle to interpersonal distinction. It is the guarantor of interpersonal distinction. It is even the guarantor of an interpersonal distinction that opens up to interpersonal presence.

---

53 This return outward also casts a new light over Thomas's hierarchy of creatures. In §§2–7, Thomas had moved up from inanimate things to plants, then to the senses, and then to intellect; in §§9–18, he goes *back down* the scale of emanations. He begins with the intellectual emanation of a word (§9), and he ends with an image culled from "the fleshy generation of animals" (§18)—a generation he had earlier linked to the emanation of seeds and fruit from plants (see 11§8). Revelation, then, sends Thomas back down the mountain. And it opens up a dimension of the divine life that is not captured by the procession of an angelic word, but that *is* captured by the generation of fleshy offspring: distinct subsistence and personal presence.

Thomas, then, certainly presents us with a hierarchy here. Yet, in this hierarchy, the lower and less perfect member can make a crucial contribution, which the higher member—without ceasing to be higher—cannot provide. The lower member enjoys a unique dignity, and Thomas summons up the whole of living creation, from its highest instance to one of its most humble, in order to "manifest" something of the generation of the divine Word (we may see something similar in Thomas's claim that, absolutely speaking, angels image God more fully than humans do, but that human beings still image something of God that angels cannot: the generation of one subsistent person from another. See *ST* I q. 93, a. 3; and I *Sent.* d. 3, q. 3, a. 1, ad 4).

Even more, Thomas might reread animal generation when he reaches back down to it. Just before beginning his direct reflection on the Trinity, Thomas had written that in animal generation, "something which was in . . . the animal is *separated* from it," such that the offspring, "at the term of generation, is *entirely outside* the generator" (11§8). At the end of this reflection, however, he writes that at the term of generation, the animal offspring is "in fellowship with the parent as distinct from him." The Son is not separated from the Father, and He is certainly not "*entirely* outside" the Father; and so animal generation, as Thomas defines it before turning to the Trinity, has little to do with the divine generation. Yet the Son *is* "in fellowship with the [the Father] as distinct from Him." Animal generation, as Thomas defines it near the conclusion of his reflections on the Trinity, has been made apt to capture something of the divine generation. Thus, as we saw in chapter one, in this chapter of the *SCG*, Thomas allows the light of the Trinity to prompt him into a new understanding of the inner word. We see now that this same reflection on the Trinity may prompt him towards insights into further basic categories.

"HE WAS IN THE BEGINNING WITH GOD"

"In" and "With"

We can end this chapter with the passage of Scripture that stands most directly behind Thomas's psychological analogy: John 1:1. We can begin with Thomas's commentary on the opening words, "In the beginning was the Word." After reflecting at length on the meaning of "Word," Thomas begins probing the meaning of "beginning." For Thomas, this *principium* can refer to, among other things, the Father. On such a reading, the opening clause means that

> "The Son was in the Father." This is Augustine's understanding of it, as well as Origen's. The Son, however, is said to be in the Father because both have the same essence. Since the Son is his own essence, the Son is in Whomsoever the Son's essence is in. Since, therefore, the essence of the Son is in the Father by consubstantiality, it is fitting that the Son be in the Father.[54]

The Word is identical to the essence of the Father, and the preposition "in" secures this consubstantial unity.

The Gospel's second clause, "and the Word was with God," points in what might seem to be the opposite direction. First,

> the preposition "with" [*apud*] signifies the *subsistence* of its antecedent, because things that do not subsist of themselves are not properly said to be "with" another. Thus we do not say that a color is with a body, and the same applies to other things that do not subsist of themselves. But things that do subsist of themselves are properly said to be "with" another. Thus we say that a man is with a man, and a stone with a stone.[55]

---

[54] *In Ioan.*, #36.

[55] *In Ioan.*, #46.

"With," first of all, signifies subsistence. Two sentences later, Thomas adds that "with" also "asserts a distinction. For it is not proper to say that a person is with himself, but rather that one man is with another." The term "with" in John 1:1, therefore, not only signifies the subsistence of the Word; it also "signifies the distinction of the Word, which is said to be 'with God.' "[56]

So far, things seem straightforward. The language of "in" secures the consubstantial unity of the Persons, and the language of "with" secures Their subsistent distinction. Because, therefore, the Evangelist writes both that the Word was "*in* the beginning," and that the Word was "*with* God," Scripture vouchsafes both sides of the Trinitarian mystery in a single verse.

In the midst of making these points, however, Thomas had also complicated them:

> Here we should note that the preposition "with" signifies *a certain union* [*conjunctionem*] of the thing signified by its grammatical antecedent to the thing signified by its grammatical object, *just as the preposition "in" does*.[57] However, there is a difference, because the preposition "in" signifies a certain intrinsic union, whereas the preposition "with" implies in a certain way an extrinsic union. And we state both in divine matters, namely, that the Son is "in" the Father and "with" the Father.[58]

We studied this text in chapter two, where we saw that Thomas raises concerns over, yet still uses, the language of "extrinsic" for the relation between the Persons. We can emphasize now that the language of "with" points not to any bare exteriority, but to an extrinsic *union*. If I am so separated from someone else that I am no longer in her presence, then I may be distinct from her, but I am no longer *with* her. Thomas develops this point as he continues: "with . . . signifies a certain union

---

56 *In Ioan.*, #44.

57 Depending on the context, *conjunctio*, can mean "union," "friendship," or "intimacy." It can also, in contexts other than the one we have here, mean "wedlock" (see DeFerrari, *Dictionary*, 205).

58 *In Ioan.*, #45.

and fellowship [*coniunctionem et societatem*]. For when some person is said to be 'with' another, it suggests to us that there is some social union between them."[59] It is not merely that "with" secures the distinction of the Persons and "in" Their union. Instead, "with" *itself*, on its own terms, secures a sort of union between the Persons.[60]

Indeed, "with" even secures the consubstantial unity of the divine Persons: "The proposition 'with' principally signifies a personal distinction; but it also signifies *consubstantiality* insofar as it signifies a certain quasi-extrinsic union."[61] We saw in chapter two that this language of *quasi extrinsecam*, along with his language of *adest* in *SCG* IV, ch. 11, could be Thomas's most suggestive nod towards something like an interpersonal standing-outside in God. Yet we see now that "with" does not signify "a quasi-extrinsic union" in God insofar as it points towards the distinction of the divine Persons. Instead, it "signifies a quasi-extrinsic union" insofar as it points to Their consubstantial unity. They are not quasi-extrinsic despite Their unity. Instead, the sort of unity They enjoy—consubstantial unity—is *itself* a "quasi-extrinsic union." And "with," by its own logic, is apt to signify this consubstantial unity.

The more basic point, however, is that "with" had first of all been used to signify the distinct subsistence of the Son and the Father. Yet now this same word is seen to signify Their consubstantial unity. Just before the passages we just quoted, Thomas had made a similar point from the opposite direction with "in": "The preposition 'in,' as was said, principally signifies consubstantiality, as implying an intrinsic union. And, *as a consequence*, it signifies a distinction of persons, inasmuch as every preposition is transitive."[62] As a preposition, "in" is transitive: by its own inherent meaning, it points to distinction. If I am "in" another, I must be distinct from that other. If this distinction were to dissolve—if intimacy were to collapse into identity—then any being-in

---

59 *In Ioan.*, #46.

60 In *SCG* IV 5§9, Thomas writes (again with reference to John 1:1) that "with" designates not only distinction, but "association and some distinction."

61 *In Ioan.*, #45.

62 *In Ioan.*, #45.

would evaporate.[63] Indeed, "in" does not secure personal distinction despite securing consubstantiality. Instead, it signifies consubstantiality, and "*as a consequence*" it signifies a "distinction of Persons." It secures consubstantiality and it *therefore* secures personal distinction. The particular sort of unity it secures—the being-in of consubstantial unity—already *itself* includes a distinction of Persons.

"In" and "with," then, are not simply synonymous: Thomas writes that "'in' . . . principally signifies consubstantiality," whereas "'with' principally signifies a personal distinction."[64] Each term has its own principal meaning. The point is simply that the principal meaning of each is included in the meaning of the other. "In" does not secure just any sort of unity; it secures a unity in which distinction is already ingredient. Just so, "with" does not secure just any distinction; it secures a distinction in which unity is already ingredient. Thomas sums things up: "*both* of these terms designate *both* a consubstantiality in nature *and* a distinction in person."[65] In speaking the unity of the divine Persons, we cannot but speak Their distinction; in speaking Their distinction, we cannot but speak Their unity. We cannot speak either without speaking both, by virtue of the meaning of the most basic terms by which we speak either.

"HE IS WITH GOD, THAT IS, IN THE SAME NATURE"

Thomas goes deeper when he writes that the clause "and the Word was God" could be misunderstood by

> the pagans, who acknowledge many and different gods, and say that their wills are in opposition. For example, those who put out the fable of Jupiter fighting with Saturn. . . . And so to exclude this the Evangelist says, "He was in the

---

63 Again, Thomas makes the same point in the *SCG*: "if there were one person of the Father and the Son, one could not say suitably that the Father is in the Son and the Son in the Father, since the same suppositum is not properly said to be in its very self" (*SCG* IV 9§7).

64 *In Ioan.*, #45.

65 *In Ioan.*, #45.

> beginning *with* God," as if to say, according to Hilary: I say that the Word is God, not as if he has a distinct divinity, but He is *with* God, that is, *in the same nature* in which He is.[66]

In response to the charge that the Word and God are two different gods, Thomas does not remind us that the Word is *in* God. Instead, he reminds us that the Word is *with* God. "With" still principally signifies the distinction of the divine Persons. Yet the term that best expresses this distinction also demands that those Persons be "in the same nature."

This same dynamic reemerges shortly thereafter, as Thomas moves onto the phrase "through Him all things were made":

> Plato thought that the ideas of all the things that were made were subsistent, separated in their proper natures. . . . For example, he thought men existed through the separated idea of man, which he called Man in itself. So lest you suppose, as did Plato, that this idea [i.e., the Word] through which all things were made was *separated* from God, the Evangelist adds, "and the Word was *with* God."[67]

Again, the language of "with" principally secures the distinct subsistence of the Son. Yet it not only rules out a non-subsistent word; it also rules out a separately subsistent word. And it therefore secures the truth that is principally secured by "in."

The meanings of "with" and "in," then, imply and include each other so profoundly that each would lose its own meaning if the principle meaning of the other were lost. If essential unity were to splinter into separate natures, then the two supposits who remained would not only cease to be in each other; they would also cease to be *with* each other in the strictest sense. Just so, if personal distinction were to collapse into an identity of supposit, then this lone supposit would not only cease to be with anything; it would also cease to be *in* anything.

Thomas, it is true, makes most of these points without explicit reference to the Son's status as Word. Yet he makes them while commenting directly on the main Scriptural source for his psychological

---

66 *In Ioan.*, #60.

67 *In Ioan.*, #65.

analogy, and he makes them shortly after one of his most sustained treatments of the divine Word.[68] It is also true that the conclusions we can draw from these passages in his John commentary are a bit more modest and limited than those we drew from *SCG* IV, ch. 11. Yet our aim in turning to these passages has been to reinforce a fairly basic point: in Thomas's Trinity, there is no opposition between consubstantial unity and interpersonal distinction, between an "intrinsic union" and a "quasi-extrinsic union," or between perfect reciprocal interiority and subsistent interpersonal presence. Nor do these pairs run on parallel tracks. Instead, they imply and include each other, and this interpenetration is written into the most basic terms we have to speak of them.

CONCLUSION

Here at the close of part one, I hope to have established that the distinction between the Father, His Word, and Their Love is a radical one. I also hope to have established that this radical distinction is not in tension with Thomas's psychological analogy for the Trinity. I hope to have shown, that is, that Thomas's psychological analogy does not secure essential unity instead of securing the "presence" of distinct Persons Who are "quasi-extrinsic" to each other. Nor does this analogy manage to eke out some semblance of interpersonal presence despite his heavy emphasis on unity and interiority. Nor, finally, is the radical distinction of the divine Persons either juxtaposed to that psychological analogy or parachuted into it from the outside. Instead, this distinction is required by Thomas's psychological analogy; it is intrinsic to his psychological analogy; it is even demanded by the essential unity which is more obviously safeguarded by that psychological analogy.

Yet to say that distinction in God is radical is not yet to say that it is interpersonal. A chair, for example, subsists distinctly from me and exists outside of me. The distinction between the chair and me, therefore, is "radical" in the sense in which we have used the term: both the chair and I stand on our own distinct ontological "foundation."[69] Yet

---

68 See *in Ioan.*, ##25–29.
69 For this language of "foundation," recall *De Pot.*, q. 9, a. 1.

this distinction is not interpersonal. For the chair is not a person, and our relationship is not marked by any of the notes we might associate with the "interpersonal": there is no reciprocal knowledge or love, no sharing of selves, no freely offered intimacy or communion. We have seen, then, that the divine Word is present towards His Speaker; we have seen that He is "quasi-extrinsic" to His Speaker; and we have argued that there is therefore enough of a "between" in God to sustain *inter*personal relationships. Yet we still have a long way to go in order to show that these relationships are inter*personal*.

We will spend the rest of our time doing just that.

PART II

4

IMMANENT PROCESSION AS TOTAL SELF-GIVING

With all of our conclusions from part one in the background, we will now enter into the real meat of this book: we will begin to see that Thomas's psychological approach to the Trinity is a matter of total interpersonal self-giving, of reciprocal interpersonal knowledge, and of reciprocal interpersonal love. In this chapter, we will focus on self-giving. We will work through knowledge and love in the next two chapters.

We can start with an obvious point: when I conceive an inner word, I need not permanently give the whole of myself to it. Instead, I might conceive a given word for a given time, but I might then cease conceiving that particular word: I might begin understanding new things and conceiving new words. Even more, during the potentially brief span of a given word's existence, there is no obvious way in which I give everything I have to that word. The conception of human words, then, is a matter of something less than total and irrevocable interpersonal self-giving.[1]

---

[1] That said, things might be deeper than they initially appear. For a reflection on human psychological acts in terms of interpersonal communion and love, see Stephan Oster, "Becoming a Person and the Trinity," in *Rethinking Trinitarian Theology*, 346–67. Indeed, D. C. Schindler argues that, for Thomas, all human action (including the conception of words) is a preparation for interpersonal self-giving: see "The Crisis of Marriage as a Crisis

It is tempting to project this same pattern into the conception of the divine Word. Indeed, no shortage of Thomas's readers assume that because I do not give the whole of myself to my words, the Father does not give the whole of Himself to His Word. First of all, many thinkers assume that Thomas's psychological Trinity is a monopersonal Trinity, and they therefore assume that there is no room for interpersonal self-giving between Thomas's solitary God and His less-than-personal Word.[2] Others are more subtle. Balthasar, for example, writes that, for Thomas, "the eternal Father gives over his entire nature to the Son. *But because God's being is entirely intellectual, this generative giving over can take the form only of the 'verbum mentis.'*"[3] Unlike Thomas's less nuanced critics, Balthasar acknowledges that Thomas's Father gives all He has to the Son. Yet he suggests that this giving is somehow cramped by the Son's proceeding intellectually as a Word. Subtler still is Anthony Kelly. As he is focusing directly on Thomas, Kelly writes, "one of the benefits of the psychological analogy is that it leads to a beautiful understanding of the reality of the Trinity as communion, in the strongest sense of the word."[4] Yet, when Kelly proposes that we think of God "not only as communion, but as communion in self-giving," he does so "*in contrast* to the Thomistic exposition of the psychological analogy": for Kelly, Thomas's psychological analogy must be "deliberately transpos[ed]" if we are to account for self-giving.[5] Kelly, then, goes a good deal further than most: he recognizes that Thomas's psychological analogy is a matter of communion, and even

---

of Meaning: On the Sterility of the Modern Will," *Communio: International Catholic Review* 41, no. 2 (2014): 354 and 358. Schindler also meditates deeply on human words in "The Word as the Center of Man's Onto-Dramatic Task." That said, these authors would certainly agree that no matter how rich the conception of human words might be, I do not give myself to my words as straightforwardly as I give myself to, say, my wife.

2 Gunton, Moltmann, and Pannenberg, whom we discussed in the introduction, fall into this category.

3 *Theo-logic II*, 167; emphasis added.

4 *The Trinity of Love* (Wilmington, DE: Michael Glazier, 1989), 132.

5 *Trinity*, 147–48; emphasis added.

of communion "in the strongest sense." Yet even Kelly judges that there is no room for self-giving within Thomas's psychological analogy.[6]

In this chapter, I hope to show that, in fact, Thomas's psychological analogy does not rule out total interpersonal self-giving. Nor does it tamp down interpersonal self-giving. Nor, finally, does it merely leave space for interpersonal self-giving indifferently open, inviting other complementary Trinitarian frameworks to fill it in.[7] Instead, Thomas's psychological analogy is itself a matter of total interpersonal self-giving. In Thomas's Trinitarian theology, immanent procession *is* interpersonal self-giving.[8]

To see as much, I will begin by briefly running through passages where Thomas makes clear that, in a simple nature, to speak a Word or to breathe Love is to communicate the whole of one's nature to that Word or Love. Also in this opening section, I will draw out the principles that undergird these passages, and which demand that this communication of nature be a giving of self.[9] From there, I will walk

---

[6] This pattern holds not only for critics of the psychological analogy, but for its partisans as well. Jeremy Daniel Wilkins and Paul Vanier, for example, argue that Thomas's psychological approach amounts to his banishing the self-communication of goodness from the Trinity: see Wilkins, "Emanatio Intellibilis in Deo: A Study of the Horizon and Development of Thomas Aquinas's Trinitarian Theology" (PhD diss., Boston College, 2004), 187–208; and Vanier, *Théologie Trinitaire chez Saint Thomas d'Aquin. Evolution du Concept d'Action Notionelle* (Montreal: Institut d'Etudes Medievales, 1953). We will return to Wilkins and Vanier in the final section of this chapter. In a more polemical mode, George Blair argues that because Thomas's Trinity is psychological, it has no room for interpersonal giving and receiving: see "On *Esse* and Relation," *Communio: International Catholic Review* 21, no. 1 (1994): 162.

[7] We saw Levering and Waldstein take up this last position the section "Social or Psychological?" of our introduction.

[8] Though he does not draw all of the same conclusions we will draw here, White at least helps prepare the way for them when he writes of "the total self-communication of the divine essence, a communication that results from intellectual procession and production in God" (*The Trinity*, 475. See also 416 and 422n21).

[9] In some of the texts we will study, Thomas speaks of the Father as "communicating" His nature to the Son; in others, he speaks of the Father as "giving." For my part, I will generally speak of giving. There are certainly subtle—and perhaps important—differences between communicating (*communicare*) and giving (*dare*). Tracing out the differences between these terms, however, would take us somewhat afield from our main task. For our current purposes, we can stress that Thomas speaks of the divine generation both as a giving and as a communicating, and that he is willing (at least in certain contexts) to use these terms interchangcably (see *in Ioan.*, ##2114–2115). Indeed, Andrea De Maio

more slowly through a number of passages where this dynamic is developed with particular depth. Finally, I will end by taking a step back and putting what we have seen thus far into dialogue with two Trinitarian frameworks to which Thomas's psychological approach is often contrasted: first, an approach centered on the family; second, an approach centered on goodness as self-communicative.[10]

Before beginning, we should admit that Thomas never explicitly affirms that one divine Person gives Himself to another. He discusses self-giving among creatures,[11] he teaches that the divine Persons give Themselves to us,[12] he holds that the Father gives everything He has to the Son,[13] and he suggests very strongly that the Father eternally gives Himself to the Son and to the Holy Spirit.[14] Yet he never explicitly affirms this last point. That said, we will see that when Thomas gestures in this direction, he is giving expression to principles that run deep in his Trinitarian theology: for we will see that, in light of these principles, immanent procession in God *must* be a matter of total self-giving. We

---

has shown that Thomas often uses *communicare* as a synonym for both *dare* and *donare*: see *Il concetto de communicazione: Saggio de lessicografia filosofica e teologica sul tema di "communicare" in Thommaso d'Aquino* (Rome: Pontificia Università Gregoriana, 1998), 146. Again, there would be much to say here. But these points are hopefully enough to justify our using these terms interchangeably—and especially our speaking of "giving" when Thomas uses language of "communicating"—in what follows.

10 As in our last chapter, many of the passages we will study here speak of the Father and His Word; they leave the Holy Spirit as Love unmentioned. That said, some of the passages we will explore in the first and final sections of this chapter speak to the Holy Spirit, and we will have a chance to address His procession as Love when, towards the end of the first section, we run through the principles at play in this area of Thomas's thought.

11 See I *Sent.*, d. 5, q. 3, a. 1, ad 3, and d. 15, q. 1, a. 1, and d. 15, q, 3, a. 1, and d. 18, a. 1, a. 1.

12 See *SCG* IV 23§11; and *in Ioan.*, #480.

13 See *SCG* IV 5§9; and *in Ioan.*, #977. This point also comes out in the texts we will study in the second section of this chapter.

14 In *ST* I q. 38, a. 1, ad 1, Thomas argues that one can give only what one possesses. He continues that, because one possesses oneself, one can give oneself. He then specifies that, in such a case, "the gift is the same as the giver." With these points in the background, he goes on to say that the Father gives the divine essence to the Son insofar as this essence is "the Father's by way of identity": that is, the Father gives the divine essence insofar as the Father *is* the essence that He gives—which suggests that the Father gives *Himself* in giving this essence. See also *ST* I q. 42, a. 5, and q. 30, a. 2, arg. 4 and ad 4, both of which we will give in this chapter.

will have to develop Thomas a bit to see as much, but this development will be fairly straightforward.

We will, however, touch on a difficult question in pursuing this point. For to speak of "self"-giving in God might seem to imply that each divine Person is a distinct "self." Some have argued that Thomas has room for three divine selves.[15] Others disagree.[16] We cannot enter into this question. Instead, when I say that the Father eternally "gives Himself" to the Son and to the Holy Spirit, I mean that He not only gives Them all that He has; He gives all that He *is*.[17] Insofar as one's "self" is that which one is, I hope that my talk of "self"-giving will therefore be justified, even if it raises certain questions that we will have to keep open.

A second point is a bit more straightforward. There can be no giving without receiving, and so to affirm that there is self-giving in God is to affirm that there is receiving in God. Accordingly, we will see Thomas claim that the Son and the Holy Spirit receive from the Father, and we will linger a bit with the character of this receiving towards the end of this chapter's first section. In exploring this point, we will pick up on a number of socially-inclined thinkers—some of them Thomists—who argue that interpersonal intimacy and love do not only require that a lover give the whole of himself to his beloved. They argue that it requires just as much that he welcome—or receive—the whole of his beloved into his heart. Indeed, these thinkers hold that receiving is ultimately just as active and as generous—and just as richly interpersonal—as giving is, and they often develop their arguments with heavy reference to the Trinity.[18] In response to this line of reflection, however, other

---

[15] See Lonergan, *The Triune God*, 389–91; Gomes, "La Réciprocité psychologique"; and Bourassa, "Personne et conscience." These authors speak more of three divine "centers of consciousness and freedom," than of three divine "selves"—though such a "center" seems a fair summary of what most of us mean by a distinct "self."

[16] See McCabe, "Aquinas on the Trinity," 292; Te Velde, "The Divine Person(s)," 360; and Levering, *Scripture and Metaphysics*, 232n108 and *Engaging the Doctrine of the Holy Spirit*, 34.

[17] Levering defines "self-gift" in such terms in *Scripture and Metaphysics*, 137n122.

[18] See Clarke, *Person and Being*, 20–22, 82–93; "Person, Being, and St. Thomas," 611–14; Kenneth L. Schmitz, "Created Receptivity and the Philosophy of the Concrete," *The Thomist* 61, no. 3 (1997): 339–76; David L. Schindler, "Norris Clarke on Person, Being,

Thomists have argued that receiving is bound up with potency, and that Thomas can therefore speak only equivocally of "receiving" in God.[19] Without entering into this question, we can at least note that Thomas is explicit on one point: "receiving from the Father is common to the Son and to all creatures by a *community of analogy*."[20] Much more would need to be said here. Yet this passage is already enough to suggest that when Thomas speaks of receiving in the Trinity, he is not speaking equivocally; he is speaking analogously. We ought to bear this point in mind when we encounter talk of receiving in this chapter.

A final word before we begin. As we saw in part one, almost all of Thomas's readers recognize that his psychological analogy can secure the unity of the divine Persons. My claim in part one, however, was not that Thomas's psychological analogy actually privileges distinction over unity; it was that the two are equally foundational. Similarly, almost everyone recognizes that if there is giving in Thomas's Trinity, then it can only be the giving of a Speaker to His Word and of both to Their inner Love-impression. It has been recognized, in other words, that interpersonal giving in God must take the form of immanent procession. Yet, as in part one, my aim here is not to argue that interpersonal self-giving does not take the form of immanent procession but that immanent procession instead takes the form of interpersonal self-giving. Far from it: I hope to show *both* that immanent procession necessarily takes the form of interpersonal self-giving *and* that interpersonal self-giving necessarily takes the form of immanent procession. Again, my interest in Thomas's psychological analogy

---

and St. Thomas," *Communio: International Catholic Review* 20, no. 3 (1993): 580–92; "The Person: Philosophy, Theology, and Receptivity," *Communio: International Catholic Review* 21, no. 1 (1994): 172–90; and, more recently, "Being, Gift, Self-Gift (Part Two)," *Communio: International Catholic Review* 43, no. 3 (2016): 419–27. In a different vein, see John Paul II, *Man and Woman He Created Them*, 195–97.

[19] See Long, "Personal Receptivity and Pure Act: A Thomistic Critique," *The Thomist* 61, no. 1 (1997): 1–31; and "Divine and Creaturely 'Receptivity.' "

[20] I *Sent.*, d. 44, q. 1, a. 1, ad 2. Thomas again uses the language of "analogy" in *De Pot.*, q. 2, a. 5, ad 6. See also III *Sent.*, d. 4, q. 1, a. 2, qc. 2, ad 2; *in Boeth. de Trin.* q. 3, a. 4, ad 8; *SCG* IV 8§17; *de 108 art.*, q. 45; *ST* I q. 33, a. 3, ad 2 (which is especially striking in light of *ST* I q. 4, a. 3); and *in Ioan.*, #977. For more on this point, see my " 'A Mark of Perfection:' Receiving and Perfection in Aquinas's Trinitarian Theology," *The International Journal of Systematic Theology* 25, no. 3 (2023): 435–55.

does not lie in its ability to secure an interpersonal Trinity. It lies in its ability to integrate the interpersonal and the intrapersonal. In this case, my interest lies in its ability to integrate intra-mental procession and interpersonal self-giving. As in part one, I will emphasize only half of this synthesis: I will focus on the claim that immanent procession is interpersonal self-giving. Yet, again as in part one, I will do so only because this half of Thomas's synthesis has received less attention. I will also recall throughout that interpersonal self-giving is immanent procession, and my aim at every turn will be to highlight the marriage Thomas makes of these two claims.

THE PRINCIPLES
"THE DIVINE NATURE IS COMMUNICATED BY EVERY PROCESSION WHICH IS NOT OUTWARD"

We saw in chapter two that Thomas acknowledges the obvious: my human words and love-impressions do not subsist as persons alongside me. Yet we also saw that part of what makes Thomas's psychological analogy for the Trinity an *analogy*—and part of what distances it from any psychological univocity—is the fact that the divine Word and Love, unlike any created words or loves, subsist as distinct Persons. Finally, we saw that if we were to get caught up in the non-subsistence of our non-personal words and loves, or if we were to miss or to minimize Thomas's frequent affirmations that God's Word and Love *do* subsist distinctly from the Father, then we would misunderstand Thomas's psychological approach. We will see something similar now. For Thomas is alive to the fact that I do not give everything I have to my words or to my love-impressions. As he puts it, "in the conception of the [human word,] the human nature is not communicated."[21] When I conceive a word, I do not share my own human nature with that word. Instead, I give it its own nature—the nature of a word—and I keep my nature for myself. We have here, however, another infinite difference separating the divine Word and Love from human words and loves. As Thomas puts it, "All that exists in God is God, whereas the same

---

21 *De Pot.*, q. 2, a. 1.

does not belong to others. Therefore *the divine nature is communicated by every procession which is not outward, and this does not apply to other natures.*"[22] In created natures, one can speak an inner word and breathe forth a love-impression without giving one's own nature. In the divine nature, one cannot. Because of divine simplicity, immanent divine procession entails the communication of the divine nature.

Thomas makes the same point with some frequency throughout his corpus.[23] To focus on one particularly rich passage, he writes,

> In every created nature there are many modes of procession, yet the specific nature is not communicated in each of them: and the reason of this is to be found in the imperfection of created nature, inasmuch as not everything of a created nature subsists in itself: thus the word that proceeds from a man's intellect is not subsistent, nor is the love that proceeds from his will. . . . On the other hand, whatsoever is in God is subsistent, and therefore in God the divine nature is communicated in every mode of procession.[24]

We saw in chapter three that because of divine simplicity, the divine Word and Love must subsist. We see now that because They subsist, the Father communicates His nature to Them. I am not simple, and my words and loves are therefore not subsistent—which means that I do not communicate my human nature to them. Yet my inability to give the whole of my nature to my words and loves is due to my "created nature." The Father, however, *is* simple; His Word and Love, unlike mine, therefore *are* subsistent; and He, unlike me, therefore *does* communicate His own divine nature to Them. Again, to project into God the processions of my non-personal words, to which I give something less than my very own nature, would be to violate the rules of analogy and to disregard one of the basic differences between the divine nature and any created nature. I do not give my nature to my

---

22 *ST* I q. 27, a. 3, ad 2.

23 For Word and Love together, see *SCG* IV 23§13. For the Word, see *De Ver.*, q. 4, a. 4; *De Pot.*, q. 2, a. 1; and *in Col.*, #34. For Love, see I *Sent* d. 13, q. 1, a. 3, ad 3, and d. 10, q. 1, a. 1, ad 2; and *De Pot.*, q. 10, a. 2, ad 22.

24 *De Pot.*, q. 9, a. 9, ad 1, second series.

words and loves; the Father does give His nature to His Word and Love; and this radical difference ensures that Thomas's psychological analogy really is an analogy and not an exercise in univocity.

TOTAL AND IRREVOCABLE SELF-GIVING

Most basically, these passages make clear *that* the immanent processions of a divine Word and Love, unlike the processions of my human words and loves, entail the communication of nature. Yet we can push things further if we think through *why* they entail the communication of nature—and why they ultimately require a *total* communication of *self*.[25] I, as a rational creature, can conceive a word. And, when I do so, I give a certain sort of existence to that word: I give to it an accidental and intentional existence.[26] Yet I do not give my very own act of existence—my real and substantial existence—to that word. Just so, when I conceive a word in my mind, that word receives from me a certain nature: it receives the nature of a word. We just saw, however, that it does not receive from me my very own human nature. It is a word *of* a human being; it is not *itself* a human being. When I conceive a word, I have one act of existence and nature, and it has a different act of existence and a different nature.

In the simple Godhead, however, there can be no such proliferation of acts of existence or of natures. Instead, there can be only one act of existence and only one nature: the one divine existence and the one divine nature. Indeed, no more than one such divine act of existence or nature could possibly exist anywhere.[27] If, therefore, the divine Word really is divine, then the Father cannot give to His Word any existence—"intentional," "accidental," or otherwise—without giving *His very own* divine existence to His Word; nor can He give any nature to His Word without giving *His very own* divine nature to that Word.

---

[25] Thomas presents the seeds of the following argument in *SCG* IV 11§11; *Comp. Theo.* I, 41; and *LR* d. 2, q. 2, a. 4. See also *in Ioan.*, #28.

[26] For background on *esse intentionale*, see Stephen L. Brock, "Intentional Being, Natural Being, and the First-Person Perspective in Thomas Aquinas," *The Thomist* 77, no. 1 (2013): 103–33.

[27] See *SCG* I, ch. 42.

If He gave any existence or nature other than His own, then the divine Word would possess a nature or an act of existence distinct from that of the Father. In such a case, however, either the Word would not be divine or there would be two natures or two acts of existence in God—both of which are impossible.

Even more, because of divine immutability, the divine Speaker can only give His own nature and existence to His Word if He gives permanently and eternally: He cannot give His nature for a time but then later decide to take it back. Giving in God must be irrevocable.[28] More deeply still, because of divine simplicity, the existence and nature of the divine Speaker must *be* the Speaker Himself. If, therefore, the divine Speaker cannot conceive a Word without giving His own existence and His own nature to His Word, then He cannot conceive a Word without giving *Himself* to His Word. As Thomas puts it, "the Father is His own essence, and He communicates His essence to the Son."[29] In giving His nature, the Father gives that which He Himself *is*. And, finally, because there are no parts in God, this Speaker cannot give His existence, His nature, or Himself to His Word without giving the whole of His existence, the whole of His nature, and the whole of Himself to His Word.[30] Because of simplicity, nothing can be given unless everything is given. The Father, therefore, cannot speak a Word without giving everything He has, even unto Himself, to His Word—His Word Who, because of divine simplicity, must subsist as a distinct Person.

All the same points would hold for Love as well. For, like every word, every love-impression must receive its existence and its nature from the lover from whom it proceeds. Yet the only nature and act of existence that could be given to Love within the simple divine nature is the one divine nature and the one divine act of existence.[31] This nature, however, is identical both to the Father Who breathes forth

---

[28] Thomas suggests this point in I *Sent.*, d. 5, q. 3, a. 1, exp. text.
[29] *ST* I q. 42, a. 5.
[30] See *LR* d. 9, q. 1; *Super Decretalem*, n. 2; and *ST* I q. 41, a. 3.
[31] Thomas suggests this point with reference to Love in *ST* I q. 27, a. 3, ad 2.

Love and to His Word Who breathes with Him.[32] The Father and His Word, therefore, can only breathe forth Love if They give Their own divine nature and existence—and hence Themselves—to Their Love.

We come, then, to the central burden of this chapter: Thomas's decision to frame the Trinity in terms of the immanent processions of Word and Love is no threat to his rendering that same Trinity in terms of total interpersonal self-giving. Instead, in God, immanent procession itself, on its own terms, is already a matter of total interpersonal self-giving. We saw in part one that the Word Whom the Father conceives subsists distinctly, and that the Word is therefore not merely within the Father. Instead, the distinction between Them is a radical one: the Word stands eternally "present" towards the Father, and He is "quasi-extrinsic" to the Father.[33] We see now that the Father gives the whole of Himself to this radically distinct Person. In God, to speak a Word in understanding oneself or to breathe forth Love in loving oneself is to give the whole of oneself to another Person—a Person Who is entirely within oneself, yet Who, as subsistent, also stands in a certain way "outside" of oneself.

SUBSISTENT RECEIVER, ACTIVE RECEIVER

As we saw at the opening of this chapter, the interpersonal intimacy and communion in which many social Trinitarians are interested is not merely a matter of total interpersonal giving. It is also a matter of total interpersonal receiving. We also saw that, for Thomas, reception is analogously present in God, which means that the Son can be said properly to receive from the Father. Thomas's psychological approach, however, might lead to some confusion here. For we just saw that every word receives its existence and its nature from its speaker. Yet there is another respect in which created words do not receive anything from their speakers: for created words do not, strictly speaking, *do* anything. They do not act. They are accidents, and no accident anywhere acts:

---

[32] We will return to this breathing at length in chapter six.
[33] See *SCG* IV 11§18 and *in Ioan.*, #45.

only subsisting things act.³⁴ The fact that the Son receives His existence as a Word from a Speaker, therefore, might seem to suggest that His reception is less than fully active.

We will return to some of the principles at play here in chapters five and six. For now, we can remain with a single point, which comes out when Thomas writes that

> the Word of God differs from an account in the mind of a [human] artist in this: the Word of God is subsistent God. ... Therefore, the plan of the house in the mind of the [human] architect does not build the house; instead, the architect builds it through the plan. However, the Word of God, which is a plan of things made by God, *does*—since He is subsistent—*act*; there is not merely an action through Him.³⁵

I act through my words; my words do not act with me. They are not agents alongside me. The divine Word, however, because He subsists, *is* an agent. He acts as a Person distinct from the Father. Indeed, Thomas teaches elsewhere that He acts in a unique sonly way, which is distinct from the Father's fatherly way of acting.³⁶ Remaining with this passage, however, Thomas teaches that all intelligent action is through a word, and he affirms that the divine Word, like our words, is He *through* Whom His Speaker acts. Yet, unlike our words, the divine Word is subsistent, and the Word therefore is also a distinct agent *with* Whom His Speaker acts.

Thomas focuses here on creation. Yet we will see throughout chapters five and six that the same holds for God's eternal and necessary operations *ad intra*: the Word, because He is a Word, is He in Whom the Father understands and loves; yet, because He is a subsistent Word, He Himself also understands and loves as a distinct agent. For now, we

---

34 As Thomas puts it, "*actus sunt suppositorum.*" For background on this claim, see Emery, "Central Aristotelian Themes," 21n109. For a broader and more nuanced discussion, see Brian Carl, "Action, Supposit, and Subject: Interpreting *Actiones sunt Suppositorum*," *Nova et Vetera* English edition 17, no. 2 (2019): 545–65.

35 *SCG* IV 13§9.

36 See Emery, *TCHP*, 115–53.

can focus on just one point: to say that the Word receives—and receives Himself—from the Father is not to suggest that He receives Himself in the way that my words "receive" themselves and their existence from me. My words are accidents whose activity can be reduced to the activity of the substance in which they inhere. The divine Word is no such thing. When He receives Himself, He receives Himself as an agent of His own receptivity. To be sure, the Word shares His agency—as He shares all things—with the Father.[37] Even more, this agency itself is received from the Father, and it only ever exists as received.[38] There is no sense, therefore, in which the Word is an autonomous generator of His own independent activity. Yet nor is there any sense in which the Word is the inert object or accessory of another's unilateral activity. Instead, the agency that the Word receives really is His own: it is the agency of a Person Who subsists distinctly from—and Who therefore exists in a way "outside of"—His Giver. It is the agency of a Person Who "does—since He is subsistent—act."[39] And so the Word's reception of Himself from the Father, along with the Father's gift of Himself to His Word, really is interpersonal.

We will turn soon to a text where the Word's reception from the Father is front and center, and we should keep this point in mind when we do so. Returning to our main concern, however, we have seen that Thomas's principles demand the convertibility of intra-mental divine procession and interpersonal self-giving in God. We have also run briefly through a few texts where Thomas tells us plainly that immanent procession in God entails the communication of the divine nature. We can now dive more deeply into a set of texts where Thomas presents an even more intimate and developed marriage of immanent psychological procession and total interpersonal self-giving.

---

[37] Indeed, in the divine generation (that is, in the activity in which the Father gives Himself and the Word receives Himself), there is but one action to which both Father and Son are really identical—though They are identical to it in different ways. See *De Pot.*, q. 2, a. 5.

[38] Indeed, *everything* in the Son exists as received and as receiving. We will return to this point in chapter five.

[39] *SCG* IV 13§9.

THE PASSAGES
"His Very Own Whole Fullness"

We can begin with a briefer text from the *SCG*, which comes three chapters after Thomas's extended meditations on the divine Word in book IV, ch. 11. In light of his conclusions in ch. 11, Thomas writes that "because the Son of God's generation is not material, but intelligible, it is now stupid to doubt whether the *Father gave His nature wholly* or partially. For, manifestly, if God understands Himself, His very own whole fullness must be contained in His Word."[40] Because the Son's generation is intelligible, and because "God understands Himself," it follows that "the Father gave His nature wholly" to the Son. These psychological premises secure a total interpersonal gift from the Father to the Son.

Especially noteworthy here is the fluidity with which Thomas moves from the psychological to the interpersonal and back again. He begins with the psychological language of intelligible generation; he argues that, because of the intelligibility of the divine generation, the Father must give His whole nature to the Son; and he ends by returning again to the psychological language of divine self-understanding in order to argue further for the totality of this gift. The logic seems to run such that, because the Father understands the whole of Himself, His Word must contain "His very own whole fullness"—and Thomas seems to assume that the Word can only contain this whole fullness if the Father *gives* Him His very own whole fullness. Thomas does not tell us explicitly that, in God, self-understanding is a matter of total self-giving. Yet he does tell us that we would be "stupid" if we failed to see that, because the divine generation is intelligible and because God understands Himself—and, at least in this passage, for no other reason—the Father must give all He has to His Word.

Two sentences later, Thomas reinforces this point from the opposite direction. He writes that,

---

[40] *SCG* IV 14§4.

> *because divine generation is not material,* clearly there need not be in the Son of God something which receives and something else which is the nature received. For this necessarily happens in material generations, insofar as the matter of the generated receives the form of the one generating. But, in *an intelligible generation,* such is not the case. For a word does not arise within an intellect as though one part of it is previously understood as receiving from the intellect, and another part is understood as flowing from the intellect. Instead, *the word in its entirety has its origin from the intellect,* as even in our case one word *in its entirety* has its origin from others—a conclusion, for example, from principles. Where one thing in its entirety rises from another there is no marking off a receiver from the thing received, but the entire thing which arises is from him from whom it rises.[41]

We just saw that because the divine generation is intelligible, the Father gives all He has to His Word. We see now that because the divine generation is intelligible, the Son receives all He has from the Father.

To elaborate, Thomas explains that there are some givings and receivings in which the receiver first exists and then subsequently receives a gift into herself. In such cases, some aspect of the receiver exists independently of her receiving: the receiver herself precedes both her act of receiving and the gift received. As Thomas puts it, there is "something which receives and something else which is the nature received." This pattern holds even in material generations. In such generations, the receiver herself, as a subsisting thing, only comes into existence when she receives existence from her generator. Yet, even here, the matter of which she is formed precedes her reception. There is some dimension of the receiver that already exists before she begins receiving.

No such possibility, however, exists in the divine generation—and it is *because the Son is a Word* that this possibility is shut down. Because this generation takes the form of the immanent procession of a Word, there can be no substratum or inner sanctum of selfhood in the Son that is set apart from His receiving: for there is no dimension of *any* word *anywhere* that precedes its reception of existence from its speaker.

---

[41] *SCG* IV 14§5.

As Thomas explains, "the word in its entirety has its origin from the intellect." Because the divine Word is a word, He cannot have—and He cannot be—anything but what He receives in being conceived: because the Son proceeds as a Word, it is impossible to "mark off a receiver from the thing received."[42]

Thus, from one direction, because the divine generation is intelligible, everything in the divine Speaker is given to His Word; from the other, because the Son is a Word, everything in Him is received from His Speaker. The whole of the Speaker must be given to another, and the whole of the Word must be a gift from another. The meaning of a Word and of intelligible generation demand it.

"We Have an Example of This Communication in the Intellect"

We see a more developed marriage of immanent procession and interpersonal giving in a text from the *De Potentia*, where Thomas asks whether there is a generative power in God. Thomas begins,

> I answer that it is in the nature of every act to *communicate itself* as far as possible. Every agent, therefore, acts insofar as it is in act: while to act is nothing else than to communicate as far as possible that whereby the agent is in act. Now the divine nature is supreme and most pure act. Hence *it communicates itself as far as possible*. It communicates itself to creatures by likeness only: this is clear to anyone, since every creature is a being according to its likeness to it. Moreover, the Catholic Faith asserts another mode of communication of the divine nature, in that the divine nature itself is communicated by a quasi-natural communication: so that as one to whom humanity is communicated is a man, so

---

[42] White points in this direction when he writes that the Son "eternally *receives* all that he is from the Father, as his eternal Word, in whom the Father knows all things" (*The Trinity*, 473). Ratzinger draws a set of richly interpersonal conclusions from similar points—and he therefore builds on the insights of Clarke, Schmitz, and Schindler which we mentioned above—in *Introduction to Christianity*, 184–90.

the one to Whom divinity is communicated is not only like God, but is truly God.[43]

Thomas opens this corpus with the fullest possible self-communication: because the divine nature is "supreme and most pure act," it "communicates itself as far as possible." It communicates itself "by likeness only" in creation. Yet it also communicates itself in a "quasi-natural communication," and the one Who receives from this communication is "not only like God, but is truly God." This receiver, however, can only be "truly God" if He receives, and hence possesses, the whole of the divine nature. Yet He can only receive the whole of that nature if the giver gives the whole of His own nature—which means that we have here a *total* communication of the *whole* divine nature.

As Thomas continues, however, his reflections turn psychological. Immediately after the words we just quoted, he introduces two differences between the communication of the divine nature and any communication of any created nature. First, because "the divine nature itself is subsistent," it follows that, "in the communication of the divine nature, there is no need of anything material for subsistence." Second, "because again the divine essence is its own being, it does not receive being from the supposit in which it is: so that by virtue of one and the same being it is in both the communicator and the one to whom it is communicated; and, in this way, it remains identically the same in both." Because of simplicity, the quasi-natural communication of the divine nature must be removed from matter, and both the giver and the receiver must share identically the same nature.

It is here that this passage begins to be interesting for us. In order to account for such an immaterial communication within a single nature, Thomas continues, "we have an example of this communication, and that most becomingly, in the intellect." We need not detail every twist and turn in Thomas's argument. Instead, we will stick to the points most important for us. First, Thomas explains that, in any act of understanding, the thing understood communicates its form to the intellect. He continues that, when intellect understands itself, there is a

---

43 *De Pot.*, q. 2, a. 1. Until otherwise indicated, all citations to follow are from the corpus of this article.

communication of a concept "from the intellect understanding into the intellect receiving it." The communication of this concept—the concept Thomas identifies as "the word of the intellect"—is immaterial, and it remains within the one nature of the mind from which it proceeds and into which it proceeds.

Taking a step back, Thomas had just established that the communication of the divine nature must be removed from matter and must remain within a unity of existence. He now argues that if we attend to the conceptions of our words, we can see an example of an immaterial communication within a unity of essence and existence. And, accordingly, Thomas continues by affirming that the generation of the divine Son is, in fact, the conception of a divine Word: "even as when our intellect understands itself there is in it a word proceeding and bearing a likeness to that from which it proceeds, so, too, in God there is a Word bearing the likeness of Him from Whom it proceeds."

Thomas continues, however, by clarifying that God's Word is not our word. First, our words are "not identified with the essence of our intellect." Second, "the human nature is not communicated" to our words when they proceed. In God, however, the Word *is* identical to the divine intellect. Just so, "the divine nature itself is its intellectuality, wherefore a communication that takes place in an intellectual manner *is* also a communication by way of nature, so that it can be called a generation." Unlike us, God communicates His nature to His Word. It follows, therefore, that the Word Who receives the divine nature is a "subsistent Son."[44]

Looking over this article as a whole, Thomas begins with the total self-communication of the divine nature. He reasons, however, that such a total self-communication can only be truly divine—that is, it can only exist within a simple nature—if it is immaterial and if it remains within a single act of existence. He then introduces the divine intellect and Word in order to gain some insight into this consubstantial and immaterial self-communication. He does not, however, end with the procession of the divine Word. Instead, as he thinks more deeply through this procession, he is led back to the communication of nature

---

44 These final words are from *De Pot.*, q. 2, a. 1, ad 2.

from subsistent hypostasis to subsistent hypostasis: because of divine simplicity, the procession of a divine Word must be a communication of the divine nature, and the Word Who receives this nature must subsist as a divine Son.

Thomas, then, begins with total self-communication; he shifts seamlessly to self-understanding and to the procession of a word; and he ends by shifting back to the communication of nature to a subsistent Son. Or, better, he does not shift at all. Instead, he shows that, in God, the total communication of nature *is* the procession of a Word, and that the procession of a Word *is* the communication of nature to a subsistent Son. He begins with the premise that, as "the Catholic Faith asserts," the whole of the divine nature is communicated from divine Person to divine Person. He then thinks through the only form that this total divine self-communication could possibly take, and he concludes that it takes the form of the procession of a Word. From there, however, he thinks through the only form that such an immanent divine procession could possibly take, and he concludes that it entails the communication of nature to a subsistent Son. As Thomas thinks through each, he concludes that it must take the form of the other.[45]

"The Most Perfect Generation"

"His Whole Substance"

Things are even more developed in an article from Thomas's Roman *Scriptum* on the *Sentences*.[46] This article recalls something of the opening

---

[45] Even more, he establishes early in the corpus of this article that the divine Persons are identical to the divine nature: as he puts it, "the Godhead is the same thing as God." The divine nature, therefore, is the same thing as the God Who gives that nature—which means that, in communicating the whole of His nature, the divine giver must give the whole of *Himself*. Thomas does not take this last step here. Yet principles he lays out within this passage demand that immanent procession be not only a giving of nature, but a total giving of self.

[46] Unless otherwise indicated, all of the citations to follow will come from *LR* d. 9, q. 1. The authenticity of the Roman *Scriptum* is still being debated. For a summary of the discussion, see Pasquale Porro, *Thomas Aquinas: A Historical and Philosophical Profile*, trans. Joseph G. Trabbic and Roger W. Nutt (Washington, DC: The Catholic University of America Press, 2016), 186–88; and Torrell, *Person and Work*, 55–59. For our purposes, there seem to be enough arguments in favor of this text's authenticity for us to dive into

paragraphs of *SCG* IV, ch. 11. As in *SCG* IV, ch. 11, Thomas is setting out to understand something of the divine generation, and he lays out a hierarchy of natures in order to do so. This new hierarchy, however, is arranged very differently. The *SCG*'s hierarchy had been organized around a scale of increasingly inward emanations. This hierarchy will be organized around a scale of increasingly total acts of self-giving. Thomas, then, is certainly employing two distinct frameworks in these two passages: one of those frameworks is more obviously a matter of interiority, the other more obviously a matter of relationships between beings. There may, however, be more overlap between these two hierarchies than initially meets the eye.[47]

Thomas begins this new hierarchy by writing that "in every generation there are two things. One is common to all generations: namely, that the one generated has the nature of the one generating. . . . But the other is diverse in diverse generations." All generators share their nature when they generate, but different generators do so in different ways and to different degrees. Thomas begins with "inanimate generations," in which "the generated does not receive anything of the substance of the generator, even though it receives the nature of the generator according to species." As in the *SCG*, he gives the example of fire: "although the thing heated receives the nature of fire according to its species, it never similarly receives its substance." A fire communicates the nature of fire to that which it burns: it turns that which it burns into the same sort of fire which it itself is. But it does not transfer anything of its own substance to this new fire. The new fire, that is, does not now possess something that had previously belonged to the old fire; instead, there is now simply more fire in addition to the old fire.

Thomas turns next to generations in which "the generator hands over his nature, and *something of his substance*, to the generated; and this

---

it here, but any conclusions we draw from it might have to be marked by a certain asterisk until this question of authenticity is resolved.

47 Some have found in *SCG* IV, ch. 11 resources for a "Trinitarian ontology" (see Susan Waldstein, "Reading Natural Hierarchy in a Trinitarian Key," and, more loosely, Ulrich, *Homo Abyssus*, 375–86). They may be right to do so. Yet, for reasons I hope to make clear here, a deeper and more complete Trinitarian ontology might be possible—and insights already present (if perhaps only implicit) in *SCG* IV, ch. 11 might be brought to the surface—if *SCG* IV, ch. 11 is read together with *LR* d. 9, q. 1.

is the case in the generation in living things. For, in these, generation is brought about by a certain separation [*decisionem*]" from the generator into the generated. Unlike inanimate bodies, living things do not merely generate another living thing like themselves; they also give something of their own substance to their child. A human child, for example, is formed by the seed of the father. And, in the womb, the child takes on the flesh of her mother. Something that had belonged to the substance of the father and mother—seed and flesh—now belongs to the child. Just so, when a plant gives off its fruit and spreads its seed, it does not merely make an additional plant outside of itself; it lets go of something that had originally been a part of itself, but which is now the beginnings of a new organism. We have here not just a likeness of species. Instead, something of the generator's very own substance is handed over to the generated. Living things, then—which are more perfect than inanimate things—give more of themselves in generating their offspring than inanimate things do in generating others like themselves.[48]

Generation among living things, however, remains less than fully perfect. For a living generator gives only "*something* of his substance." He does not give his whole substance. In God, in contrast, "there is the most perfect generation, because not only is there a likeness of nature in the generator and the generated, but there is even the communication of the generator's substance, and *His whole substance*, for there are no parts in God. And, therefore, the Father gives His substance to the Son." The perfection of the divine generation outstrips the perfection of any creaturely generation. And it does so because, in the divine generation, the whole substance of the generator is totally given to the one generated. I give my son a part of my substance, but I do not give him the whole of my substance. My hands and my eyes, for example, remain my hands and my eyes. I give him his own hands and his own eyes distinct from mine. More deeply, I give him *a* human nature; I do not give him *my* human nature. My instance of human nature remains mine alone, and I give him his own discrete instance of human nature. In the generations of living creatures, then, much remains ungiven. It is only in God that the generator gives *everything*, without any exception, to the one generated. The Father cannot give only a part

---

[48] For living things are more perfect than inanimate things, see *SCG* I 97§4.

of His substance to the Son, for "there are no parts in God." Instead, He gives "His *whole* substance." Just so, the Father cannot give the Son a distinct instance of the divine nature—He cannot give a mere "likeness of nature"—for there can be no more than one divine nature. Instead, the Father has to give the Son His very own nature. Nothing can remain ungiven. And it is because everything is fully given that this generation is most perfect.[49]

Two Hierarchies, One Hierarchy

Thomas continues by shifting to more obviously psychological language. Before attending to this shift, however, we should briefly compare this hierarchy with that of the *SCG*. As in the *SCG*, inanimate bodies occupy the lowest rung of this new hierarchy. The differences between the two texts, however, are evident. In the *SCG*, inanimate bodies had been the least perfect because the emanation proper to them had been the least intimate. Here, they are the least perfect because, in the generation proper to them, the thing generated receives the least from its generator—which means that the generator gives the least of itself. It gives nothing of its substance. What had been a minimally interior emanation in the *SCG* is now a minimally total self-giving.

Even here, however, there may be a parallel between the two texts. For to say that an inanimate generator gives relatively little of itself in generating is to say that relatively little emanates *from the interior* of the generator into the generated. To use Thomas's example, nothing from *within* the fire that heats is given to the thing heated; instead, the original fire merely brings additional fire into existence. This self-giving of limited totality corresponds to an emanation of limited interiority. We should not, of course, minimize the intimacy entailed in a fire generating more fire. To give one's nature "according to species" is already to give quite a lot, and it is already to give something that is profoundly intimate to oneself. Indeed, the form of fire that the fire shares is more intimate to the fire than a mother's flesh is to the

---

[49] Thomas elsewhere links the perfection of the divine generation to the totality of the Father's communication (again with reference to simplicity): see *ST* I q. 41, a. 3; and *Super Decretalem*, n. 2.

mother.⁵⁰ Yet a fire gives less, and it gives less intimately, than living generators who are higher up the hierarchy give. First of all, a mother gives of her flesh over and above *also* sharing her form with her child. She gives as intimately as the fire does, yet she also gives beyond this common baseline giving. Secondly—and more importantly—a fire does not give *its very own instance* of a fiery nature to a new fire; it creates a new fire with a new instance of fiery nature. The mother, in contrast, gives her very own flesh to her child. This living generation, therefore, is more intimate: because living parents give *more* of themselves, they give *more intimately* from within themselves.

And, because the Father gives the *whole* of Himself, His self-giving is *wholly intimate*. First of all, He gives the whole of the nature that He Himself *is*, and this nature is incalculably more intimate to Him than my seed is to me, than a fruit is to a tree, or than any creaturely form is to any creature. As Thomas puts it elsewhere, the Father shares with the Son "the most secret things of the fatherly nature and essence."⁵¹ His giving is infinitely intimate. The Son, in turn, like everything generated, emanates from His generator. Yet, unlike anything else that is generated, He emanates within "the most secret things" of His generator. And He does so *because* His generator gives Him everything He has. It is because the Father gives to the Son the whole of His very own essence and substance that the Son is identical to the Father's own essence and substance; yet it is because the Son is identical to the Father's essence and substance that the Son is perfectly within the Father.⁵² In the divine generation, the Father gives all He has to the Son Who emanates from Him, and the Son's emanation *therefore* remains perfectly interior to the Father. We are not faced with a choice between total interpersonal self-giving and perfectly interior emanation. Instead, a total act of interpersonal self-giving, because it is total, takes the form of a perfectly interior emanation.⁵³

---

50 Even at the bottommost rung of nature, therefore, we find some degree of intimate self-giving. This point might be relevant to the question of "Trinitarian ontology" in this text.

51 *In Ioan.*, #218.

52 See *ST* I q. 42, a. 5.

53 Thomas does not, admittedly, use the language of "Person" in *LR* d. 9, q. 1, and so one might object to our talk of "interpersonal" self-giving. By this point in the *LR*, however,

"The Word of His Intellect"

This point becomes more evident as Thomas continues, and as he begins speaking more directly to our main concern:

> We can make this clear as follows: for God is intellect itself, and His existence is His understanding. Whenever anyone understands, he forms the word of his intellect. If, therefore, God understands, He must form the Word of His intellect; and, because God's understanding is His essence, this Word must therefore have the nature and substance of the Father. And because God understands the whole of Himself, the Word therefore has the whole nature of the Father. In us, on the other hand, because our understanding is other than our existence, our word therefore is not the same as us and does not have our nature.

Thomas had just shown that the divine generation is a matter of total self-giving. Once he reaches the pinnacle self-giving, however, his reflections take a psychological turn. He speaks at length of the divine Word and the divine intellect, and he draws a parallel between the generation of the Son and the conception of the Word: just as the perfection of the divine generation demands that the Father give His whole nature to the Son, so the perfection of the divine self-understanding—"because God understands the whole of Himself"—demands that the Word have "the whole nature of the Father." As in our *De Potentia* text, however, Thomas does not begin a new set of reflections when he shifts to this psychological register. Instead, he only introduces the psychological at all in order to illuminate the interpersonal: he transitions to the procession of a Word because this procession can "make clear" the total self-giving of the Father to the Son.

One might object, however, that, even though Thomas claims to be illuminating the interpersonal by way of the psychological, he actually ends up absorbing the interpersonal into the psychological. For it might seem that, just as Thomas is on the verge of introducing

---

he had already written that in God, there are "three Persons: namely, the Father, the Son Who proceeds by way of intellect, and the Holy Spirit by way of will and love" (d. 2, q. 2, a. 4, ad 3).

full-bodied interpersonal giving and receiving in God, he hastens to clarify that the only thing that giving and receiving in God can *really* mean is that a Word proceeds within the mind of His Speaker. The conclusion of the corpus, however, suggests otherwise: "Therefore, although in God the one generated is perfectly assimilated to the one generating, and has the whole of the generator's nature, nevertheless there still remains there the distinction through relations, by which the one generating is distinguished from the one generated insofar, of course, as one is *giving* and the other is *receiving*." Thinking through the logic of generation, giving, and receiving had prompted Thomas to introduce the intellect and its word. Now, thinking through the logic of the divine intellect and its Word leads him back to talk of generation, giving, and receiving. It leads him to the conclusion that the Father gives to the Son, that the Son receives from the Father, and that They are distinct from each other by virtue of this giving and receiving. The interpersonal organically opens up to the psychological, and the psychological—far from eclipsing the interpersonal or sanding off its edges—opens back up to the interpersonal. Yet Thomas can only shift with this fluidity because the interpersonal ultimately *is* the psychological, and the psychological ultimately *is* the interpersonal. In God, total interpersonal self-giving takes the form of the immanent procession of a Word, and the immanent procession of a Word takes the form of total interpersonal self-giving. As we saw in the first section of this chapter, principles that are bedrock to Thomas's Trinitarian theology demand that these two registers must coincide. We see now that, in light of this coincidence, Thomas can move from one register to the other and back again without batting an eye.

From Father to Speaker, from Speaker to Father

We can draw our strongest conclusions by highlighting one more parallel between this text and the *SCG*. In chapter three, we had ended our study of *SCG* IV, ch. 11 with Thomas's claim that the Word stands eternally present to the Father. Ch. 11, however, does not end with this talk of presence. Instead, it ends in the next paragraph, where Thomas writes that "to *give* the nature and species to the offspring belong to the father, whereas to conceive and bring forth belong to the mother as patient and recipient."[54] Thomas continues by reasoning that, because the Word proceeds insofar as "God understands Himself," and because "the divine intellect is not in potency but is only actual," the divine Speaker is a divine Father—Who, as a father, gives His nature to His Word. Thomas never abandons his psychological terms as he introduces this giving of nature from Father to Son. Instead, he justifies this interpersonal giving with reference to his psychological terms: it is because the divine Word proceeds as "God understands Himself" that the divine Speaker is a Father Who gives His nature to His Word. It is not the interpersonal instead of the intrapersonal. Instead, self-understanding vouchsafes interpersonal giving.

Taking a step back, Thomas had begun ch. 11 by sketching a hierarchy of increasingly interior emanations, and this hierarchy had concluded in 11§7 with the summit of interiority and of unity: it had concluded with the emanation of the divine Word within the identity of the divine essence. Thomas then spends 11§§9–19 thinking through the shape that such an emanation takes within a simple nature. And, in so doing, he shows that the perfectly interior emanation of a divine Word—without ceasing to be perfectly interior, and without ceasing to be the procession of a Word—is an interpersonal giving of nature. Indeed, he says enough to ensure that it is a *total* interpersonal *self*-giving, and that the Persons Who give and receive are so distinct that one can stand present to the other.[55] Now, in this new hierarchy, he lays out a scale of increasingly total communications of nature, and he ends with the summit of self-giving: he ends with the Father's giving "His whole substance" to the Son. Yet he continues by thinking through the shape of such a total self-giving. And, in so doing, he shows that

---

54 *SCG* IV 11§19. Thomas's take on biology and gender might, of course, be inadequate, but we will have to leave those questions to the side.

55 The totality of this giving was established earlier in *SCG* IV, ch. 11, where Thomas had reflected at length on the simplicity of the divine nature (see especially 11§11); in so doing, he had guaranteed that the divine nature can only be given if it is wholly given. The fact that it is an act of *self*-giving follows from Thomas's teaching that the divine Speaker *is* the divine nature ("God is both His essence and His act of being": 11§12. See also 11§11), which ensures that this Speaker can only give His nature if He gives Himself. Finally, this giving must be interpersonal insofar as the Word subsists in the intellectual divine nature, and insofar as a person is "a subsistent thing in intellectual natures" (IV 10§6).

the perfectly total self-giving from Father to Son—without ceasing to be a total self-giving, and without ceasing to be between distinct Persons—is the procession of a Word within the one divine mind. In the *SCG*, Thomas thinks through the immanent procession of divine Word, and he arrives at the total interpersonal self-giving of the Father to the Son; in the Roman *Scriptum*, he thinks through the total interpersonal self-giving of the Father to the Son, and he arrives at the immanent procession of a Word. No matter which side Thomas begins from, he ends with a synthesis of both. And, again, the interpersonal and the psychological can flow so fluidly into and out of each other because, in God, immanent psychological procession *is* total interpersonal self-giving, and total interpersonal self-giving *is* immanent psychological procession.

Passages and Principles

Taking a step back, our most basic conclusion here was already guaranteed by the principles we laid out in the first section of this chapter: to conceive a word is, by definition, to give existence to that word; in God, there can be no existence—and hence no existence can be given—except the one divine act of existence; because it is simple, this existence can only be given if it is wholly given; again because of simplicity, the one who gives existence must *be* the existence He gives, which means that He must give Himself to His Word in giving existence to His Word; and, because the existence that the Word receives is self-subsistent, the Word Himself must subsist as a distinct Person. The passages we have studied in this section, therefore, only shine the spotlight on a conclusion that follows unavoidably from principles basic to Thomas's Trinitarian theology and doctrine of God. I hope, however, that these passages have not been redundant. For, if nothing else, they suggest that Thomas was fully aware of, and comfortable with, the marriage that his principles arrange between immanent psychological procession and total interpersonal self-giving. Thomas's principles do not merely carry a set of implications of which he himself was unaware, with which he would have been uncomfortable, and which, had he recognized them, might have prompted him to revise his principles. Instead, Thomas himself draws attention to these implications. He may never come out and tell us that in God, immanent procession is a matter of total interpersonal self-giving. Yet he suggests that we would need to be "stupid" not to see that this conclusion follows on his principles.[56]

In light both of these principles and of these passages, then, I hope that the basic point has been established: Thomas's psychological categories do not prevent him from rendering the divine life in terms of total interpersonal self-giving. Nor do interpersonal self-giving and immanent procession run on parallel tracks, as though each left room for the other but neither had anything to do with the other. Instead, Thomas's psychological categories are *themselves* interpersonal categories: the immanent procession of the Word is *itself* the divine Speaker's giving all He has, even unto Himself, to a radically distinct Person. The meaning of immanent procession in God and of total self-giving in God demand that neither can exist except as the other.[57]

---

[56] See *SCG* IV 14§4.

[57] A final set of passages is less directly relevant to our question but is still worth mentioning briefly. First, Thomas writes that "this is the proper mark of friendship: that one reveal his secrets to his friend. For, since charity unites affections and makes, as it were, one heart of two, one seems *not to have brought forth* [*protulisse*] *to the exterior of his heart* that which he reveals to a friend" (*SCG* IV 21§5; Thomas makes an almost identical point in *in Ioan.*, #2016. He uses "*protulit*" for the eternal procession of the Word in *ST* III q. 45, a. 4, ad 1). My secrets proceed—or they are "brought forth"—from me to my friend; yet they remain within my heart. Indeed, they remain within my heart because my heart *itself* belongs to my friend. This procession is both totally immanent and totally interpersonal. Thomas, it is true, registers this point in order to illuminate not the eternal processions of the divine Persons, but the Holy Spirit's role in the economy. Still, this passage appears within his Trinitarian theology, and it suggests that even among creatures, an immanent procession can be fully interpersonal without thereby ceasing to be immanent.

We perhaps see something similar when Thomas writes, "when I speak to others, my mind goes out to them, yet it does not leave me; and when I am silent, in a certain sense I return to myself, yet I still remain with those to whom I spoke" (*in Ioan.*, #1872). Whenever I speak to another person, my mind "goes out" from myself to her, even as it remains within me; whenever I cease speaking, I proceed from her back to myself, even as I remain with her. I never leave myself in either of these processions; yet I really proceed to and from another. Again, this procession—which takes place every time I speak to another human being—is both totally immanent and totally interpersonal.

In neither of these passages, of course, is Thomas speaking directly to the eternal relations of the divine Persons, and in neither does he use the language of self-giving. In both, however, he shows that even in creatures, there is no conflict between a procession's being immanent and its being interpersonal.

A FAMILY TRINITY AND SELF-DIFFUSIVE GOODNESS

We can end this chapter by taking a step back. For the texts we just explored, along with others we have explored throughout this study, can put Thomas's psychological approach in dialogue with a pair of Trinitarian frameworks to which it is often opposed: first, a Trinitarian theology that takes its bearings from the family; second, one that takes its bearings from the self-communication of goodness.[58]

PSYCHOLOGICAL TRINITY AS FAMILIAL TRINITY

Psychological, Interpersonal, Familial

Amidst the surge of social Trinities that have emerged over the past few decades, a good deal of attention has been paid to the family as an analogy for the Trinity.[59] For our part, we have seen familial language crop up throughout this chapter. For most of our reflections have not revolved around interpersonal self-giving in the broadest or most general terms; they have revolved around the self-giving of a Father to a Son. Seeing as much can bring us to the first, and most basic, point: insofar as "fatherhood" and "sonship" are familial terms, Thomas's Trinity is very much a "familial" Trinity.[60] God the Father, after all, really is a Father, and God the Son really is a Son: "fatherhood" and "sonship" are predicated properly of God, and there is a community of analogy

---

[58] In what follows, I will explore the question of the Trinity and the family only insofar as it touches on Thomas's psychological analogy. In "The Family as an Image of the Trinity in Aquinas," *Communio: International Catholic Review* 49, no. 2 (2022): 299–330, I speak more broadly to the Trinity and the family. I also deal with *ST* I q. 36, a. 3, ad 1, and q. 93, a. 6, ad 2 (where Thomas seems to reject the family as an image of the Trinity), and I dive deep into passages that reinforce the conclusions we will draw here (especially q. 93, a. 3).

[59] See Angelo Cardinal Scola, *The Nuptial Mystery*, trans. Michelle K. Boras (Grand Rapids, MI: Eerdmans, 2005), 48–50; and Ouellet, *Divine Likeness*, 26–33.

[60] Some contemporaries have seen an analogy for the Trinity not only in fatherhood and sonship, but also in marriage and sexual difference (see Scola, *The Nuptial Mystery*, 42–52). We will see here that Thomas's Trinity can certainly accommodate—indeed, it even centers around—the "familial" language of fatherhood and sonship. There seems to be less room, however, for nuptial language (though see my "The Family as an Image of the Trinity in Aquinas," 328–29).

binding creaturely fatherhood and sonship to divine fatherhood and sonship.[61] Indeed, it is not merely that fatherhood and sonship are properly present both in God and in creatures. Instead, "the *perfect essence* of fatherhood and sonship is to be found in God the Father and God the Son," and " 'generation and 'fatherhood,' like the other terms properly applied to God, are said of God *before* creatures as regards the thing signified."[62] Fatherhood and sonship are not merely present in God. They are present more fully and more properly in God than they are in any creaturely father or son.[63]

Given the prominence of fatherhood and sonship in Thomas's Trinity, one might expect advocates of a familial Trinity to identify Thomas as an ally. Once again, however, his psychological analogy stands as a stumbling block. Indeed, because of Thomas's psychological approach, family Trinitarians generally cast him as a barrier or a foil to the familial Trinities they are after: they seem to assume that because Thomas's Trinity is psychological, it cannot be familial.[64] We, however, have seen enough to draw a very different conclusion. For we have seen enough to suggest that, because of the specific way in which Thomas's Trinity is psychological, it *must* be familial. To be more precise, we have stressed throughout this chapter that Thomas's psychological Trinity is already an interpersonal Trinity. Yet we have also seen—and we can now emphasize—that his psychological Trinity is already a *familial*

---

[61] See Emery, *TTTA*, 160–63, 205–9; Dominic Legge, *The Trinitarian Christology of St. Thomas Aquinas* (Oxford: Oxford University Press, 2017), 83–84; and John Baptist Ku, "St. Thomas Aquinas's Treatment of the Name "Father" in ST I, q. 33, a. 2," *Nova et Vetera* English edition 9, no. 2 (2011): 438–48.

[62] *ST* I q. 33, a. 3; *ST* I q. 33, a. 2, ad 4.

[63] For more here, see Ku, "St. Thomas Aquinas's Treatment of the Name 'Father,' " 445–48. Durand writes that, for Thomas, "Fatherhood and filiation as such are found first and foremost in the heart of the Trinity, and the human correspondents (fatherhood—maternity and filiation) are participations in these perfect modes of existence that are proper to God alone" ("The Theology of God the Father," 377). In *ST* I q. 13, a. 6, s.c.; and I *Sent.*, d. 22, q. 1, a. 2, s.c. 1, Thomas presents "fatherhood" as the paradigm of the pattern by which all names—"goodness," "existence," "intellect," and so on—are to be predicated properly of God. Even more, Thomas writes that "the fatherhood present in creatures is, as it were, nominal or vocal; but the divine fatherhood, by which the Father gives His whole nature to the Son without any imperfection, this is true fatherhood"—which suggests that fatherhood is *only* truly present in God the Father (*in Eph.*, c. 3, l. 4).

[64] See Ouellet, *Divine Likeness*, 20–25.

Trinity. For fatherhood and sonship, by definition, signify the giving and receiving of a common nature between distinct hypostases.[65] And we have seen that in Thomas's Trinitarian theology, a Speaker cannot conceive a Word unless He gives His nature to His Word, and unless His Word subsists distinctly from Him. Thomas's psychological analogy, therefore, does not merely require the total self-giving of one Person to another. It requires the total self-giving of a Father to a Son.[66]

Of course, it is no less true that in Thomas's Trinitarian theology, a Father's giving His nature to His Son necessarily takes the form of a Speaker's conceiving a divine Word. If the psychological is familial, then the familial is no less psychological. For our purposes, however, we can focus on one direction: in Thomas's Trinity, a Speaker is necessarily a Father, a Word is necessarily a Son, and inner speech within one's heart is necessarily the birth of such a Son. The psychological is necessarily familial, and the familial is necessarily psychological.

"The Name 'Son' Insinuates His Consubstantiality"

We can go deeper into the interpenetration of the psychological and the familial if we note that, in an echo of a scheme we have seen throughout this study, it is sometimes alleged that a psychological Trinity can secure the Persons' unity of essence but not their personal distinction, whereas a familial Trinity—like social Trinities more broadly—can capture Their personal distinction but not Their essential unity.[67] And it is therefore implied that in plighting his troth to the psychological, Thomas opts for unity at the expense of distinction. We saw all through part one that, at least so far as Thomas is concerned, this scheme misses the mark on the psychological and the social more broadly. We will

---

[65] See *in Ioan.*, #2112. See also *in Ioan.*, #1462; *SCG* IV 8§9, and 23§12; and III *Sent.*, d. 4, q. 1, a. 2, qc. 1. For the real distinction between a giver and a receiver, see I *Sent.*, d. 5, q. 3, a. 1, ad 3, and d. 18, q. 1, a. 1.

[66] This point was especially evident in our readings of *SCG* IV, ch. 11 both in this chapter and in chapter three. Thomas again shows that a divine Speaker and Word are necessarily a divine Father and Son in *ST* I q. 29, a. 2; *Comp. Theo.* I, 38–40; *in Ioan.*, #29; and, more briefly, *De Pot.*, q. 9, a. 5.

[67] See, somewhat indirectly, Ouellet, *Divine Likeness*, 24. More generally, see van den Brink, "Social Trinitarianism," 333 and 347.

see now that it becomes even more problematic when it is applied to the familial.

To see as much, we can turn to passages where Thomas runs through the range of names that, following Scripture and Tradition, he uses for the second divine Person: Son, Word, Image, and Splendor. He explains that

> the Son's nativity, which is His personal property, is signified by different names, which are attributed to the Son to express His perfection in various ways. To show that He is *of the same nature as the Father*, He is called the *Son*; to show that He is co-eternal, He is called the Splendor; to show that He is altogether like, He is called the Image; to show that He is generated *immaterially*, He is called the *Word*. All these truths cannot be expressed by only one name.[68]

In a parallel passage from his commentary on John, Thomas puts the matter in stronger terms: he writes that "we call Him 'Son' " in order to secure His "*identity of nature*" with the Father; he continues that "the name 'Son' insinuates His *consubstantiality*"; and he concludes that "we call Him 'Son' to show that He is of the *same nature* as the Father."[69] We use the name "Word," in contrast, to show that "He is generated immaterially."[70]

Thus, when Thomas inquires directly into the facets of the divine life that are secured by the language "Word" in contrast to "Son," he does not tell us that "Word" secures unity or interiority but leaves subsistent distinction underdeveloped. Instead, "Word" secures immateriality, without any reference either to essential unity or to personal distinction.[71] More striking still, the language of "Son" does not secure personal distinction but leave doubts as to consubstantial unity. Instead,

---

68 *ST* I q. 34, a. 2, ad 3.

69 In Ioan., ##41–42.

70 In Ioan., #42.

71 In *ST* I q. 42, a. 2, ad 1, "Word" secures impassibility and coeternity (the latter of which is usually correlated with "splendor"). Even here, however, "Word" does not secure the essential unity of Father and Son; it secures the impassibility and eternity of the Son.

the particular facet of the Triune life that the logic of sonship is most apt to secure is—consubstantial unity!

If, therefore, Thomas privileges the "psychological" over the "familial," then it is not because he lopsidedly privileges unity and interiority over distinction and outwardness. First of all, we have seen repeatedly that his psychological categories *themselves* do not lopsidedly privilege unity over distinction; instead, they secure both essential unity and interpersonal distinction. We see now that the familial language of father-son does not lopsidedly privilege interpersonal distinction over consubstantial unity. If anything, it does the opposite. Personal distinction goes all the way to the foundation of Thomas's psychological categories, and consubstantial unity goes all the way to the foundation of his familial categories.

Two Centers

That said, when push comes to shove, it remains that Thomas ultimately gives pride of place to the psychological. He writes that, of all ways of articulating the divine generation—including the language of fatherhood and sonship—"the procession of the word from the intellect most exactly represents" it.[72] Thomas's psychological analogy may itself be familial. Yet, insofar as the psychological and the familial are logically distinct, the emphasis seems to fall on the psychological.

I have no intention of denying this primacy of the psychological. Indeed, the whole of this study is premised on the claim that Thomas's mature Trinitarian theology is first and foremost psychological. Yet it is also premised on the claim that the psychological itself already includes more of the interpersonal—or, here, more of the familial—than is generally recognized. We can end this section by suggesting that this interpenetration of the psychological and the familial might complicate the primacy of the psychological.[73]

---

72 *ST* I q. 42, a. 2, ad 1.

73 John Baptist Ku emphasizes the priority of the psychological, arguing that the language of "Son" in Thomas's Trinitarian theology ought always to be read in terms of "Word" (see "St. Thomas Aquinas's Treatment of the Name 'Father,' " 448–50). I completely agree. I would simply add that, as we will see, the priority of the Word is not unilateral, and the language of "Word" ought also always to be read in terms of "Son."

The first thing to note is that this primacy of the psychological is not merely affirmed in a single stray passage. Instead, it is evident in the concrete details of Thomas's Trinitarian theology. In the *Summa*, for example, Thomas establishes that the first procession in God is the conception of a Word, before he establishes, through arguments drawn from the nature of a word, that this procession is the generation of a Son.[74] Just so, the first question devoted to the second Person centers around the name "Word," and there is no similarly detailed inquiry into the name "Son."[75] Again, "Word" comes first.

If we attend to other details, however, things become more complicated. Returning to q. 27, Thomas uses the language of sonship well before he ever introduces the divine Word: he writes that, according to Arius, "the *Son* proceeds from the Father as His primary creature, and the Holy Spirit proceeds from the Father and the *Son* as the creature of both. In this sense neither the *Son* nor the Holy Spirit would be true God: and this is contrary to what is said of the *Son*."[76] Talk of "Son" and "Father" continues to abound through the opening sentences of this passage, and Thomas only so much as mentions the procession of a Word after he has spoken at length of the Father and the Son. Similarly, although q. 34 is devoted to the name "Word," Thomas explains in the prologue to this question, "We next consider the Person of the Son. Three names are attributed to the Son—namely, 'Son,' 'Word,' and 'Image.' The idea of Son is gathered from the idea of Father [which had just been treated in q. 33]. Hence it remains for us to consider Word and Image."[77] By the time Thomas treats of the name "Word" in q. 34, he had already—albeit indirectly—treated of the name "Son" in q. 33. More deeply, all through this passage, where Thomas is setting out the framework for his treatment of the second Person, the name "Son" enjoys a clear preference: "We next consider the Person of the *Son*. Three names are attributed to the *Son*—namely, 'Son,' 'Word,' and 'Image.'" "Son" is the default name given to the second Person, precisely at the

---

74 See *ST* I q. 27, aa. 1-2.
75 See *ST* I q. 34.
76 *ST* I q. 27, a. 1.
77 *ST* I q. 34, prol.

point where Thomas is discussing, at the most basic level, how He is to be named. We find the same dynamic when Thomas runs through the various names of the second Person: "the *Son's birth*, which is His personal property, is signified by different names, which are attributed to *the Son* to express His perfection in different ways."[78] Again, the default name, as Thomas is poised to run through the various names of the second Person, is "Son."

So too in the *SCG*. We saw in chapter three that the name "Word" enjoys a certain priority over "Son" in book IV, ch. 11: God is first mentioned here with reference to His "intention understood," and the language of "Word" remains at the fore even as Thomas dives into the logics of "Image" and "Son."[79] At the same time, however, ch. 11 is preceded and prepared for by nine chapters in which "the names of 'fatherhood and 'sonship' in the divinity" clearly figure foremost.[80] Indeed, the whole of book IV, ch. 11 is crafted in response to those who would "attack divine *generation*," and the chapter itself is titled, "How *generation* in God, and how what is said of the *Son* of God in Scripture, is to be understood."[81] There is a way in which "Word" comes first and frames the discussion as a whole. Yet there is also a way in which "Son" comes first and frames the discussion as a whole.[82]

---

[78] *ST* I q. 34, a. 2, ad 3. See also q. 42, a. 2, ad 1; and *in Ioan.*, #42: "we give *the Son* various names to express his perfection."

[79] The language of "intention understood" first appears in *SCG* IV 11§5.

[80] See chs. 2–9; the quote is from IV 2§2.

[81] IV 10§15; IV 11, title. For background on the titles of *SCG* IV, see volume XV of the Leonine Edition, xxvi-xxxviii.

[82] One might argue that, if Thomas sometimes begins with "Son" (as is *SCG* IV, chs. 2–9 and the opening of *ST* I q. 27, a. 1), then it is because He begins with Scripture. Yet one might object that once this Scriptural preamble is out of the way, he shifts to the language of "Word" as he gets down to the real business of systematic theology. We have already seen enough to challenge any facile correlation of "Son" to Scripture and "Word" to something else (systematics, philosophy, etc.): recall especially the section "Whence the Word?" in chapter one, and see Emery, *TA*, 271–319. For now, we can make a more basic point: Thomas is insistent that he only uses the language of "Word" at all because this language is given to us by Scripture (see Levering, *Scripture and Metaphysics*, 144–64). If he begins with Scripture, therefore, he might just as easily begin with "Word" as with "Son," and the fact that "Son" often precedes "Word" in his theology seems to be a function of something deeper than this objection would suggest.

All that said, I am by no means arguing that the familial language of "Son" is more important than the psychological language of "Word." Again, when all is said and done, "Word" is the most fitting name for the second Person.[83] My only point is that if "Word" enjoys a priority and a centrality, then it is not a unilateral priority or an exclusive centrality. Instead, it is a reciprocal—though ordered—priority, and it is a shared centrality. "Word" and "Son" are each central; "Word" and "Son" are each prior to the other; "Word" and Son" each need to be read in light of the other—even as "Word" is ultimately the most fitting name.

Thus, even insofar as these familial and psychological registers remain rationally distinct, there is no conflict between them. Instead, each allows the other to stand center stage. The deeper point, however, is that these registers, again insofar as they are rationally distinct, are inseparable. The logic of Thomas's psychological terms demands that they be familial, and the logic of his familial terms demand that they be psychological: there can be no conception of a divine Word that is not the total giving of nature between a Father and Son, and there can be no total giving of nature that is not the conception of a Word. The psychological is already familial and the familial is already psychological. Things are a good deal more complicated regarding contemporary talk of the Trinity in terms of marriage.[84] Yet, at least so far as fatherhood and sonship are concerned, to propose a conflict between the psychological and the familial in Aquinas—or to claim that his Trinity is psychological instead of familial—would be to misunderstand both his familial language and his psychological analogy.

Bonum Diffusivum Sui per Modum Intellectus et Voluntatis

If Thomas's psychological Trinity is often contrasted to a familial Trinity, then it is contrasted just as often to a Trinity centered on

---

[83] *ST* I q. 42, a. 2, ad 1 is enough to establish this point.

[84] Though, again, see my "The Family as an Image of the Trinity in Aquinas," 328–29.

the self-communication of goodness.[85] Jeremy Daniel Wilkins offers a particularly subtle version of this reading. He admits that talk of goodness as self-communicative is present in Thomas's early thought. Yet, according to Wilkins, Thomas's Trinity has less and less room for the self-communication of goodness as it becomes more and more psychological. Indeed, according to Wilkins, Thomas's embrace of the psychological in the *Summa* brings about "the total elimination of the self-diffusive good from the conception of the divine processions."[86]

We have already seen that Thomas's psychological categories are themselves a matter of total self-communication. And it seems plain enough that the divine nature, which is communicated in the processions of Word and Love, is supremely good. Thomas's psychological categories, therefore, demand that the supremely good divine nature be supremely communicated from divine Person to divine Person. This point might already be enough to push back on any facile opposition between the self-communication of goodness and Thomas's psychological categories. Yet it leaves certain questions open. For, if we were to

---

[85] See, for example, Rik van Nieuwenhove, "In the Image of God: The Trinitarian Anthropology of St Bonaventure, St Thomas Aquinas, and the blessed Jan Van Ruusbroec," *Irish Theological Quarterly* 66, no. 2 (2001): 111–13.

[86] "Emanatio Intellibilis," 261. Wilkins draws on Paul Vanier, who had drawn the same conclusion in *Théologie Trinitaire*. We will see in chapter six that M. T.-L. Penido proposes a similar historical development regarding mutual love in God. Remaining with self-communicative goodness, Wilkins notes (truly enough) that Thomas's treatment of generation in the earlier I *Sent.*, d. 4, q. 1, a. 1 and *De Pot.*, q. 2, a. 1 center around the self-communication of goodness, whereas the later *ST* I q. 27, a. 2 makes no mention of it. He concludes, however, that Thomas's thought evolves from a self-communicative-goodness approach in the first two texts to a merely psychological approach in the *ST*. He seems on solid enough ground regarding the *Sentences* commentary. Yet, regarding the *De Pot.*—which comes before the *ST*, but after Thomas had discovered his mature theology of the Word and after he had embraced a psychological Trinity in the *SCG*—things are more complicated. For there are also a number of texts *before* the *De Pot.* where, as in the *ST*, Thomas's treatment of divine generation makes no mention of goodness as self-diffusive and instead centers entirely on the immanent procession of the Word (see *Comp. Theo.* I, chs. 37–44; *de rationibus fidei*, ch. 3; and, of course, *SCG* IV, ch. 11). The shift from *De Pot.*, q. 2, a. 1 to *ST* I q. 27, a. 2, therefore—at least so far as the role of self-communicative goodness in the divine processions is concerned—might be a matter of something more complicated than mere linear historical development, and the prominence of self-communicative goodness in *De Pot.*, q. 2, a. 1 might be a function of something deeper than the relative immaturity of the text. In what follows, I will draw out passages from the *ST* that further complicate Wilkins's thesis.

stop there, we could say both that the divine nature is supremely good and that it is totally communicated; yet we could not say that it is totally communicated *because* it is supremely good. The meaning of goodness as self-diffusive would not in any way account for this communication. Instead, a nature that happened to be supremely good would happen to be communicated by way of intellect and will.

We will ask here whether we can say more. For it is certainly true that the self-communication of goodness looms larger in the thought of, say, a Bonaventure than it does in Thomas's mature Trinitarian theology. Just so, it is undeniable that the place of self-communicative goodness in Thomas's Trinity changes—and that it becomes less prominent—over time. This shift, moreover, is obviously bound up with Thomas's embrace of a psychological Trinity. We saw in chapter one that, in his *Sentences* commentary, the conception of a Word figures only marginally in his Trinity. We can note now that, in this same commentary, the self-communication of goodness sometimes takes center stage.[87] In Thomas's mature thought, in contrast, his psychological language moves front and center, and self-communicative goodness becomes less obviously prominent. It might seem reasonable, therefore, to conclude that Thomas's psychological approach crowds out the self-communication of divine goodness. Such a conclusion, however, would be overhasty. To see as much, we will show first that, within his mature Trinitarian theology, Thomas affirms—albeit indirectly—that the whole of the divine nature, because it is supremely good, is communicated from divine Person to divine Person. After showing as much, we will see that Thomas's psychological categories do not replace the self-communication of goodness. Instead, they preserve, and they assume up into themselves, the self-communication of goodness.

Bonum Diffusivum Sui

The first point to note is that Thomas, all the way through the end of his career, holds that goodness, by definition, is self-communicative.

---

[87] See Wilkins, "Emanatio Intelligibilis," 194–97.

He puts the matter in the strongest of terms in the *Tertia Pars*: "it belongs to the *ratio* of goodness that it communicate itself to others."[88]

So far as Thomas's mature Trinitarian theology goes, however, the self-communication of goodness is usually invoked in objections.[89] Thomas's response to these objections, however is sometimes instructive.[90] We will focus on an objection that runs all through Thomas's Trinitarian theology: it appears once in the *Sentences*, once in the *Summa*, and three times in between.[91] This objection always follows the same pattern: as Thomas puts it in the *Summa*, "it is from the infinite goodness of the Father that He communicates Himself infinitely in the production of a divine Person. But also in the Holy Spirit there is infinite goodness. Therefore the Holy Spirit produces a divine Person; and that Person another; and so to infinity."[92] Thomas here puts his finger on a problem with which any *bonum-diffusivum-sui*-centered Trinitarian theology must contend: if the Holy Spirit is infinitely good, why does He not communicate Himself infinitely to a fourth divine Person?

Thomas almost always responds in the same way.[93] In the *Summa*, this response runs as follows:

> This argument *would prove* if the Holy Spirit possessed another goodness apart from the goodness of the Father; for then, if the Father produces a divine Person *by His*

---

[88] *ST* III q. 1, a. 1. For more texts to this effect, see Clarke, *Person and Being*, 6–13.

[89] One important exception is *De Pot.*, q. 9, a. 9, s.c. 3 (second series), which Thomas accepts in the final words of the article (*"Alias rationes concedimus"*).

[90] In the most famous such response, Thomas clarifies that the self-communication of goodness cannot provide natural reason with a proof of the Trinity (see *ST* I q. 32, a. 1, ad 2). None of the points we will draw from other passages are incompatible with this point (though, as we will see at the end of this chapter, there may be a certain tension at work here).

[91] See I *Sent.*, d. 10, q. 1, a. 5, arg. 3; *SCG* IV 26§5; *De Pot.*, q. 9, a. 9, arg. 14, and arg. 17; and *ST* I q. 30, a. 2, arg. 4.

[92] *ST* I q. 30, a. 2, arg. 4.

[93] Thomas offers versions of the response we will study here in I *Sent.*, d. 10, q. 1, a. 5, ad 3; *SCG* IV 26§5; *De Pot.*, q. 9, a. 9, ad 17; and *ST* I q. 30, a. 2, ad 4. The only time he responds to this same objection in any other way is in *De Pot.*, q. 9, a. 9, ad 14. The fact that this last passage comes so shortly before *De Pot.*, q. 9, a. 9, ad 17, however, makes clear that there is no ultimate conflict between this text and the ones on which we will focus here.

goodness, the Holy Spirit also would do so. But the Father and the Holy Spirit have one and the same goodness. Nor is there any distinction between Them except by the personal relations. Therefore goodness belongs to the Holy Spirit as though had from another, and it belongs to the Father as *the principle of its communication to another*.[94]

This response is very rich, and it brings to the fore a point we mentioned in chapter two that will be important for us in chapters five and six: the one divine goodness, though it is identically "one and the same" in all three Persons, exists in each Person in a distinct way. As Thomas puts it here, it exists in the Holy Spirit "as though had from another," and it exists in the Father "as the principle of its communication to another."

For now, however, we can focus on just one point: in his response, Thomas accepts the objector's premise that because the Father is infinitely good, He communicates the whole of His goodness to another divine Person. Indeed, if the Father's goodness were not the reason for this communication, then Thomas could have simply told us so: he could have clarified that while the Father communicates Himself infinitely, He does not do so because He is infinitely good. Doing so would have opened up a far simpler and easier route to the conclusion that the Holy Spirit's infinite goodness does not require that He produce a fourth divine Person. Thomas, however, does not make this move. Instead, he begins by conceding that the Holy Spirit's goodness *would* require Him to produce a fourth Person "if the Holy Spirit possessed another goodness apart from the goodness of the Father." Supreme goodness, it seems, *is* supremely self-communicative, and an additional instance of supreme goodness *would* need to be communicated to a fourth divine Person. The Holy Spirit's goodness, in other words, *is* supremely communicated: it is communicated from the Father to the Holy Spirit, and this communication is enough to satisfy the self-communicative requirements of goodness. If, however, the Holy Spirit had a separate goodness that had *not* already been wholly communicated to Him, then He *would* need to communicate it to a fourth divine Person—for supreme goodness is supremely self-communicative. Again, "This

---

[94] *ST* I q. 30, a. 2, ad 4.

argument *would* prove if the Holy Spirit possessed another goodness apart from the goodness of the Father."

In any event, after this opening remark, Thomas spends the whole of his response wrestling with a double claim: first, the Father's goodness is the reason He communicates His nature to the Holy Spirit; second, the Holy Spirit does not produce a fourth divine Person, even though He is just as good. Yet Thomas only needs to wrestle with this tension because *the Father's goodness is the reason He communicates His nature to the Holy Spirit*. Indeed, as he works through this tension, Thomas ends up affirming, at least indirectly, that "the Father produces a divine Person *by His goodness*." He reiterates this point more directly as he continues: he affirms that the divine goodness "belongs to the Father as *the principle of its communication* to another divine Person." It is not merely that the divine nature, which happens to be infinitely good, happens to be communicated from divine Person to divine Person. Instead, the Father communicates His nature "by His goodness," and this goodness is the reason for—or the "principle of"—its own infinite communication. Because goodness is self-communicative, the whole of the supremely good divine nature is communicated from divine Person to divine Person.

Towards the end of the *De Potentia*, Thomas raises a similar objection: "it belongs to perfection in creatures to communicate nature. ...Therefore to communicate the divine nature belongs to perfection in God, and consequently it must be attributed to the Holy Spirit. Therefore a Person proceeds from the Holy Spirit."[95] Here, Thomas speaks of perfection instead of goodness. Yet goodness and perfection are closely related, and the self-diffusiveness of goodness is therefore closely related to the self-diffusiveness of perfection.[96] Thomas's response here echoes the one we just studied: "Just as the *communication* of the divine nature from the Father to the Son *belongs to perfection*, so too to perfectly receive the communicated nature belongs to perfection in the Holy Spirit."[97]

---

[95] *De Pot.*, q. 9, a. 9, arg. 17. According to Wilkins, Thomas's Trinitarian theology is already fully mature and exclusively psychological by q. 9 of the *De Pot*. (see "Emanatio Intelligibilis," 200n102 and 205).

[96] For the link between perfection and goodness, see *ST* I q. 5, a. 1.

[97] *De Pot.*, q. 9, a. 9, ad 17.

Again, this response is very rich, and it trades on Thomas's teaching that the Father is perfect as communicating His nature, whereas the Holy Spirit is perfect as receiving that nature. Yet, in laying out this dynamic, Thomas implicitly accepts the objector's premise that "to communicate the divine nature belongs to perfection in God." Indeed, he explicitly affirms in his response that the Father's communication of His nature "belongs to" the supreme divine perfection. God's absolute perfection does not just happen to be communicated; it is communicated *because* it is absolutely perfect. This self-communication "belongs to perfection."[98]

Per Modum Intellectus et Voluntatis

Yet one could raise an objection. For it may be that, even in the *Summa*, Thomas affirms that the divine goodness, as it exists in the Father, is the "principle" of its own communication. Yet he makes this point only indirectly, and he does so only in response to a fairly arcane objection. When he sets about laying down the main lines of his Trinitarian theology, he does so according to his psychological categories, and he makes no use at all of the communication of goodness. These psychological terms might not, therefore, demand Wilkins's "total elimination of the self-diffusive good from the conception of the divine processions."[99] Yet they do seem to leave the self-diffusive good marginalized and on the cusp of elimination.

Again, it is true that the self-communication of goodness surfaces only rarely in Thomas's mature Trinitarian thought. At the same time, however, this self-communicative goodness is not merely wedged into the cracks left open by Thomas's psychological categories. Instead, certain passages suggest that the self-communication of goodness is intrinsic to, and is assumed up into, those psychological categories. We already saw as much earlier in this chapter: in *De Potentia*, q. 2, a. 1, Thomas begins with the total self-communication of pure actuality; he explains that this total self-communication takes the form of the conception of a divine Word; and he concludes that this conception,

---

98 In a move that goes beyond any neo-Platonic association of goodness with self-communication, Thomas also affirms that the Holy Spirit's reception of the divine nature belongs equally to perfection—a point that might itself carry interpersonal implications.

99 "Emanatio Intellibilis" 261.

in turn, is the communication of nature to a subsistent Son. Total self-communication is psychological procession, and psychological procession is total self-communication.[100]

A similar point comes out in the *Summa*, right where Thomas might appear to be sidelining the self-communication of goodness in favor of a psychological approach. This passage comes in the last article of the *Summa*'s first Trinitarian question. Thomas had just shown that there is one procession in God by way of intellect and another by way of will, and he is asking whether there are any additional processions in God. He raises the objection that "goodness seems to be the greatest principle of procession, since goodness is diffusive of itself. Therefore there must be a procession of goodness in God."[101] His response, however, seems to deny that the self-communication of goodness can account for—or be so much as involved in—the processions of the divine Persons. He responds that "goodness belongs to the essence and not to the operation, unless considered as the object of the will. Thus, because the divine processions must be denominated from certain actions, no other processions can be understood in God according to goodness and the like attributes except those of the Word and of Love, insofar as God understands and loves His own essence, truth, and goodness."[102] Earlier in the same question, Thomas had explained that "all procession is according to some sort of action."[103] Because goodness is not an operation, goodness seems unable to account for the processions of the divine Persons.

To get a handle on Thomas's response, however, we should first recall that, in this article, he is asking whether there is any divine procession in addition to the processions by way of intellect and will that he had already explored. Accordingly, the objector is not merely

---

100 Again, actuality and goodness are closely related (see *ST* I q. 5, a. 1). Wilkins acknowledges that, in this passage, Thomas integrates the psychological into self-communicative goodness (see "Emanatio Intellibilis," 200). Yet he argues that this integration gives way to a monopoly of the psychological by the end of the *De Pot.* and into the *ST*. Without denying certain respects in which Thomas's thought develops across these texts, I hope to show now that some version of this integration remains alive and well through the *ST* (and, as we will see presently, through the end of the *De Pot.* as well).

101 *ST* I q. 27, a. 5, arg. 2.

102 *ST* I q. 27, a. 5, ad 2.

103 *ST* I q. 27, a. 1.

alleging that the self-communication of goodness might account for the divine processions. Nor is he arguing merely that the divine nature communicates itself infinitely because it is infinitely good. Instead, he is arguing that there is a divine procession *in addition* to the processions by way of intellect and will: he is proposing a *third* divine procession of a *fourth* divine Person Who would proceed *not* by way of intellect or will *but* by way of goodness.

Thomas, of course, responds by denying that there is any procession in God in addition to those of Word and Love. Yet he does not thereby deny that there is procession in God "according to goodness." Far from it: he actually affirms—though, again, indirectly—that there *is* a procession in God according to goodness. He writes that there is no procession "*according to goodness* and the like attributes *except* those of Word and Love." There is no procession according to goodness *in addition to* the processions of Word and Love. Yet nor are there processions of Word and Love *instead of* procession according to goodness. Indeed, to say that there is no procession "according to goodness . . . except those of Word and Love" is to affirm that the processions of Word and Love are *themselves* processions "according to goodness." Goodness, in other words, "belongs to the essence and not to the operation, unless considered as the object of the will." Yet, insofar as goodness *is* the object of the will, goodness *does* belong to operation—and therefore there *is* procession in God according to goodness. Thomas reiterates this point in the closing words: he writes that the processions of Word and Love are processions "according to goodness" insofar as in these processions, "God understands and loves His own essence, truth, and goodness." These immanent processions are according to goodness only because, in them, goodness is understood and loved. Yet, because goodness is understood and loved in them, they really are processions "*according to goodness.*"[104]

---

[104] Vanier acknowledges the force of this passage, and he even writes that, in the *ST*, the self-communication of goodness is "included in the processions of intellect and will." Yet he does so in the course of arguing that, in the *ST*, Thomas "rejects the analogy of the communication of being, precisely because it is not an immanent procession" (*Théologie Trinitaire*, 64. See also Wilkins, "Emanatio Intelligibilis, 207–8). For Vanier, immanent procession cannot be a communication of being from hypostasis to hypostasis—which means that this passage cannot ultimately have room for the self-communication of

There is, of course, no talk of goodness as self-communicative here. Yet Thomas's conclusion picks up on a commitment that runs through the whole of his corpus: as he puts it early in the *Summa*, "Goodness is said to be self-diffusive in the sense that an end is said to move."[105] There would obviously be a great deal to say about goodness, self-communication, and final causality in Thomas.[106] For our purposes, we can make just one point: everything communicates its goodness insofar as it is inclined to its goodness as an end.[107] An intellectual nature, however, is inclined towards its end *insofar as it understands and loves it*.[108] An intelligent agent understands and loves his goodness, and, because he loves his goodness, he wants there to be more of it once he himself fully possesses it.[109] An intelligent agent, that is, communicates his goodness only insofar as he understands and loves his goodness. To say, therefore, that the processions of Word and Love are processions "according to goodness . . . insofar as God understands and loves His own essence, truth, and goodness," is not to deny that they are processions of goodness insofar as goodness is self-communicative. Instead, it is to specify the way in which they *are* processions of self-communicative goodness: it is to recall that the good of an intellectual nature is only ever self-communicative insofar as it is understood and loved.[110]

---

goodness. We have argued, however, that immanent procession *must* be a communication of being from hypostasis to hypostasis.

105 *ST* I q. 5, a. 4, ad 2.

106 For some helpful background information, see Bernhard-Thomas Blankenhorn, "The Good as Self-Diffusive in Thomas Aquinas," *Angelicum* 79 (2002): 803–37.

107 See *ST* I q. 19, a. 2.

108 See *ST* I-II q. 26, a. 1.

109 See *in div. nom.*, c. 4, l. 5: "it belongs to a perfect agent to act through the love of that which it possesses. And, because of this, [Dionysius] adds that beauty, which is God, is the effective and moving and containing cause, 'by a love of its own beauty.' For, because He has His own beauty, He wants to multiply it, so far as possible, by communicating its likeness." God loves His goodness (here, His beauty). And, because He is perfect, He perfectly possesses all the goodness that could possibly be possessed. His love, then, motivates Him not to seek more goodness for Himself, but to share His goodness with others.

110 Some have suggested that because Thomas's goodness is self-communicative as a final cause, it is not *really* self-communicative. Blackenhorn responds to this argument in "The Good as Self-Diffusive."

The language of goodness as self-communicative, then, may not be explicitly present in Thomas's response. It had, however, been explicit in the objection to which Thomas is responding—"goodness seems to be the greatest principle of procession, since goodness is diffusive of itself"—and Thomas has this objection in mind throughout his response.[111] It is perhaps no surprise, therefore, that we can find evidence of self-communicative goodness if we dig a bit into the claims Thomas *does* explicitly register in his response.[112]

Again, none of this is to deny that Thomas's Trinitarian theology undergoes massive transformations from his *Sentences* commentary to his mature thought. We also need not ignore the fact that the self-communication of goodness becomes less obviously prominent once Thomas's mature doctrine of the Word emerges in the *SCG*. Instead, we need only point out that Thomas does not simply banish the self-communication of goodness from his mature thought. He brings it to the surface of his mature thought only rarely. Yet, in some of these surfacings, he suggests that his psychological approach does not crowd out or replace the self-communication of goodness. Instead, his psychological approach integrates the self-communication of goodness. For Thomas, the supreme divine goodness, as supremely good, communicates the whole of itself insofar as it is known and loved in the processions of Word and Love.[113]

---

111 *ST* I q. 27, a. 5, arg. 2.

112 We find perhaps the deepest—but also the most complicated—integration of self-communicative goodness and the psychological analogy in *De Pot.*, q. 9, a. 5, ad 23, and ad 24 (which comes in the part of the *De Potentia* that Wilkins identifies as fully mature, and so as fully psychological). These passages are very complicated, and talk of self-communication never surfaces explicitly in them. Even more, they unfold in dialogue not with the principle that goodness is self-diffusive, but with the claim that there can be no joy in goodness unless it is shared. We therefore cannot treat these passages here. Yet we can at least note that, in them, Thomas affirms that the Father would have no joy in His own goodness—and even that "there would be no absolute perfection in God"—if the Father did not share His goodness with the Son. For more on these texts, see my "Does Goodness Require Another? On an Unexplored Corner of Aquinas's Trinitarian Theology," *Communio: International Catholic Review* 47, no. 2 (2020): 368–98.

113 There may be another route to the same conclusion. For it is clear enough that supreme goodness, by its own logic, could not be perfectly good unless it were simple, purely actual, and intelligent (see Long, *The Perfectly Simple Triune God*, 21). If, however, these readings hold any water, then a simple and intelligent nature could not be simple

Moreover, Thomas's psychological approach may help to refine, and to clarify the character of, supremely self-communicative goodness. For this psychological language makes especially clear that when supreme goodness is supremely communicated, it is not diffused blindly or mechanically. It is not the sun giving off light. Instead, it is a fully inter*personal* giving. When it is given, the understanding and will of the giver are front and center. Indeed, they are front and center in a way that outstrips anything we might find among created persons. As a created person, my understanding and will can—and should—be present and engaged in my self-giving. When the Father gives Himself, however, His understanding and will are not merely involved in His giving. Instead, they are the acts *by way of which* He gives Himself. Understanding and will are, as it were, the avenue and atmosphere of His self-giving. The total self-communication of infinite goodness—which has goodness as its "principle," which is communicated "according to goodness," and which "belongs to perfection"—is not only shot through with intellect and will; it is *per modum intellectus and voluntate*.[114]

CONCLUSION

Again, I hope to have opened up space for Thomas's psychological Trinity to dialogue both with familial Trinities and with *bonum-diffusivum-sui* Trinities. Yet my main goal has been more focused: it has been to show that Thomas's psychological Trinity is already a Trinity of total interpersonal self-giving. If such total self-giving can be cast in terms of familial relationships or in terms of self-communicative goodness, then so much the better. But we ultimately need to establish only one thing: that this self-giving is real, that it is total, and that it is interpersonal. We have already seen that this self-giving is *inter*personal insofar as the giver and receiver subsist distinctly in a rational nature,

---

and intelligent—and therefore could not be supremely good—apart from the procession of a personal Word, a procession that, as we have seen at length, necessarily entails the communication of the divine nature. This route is a bit roundabout. Yet it might lead to the conclusion that the very logic of supreme goodness demands that it could not be supremely good unless it were totally communicated from divine Person to divine Person.

114 *ST* I q. 30, a. 2, ad 4; *ST* I q. 27, a. 5, ad 2; and *De Pot.*, q. 9, a. 9, ad 17.

and insofar as the receiver is a distinct agent of His own receptivity. And we hinted at the very end that it is inter*personal* insofar as it is entirely a matter of understanding and of will. We will now deepen this point by attending more closely to understanding and will.

5

SELF-KNOWLEDGE AS INTERPERSONAL KNOWLEDGE AS INTERPERSONAL SELF-GIVING

As we saw in the introduction, some contemporary figures define personhood in terms of self-giving.[1] On such a reading, our previous chapter would go a long way towards establishing that Thomas's Trinity is an inter*personal* Trinity. For we saw that the divine Speaker gives the whole of Himself to His Word, and we suggested this Word, with His Speaker, gives the whole of Himself to Their Love. Elsewhere in his thought, Thomas may offer further openings towards such a self-giving-centered account of personhood.[2] As we already mentioned, however, Thomas defines personhood not first in terms of self-giving, but in terms of subsistence in a rational nature.[3] To subsist in a rational nature, however, is—among other things—to be able to understand and to will. For Thomas, then, personhood is bound up very tightly with intellect and will. In this chapter and the next, I will

---

[1] See Norris Clarke, "Person, Being, and St. Thomas," 610.

[2] See Clarke, "Person, Being, and St. Thomas," 609–11; Oster, "Becoming a Person and the Trinity"; and Schindler, "The Crisis of Marriage," 354 and 358.

[3] See Emery, "On the Dignity of Being a Substance"; and *TTTA*, 104–11.

ask whether Thomas's psychological analogy is inter*personal* insofar as it has space for three distinct Persons Who each understand and will.

In this chapter, we will focus on understanding. We will see, first, that all three of Thomas's divine Persons understand in the one divine act of understanding. Thomas makes this point explicitly, and it is already enough to show that his psychological Trinity is interpersonal. Yet we will be able to go deeper by thinking through a number of principles that appear throughout Thomas's Trinitarian theology. For these principles will allow us to see that divine knowledge is interpersonal not only insofar as a Speaker, His Word, and Their Love all understand in it; it is interpersonal also insofar as this Speaker, Word, and Love all understand *each other* in it.

To say that the divine Persons know each other, however, is not to deny that They know Themselves. Instead, each knows the others and knows Himself. Indeed, it is here that we will see our deepest marriage yet of the interpersonal and the intrapersonal. For, in Thomas's psychological Trinity, each Person does not merely know Himself *and* know another Person. Instead, each knows Himself *in* knowing another, and each knows another *in* knowing Himself.[4]

This claim may not sound so novel. Indeed, long-established readings of Thomas have room for a certain synthesis of self-knowledge and interpersonal knowledge in God.[5] Each divine Person, after all, must understand the divine essence.[6] And, because each Person is identical to this essence, each knows Himself in knowing His essence. Yet, because both of the other divine Persons are also identical to the same essence, each Person must know the others in knowing His own essence. No divine Person, then, can know Himself or His own essence without knowing the other Persons.

---

[4] In this chapter, the Holy Spirit will be pushed even further to the sidelines than He had been in any of our previous chapters. This point may not be so surprising, for we will speak here of intellect, and it is the Son Who proceeds by way of intellect. I will, however, speak briefly of the Holy Spirit at the very end of this chapter, and we will focus on Him at great length in our next chapter.

[5] Thomas lays out the following dynamic in *in Ioan.*, #1065 and *in I Cor.*, #107.

[6] See *ST* I q. 14, a. 2.

This point is already quite rich. Yet it is also limited. First of all, it might ensure that interpersonal knowledge is present in God. It might even suggest that interpersonal knowledge is inextricable from self-knowledge. Yet it also makes interpersonal knowledge a function of self-knowledge. Each Person would most basically know His own essence. And, as a logically subsequent consequence of this primordial self-knowledge, each would know the others. Self-knowledge would be fundamental; interpersonal knowledge would be derivative.[7]

Perhaps more importantly, each Person would know the others only insofar as They are identical to His own essence—not insofar as They are distinct Persons. In knowing Himself, the Father would know the Son only insofar as the Son is God. He would not know the Son insofar as the Son is a Son: He would not know the Son insofar as the Son subsists distinctly from Himself. Indeed, when the Father knew the Son, all He would see in the Son is *His own* essence—the essence that is identical to the Son but that is also identical to the Father. To put the matter bluntly, when He saw another Person, all He would really see is more of Himself. Interpersonal knowledge, then, would not merely be derivative. It might even be illusory: it might ultimately collapse back down into self-knowledge.[8]

Such a scheme, then, can take us only so far towards a synthesis of self-knowledge and interpersonal knowledge in God. Happily, however, Thomas offers resources for something deeper. And he offers them in what might seem to us the unlikeliest of places: the details of his psychological analogy for the Trinity.

To see as much, we will spend this chapter diving more deeply into Thomas's theology of the Word. To begin, we will explore the place of a

---

[7] The same limit would hold in another possible route towards integrating self-knowledge and interpersonal knowledge. In knowing Himself, the Father cannot but know Himself *as Father* (see *De Ver.*, q. 2, a. 3, ad 7). And, because "whoever knows one relative term knows the other" (I *Sent.*, d. 1, q. 2, a. 2), the Father must know the Son *as Son* in knowing Himself as Father. Just so, the Son must know the Father as Father in knowing Himself as Son. Again, these principles are very rich. Yet, if we were to content ourselves with them, each Person's knowledge of the others would be built on a more basic self-knowledge.

[8] M. T.-L. Penido, who sets himself against any talk of interpersonal reciprocity in God, invokes just this point in arguing that mutual love in God is ultimately reducible to self-love: see "Gloses sur la procession," 59. We will return to Penido in our next chapter.

word in the act of understanding more broadly. In our first section, we will see that the conception of a word is not merely a consequence of a logically prior act of understanding. Instead, the two are equally and reciprocally foundational: in Thomas's mature thought, intellect both conceives a word by understanding and understands by conceiving a word. Next, we will explore in more detail the specific role a word plays in understanding: we will see that a word is itself understood in the act of understanding, and we will see that a word is that in which intellect understands whatever it understands. Having laid this foundation, we will turn to God. First, we will see that these features of a word hold analogously in the divine Word. Then, in light of these features of a word, we will see that the Father can only know Himself in knowing His Word, and that He cannot know His Word without thereby knowing Himself. From there, we will see that the Word, because He is a Word, cannot know Himself without thereby knowing the Father, and that He can only know the Father in knowing Himself. We will then take a step back and see that when each Person knows the other, He knows that other as other. Finally, we will see that self-knowledge and interpersonal knowledge are inextricable not only from each other, but also from total interpersonal self-giving. We will see that the one perfect act of divine understanding is a marriage of self-giving, of self-knowledge, and of reciprocal interpersonal knowledge; we will see that none of these elements can exist without the others and that none can be reduced to the others; and we will see that each is just as logically basic as the others.[9]

---

9 In what follows, I will speak at length of the role of a word in understanding, and I will argue that, for Thomas, the structure of understanding demands that no one—not even, analogously, the divine Persons—ever understands anything except in his word of that thing. This is not, however, to claim that, because of the structure of understanding, no one *could* ever understand anything except in his word of that thing. This latter claim might suggest that reason could discover the Trinity based on the structure of understanding. We mentioned readers of Thomas who have hazarded this claim in note 9 in chapter three. For our current purposes, however, we can leave open the possibility that reason might be unable to discover that there is a Word in God, and we can make a more modest claim: given that, with Revelation, we see that a Word exists in God (and given the nature of the Word, and given that this Word is spoken in the Father's act of self-understanding), it follows that the Word is that in which the Father understands. None of our conclusions here, therefore, will touch directly on—or depend on the answer to—these difficult questions of faith and reason.

All that said, I should admit that while Thomas points clearly towards some of the conclusions we will draw—especially concerning the role of the Word in the Father's self-knowledge—we will draw other conclusions—especially regarding the role of the Father in the Word's self-knowledge—that he never makes explicit. Yet we will see that even these latter conclusions are suggested in any number of texts from Thomas's Trinitarian theology, and we will argue that they are implied—and even demanded—by any number of principles fundamental to Thomas's psychological analogy. We may, therefore, need to develop Thomas in order to reach some of our conclusions. Indeed, we may end up, at most, finding resources in Thomas for conclusions he does not draw himself. Yet those resources are real, and my claim is that, in drawing these conclusions, I am merely digging up treasures that are already contained—even if they are sometimes buried fairly deep—in Thomas's thought itself.[10]

---

[10] Indeed, I am not the first to point towards some of the conclusions we will draw here. Rowan Williams argues that, for Thomas, divine understanding entails intra-divine self-giving: see "What does Love Know? St. Thomas on the Trinity," *New Blackfriars*, 82 (2001): 260–72. Williams's argument, however, is based only loosely on Thomas's actual texts, terms, and specific commitments. Even more noteworthy are Cirilo Folch Gomes ("La Réciprocité psychologique") and François Bourassa ("Sur la Propriéte de l'Espirit, Questions Disputées," pts. 1 and 2, *Science et Esprit* 28 [1976]: 243–64; 29 [1977], 23–43; and "Le Saint-Espirit, 'Communion du Père et du Fils,' " pts. 1 and 2, *Science et Esprit* 29 [1977]: 251–81; 30 [1978]: 5–37). Gomes and Bourassa have done a remarkable job identifying a robust sense of interpersonal knowing and loving at the center of Thomas's Trinitarian thought, and they have done so in dialogue with his psychological language. Bourassa even briefly suggests that the role of a word in knowledge demands that divine self-knowledge be interpersonal knowledge: see "Personne et conscience," 706–7. That said, Bourassa and Gomes leave most of the specific points we will discuss here either untouched or undeveloped. Bourassa can also be a bit imprecise (he refers to the Son as the "thought" of the Father: see, for example, "Personne et conscience," 689), and he sometimes juxtaposes—and he even sometimes opposes—the interpersonal to the psychological (see note 14 in chapter six).

José Luis González Alió, finally, has gone further than anyone else in showing that because God's knowledge is "*in verbo*," it must be interpersonal: establishing this point is the main burden of "La santísima Trinidad, comunión de personas," *Scripta Theologica* 18, no. 1 (1986): 11–115; laying the foundation for it is the aim of "El entender como posesión: La función gnoselógica del verbo mental," pts. 1 and 2, *Sapientia* 43 (1988): 243–68; 332–68; see especially 245. This point also appears more briefly in "La visión beatífica como realidad trinitaria," *Scripta Theologica* 19, no. 3 (1987): 597–631. That said, while González Alió finds in Thomas's doctrine of the Word the "metaphysical foundation" for interpersonal knowledge in God (see "Santísima Trinidad," 66–67 and 113; "entender como posesión," 368), he also argues that Thomas himself ultimately shuts

IN THE BEGINNING WAS THE WORD

We saw in chapter one that Thomas's theology of the Word develops over his career. In his *Sentences* commentary, a word is merely a cipher for the intelligible species or for the act of understanding. Beginning in the *SCG*, it is a really distinct element of intellect. We can note now that over the same period of time, the place of a word in the structure of understanding evolves as well. Early in Thomas's career, a word is present in the act of understanding, but not at its foundation. He writes it in his *Sentences* commentary that

> in the operations of intellect, there are certain degrees. For first, there is the simple intuition of intellect in knowing the intelligible thing, and this simple intuition never has the nature of a word. Second, there is the ordination of this knowledge towards manifestation: either manifestation to another, according to which someone is said to speak to another; or manifestation to oneself, according as it happens that someone even speaks to himself.[11]

As Thomas goes on to explain, it is only in this second moment that one can speak of a "word" in understanding: at this point in his career, the word comes after the act of understanding. Thomas puts the matter more concisely in the *De Veritate*: "conception itself is an effect of the act of understanding."[12] First we understand, and then we conceive a word as an effect of our understanding.

Some readers of Thomas have argued that we have here Thomas's definitive position on the place of a word in the act of understanding.[13]

---

down the possibility of interpersonal knowledge in God (see "Santísima Trinidad," 14, 42, 48–50, 63, 83, 85; he also contrasts Thomas and John Paul II on this score: see 50, 79, 84). González Alió, then, sees in great depth some of the steps along the argument we will lay out here. Yet he denies the main conclusions we will draw from them.

11 I *Sent.*, d. 27, q. 2, a. 1.

12 *De Ver.*, q. 4, a. 2.

13 Most important here is Lonergan. We will see that Lonergan has anticipated some of the points we will make in our next section. Yet we will differ from him here. To focus on our current point, Lonergan writes that words "proceed from acts of understanding"

And they are right that, through the end of his career, Thomas presents the word as arising from the act of understanding. In a set of mature texts, he writes that "the intellect, *by understanding*, conceives and forms the intention or definition understood, which is the inner word";[14] "that is properly called an inner word which the one understanding forms *by understanding*";[15] and "the Father *by understanding* . . . conceives the Word."[16] The act of understanding is more logically basic than the conception of a word: a speaker conceives a word by understanding.

Yet Thomas also complicates things. As he puts it in the *Comp. Theo.*, "God understands Himself *by conceiving* His intelligible Word."[17]

---

and "proceed from understanding": *The Collected Works of Bernard Lonergan*, vol. 2, *Verbum: Word and Idea in Aquinas*, ed. Fredrick E. Crowe and Robert M. Doran (Toronto: University of Toronto Press, 1997), 56–57. See also 50–51. Others who follow Lonergan take a similar tack: see Wilkins, "Emanatio Intellibilis," 161, 249, and 101n108. Wilkins makes the same point in "Method, Order, and Analogy," 580.

We will spend the rest of this section exploring texts from Thomas's mature thought where he suggests that the word is just as foundational as the act of understanding. In addition to these texts, however, there are deeper reasons to be skeptical of Lonergan's reading. We will see some of these reasons in our next section. For now, we can note that if it were simply true that words "proceed from understanding," then it would follow that the divine Word proceeds from the divine act of understanding. Yet the divine Word *is* the divine act of understanding, and nothing can proceed from itself. The Word, instead, proceeds from the divine *Speaker*. Thomas extends this point to all words when he writes, "That is properly called an inner word which *the one understanding* forms by understanding" (*in Ioan.*, #25). The word is not formed by the intellect, by its act of understanding, or by its knowledge; it is formed by the person who understands (see also *ST* I q. 93, a. 6: "the uncreated Trinity is distinguished by the procession of the Word from *the Speaker*." This point also appears in a. 8).

That said, Lonergan cites mature texts where Thomas says that a word proceeds from knowledge (see *ST* I q. 27, a. 1 and q. 34, a. 1, both of which we discussed briefly in note 49 in chapter one). Both of these texts might need to be qualified in light of the point we just made, in light of texts we will explore presently, and in light of points we will explore in our next section. At the end of the day, however, even if Lonergan's reading of Thomas turns out to be right, our main conclusions in this chapter will still largely hold. Yet these conclusions can only be cast in the strongest terms if we show here that the conception of a word is just as logically basic as the act of understanding.

14 *SCG* IV 11§13.

15 *In Ioan.*, #25.

16 *ST* q. 34, a. 1, ad 3. See also ad 2.

17 *Comp. Theo.* I, 43.

In Thomas's mature thought, God conceives a Word by understanding, yet God also understands by conceiving a Word.[18]

Indeed, Thomas affirms both sides of this claim in the same passage—which suggests that we have here something more interesting than a mere contradiction. And not just any passage: both sides of this claim appear back-to-back in the first text where Thomas articulates his mature account of a word. In *SCG* I, ch. 53, and so with an eye to drawing conclusions concerning the divine Word, Thomas writes that the intellect "by an act of understanding forms within itself a certain intention of the thing understood."[19] Yet he continues that "the intellect, by forming such an intention, understands the thing."[20] Intellect forms a word by understanding, and intellect understands by forming a word. The act of understanding and the formation of a word are reciprocally foundational: each precedes and grounds the other.

Thomas reiterates this point a few chapters later, when responding to an Arian argument that nothing that is generated can be eternal:

> the word conceived by our intellect does not proceed from potency to act except insofar as intellect proceeds from potency to act. Nevertheless, it also does not arise in our intellect except as it exists in act; rather, *as soon as* intellect exists in act, there is a word conceived therein. . . . Hence, clearly also, generation does not prevent the Son of God from being true God, nor from being Himself eternal. Rather, it is necessary that He be coeternal with God whose Word He is, for an intellect in act is never without its word.[21]

Intellect does not first exist in act by actually understanding a thing, and it does not subsequently conceive the word as the fruit of an

---

[18] Emery points towards this second half of our claim when he writes, "In human knowledge, the grasp of truth *presupposes* the conception of the word. . . . Knowing the truth as such depends therefore on the word (and not only on the so-called intellectual *species*), since it is in the word that the intellect grasps the reality as it is" (*TCHP*, 80). Emery might hesitate to apply these points to the divine Word. Yet he at least suggests that Lonergan's unilateral priority of understanding is open to being questioned.

[19] *SCG* I 53§3.

[20] I 53§4.

[21] *SCG* IV 14§3.

actuality that is already complete—or even just inchoate—before the conception of a word. Instead, an intellect without a word is an intellect in potency: "an intellect in act is never without its word." From the other direction, however, a word does not actually exist before intellect actually understands: the word does not come first as a sort of steppingstone towards understanding-in-act. Instead, a word is only conceived when intellect actually understands, and intellect only actually understands when it conceives a word: intellect actually understands and the word actually exists at the same time.

Indeed, if the conception of a word merely followed on the act of understanding, then Thomas's argument in this passage would fall apart. For he only introduces the conception of a word in order to argue that the Son is coeternal with the Father. Thomas could have secured this point by citing divine immutability: he could have admitted that, in us, the conception of a word is subsequent to the act of understanding, but he could have clarified that there can be no succession in God, and that the divine Word must therefore be coeternal with the Father. Yet Thomas cites not divine immutability, but the structure of understanding: he argues that, even in us, there is no unilateral succession between the conception of a word and the act of understanding. Instead, the two are simultaneous: each must arise "as soon as" the other arises, or neither will arise at all.

This simultaneity will prove pivotal in what follows. For our part, however, we will focus a bit more on the priority of the word, and we will run through a few more passages where Thomas points towards this priority. For, again, it is this half of our paradox that has been denied by some of Thomas's readers, and it is this half that will be most important for our conclusions later in this chapter. First, at the end of Thomas's career, and again in order to secure the eternity of the Son, he writes that "God did not first exist and then begin to generate a Word: for, since the generation of the Word is nothing other than an intelligible conception, it would follow that God would be understanding in potency before understanding in act, which is inadmissible."[22] An intellect does not first understand and then conceive a word. Instead, before it conceives a word, it does not *actually* understand at all. Thomas

---

22 *In Ioan.*, #41.

enters into more detail when he writes, "the action of understanding is not exercised without something being conceived in the mind of the one who understands, and this is called the word: since before a concept of some kind is fixed in the mind we are not said to understand, but to think about a thing in order to understand it."[23] Again, we do not first understand and then conceive a word; we only understand once we have conceived a word of the thing we understand.[24] In a different vein, Thomas writes that intellect "forms the word in order to understand the thing," and that "the intellect forms its concept of the thing in order that it might know the thing."[25] The word is not merely an effect of understanding. Instead, the word is conceived in order that understanding might come about.[26]

One more paradox can be drawn out of this final passage. Just two sentences after writing that "the intellect forms its concept of the thing in order that it might know the thing," Thomas continues that the word "differs from the act of the intellect, because it is considered as the term of the action, and as something constituted thereby."[27] A word exists "in order that" understanding might come about, which suggests that the word precedes understanding. Yet the word is "constituted" by understanding, which suggests that understanding precedes the word. The word exists in order to bring about that which constitutes it—which is precisely the paradox in which we are interested here.

This paradox, finally, reinforces an important point. For it is not merely that the word is conceived "as soon as" intellect understands.[28]

---

23 *De Pot.*, q. 9, a. 9.

24 There is, of course—at least in us—some mental activity before the conception of a word: we "think about a thing in order to understand it." Yet this "thinking about" is *not* understanding. More importantly, I am ultimately interested in God, in Whom there is no preliminary "thinking about." There is only conception and understanding, and Thomas is clear here that no such understanding exists without the conception of a word.

25 *Quodl.* V, q. 5, a. 2, ad 1; *De Pot.*, q. 8, a. 1.

26 This language of "in order to" might entail its own sort of reciprocal priority. Thomas writes that "the end is indeed first in the order of intention, but last in the order of execution" (*ST* I-II q. 25, a. 1). In one respect, an end follows on things ordered to it; in another, it precedes them.

27 *De Pot.*, q. 8, a. 1.

28 *SCG* IV 14§3.

If it were, then the word could still be an effect of understanding. It would be an effect that comes into existence simultaneously with its cause, but it would still depend unilaterally on its cause.[29] In such a case, there would be no temporal priority between the two, but there would still be a logical priority.[30] In fact, however, these passages suggest that even any *logical* priority is reciprocal. Again, intellect conceives a word "in order to understand" and "in order that it might know the thing"; it understands "by conceiving" "by forming" a word.[31] Word and understanding are not merely temporally simultaneous; each is brought about by the other. Even logically speaking, they are equally foundational.[32]

We can begin to appreciate the importance of this reciprocal priority, and we will uncover principles that reinforce it—and that make even clearer that a word cannot follow unilaterally on the act of

---

[29] It would be like a fire that gives off heat from the moment it comes into existence, yet still remains the cause of the heat.

[30] Lonergan takes this position: "understanding and inner word are simultaneous, the former being the ground and cause of the latter" (*Verbum*, 51). The only support for this claim Lonergan offers is a reference to *SCG* IV 14§3. This text certainly establishes that the word is simultaneous with the act of understanding. Yet it does not establish that the word is unilaterally grounded in and caused by the act of understanding.

[31] These texts come from *Quodl.* V, q. 5, a. 2, ad 1; *De Pot.*, q. 8, a. 1; *Comp. Theo.* I, 43; and *SCG* I 53§4, respectively.

[32] We will spend much of this chapter drawing out the implications that this reciprocal priority carries for the divine understanding. Yet it might also carry implications for human understanding. As we saw in note 76 in chapter two, the inner word not only remains within the mind; it also already bears a reference to audible speech. It is therefore the element of human intellect that is most directly oriented towards speech between human beings—or towards interpersonal communication. Thomas suggests the same in his early career when he speaks of the inner word in terms of "manifestation to another" (I *Sent.*, d. 27, q. 2, a. 1). In his early thought, however, this manifesting word is conceived *after* we understand something in ourselves. An ordination towards interpersonal communication is present, but it is derivative. In Thomas's mature thought, this ordination towards the interpersonal goes all the way to the foundation of the act of understanding: whenever we know anything, we just as basically conceive a word that inclines us towards sharing this knowledge with others. We may, then, find here a created echo of the marriage of the interpersonal and the intrapersonal that we are tracing out in God. Indeed, insofar as Thomas's mature doctrine of the Word is a fruit of his encounter with Revelation, we may have here another example of Revelation's prompting him to rethink a basic "philosophical" category: in this case, the relationship between interior thought and exterior communication.

understanding—by turning now to the word's specific role in the act of understanding.[33]

IN THE WORD WAS UNDERSTANDING
"The Existence of the Intention Understood is the Very Act of Being Understood"

We will focus on two points. First, the word is the immanent terminus of the act of understanding, which is itself understood in the act of understanding.[34] Second, the word is that *in* which intellect understands whatever it understands.

The first point appears already in the *De Veritate*, where Thomas writes that "our intellectual word, which enables us to speak about the divine Word by a kind of resemblance, is that at which our intellectual operation terminates. This is the very thing understood [*ipsum intellectum*], which is called the conception of the intellect."[35] Similarly, the word is the "terminus of the act of understanding," and it

---

[33] We should flag here a point that will become very important later in this chapter: it is only in creatures that word and understanding bring each other about. In God, Word and understanding are really identical. Indeed, to say that the divine Word is "brought about" by understanding would be to say that the divine Persons proceed from the divine essence; to say that understanding is "brought about" by the Word would be to say that the essence proceeds from a Person—both of which are inadmissible (see Emery, *TA*, 190–92). That said, the *real* distinction between created words and created acts of understanding corresponds to a *logical* distinction between the divine Word and the divine understanding. There can be no real priority between Word and understanding, for nothing can be prior to itself. Yet, insofar as they are logically distinct, there can be a reciprocal priority between them. Throughout this chapter, we should bear in mind that any such priority is only logical. Still, logical priorities matter, and we should therefore pay attention to them: for one example of a logical priority brimming with practical and political implications, see D. C. Schindler, *The Politics of the Real* (Steubenville, OH: New Polity Press, 2021), 24–25; for more on logical distinctions in Aquinas more broadly, see Russell L. Friedman, *Intellectual Traditions at the Medieval University: The Use of Philosophical Psychology in Trinitarian Theology among the Franciscans and Dominicans, 1250–1350* (Leiden: Brill, 2013), 55–61.

[34] Regarding the word as terminus, we will run through only a few texts here. For a more thorough discussion, see José Luis Fernández Rodríguez, "El Concepto en santo Tomás," *Anuario Filosófico* 7 (1974): 157–68. Lonergan also speaks of the word as the "object" of understanding in *Verbum*, 18–19.

[35] *De Ver.*, q. 4, a. 2. See also q. 4, a. 1.

is "understood" in this act.[36] Understanding terminates in the word, and the word is understood in the act of understanding. As we will see shortly, Thomas is also very clear that when intellect understands, it understands things-in-themselves. Yet, as we see now, it understands things-in-themselves by understanding its words of those things.

We see the same point in the *SCG*, and so in Thomas's mature account of the word. First, Thomas writes that "this intention understood is a quasi-terminus of intelligible operation."[37] Thomas continues referring to the word as the "intention *understood*" all through *SCG* IV, ch. 11, which further suggests that this word is itself understood in the act of understanding.[38] He also extends this language explicitly to the divine Word.[39] Indeed, in light of this language, he even refers to the divine Word as "*Deus intellectus.*"[40] Finally, especially noteworthy from the *SCG* is Thomas's claim—which he sets down three times—that "the *existence* of the interiorly conceived word, or the intention understood, is its very act of *being understood*";[41] "the *existence* of the intention understood consists in the very act of *being understood*";[42] and, most briefly, "the *existence* of the intention understood is the very act of *being understood.*"[43] Even among composed creatures, a word is not a thing that exists and that is subsequently understood. Nor even are its existence and its being-understood two things that coincide temporally. Instead, its existence *is* its being understood.[44]

---

36 *De Ver.*, q. 3, a. 2.

37 *SCG* I 53§4.

38 See IV 11 §§5–7, 9–11, and 13. See also I 53§§4–5. This language also appears outside of the *SCG*: see *Comp. Theo.* I, 52; and *de sensu et sensato* I l. 2, n. 14.

39 See *SCG* I 53§5, and IV 11§§5, 7 and 13.

40 See *SCG* IV 11§§9 and 11. Of course, all three divine Persons are understood in the divine act of understanding. This language, however, suggests something of how intimately being understood enters into the fabric of a word—and, therefore, of the divine Word.

41 *SCG* IV 11§11.

42 IV 11§11.

43 IV 11§6.

44 González Alió explores this last point at some length in his articles cited above.

This last point can deepen the conclusions we just drew about the priority of the word. For we just saw that the conception of a word is just as basic as the act of understanding. We see now that a word's being understood is just as basic as its existence. Intellect, then, cannot first understand something and only subsequently conceive its word. Yet nor can it first understand something and only subsequently *understand* its word. For a word cannot exist—and so it cannot be conceived—without already, and just as basically, being understood. Again, its existence *is* its being-understood. Both the word's being-conceived and the word's being-understood, therefore, go to the foundation of the act of understanding.

We will return to this point shortly. Returning, however, to our current question, Thomas uses his strongest language in the *De Potentia*.[45] First, he reiterates his claim that the word is the "terminus" of the act of understanding.[46] More deeply, when he is asking whether there are multiple Persons in God, he refers to the word—and *not* to the thing itself that is understood—as that which, in the act of understanding, is primarily understood and as that which is understood through itself: the word is "*primo et per se intellectum.*"[47] Thomas argues that this *per se intellectum* cannot be "the thing that is known by the intellect. For this thing is at one time only potentially understood, and it is outside the person who understands; as when a man understands a material thing, for instance a stone, an animal, or something of the kind. The thing understood, however, must be in the person who understands and must be one with him." When I understand a stone, this stone—that is, the thing-in-itself which I am understanding—really is understood. Yet it is not understood *first*, and it is not understood *through itself*. It is not the primary object of my understanding. Thomas gives two reasons for this conclusion. First, a stone may be understood, but it can also exist independently of my understanding it: it is "at one time only potentially understood" by me. My inner word, in contrast, only

---

[45] Lonergan identifies this passage as the "most downright affirmation" that the word is the object of understanding (*Verbum*, 19).

[46] *De Pot.*, q. 8, a. 1.

[47] *De Pot.*, q. 9, a. 5.

exists at all insofar as I understand it. Second, Thomas follows Aristotle in teaching that understanding terminates within the intellect that understands.[48] With this point perhaps in the background, Thomas argues that the *primo et per se intellectum* must be "in the person who understands." It therefore cannot be the stone that I understand, for this stone exists outside of my intellect. A word, in contrast, only ever exists within the person who understands.[49]

Thomas continues by bringing the word to the fore: he writes that "that which is *primo et per se intellectum* is something that the intellect conceives within itself about the thing understood." He then clarifies that "this concept of the intellect is called the interior word." The *primo et per se intellectum*, therefore, is the word. It is not merely that intellect, when it understands something, principally or initially understands the thing itself, but that it also, in a derivative or less intense way—or in a logically subsequent step—understands its word of that thing. Instead, whenever intellect understands, it is the word that is understood *primo et per se*. The word is not only understood; it is understood primally and in a privileged way.

These passages should be enough to establish our first point: whenever intellect understands anything, it understands its word of that thing. Indeed, it understands its word just as basically as it understands the thing itself that is imaged in that word.

In the Word

That said, Thomas by no means suggests that because the word is *primo et per se intellectum*, the thing itself is somehow less than fully known. Instead, he is very clear that understanding is an intimate encounter between mind and thing.[50] The point to stress now, however, is that

---

48 See *De Ver.*, q. 1, a. 2.

49 Lonergan offers some helpful reflections here in *Verbum*, 18. Commenting on the same text, Paissac writes that "the word is the object; we should say it is pure object; the thing, of itself, is not an object; but, thanks to the word, one can speak of the thing known. The thing . . . is not a pure object" (*Théologie du Verbe*, 196).

50 For some deep reflections here, see Joseph Pieper, *Living the Truth*, trans. Lothar Krauth (San Francisco: Ignatius, 1989).

the mind unites itself to things *in its words* of those things. As Emery puts it, the act of understanding "consists in a union, an assimilation. . . . This union with the thing known abides in the intimacy of the word within the intellect itself. The intellect unites itself to the known thing through the word which abides within itself."[51] "It is through the word that we 'unite' ourselves to the known reality."[52] We know things in themselves; yet we know them *through* our inner words.

Most importantly, it is not merely that intellect knows the thing itself in one act of understanding, and that it knows its word of that thing in a second discrete—but simultaneous—act of understanding. Instead, it is *through* its word of a thing that intellect unites itself to that thing. Or, better, it is *in* its word. To put things more precisely, intellect understands *by* the species that is the principle of understanding. It does not understand *by* its word, for its word is not the principle of understanding. Instead, the word proceeds by way of understanding, and intellect therefore understands *in* its word.[53] Thomas writes that the word "is compared to the intellect, not as that by which the intellect understands, but as that *in* which it understands, because it is *in* what is thus expressed and formed that intellect sees the nature of the thing understood."[54] On the one hand, intellect "sees the nature of the thing understood" in the word. This word does not trap intellect within itself; it puts intellect in contact with things outside of itself. On the other hand, intellect does not need to push its word out of the way in order to enjoy an unobstructed view of things in themselves. Instead, it is *in* the word—and it is *only* in the word—that the intellect sees things in themselves.

It is not a question, therefore, of the act of understanding being directed either to the word within the mind or to a thing outside the mind. Rather, *because* the act of understanding is directed to its own immanent word, it reaches out to things in themselves. As Thomas had

---

51 *TTTA*, 59.

52 *TTTA*, 184. See also Lonergan, *Verbum*, 20–21.

53 See Emery, *TTTA*, 183–84; and White, *The Trinity*, 473.

54 *In Ioan.*, #25. Thomas makes this point less directly and prominently in the *ST*, where he writes of "the thing understood, which *in* the word uttered is manifested to the one who understands" (I q. 34, a. 1, ad 3).

put it earlier in his career, "the intellectual conception is not only that *which* is understood, but also that *by* which the thing is understood. Consequently, that which is understood can be said to be both the thing itself and the conception of the intellect."[55] The word itself is understood. Yet, in being understood, it allows us to understand the thing itself.

These conclusions, finally, can help to reinforce our conclusions from our first section on the priority of the word. For, if the word is the object of the act of understanding, if it is the *primo et per se intellectum*, and if it is that in which intellect understands, then its conception cannot—even logically speaking—follow unilaterally on the act of understanding. If it did, then the act of understanding would exist before its object: understanding would exist before the thing understood existed. Yet there can be no act of understanding without the thing understood in it: understanding must have an object, or it cannot exist at all. To say otherwise would be like saying I hold my son before my son exists. Just so, the act of understanding cannot see anything unless that *in* which it sees things already exists. To say otherwise would be like saying I see my face in a mirror before the mirror exists. Again, it is only in its word that intellect makes contact with things in themselves. Even logically speaking, therefore, this contact cannot precede the word in which it takes place. And so we seem to be on even firmer ground in saying that the conception of a word goes all the way to the logical foundation of the act of understanding.

Our Words, God's Word

We have already seen that immense differences separate the divine Word from any created word. One might suspect, therefore, that the features of a word we have unearthed here—its being understood in the act of understanding and its being that in which intellect understands—could be features that are limited to our words and that do not hold in God's Word. In fact, however, almost all of the passages we have quoted in this section have come from the thick of Thomas's Trinitarian theology:

---

55 *De Ver.*, q. 4, a. 2, ad 3.

they come either as Thomas is speaking with direct reference to the divine Word or as he is in the process of introducing the divine Word.[56] These features of a word are not bound up with created imperfections, and they need not therefore be kept at arm's length from the divine Word. Instead, these features come to the fore as Thomas has the divine Word directly in mind.

Even more, both when Thomas tells us that a word is *"primo et per se intellectum"* and when he tells us that the word is that "in which" intellect understands—that is, when he registers two of the claims that will be most important for our conclusions here—he continues by immediately introducing the divine Word, and he highlights certain differences that separate the divine Word from created words.[57] In the first text, he clarifies that the divine Word, unlike any created word, is one, is perfect, shares the essence of the divine intellect, and is the Son of His Speaker.[58] In the second, he specifies that the divine Word is always in act, is one, is perfect, is identical to the divine essence, and is therefore subsistent.[59] Yet as he is cataloguing these differences between human words and the divine Word, Thomas never so much as hints that there might be any respect whatsoever in which the divine Word, as a word, is not understood in the act of divine understanding. Nor does he hint that the divine Word is not that in which God understands. If these differences obtained, then Thomas could very easily have noted them, for they were fresh in his mind as he was listing the differences that *do* obtain between human words and the divine Word. The fact that he makes no mention of these features strongly suggests that they do not, in fact, separate God's Word from our words. They seem to be not points of analogous differences that rule out any univocity between our words and God's Word, but points of analogous contact that rule out any equivocity between our words and God's Word.

---

[56] The only exceptions are *De Ver.*, q. 3, a. 2 and *Quodl.* V, q. 5, a. 2, ad 1. Every other text comes from Thomas's Trinitarian theology.

[57] For a more general review of these differences between human words and the divine Word, see White, *The Trinity*, 474–76.

[58] See *De Pot.*, q. 9, a. 5.

[59] See *in Ioan.*, ##26–28.

Keeping in mind the limits of analogy, it seems safe to conclude, at the very least, that the divine Word, because He is a word, is somehow understood in the divine act of understanding, and that the divine Word somehow stands as that in which—or as He in Whom—God understands whatever He understands.

"ACTUS SUNT SUPPOSITORUM"

Of course, even here, the infinite differences of analogy apply. For if the divine Word is understood, or if He is that in which God understands, then He is understood in a way that remains incomprehensible, and which differs infinitely from anything we encounter among our created words. Again, these differences are legion. Yet prominent among them is the subsistence of the Word. The divine Word is not only understood in the one divine act of understanding, and He is not only that in which another Person understands. He also subsists as a Person. And He Himself therefore understands in the very act of understanding by way of which He proceeds.[60]

---

[60] This point is especially important because, in what follows, we will draw strong conclusions from the structure of divine understanding. One might therefore suspect that we are venturing beyond the strict limits Thomas sets on our knowledge of the Trinity (for more on the scope of our knowledge of the Trinity in Aquinas, and for respects in which Thomas's Trinitarian theology both is and is not apophatic, as well as ways in which he steers between one set of contemporaries who were inadequately apophatic and another set who were excessively apophatic, see White, *The Trinity*, 374–91, 452–53). In response, we should first reiterate the point we just made: we will insist that the divine Word, because He is a word, is understood in the divine act of understanding. We will also insist that, because this Word is a word, God understands in Him. Yet we will do so only because, as we just saw, Thomas gives us warrant to do so. Second, we should highlight a point we have seen repeatedly through this study, a point that will come to the fore momentarily: our conclusions here will not stand at odds with the analogy between human and divine understanding. Nor will they trade on a tacit univocity. Instead, they will depend on analogy: they would collapse if analogy gave way to univocity. A univocal divine Word, after all, would be like human words: it would be non-subsistent. Only an analogous divine Word can subsist as a Person distinct from His Speaker—and, as we will see, all of our conclusions in this chapter will stand or fall with the subsistence of the divine Word. Finally, we should clarify a more basic point: all through this chapter, our knowledge will remain radically limited. On the one hand, because the divine Word is, in fact, a word—that is, because "Word" is said of Him not univocally but analogously—we can say *that* He is understood and *that* God understands in Him. On the other hand, we cannot know *how* He is understood or *how* God understands in Him: the mode of divine understanding remains beyond our reach. All we can say—or

We will return to this point at length soon. For now, we should begin by clarifying our language. Thus far, we have said that the word is that in which intellect understands. Yet this language is imprecise. For intellects are accidents, and we saw in our last chapter that accidents do not, strictly speaking, *do* anything. It is not intellects that understand in their words; it is subsistent persons who, with their intellects, understand in their words.

For our purposes, this point is most important for God. The divine intellect does not understand, for the divine intellect, as intellect—like the divine essence, as essence—does not act at all. As Thomas puts it with reference to the divine Son, "to act is not attributed to the nature as agent, but to the Person, since 'acts belong to supposits and to singulars.' "[61] The axiom *"actus sunt suppositorum"* redounds all through Thomas's work: action, by definition, belongs to subsisting supposits.[62] And because, in God, the Persons are supposits of the divine nature, it is the divine *Persons* Who act in every divine action—including the essential act of understanding common to all three.[63]

In God, therefore, it is not an impersonal divine essence or intellect that understands. Indeed, there *is* no impersonal divine essence or intellect: there is no essence or intellect that exists in any way before, behind, or beneath the three Persons. Instead, there is a divine essence and intellect that exists—and that *only* exists—in and as the three Persons Who exist and understand.[64] Even more, and to focus on

---

stammer—is that because the divine Word is a word, He is *somehow* understood in the divine act of understanding, and God *somehow* understands in Him.

61 *ST* III q. 20, a. 1, ad 2.

62 As Emery points out, Thomas first invokes this principle in the context of Trinitarian theology (see "Central Aristotelian Themes," 21). Brian Carl identifies some of the finer points that are up for debate surrounding the interpretation of this axiom (see "Action, Supposit, and Subject"). Yet the very basic point on which we will focus is uncontroversial.

63 González Alió, extending the logic of *ST* I q. 39, a. 3 and *De Pot.*, q. 9, a. 6, can write that there are in God *"tres habentes intelligere vel actum intelligendi"* ("Santísima Trinidad," 68). That said, there is of course no real composition in God between essence and supposit. Yet, insofar as there is a rational distinction between essence and Person, the Persons can be thought of as subsisting supposits, and the essence as the nature in which They subsist.

64 See Emery, *TTTA*, 44–48. We will return to this point in the final section of this chapter.

intellect, the one divine intellect exists in each of those Persons in a distinct way. As Thomas puts it, "As the Father is God generating and the Son is God generated, so must we say that the Father is wise as conceiving, while the Son is wise as conceived. For the Son, in that He is the Word, is a conception of a wise being."[65] The Son not only *is* a Word; the Son understands—or "is wise"—*as* a Word. The Father understands as conceiving a Word, and the Son understands as the Word Who is conceived.

We will explore similar texts, along with the principles behind them, later in this chapter. For now, we can shift our attention to the divine Persons Who understand in order to see that, in Thomas's psychological analogy, interpersonal knowledge goes just as deep as self-knowledge.

UNDERSTANDING ONESELF IN ANOTHER

UNDERSTANDING ONESELF *IN ANOTHER*

We can begin with a point on which there is no disagreement: divine knowledge is fundamentally self-knowledge.[66] God certainly knows creatures. Indeed, He knows them perfectly. Yet He knows them as a consequence of knowing His own essence.[67] As we just saw, however, to say that "God" knows the divine essence is not to say that an impersonal divine essence or intellect knows itself; it is to say that the Father, the Son, and the Holy Spirit, each of Whom is identical to the divine essence, know that essence. We can begin, then, with the Father: what the Father knows first and foremost is the essence that He Himself is. In the Father, divine knowledge is fundamentally self-knowledge.

This point is crucial, and I have no intention of denying it. Indeed, part of my ultimate conclusion in this section will be that perfect knowledge in the Father *is* fundamentally self-knowledge. Yet I also hope

---

65 *De Pot.,* q. 9, a. 9, ad 6.
66 See *SCG* I, ch. 48.
67 See *ST* I q. 14, a. 5.

to show that, because the Father understands "as producing a Word," this self-knowledge is just as fundamentally interpersonal knowledge.[68]

It is here that our conclusions from the beginning of this chapter come into play. Again, for Thomas, the conception of a word is just as logically foundational as the act of understanding; a word is understood in the act of understanding and its very being is its being-understood; and a word is that in which the one who speaks it understands. Thomas gives us every reason to conclude that these features of a word hold analogously in the divine Word. And he therefore gives us every reason to conclude that, because the Father understands as conceiving a Word, His act of conceiving this Word must be just as logically basic as His act of understanding Himself. Even logically speaking, He does not understand Himself and *then* produce a Word; He understands Himself "*as* producing a Word."[69] This act of producing a Word goes all the way to the foundation of His self-understanding. Yet, because a word itself is understood in the act of understanding, and because it only ever exists as already understood by its speaker, it is not only the Father's act of *conceiving* a Word that goes to the logical foundation of His self-knowledge. His act of *understanding* a Word goes just as deep. Again, a word is not conceived and *then* understood; it is conceived *as* understood: its being understood is its very existence. The Father, therefore, does not understand Himself and *then* understand His Word; He understands Himself *as* understanding His Word, and He understands His Word just as basically as He understands Himself. Finally, because all understanding is in a word, the Father must understand whatever He understands—including Himself—in the Word He conceives. Again, He does not understand Himself and *then* understand His Word. Yet nor does He understand Himself and *also*, or at the same time, understand His Word. Instead, He understands Himself *in* His Word.

Again, these conclusions hinge on certain points of analogous contact between our words and the divine Word: the divine Word is that in which His Speaker understands; He is understood in the divine

---

68 *ST* I q. 34, a. 2, ad 4.

69 *ST* I q. 34, a. 2, ad 4.

act of understanding; His existence is His being-understood; and His conception is just as logically basic as the act of understanding in which He is conceived. Yet our ultimate conclusions will hinge just as much on a point of analogous difference between our words and God's Word.[70] For God's Word, unlike our words, is a distinct Person. To say, therefore, that the Father understands Himself as understanding His Word is to say that He understands Himself as understanding *another Person*. Just so, to say that He knows His Word just as basically as He knows Himself is to say that He knows *another Person* just as basically as He knows Himself. Finally, to say that He only knows Himself in His Word is to say that He only knows Himself *in another Person*. He knows Himself *as* knowing another, and He knows Himself *in* knowing another—another Who is radically distinct from Him, Who stands "present" to Him, and Who is "quasi-extrinsic" from Him.[71]

It is true that Thomas never comes out and writes explicitly that, because of the role of a word in knowledge, the Father's self-knowledge is just as basically interpersonal knowledge. Yet, first of all, my claim is that all of these conclusions follow on principles he lays out in the thick of his Trinitarian theology. Perhaps more strikingly, there are two sets of passages where Thomas points quite clearly in this direction. In one set, he writes that "the Father is revealed to all by means of the Word Incarnate; but the eternally generated Word has manifested Him to Himself";[72] that "God understands Himself by conceiving His intelligible Word";[73] and that "the Word of God is God's very concept, by which He understands Himself and other things."[74] The Father's act of self-understanding does not in any way circumvent or sideline His Word. Nor does the Father, even logically speaking, first understand Himself and subsequently understand His Word. Instead, the Father

---

[70] Again: our conclusions here will not backdoor a tacit univocity; they would be upended by any such univocity.

[71] *SCG* IV 11§18 and *In Ioan.*, #45.

[72] *De Ver.*, q. 4, a. 1, ad 5. Thomas is comfortable here drawing a parallel between this intra-Trinitarian manifestation and the Son's revelation of the Father in the economy.

[73] *Comp. Theo.* I, 43.

[74] *In Heb.*, #564.

understands Himself *by* His Word—the Word Who "manifest[s] Him to Himself."

Indeed, in a second set of passages, Thomas argues that the Word enters so intimately into the Father's self-knowledge that the Father could not know Himself without the Word. He writes that "if at any time there were no Word in God, then during that time God would not understand Himself."[75] Similarly, he writes that "the Arians, who separate the Word from God, were foolish, because, if they had been right, God would not have known Himself."[76] He uses even stronger language: "No one can say that God has not a Word, because such would make God most foolish."[77] He also writes that a God without a Word would not be "an intelligent being" but would instead be "mindless."[78] Finally, in a passage we already gave earlier in this chapter, he tells us that "God did not first exist and then begin to generate a Word: for, since the generation of the Word is nothing other than an intelligible conception, it would follow that God would be understanding in potency before understanding in act, which is inadmissible."[79]

There would be a great deal to say about these passages, all of which are very rich, but we cannot treat them in any detail beyond rattling them off in rapid succession.[80] At the very least, however, we can note that they militate against an account of the divine understanding in which—perhaps because of divine simplicity—the Father would

---

75 *Comp. Theo.* I, 43.

76 This passage comes from the sermon *Seraphim Stabant*: see *The Academic Sermons*, trans. Mark-Robin Hoogland (Washington, DC: The Catholic University of America Press, 2010), 166.

77 *In Symb. Apost.*, a. 2.

78 *De Pot.*, q. 10, a. 1.

79 *In Ioan.*, #41.

80 We can note, however, that all of these passages are compatible with Thomas's claim (following Augustine) that the Father is not wise *by* the Son (see, for example, *ST* I q. 37, a. 3, ad 1 and q. 39, a. 7, ad 2). First of all, even in these passages, the Son is not the *principle* of the Father's understanding (which is the error to which Thomas fears the language of "by" might lead); He is the Word Who *proceeds* in this understanding. Yet these passages make clear that, without His Word, the Father would not understand Himself at all. More technically, the Father does not, strictly speaking, understand *by* His Word; He understands *in* His Word. Yet the Word is so necessary for His self-understanding that Thomas is comfortable using the language of "by His Word."

understand Himself otherwise than by His Word or in His Word.[81] Even more, they militate against a scheme according to which the Father would first understand Himself fully—or even inchoately—and then, as a consequence of this primordial self-knowledge, conceive a Word Whom He might also understand in a logically subsequent moment. For, in these texts, Thomas is explicit that the Father understands Himself by His Word, that this Word manifests the Father to Himself, and that the Father's self-understanding would collapse without His Word. Indeed, they suggest that the Father could not understand *anything*, on any level—no matter how inchoately—without His Word: a Wordless God would be "mindless" and "most foolish," and He would only understand anything "in potency." These texts therefore suggest that the conception of a divine Word goes just as logically deep as the Father's act of self-understanding. Because, moreover, a word cannot be conceived without thereby—and just as basically—being understood by its speaker, these passages suggest that the Father's act of *understanding* His Word goes just as logically deep as His act of understanding Himself.

The most basic point, however, is that these passages give voice to the principles we surveyed through the first sections of this chapter. Again, all of these principles are basic to Thomas's rendering of a word, and Thomas seems to extend all of them analogously to the divine Word. Indeed, given these principles, it should perhaps come as no surprise that Thomas can stake these claims concerning the role of the divine Word in the Father's self-understanding. These principles can make sense of these passages, and these passages give us further reason to conclude that these principles hold analogously in God—and to conclude that, when Thomas laid these principles out, he was at least generally aware of the implications they carry. Reading these principles and these passages together, we can return to our first major conclusion. Again, the divine Word is a Word unlike any other: He is a Person Who subsists distinctly from His Speaker. Yet because He is the Word of the Father, and because of what a word is, the Father can only know Himself if He thereby, and just as fundamentally, knows

---

[81] González Alió, for all the richness of his reading of Thomas, ultimately accuses Thomas of following such a route.

this other Person—a Person Who remains entirely within the Father, yet Who also stands present to the Father from the "outside."

Even more, the Father does not merely both know Himself and know this other Person in two logically distinct, but logically equiprimordial, acts of understanding. Again, even in us, there is but a single seamless act wherein we know a thing in our word of that thing. So much the more in the simple and immutable divine nature. Again, the Father does not know Himself *and* know His Word. He knows Himself *in* knowing His Word—not only because there is no real distinction in God, but also because there is no real distinction in us between our act of knowing our word and our act of knowing the thing imaged in that word. There is not one logically distinct act by which the Father knows Himself and a second logically distinct act by which He knows another Person. Instead, He knows Himself *in* knowing another Person: His self-knowledge *itself* passes through another Person Who manifests Him to Himself.

Understanding Oneself in Another Person

That said, it is just as important to stress that the Father really does know *Himself* in knowing another Person. Again, my claim here is not that the Father's self-knowledge is subordinated or subsequent to interpersonal knowledge. Instead, my claim is that, even logically speaking, interpersonal knowledge is not subordinated or subsequent to self-knowledge. Even logically speaking, they are equally foundational. The Father, then, can only know Himself if He just as basically knows another Person; but He can only know another Person if He just as basically knows Himself. As Thomas puts it, "the Son manifests Himself and the Father at the same time, because the Son is the Word of the Father."[82] It is not first the Father and then the Son. Yet nor is it first the Son and then the Father. It is both at once—and not merely because there can be no real succession in the immutable God. Instead, it is both at once "because the Son is the *Word* of the Father," and because,

---

82 *In Ioan.*, #1937. The context of this claim is the economy, but the grounding of the claim ("because the Son is the Word of the Father") seems to carry implications for the eternal Trinity.

even logically speaking, a word and the thing imaged in that word are known simultaneously.

We can come to the same point if we recall that, as we saw in chapter three, all words are images that represent the thing made known in them.[83] One does not, however, see an image and *then* see the thing represented by that image. Instead, one sees the thing represented *in* seeing the image.[84] The divine Word, however, is not merely one more image; He is the Image *par excellence*. As Thomas puts it, "our intellect frequently understands both itself and other things imperfectly, whereas God's act of understanding cannot be imperfect. Hence God's Word is perfect, representing all things perfectly, whereas our word is often imperfect."[85] The divine Word not only represents the Father; He represents the Father perfectly. To see Him is to see the Father.

Again, even our words, to the extent that they are perfect words and true words, are transparent to the things they make known. So much the more in God, where the uniquely perfect Word is uniquely transparent to the Father. The Father, then, cannot but *already* see the whole of Himself in seeing His Word. We saw above that the Father cannot know Himself except in knowing another Person. We see now that, in knowing this other Person, He cannot but know Himself.

Seeing Himself, Seeing His Word

All that said, it is just as important to clarify that the Word does not melt into the Father's self-knowledge: when Father sees His Word, He does not merely see Himself. Again, "the Son manifests *Himself* and the Father at the same time, because the Son is the Word of the Father."[86] The Word Himself is made known when He makes the

---

83 Recall *SCG* IV 11§§14–15; and *ST* I q. 35, a. 2.

84 See *ST* III q. 25, a. 3. This passages also highlights a respect in which, when one sees an image, one sees that image as a thing-in-itself: one sees it as distinct from its exemplar. The image, that is, does not merely reduce back to the exemplar.

85 *De Pot.*, q. 9, a. 5. See also *in Ioan.*, #26 and *de rationibus fidei*, ch. 3 for the divine Word as a uniquely perfect word. In *de Ver.*, q. 4, a. 4, the Son is called "a true word" because "whatever is contained in the Father's knowledge is necessarily and *entirely* expressed" by Him.

86 *In Ioan.*, #1937.

Father known. He is perfectly transparent, but He is not invisible. Still less is He a mere means—even an indispensable means—to another's self-knowledge.[87] Instead, He is subsistent, and He therefore has a solidity and an existence-in-Himself that infinitely outstrips anything we encounter in our human words.

The deepest point, however, is that the Word *must* be perfectly solid in Himself *because* He is perfectly transparent to the Father. Just so, He must be perfectly transparent because He is perfectly solid. The Word can only be a perfect image—that is, He can only be perfectly transparent—because He is perfectly like the Father. Yet He can only be perfectly like the Father because, unlike created Words, He contains—and *is*—the whole essence of the Father.[88] As we saw throughout chapter three, however, it is because the Word is identical to the Father's essence that He is a subsistent Word. There is but a single reason, therefore, that the Word both subsists distinctly from the Father and is perfectly transparent to the Father: the consubstantiality of Word and Father.

The Word's perfect transparency to the Father, therefore, is no threat to the Word's integrity and solidity in Himself. Nor is it a threat to the Father's knowing the Word as a Person distinct from Himself. Instead, if the Word were anything less than perfectly transparent to the Father, then He would be something less than identical to the Father's self-subsistent nature, and He therefore would not subsist as a Person distinct from the Father. My self-knowledge is imperfect because my words of myself are not perfectly transparent to me. Yet they are not perfectly transparent to me because they do not share my nature, and because they therefore do not subsist as persons alongside me. From the other direction, the Word only perfectly mirrors and expresses His Speaker because the Word shares the nature of His Speaker, and because He is therefore a Person distinct from His Speaker. The Father sees nothing but Himself in seeing His Word *because* His Word is a distinct Person. Thus, the fact that the Word subsists "outside" of the

---

[87] In God, everything is an end in itself and nothing is a means to some further end: see *ST* I q. 42, a. 2, ad 5.

[88] See *in Ioan.*, #1887.

Father is no threat to the Father's knowing Himself perfectly in His Word; it is a condition for the Father's knowing Himself perfectly in His Word. The Father can *only* know Himself perfectly because He looks "outside" of Himself towards a Word Who stands present to Him.[89]

UNDERSTANDING ANOTHER IN ONESELF

We see the same thing, though from the opposite direction, with the Son. First of all, the Son eternally understands both Himself and the Father. This point comes out with particular fullness in Thomas's commentary on John, where he writes that "the Son knows the Father most perfectly, just as He knows Himself most perfectly,"[90] and that "all knowledge comes about through some likeness. . . . Now the Son has the most perfect likeness to the Father, since He has the same essence and power as the Father does; and so He knows the Father most perfectly. . . . Thus, just as He knows Himself perfectly through His essence, so 'I know Him' perfectly through the same essence."[91] Just as the Father eternally knows both Himself and the Son, so the Son eternally knows both Himself and the Father.

These texts already take us a good deal further than some of Thomas's critics allege he can go. For, to hear those critics tell it, because the Son is a Word, He cannot be a distinct agent of understanding: He can know neither Himself nor the Father.[92] Thomas argues otherwise. In these passages, however, Thomas registers this point with reference not to his psychological categories but to the familial language of Father

---

[89] In "As Kingfishers Catch Fire," Gerard Manley Hopkins finds in creatures a similarly paradoxical marriage of existence-in-oneself and transparency-to-another. For Hopkins, when the Father sees a given creature, He sees "Christ . . . / Lovely in limbs, and lovely in eyes not his"; yet, in manifesting Christ, this same creature "Selves—goes itself; *myself* it speaks and spells / Crying *Whát I dó is me*." To be fully oneself—to "do" oneself and to "self" as a unique self, distinct both from God and from every other creature, is to be a transparent window through which the Father sees the incarnate Son.

[90] *In Ioan.*, #1063.

[91] *In Ioan.*, #1065. See also ##1149, 1216, 1284, 1398, and 1414.

[92] Gunton, Moltmann, and Pannenberg, all of whom we discussed in the introduction, criticize Thomas in these terms.

and Son. If we were to limit ourselves to these passages, therefore, we might give the impression that Thomas's Trinitarian thought has room for interpersonal knowledge only to the extent that it has room for nonpsychological approaches to the Trinity. Yet these passages would also leave us with an interpersonal knowledge that was either juxtaposed to or derivative of self-knowledge: they would leave us either with a Son Who knows Himself and Who *also* knows the Father, or with a Son Who knows His own essence and Who *therefore* knows the Father with Whom He shares that essence. They would leave us, in other words, with the scheme with which we began this chapter.[93]

Happily, however, we need not limit ourselves to these passages. Instead, by going deeper into Thomas's psychological categories, we can find resources for a far more intimate marriage of interpersonal knowledge and self-knowledge in the Son.

"Wise as Conceived"

The first point to note is that Thomas does not merely sideline the Son's status as Word when he speaks of Him as an agent of understanding. First of all, we saw in our last chapter that "the plan of the house in the mind of the [human] architect does not build the house; the architect builds it according to the plan. However, the Word of God, which is a plan of things made by God, does—since He is subsistent—act; there is not merely an action through Him."[94] The Father, like us, acts through His Word; yet His Word, unlike our words, is subsistent. His Word therefore acts. He even acts—and He even understands—in the very act of understanding by way of which He proceeds: "the Word

---

[93] Thus, perhaps surprisingly, in the passages where Thomas is commenting on the Gospel, and where he is working with the register of "Father-Son"—that is, where we might expect him to be most "interpersonal"—he opens up room only for a limping synthesis of self-knowledge and reciprocal knowledge. As we will see, he opens a path towards something deeper in dogmatic contexts, where he is speaking in the psychological register of "Speaker-Word." This point can help to further undermine the opposition between the "Scriptural" and the "dogmatic" that we have mentioned at several points, along with the opposition between the "familial" and the "psychological" that we saw in chapter four.

[94] *SCG* IV 13§9.

understands Himself."[95] It is not merely that the Word understands insofar as He is a Son but that He is something less than a distinct agent of understanding insofar as He is a Word. Instead, the Word understands as a Word.

Indeed, as a Word, He understands in a distinct and personal way. As Thomas puts it, the Son "understand[s] as the Word proceeding" and the Son is "intelligent, not as producing a Word, but as the Word proceeding."[96] The Son's status as Word does not threaten His agency in understanding; it specifies His agency in understanding. The Son understands as the Word Who proceeds in His own act of understanding.[97]

It is because He understands as a Word that all of our conclusions here will follow. Again, "the Word understands Himself."[98] Yet, because the self Whom He understands is the Word of the Father, this self is the image—and the perfectly transparent image—of the Father. We just

---

[95] *SCG* IV 13§3.

[96] *ST* I q. 37, a. 1, ad 4; *ST* I q. 34, a. 2, ad 4. See also *De Pot.*, q. 9, a. 9, ad 6; and *SCG* IV 26§5.

[97] These passages also speak to a question that has long dogged psychological analogies for the Trinity: if a word proceeds in every act of understanding, and if a simple Word is a subsistent Word, then why does an additional subsistent Word not proceed from the Son when He understands? And why does a third subsistent Word not proceed from this second Word—and on and on to infinity? Rahner raises this objection in *The Trinity*, 19. For other examples, see John McDermott "Is the Blessed Trinity Naturally Knowable? St. Thomas on Reason, Faith, Nature, Grace, and Person," *Gregorianum* 93, no. 1 (2012): 148; Craig, "Toward a Tenable Social Trinitarianism," 91–92; and Williams, "Augustine, Thomas Aquinas, Henry of Ghent and John Duns Scotus," 48–49, 72–73. Thomas, however, anticipates this objection. Indeed, he raises it *as* an objection in his Trinitarian theology, and all of the passages we just cited in the previous note come in response to this objection (for the objections, see *ST* I q. 34, a. 2, arg. 4; *De Pot.*, q. 9, a. 9, arg. 6; and *SCG* IV 13§2 and IV 26§5). In all of his responses, Thomas explains that, whereas the Father understands as speaking a Word, the Son understands as the Word spoken by the Father—and *not* as speaking His own Word. Without going too deep into this area of Thomas's thought, we can at least note one point: Rahner's objection assumes that the divine Persons all understand *in the same way*. Behind this objection, that is, lies an assumption that the divine understanding is undifferentiated in the three Persons: it is not inwardly shaped by Their relations. For Thomas, in contrast, the divine understanding *only ever exists according to these relations*: understanding exists in the Father as giving existence to His Word, it exists in the Son as receiving existence as a Word, and it exists in the Holy Spirit as receiving existence as the Love that follows on understanding. For Thomas, the divine relations shape the one divine act of understanding through and through—and the Son can therefore understand without producing His own Word.

[98] *SCG* IV 13§3.

saw that, because of this transparency, the Father cannot understand His Word without thereby already understanding Himself. We see now that because of this same transparency, the Word cannot understand Himself without thereby already understanding the Father. For the Word does not image an impersonal divine essence: the Word *is* the divine essence, and nothing can be the image of itself.[99] Instead, the Word images the Father, and it is the Father Who is known in knowing the Word.[100] In knowing Himself, therefore, the Word cannot but already know the Father.

We can reinforce this point if we recall that a knower, in a single act of understanding, knows a thing in knowing his word of that thing. If the divine Word really is a Word, therefore, then no one—not even the Word Himself—can know this Word without already knowing the Father. If He did, then He would know a word, but He would not know the thing imaged by that word—which is impossible. For the Son as much as for the Father, to understand oneself is already, and just as basically, to understand another Person.

At the same time, and for the same reasons, the Son can only understand this other Person if He just as basically understands Himself. Again, no one—not even, analogously, the divine Persons—ever understands anything except in understanding his word of that thing. The Son, therefore, just like the Father, can only understand the Father if He understands the Word in which the Father is represented. But the only Word in which the Father is represented is—the Son Himself! The Word, therefore, can only see the Father if He sees Himself. In turning to Himself He is turned to the Father; yet He cannot turn to the Father without turning to Himself.

Reciprocal Knowledge

In God, then, it is not merely that one Person knows *an*other in knowing Himself. Instead, two Persons know *each* other in knowing Themselves. Taking a step back, we saw in our last chapter that in

---

[99] Thomas writes that "for a true image it is required that *one* proceeds from *another* like to it in species" (*ST* I q. 35, a. 1).

[100] For this last point, in the context of the economy, see *in Ioan.*, #830.

God, immanent procession is a matter of interpersonal self-giving: a Speaker cannot speak a Word without giving the whole of Himself to His Word. Immanent procession, however, is not a matter of *reciprocal* self-giving. The Word actively receives Himself in being spoken, but He does not give Himself back to His Speaker.[101] Now, however, we see that the Speaker knows Himself in speaking His Word, and that the Word knows the Speaker back in being spoken. In knowing Himself, each Person knows another Person Who knows Him in return.

For all that, however, Word and Speaker know each other in a single act of understanding to which each is identical. We will return to this point in a moment. For now, we can note that, as we have seen, this one act of understanding follows the same course in both Persons: in this one act, both the Father and the Son understand the Father in His Word. In the Father, this pattern of understanding means that He understands Himself in another Person Who is His Word; in the Son, this same pattern means that He understands another Person in understanding the Word that He Himself is. In both, however, the same pattern is constant: both understand the Father in understanding the Father's Word. Indeed, because there is but one act of understanding between the Father and the Son, it may be that this pattern *must* be constant. In any event, the point is that nothing we have said here need undermine the strict unity of understanding in the Father and the Son. The two Persons understand in distinct ways, and They understand from, as it were, opposite directions. Yet They both understand the Father in understanding His divine Word, and They both understand in—and They are both ultimately identical to—a single act of understanding.[102]

---

101 See *De Pot.*, q. 10, a. 4, ad 10: "the Father receives nothing from the Son." Though, as we saw in chapter three, Durand finds room in Thomas for a "return" of the Son to the Father: see Durand, "The Theology of God the Father," 376.

102 It might sound strange to claim that the Son is the Word in Whom the Son Himself understands. Yet this claim might find an echo when Thomas writes that the "the Holy Spirit loves Himself by Himself" (*de 108 art.*, q. 59; see also q. 60). We will unfold some of the subtleties involved in this passage in chapter six. For now, we need merely note that, if the Holy Spirit is the Love-impression by Whom the Holy Spirit Himself loves then it should make sense to say that the Son is the Word in Whom the Son Himself understands.

Thomas perhaps points in the same direction when he is commenting on Heb 1:3 ("The Son . . . upholds all things by the word of His power"). He writes that, "just as the Father

AS OTHER

With these points in mind, we can return to the scheme we laid out in the beginning of this chapter. Again, in this synthesis, interpersonal knowledge would be derivative of a more basic self-knowledge, and each divine Person would enter into the other's self-knowledge only insofar as all three are identical to a single essence. Since sketching this scheme, we have argued that Thomas's psychological analogy gives us an interpersonal knowledge that is just as basic as self-knowledge. We can suggest now that this same psychological analogy gives us an interpersonal knowledge that springs not only from essential unity but also from personal distinction. According to Thomas's psychological categories, the Father knows the Son in knowing Himself not only because the Son, like the Father, is identical to the Father's own essence. Instead, He knows the Son in knowing Himself because the Son, unlike the Father, is the *Word* of the Father. It is the Son's status as Word—which accounts for His distinction from the Father—that plants Him at the foundation of the Father's self-knowledge. Just so, the Son knows the Father in knowing Himself because the Father, unlike the Son, is imaged in the divine Word. When the Father and the Son know each other, therefore, They certainly know each other as united in the same essence. Yet Thomas's psychological analogy demands that They also—and that They just as basically—know each other *as other*.

Yet one might still raise an objection. For even if the Persons know each other as distinct Persons, They are still all identical to the same essence. Indeed, because of simplicity, none of the divine Persons is *anything but* the essence He shares with the others. It may be, therefore, that the Father cannot know Himself without knowing His Word. Yet it seems like all He could possibly know in His Word is His own essence. All He could see in another is more of Himself.

---

produced all things by the Word . . . so the Son, *by the same Word that He is*, made all things" (*in Heb.*, #33). He continues, "'by the Word of His power,' i.e., *by Himself* Who is the powerful Word" (#35). Thomas is comfortable saying that the Word creates by the Word that He is. It seems no less of a stretch to say that the same Word understands in the Word that He is.

The deepest response to this objection trades on the distinct ways of knowing that we have mentioned throughout this chapter. As we have seen repeatedly, the one divine act of understanding exists in distinct ways in the Father and in the Son. We can return now to a point we mentioned in chapter two: "[it is true that] whatever the Father has the Son has, but not that the Son has it in the same order as the Father. For the Son has as receiving from another; whereas the Father has as giving to another."[103] Everything in the Father exists in Him as giving to the Son; everything in the Son exists in Him as receiving from the Father. Even the divine essence is caught up in this pattern: "the same *essence* is fatherhood in the Father and sonship in the Son."[104] We saw above that there is never any bare or impersonal divine intellect that understands itself. Instead, the only ones Who understand are the Father, the Son, and the Holy Spirit, each of Whom understands in a distinct way. So too the divine essence. This essence is no fourth thing in God, and it exists in no way beneath, before, or independent of the divine Persons.[105] It is the essence *of* the three Persons, and it only ever exists *as* those three Persons: it exists as fatherhood in the Father, as sonship in the Son, and as proceeding in the Holy Spirit, and it never exists anywhere else or in any other way.

When the Father sees the Word, therefore, He sees nothing but His own essence. He sees nothing alien to Himself, and He sees nothing that He Himself does not already contain within Himself. Yet He does not see an impersonal or generic divine essence—for there *is* no impersonal or generic divine essence. Instead, when He sees His own essence *in* the Word, He sees that essence *as* the Word: He sees His own essence existing according to the relation by which His Word is distinct from Himself. Again, this relation is not a sort of film overlaying the

---

[103] *In Ioan.*, #2112. For more on these points, see Legge, *Trinitarian Christology*, 111–22; White, *The Trinity*, 394, 446, and 450, and "Divine Simplicity and the Holy Trinity," *International Journal of Systematic Theology* 18, no. 1 (2016): 87; and Hankey, *God in Himself*, 130–31. See also Bourassa, "Sur la Propriéte de l'Espirit," pt. 2, 27 and 36–43; and Gomes, "La Réciprocité psychologique," 162–63.

[104] *ST* I q. 42, a. 6, ad 3. See also q. 42, a. 4, ad 2.

[105] As Emery puts it, "the essence . . . is, from one end to the other of the treatise [on God] 'the unique essence *of three persons*,' numerically one, subsisting in each of the persons, never outside of the persons with whom it does not number" (*TA*, 198; emphasis added).

divine essence in the Word; it *is* the divine essence in the Word. The "essence *is* . . . sonship in the Son."[106] There is no corner or crevice in the Word, therefore, in which the Father might possibly see anything other than His Word—or in which He might possibly see something other than a Person distinct from Himself. Just so, when the Son sees His own essence in the Father, He sees that essence as fatherly and as fatherhood. He sees the Father as a Person distinct from Himself. Interpersonal knowledge in God, therefore, really is interpersonal. No divine Person sees anything but His own essence in any of the other Persons; yet no divine Person sees anything but another Person when He sees His own essence in that Person.[107]

UNDERSTANDING ANOTHER, UNDERSTANDING ONESELF, GIVING ONESELF

We can add a final dimension by recalling the conclusions of our last chapter. We saw throughout that chapter that in God, a Speaker

---

106 *ST* I q. 42, a. 6, ad 3.

107 These points open up a final paradox. On the one hand, because the Son is a Word, He is far more intimate to the Father's act of understanding than any other human being could possibly be to my act of understanding. I conceive a word of my friend when I know him. My friend, however, never *is* the word I conceive. The Son, therefore, as the Father's Word, is involved in the Father's understanding far more intimately than any human being (or angel) is involved in another human being's (or angel's) understanding. Yet, for the same reason—because the Son is the Father's Word—the divine act of understanding is *itself* interpersonal in a way that has no parallel in interpersonal knowledge among creatures. When my friend and I understand each other, we each understand another person. Yet we do so in the same way: we both understand as conceiving a word. My relationship to my friend does not govern the way in which I understand him—let alone govern the way in which I understand all that I understand. It is only in God that the relationship between the Persons Who know each other shapes Their respective ways of knowing: all the Father's knowledge is in relation to His Word (He understands as producing a Word), and all the Word's knowledge is in relation to His Father (He knows as the Word proceeding from the Father). Thus, we saw all through part one that intimacy and distinction are not opposed in Thomas's Trinity. We see the same point now: the divine Word is intimately ingredient in His Speaker's act of understanding in a way that outstrips anything to be found between two created persons; yet the distinction between Word and Speaker enters into Their act of understanding—and so Their act of understanding is *itself* shot through with interpersonal distinction—in a way that also outstrips anything found between two created persons.

cannot conceive a Word without giving Himself to His Word. We see now that, because of the nature of a word, the conception of the divine Word goes all the way to the logical foundation of the divine act of understanding—which means that *interpersonal self-giving* must go to the logical foundation of divine understanding: for in God, intra-mental conception *is* interpersonal self-giving. Understanding in God, therefore, is not only a marriage of self-knowledge and interpersonal knowledge. It is a marriage of self-knowledge, interpersonal knowledge, and interpersonal self-giving.

And it is a marriage in which all three dimensions are equally and reciprocally foundational. We do not first understand something and only subsequently conceive a word of that thing or understand that word. Nor do we first conceive a word of something and only then understand our word or understand the thing. Nor, finally, do we first understand our word and only then understand the thing or conceive our word. Instead, we conceive our word, we understand our word, and we understand the thing all at once. Or, perhaps better, in conceiving our word, we already understand our word and we already understand the thing imaged in it; in understanding our word, we already conceive our word and we already understand the thing; and, in understanding the thing, we already conceive our word and we already understand our word.

Even in us, then, all three of these moments coincide, depend on each other, and indwell each other. In God—in Whom understanding one's Word is understanding another Person, and in Whom conceiving a Word is giving the whole of oneself to another Person—they do the same. Yet they do so not only because they are really identical, and not only because God is simple or immutable. Instead, they do so because, even as logically distinct, these three moments are equally and reciprocally foundational.

Thus, beginning with the Father, the Father cannot understand Himself unless He already understands His Word and unless He already gives Himself to His Word. Yet He cannot understand His Word unless He already understands Himself in His Word and unless He already gives Himself to His Word. Finally, He cannot give Himself to His Word unless He already understands His Word and unless He already understands Himself in His Word. Giving the whole of oneself to another Person, understanding that other Person, and understanding oneself in that other Person are all really identical. Yet, insofar as they are logically distinct, they are reciprocally foundational: each comes before all the others.

Just so, the Son cannot understand Himself unless He already understands the Father in Himself, unless He already receives Himself from the Father, and unless He receives all that the Father has. Yet He cannot understand the Father unless He already understands Himself, unless He already receives Himself, and unless He already receives all that the Father has. Finally, He cannot receive Himself from the Father, and He cannot receive into Himself all that the Father has, unless He already understands Himself and unless He already understands the Father in understanding Himself. Receiving oneself, receiving another Person into oneself, understanding oneself, and understanding another Person from Whom one has received oneself are all reciprocally foundational in the one divine act of understanding as it exists in the Son.

In both divine Persons, therefore, each element—self-knowledge, reciprocal interpersonal knowledge, and giving the whole of oneself to another Person or receiving the whole of oneself from another Person—enters into the logical fabric of all the others. Again, it is not merely that divine simplicity demands that these facets be really identical. The details of Thomas's psychological analogy also demand that even insofar as these facets are logically distinct, they must be equally and reciprocally foundational, to the point that none could exist without the others.

CONCLUSION

To speak of knowledge in the Father and the Son, however, is to speak incompletely. For there are not only two divine Persons; there are three. It need hardly be said that the Holy Spirit has faded into the background over the past several chapters. It is now time for Him to take center stage. Indeed, it is only by turning to the Holy Spirit that we will uncover the deepest interpenetration of the interpersonal and the intrapersonal.[108]

---

108 Though we cannot say much about the Holy Spirit and the divine intellect, we should at least say a word or two. First of all, Thomas teaches that because the Holy Spirit is a

divine Person, He understands Himself, the Father, and the Son (see *in I Cor.*, #107). As we saw above, however, Thomas offers insights into the ways in which the divine act of understanding exists in the Father and the Son. He never offers any comparable insights regarding the Holy Spirit. To say anything here, we will therefore need to extend Thomas's principles into conclusions that Thomas himself does not draw.

To begin, we saw that the Father understands as conceiving a Word and that the Son understands as the Word conceived. It seems that the Holy Spirit, for His part, must understand as the Love Who proceeds from both. Saying more is difficult. Yet we can perhaps suggest that because of the structure of understanding, the Holy Spirit can only understand at all if He understands in a word. Thus, given that there is only one Word in God, it seems that the Holy Spirit must understand in the one divine Word. Yet, in understanding the divine Word, He must already understand the Father: for the Word is transparent to the Father. To understand the Father in understanding the Word, however, is to understand the Father *in relation* to the Word and the Word *in relation* to the Father: it is to see the bond between the Father and the Son. Yet the Holy Spirit Himself *is* this bond. The Holy Spirit, therefore, in one act of understanding, would know Himself *in* knowing the Father *in* knowing the Son. Even more, He would know Himself, the Father, and the Son insofar as each is distinct from the others: He would know the Father as Speaker, the Son as Word, and Himself as Their bond of Love.

Indeed, if this logic holds, then it may be that the Father and the Word also know Their personal Love-bond in knowing Themselves and each other. Thomas might suggest as much when he writes that "knowledge of the Father includes, in a way, knowledge of the Son, for He would not be Father if He did not have a Son; and the bond between Them is the Holy Spirit" (*ST* II-II q. 1, a. 8, ad 3).

6

SELF-LOVE AS INTERPERSONAL LOVE AS INTERPERSONAL COMMUNION AS INTERPERSONAL SELF-GIVING AS INTERPERSONAL BEING-GIVEN

As we saw in our last chapter, Thomas's principles can yield a number of conclusions regarding self-knowledge and mutual knowledge in God. Thomas himself, however, never directly asks whether the divine Word has anything to do with interpersonal knowledge. Things are different with Love. Thomas asks regularly whether the Holy Spirit proceeds as the mutual Love of the Father and the Son: this question emerges in his commentary on John, but it also figures prominently in such dogmatic contexts as his *Sentences* commentary, the *De Potentia*, and the *Summa*.[1]

---

[1] Thomas was not the only scholastic to take on this question directly, and the prominence of this question among his contemporaries may help to explain why he engages with it so consistently. For more on this historical background, see Emery, *TTTA*, 238–39; and Anthony Keaty, "The Holy Spirit Proceeding as Mutual Love: An Interpretation of Aquinas' *Summa Theologiae* I.37," *Angelicum* 77 (2000): 533–57.

Perhaps because of this prominence, Thomas's readers have paid more attention to mutual love than they have to mutual knowledge. They have not, however, done so with one voice. On one extreme stands M. T.-L. Penido.[2] Penido acknowledges that mutual love enjoys pride of place in the *Sentences*, and he recognizes passages in the *De Potentia* where Thomas integrates the interpersonal and the psychological. Yet he argues that Thomas's most mature thought is psychological *instead of* interpersonal. Penido admits that Thomas speaks of mutual love in the *Summa*. He also admits that, in the *Summa*, each Person is identical to the same goodness, which means that "each Person cannot love Himself without loving the others."[3] Yet Penido insists that, on the terms of Thomas's mature thought, any talk of mutual love "approaches metaphor": in reality, all God ever loves is His own goodness.[4] Even when the Father loves the Son and the Son the Father, each merely loves His own goodness, and Thomas's language of "mutual love" is but a cipher for this self-love.

Penido was not alone in advancing such a reading.[5] Yet he did not go unchallenged. François Bourassa headed the countercharge by arguing that even in Thomas's mature theology, self-love and mutual love are equally foundational.[6] H. C. Schmidbaur went even further: he proposed that the Holy Spirit's procession is a matter of mutual love instead of self-love.[7]

---

2 See "Gloses sur la procession d'amour dans la Trinité"; and "A Propos de la procession d'amour en Dieu."

3 "Gloses sur la procession," 59.

4 "Gloses sur la procession," 59.

5 For other figures who align with Penido, see Anthony Keaty, "The Holy Spirit Proceeding," 533n1.

6 See "Sur la Propriéte de l'Espirit"; "Le Saint-Espirit, 'Communion du Père et du Fils'"; "Le Saint-Esprit unite d'amour du Père et du Fils"; and "Dans la communion de l'Esprit Saint," pts. 1–3, *Science et Esprit* 34, no. 1 (1982): 31–56; 34, no. 2 (1982): 135–49; 34, no. 1 (1982): 239–68. For others in Bourassa's camp, see Keaty, "The Holy Spirit," 535n6.

7 As Emery puts it, Schmidbaur wants "to see in the mutual love of the Father and the Son, to the exclusion of the love that God has for Himself . . . the only authentic explication of Thomas concerning the procession of the Spirit." Quoted from Emery's review of *Personarum Trinitatis: De trinitarishe Gotteslehre des heiligen Thomas von Aquin* (St. Otillien: EOS Verlag, 1995), *Revue Thomiste* 96 (1996), 692.

More recently, a new path has emerged. This third way seems to have achieved the status of a new consensus, and we can therefore spend a bit more time with it. Emery sums up the matter well: "St. Thomas shows the property of the Holy Spirit as Love by considering the love through which God loves His own goodness, and then by reflecting on the mutual love of Father and Son, the second theme being founded on the first."[8] Torrell had already claimed the same: "Thomas introduces [mutual love] in a second phase of his explanation, after establishing it on a more solid metaphysical and conceptual basis: the love that God has for his own goodness."[9] Mutual love in God is real: it is no mere metaphor, and it is no cipher for self-love. Yet this mutual love is built on the more logically basic foundation of self-love.[10]

In the decades since Torrell first proposed this middle way, no one has challenged it. Instead, readers of Thomas have flocked to it. Most important here is Kenneth M. Loyer, who argues for this position in even more depth and detail than either Emery or Torrell had.[11] Emmanuel Durand, John Baptist Ku, and Matthew Levering have also, in briefer engagements, thrown their weight behind it.[12] For our part, we can turn to a passage where Emery articulates his position in a bit more detail:

> the idea of "mutual love" . . . as the immediate entrance to the study of the person of the Holy Spirit as love cannot be congruent to the purpose of disclosing the *unity* of an

---

8 *TTTA*, 237.

9 *Spiritual Master*, 186. See also 183–88.

10 Of course, for Thomas, those who have not encountered Revelation can conclude that God loves Himself, but they cannot know of any mutual love in God. In this sense, self-love *is* logically prior to mutual love, at least in our understanding of the mystery. Yet Torrell and Emery go further: they claim that *within* Thomas's Trinitarian theology, and in his treatment of the procession of the Holy Spirit, self-love is more logically basic than mutual love.

11 See *God's Love through the Spirit: The Holy Spirit in Thomas Aquinas and John Wesley* (Washington, DC: The Catholic University of America Press, 2014), 101–40.

12 See Durand, *La Périchorèse des personnes divines* (Paris: Cerf, 2005), 183, 259–61, and 342–44; and Ku, *God the Father in the Theology of St. Thomas Aquinas* (New York: P. Lang, 2013), 265. In *Engaging the Doctrine of the Holy Spirit*, Levering does not take up this question up directly; but he alludes to it (see 91n91), and he cites Emery and Loyer at almost every turn in his treatment of *ST* I q. 37 (see 99–103).

> *immanent* procession.... This is why Thomas takes as his point of departure the case of the procession of the "imprint" of love which comes about in the will of the lover. When it is transposed into God, the imprint of love which arises from *God's love for Himself* can be understood as a subsistent relation, the very person the Holy Spirit is. Once he has set these bases into position, Thomas can erect the *second tier* of his analysis, and show that the Father and the Son love each other through the Holy Spirit.[13]

There can be no doubt that, at least in the *Summa*, Thomas begins his pneumatology with the immanent procession of a love-impression. For Emery, however, this immanent procession is a matter merely of "God's love for Himself." On this point, moreover, he is joined by Bourassa as well as by Penido. Indeed, everyone who has weighed in on this question, no matter how opposed their ultimate conclusions might be, shares a common assumption: they all assume that Thomas's psychological analogy is a matter merely of self-love and that Thomas only introduces mutual love insofar as he introduces nonpsychological language.[14] For Penido, this nonpsychological language is ultimately a cipher for the psychological; for Bourassa, it is real and equally foundational; for Emery and company, it is real, but it is a "second tier" built on the foundation of the psychological. For all parties, however, the immanent procession of a Love-impression is a matter of self-love alone.

We have already seen enough to call this common assumption into question. Indeed, we have spent this whole study arguing that Thomas's psychological analogy itself is already interpersonal. We will

---

[13] *TTTA*, 236; emphasis added. Emery makes a similar point in *TTTA* 235. See also Loyer, *God's Love*, 135 and 140. We will spend part of this chapter pushing back against this reading of mutual love as a "second tier," but we will not be able to speak to every argument Emery and Loyer offer in its favor. For a fuller response to it, see my "A Second Tier? Aquinas on Mutual Love in the Procession of the Holy Spirit," forthcoming in *Nova et Vetera*.

[14] This point runs all through Penido: see "Gloses sur la procession," 48 and 62. Bourassa is more subtle. Yet he still proposes a version of the mutually extrinsic "complementarity" that we saw in the section "Social or Psychological?" in our introduction. See, for example, "'communion' du Pêre et du Fils," I, 276–80, and II, 11–13, 36; "Sur la Propriété," II, 28–29. Bourassa also sometimes succumbs to the temptation of opposing the psychological and the interpersonal: see "Sur la Propriété," 34–36.

see now that this pattern holds in the procession of Love no less than it does in the procession of a Word. Indeed, it is only in the procession of Love that we find the fullest flowering of the interpersonal within the psychological. We will begin by seeing that the procession of an inner Love-impression in the simple divine nature is already a matter of interpersonal love. Because of the role of a word in the procession of love—that is, because of the details of Thomas's psychological analogy—neither the Father nor the Son can love Himself unless the other loves with Him. Just so, neither can love Himself unless He is loved by the other. After seeing as much, we will add another dimension: we will see that the procession of divine Love is not merely a marriage of self-love and interpersonal love. It is also a marriage of both to total interpersonal self-giving: in this procession, Speaker and Word give Themselves together to Their subsistent Love. Even more, this self-giving is inextricable from the interpersonal communion of the two givers. After tracing out this self-giving, we will add still another dimension: we will see that the procession of Love is a matter of interpersonal giving not only insofar as two Persons give Themselves to a third, but also insofar as this third Person is Himself given by the first Person to the second Person. From there, we will end by proposing that all of these interpersonal elements are ingredient not only in the immanent procession of a divine Love-impression but in God's essential love as well. Indeed, we will suggest that these interpersonal notes go all the way to the logical foundation of God's essential act of loving His own goodness.[15]

---

15 After His long absence, the Holy Spirit will return in force in this chapter. Yet one might complain that, even here, He remains somewhat in the background. One might also complain that He does not *do* much in this chapter. For, through much of this chapter, it will be the Father and the Son Who love each other and Who give Themselves. Indeed, when we discuss the Holy Spirit as given by the Father to the Son, it might seem that we are reducing the Holy Spirit to a thing that is passively given from one Person to another (though, as we will see, He is not a "possession"). In response, we should note that Thomas's Holy Spirit *is* active: He, for example, loves in the act of love by way of which He proceeds (see *ST* I q. 37, a. 1, ad 4). More deeply, we will see that, because He is a Love-impression, He unites the Father and the Son in communion—a very active role. Most deeply, however, to say that the Holy Spirit is mostly "passive" in divine love is not to say that He is less important than the others. Thomas Weinandy argues that such "passivity" is a matter of imperfection, and he attempts to carve out an "active" role for the Holy Spirit: see *The Father's Spirit of Sonship* (New York: T&T

As in our last chapter, reaching these conclusions will certainly require that we develop Thomas: we will spend most of this chapter unfolding his principles in order to draw conclusions that Thomas himself never makes explicit. Indeed, our conclusions here will require even more creative development than those of our last chapter did. Even more, because Thomas speaks less directly of a love-impression than he does of a word, our conclusions will sometimes require that we gather together a good number of threads. Our arguments will therefore sometimes be less elegant than those of our previous chapter, and our conclusions will sometimes be more tentative. Yet, as in our previous chapter, I hope to show that the conclusions we will draw here really do follow on—or are at least suggested by—Thomas's principles. We will have to do quite a bit of digging to unearth them, but I hope to show that everything we dig up is buried in Thomas's psychological analogy for the Trinity.

SELF-LOVE AS INTERPERSONAL LOVE

LOVE FROM A WORD

We can begin by defining some terms. As we saw briefly in chapter one, Thomas acknowledges the limited range of our language for love: whereas we have different terms to distinguish "understanding" from "speaking" and from the "word" that proceeds in understanding, we have no such terms for love.[16] Instead, "essential love," which corresponds to "understanding," points to the relation between the lover and the thing he loves. "Notional love," which corresponds to "speaking," points to the act of breathing forth a love-impression. "Personal love," which corresponds to "word," points to the love-impression that proceeds

---

Clark, 1995). In fact, however, this "passive" role might be just as important—and just as dignified—as the "active" roles played by the Father and the Son: see David Liberto's response to Weinandy in "Person, Being, and Receptivity: W. Norris Clarke's Retrieval and Completion of Thomas's Thought," in *Aquinas as Authority: A Collection of Studies Presented at the Second Conference of the Thomas Instituut te Utrecht, December 14–16, 2000* (Leusden-Zuid: Thomas Instituut te Utrecht, 2002), 201–11.

16. For the following points, see *ST* I q. 37, a. 1; and Emery, *TTTA*, 62–69, 227–33.

in the act of love. In God, essential love is the act in which all three Persons love the divine goodness. Notional love is the act in which the Father and the Son breathe forth the Holy Spirit. And personal love is the Holy Spirit Himself Who proceeds as a Love-impression.

This interplay of love taken essentially, notionally, and personally will reemerge throughout this chapter. We ought therefore to keep it firmly in mind. For now, however, we will focus on notional and personal love. We will focus, that is, on the procession of the Holy Spirit as Love. We can begin with the role a word plays in any such procession of love. As Thomas puts it in the *Summa*,

> Though will and intellect are not diverse in God, nevertheless it is of the *ratio* of will and of intellect that the processions which are according to the action of each should exist in a certain order. For there is no procession of love except as ordered to the procession of the word; for nothing can be loved by the will unless it is conceived in the intellect. Therefore . . . , because *it is of the ratio of love that it not proceed except from the concept of intellect*, there is a distinction of order between the procession of Love and the procession of the Word in God.[17]

As we saw in chapter one, it belongs to the *ratio* of a word that it proceed from a speaker who understands. We see now that procession belongs to the *ratio* of love as well. Yet love proceeds not only from the lover who loves. It proceeds also from his word of the beloved thing. Indeed, "the *ratio* of love" demands that love cannot proceed at all unless it proceeds from a word.[18]

---

[17] *ST* I q. 27, a. 3, ad 3.

[18] Thomas offers similar arguments regarding word and love throughout his corpus: see *ST* I q. 36, a. 2; *SCG* IV 19§8; *Comp. Theo.* I, 49; *de rationibus fidei*, ch. 4; and *De Pot.*, q. 10, a. 4. See also Emery, *TTTA*, 286–88. It will also be important for us that love proceeds not only from a word, but from the lover who speaks that word: as Thomas puts it, "words proceed from the speaker, and love from the lover" (q. 10, a. 1), and "the act of willing is exercised by love proceeding from the lover through his will" (q. 9, a. 9. See also *Comp. Theo.* I, 49 and 52). In *SCG* IV 19§8, Thomas might point in a different direction: he seems to suggest that love proceeds from the word and from the beloved thing. Here, however, we will focus on self-love, in which the beloved thing is the lover

Thomas is clear here that this pattern holds analogously in God: because of "the *ratio* of love," the divine Love-impression cannot proceed unless He proceeds from the divine Word. As in God, so in us. In us, however, our words are merely a part of us: they are accidents that do not act and that do not love us in return. The whole drama of my self-love, then, can play out within a single person: me.[19] Not so in God. We will see soon that the Love Who proceeds in God is a distinct Person. We can begin, however, by recalling that the Word from Whom Love proceeds—and without Whom Love cannot proceed—is also a distinct Person. To say, therefore, that divine Love must proceed from a Lover and from His Word is to say that Love must proceed from two Persons.

This point is already enough to yield some fairly strong conclusions, and it can already push back on the idea that, in the procession of the Holy Spirit, mutual love is a "second tier" built on self-love.[20] To see as much, we should note first that the procession of divine Love has everything to do with self-love in God: "The Father loves not only the Son, but also *Himself* and us, by the Holy Spirit. . . . He loves *Himself* and every creature by the Holy Spirit insofar as the Holy Spirit proceeds as the love of the primal goodness, according to which the Father loves *Himself* and every creature."[21] Even when the Father loves His own "primal goodness," He loves by the Love-impression Who proceeds from Him. We will see towards the end of this chapter that things are complicated and that Thomas here is referring only to notional love. In essential love, the Father loves Himself "not by the Holy Spirit, but by [His] essence."[22] For now, however, we can remain with notional and personal love. For the various positions with which we opened this chapter were concerned not with God's love more broadly, but specifically with notional and personal love: they were concerned with

---

himself—and so in which, even based on the *SCG*'s criteria, love proceeds from a word and from the lover who conceives it.

19 Though for some qualifications of this point, see Oster, "Becoming a Person and the Trinity" and Schindler, "The Crisis of Marriage," 354 and 358.

20 Quoted from Emery, *TTTA*, 236.

21 *ST* I q. 37, a. 2, ad 3. See also *De Pot.*, q. 9, a. 9, ad 13.

22 *ST* I q. 37, a. 2. For more of this language of "by" the Holy Spirit, see *ST* I q. 37, a. 2; and Emery, *TTTA*, 240–41.

the relationship between self-love and mutual love in the procession of the Holy Spirit. We can therefore focus a bit on notional and personal love before we turn to essential love at the end of this chapter.

Again, the first point to emphasize is that notional love includes self-love. It does so not only in the Father, but in the Holy Spirit—and, by extension, in the Son—as well: "the Holy Spirit loves Himself by Himself."[23] We can remain, however, with the Father. In the immanent procession of Love, the Father loves Himself by the Love-impression Whom He breathes forth. Yet, because of the nature of love, He can only breathe forth Love if He does so with His Word: again, "the *ratio* of love" demands that love cannot proceed at all unless it proceeds both from a lover and from his word. The divine Word, therefore, breathes forth with the Father the Love-impression by which the Father loves Himself: He "is not just any sort of Word, but a Word breathing forth Love."[24] This point is very basic, but it is already important for us. For it is enough to guarantee that, in the procession of the Holy Spirit, the Father does not love Himself alone. Indeed, insofar as Love cannot proceed except from a Word, the Father *cannot* love Himself alone. He can only breathe Love in His self-love if He breathes with His Word—which means that He can only breathe if He breathes *with another Person*.

This breathing-forth, moreover, is not tacked on to the act of love. Instead, in notional love, breathing-forth *is* the act of love: "when the term 'love' is taken in a notional sense, it means nothing else than 'to breathe love,' just as to speak is to produce a word."[25] So far as notional love goes, to love is to breathe. Yet, because the Father cannot breathe unless He breathes with His Word, He cannot *love* anything notionally—not even Himself—unless He loves with His Word. In the procession of the Holy Spirit, the Father can only love Himself if He loves Himself with another Person—a Person Who remains entirely within Him, yet Who also stands present to Him from the outside.

---

23 *De 108 art.*, q. 59. This point is reiterated in q. 60.
24 *ST* I q. 43, a. 5, ad 2.
25 *ST* I q. 37, a. 2.

Even more, it is *as other* that this other Person loves in the Father's self-love. The Son loves with the Father not only insofar as, like the Father, He is identical to the goodness that the Father loves. He loves with the Father also insofar as, unlike the Father, He is a Word. Even more, because the Word is a Word, He goes just as logically deep into the Father's self-love as the Father Himself does. In God, the Holy Spirit proceeds no less from the Son than He does from the Father.[26] Indeed, because the Son is the Word of the Father, the Holy Spirit could not possibly proceed any less from the Son than from the Father. Even logically speaking, love does not proceed first from a lover alone and subsequently from his word of the beloved thing. Instead, love only ever proceeds *at all* insofar as it proceeds from a word. A word goes all the way to the first logical beginning of the procession of love. The divine Word, therefore, goes all the way to the first logical beginning of the Father's self-love. Even logically speaking, the Father cannot ever, on any level, love Himself in solitude. In notional love, He can only love Himself if another Person loves with Him.

LOVING WITH ANOTHER, LOVED BY ANOTHER

We can take one more step. We can do so somewhat tentatively, for it will take us a good deal beyond any conclusion that Thomas explicitly draws. Yet Thomas's principles seem to open this path up, so we can at least scout it out provisionally. First, when the Father loves Himself, He does not love a generic or impersonal essential divine goodness: again, there *is* no generic or impersonal essential divine goodness. Instead, essential goodness only ever exists as fatherly in the Father, as sonly in the Son, and as proceeding in the Holy Spirit.[27] When the Father loves Himself, therefore, He loves the divine goodness as fatherly and as fatherhood. Indeed, because the divine goodness does not *exist* in

---

26 See *ST* I q. 36, a. 3, ad 2. In this same passage, Thomas writes that the Holy Spirit proceeds "principally" from the Father, but only insofar as the Son receives from the Father the power to breathe. We will return to this point later in this chapter.

27 See *ST* I q. 30, a. 2, ad 4, which we studied in the section "A Family Trinity and Self-Diffusive Goodness" in chapter four. See also *SCG* IV 26§5; and I *Sent.*, d. 10, q. 1, a. 5, ad 3.

the Father except as fatherly, there is no other goodness that the Father *could* love in loving Himself.

No one, however, can breathe forth a love-impression unless he loves the thing loved by that love-impression. As we will see towards the end of this chapter, the impression of a beloved thing proceeds in the affections of a lover "from the fact that anyone loves anything."[28] A specific thing makes an impression in a specific lover's affections "from the fact" that this specific lover loves this specific thing. A lover, therefore, can only breathe forth an impression of a thing if he loves that very thing. Put differently, Thomas writes that a love-impression is the presence of "*the beloved thing* in the lover": it is "the impression . . . of the *beloved* object."[29] A love-impression, therefore, can only be present in a lover—and that lover can only breathe forth love—if that lover actually *loves the thing* that makes this impression in His affections.

This point may seem obvious. Yet, if we think it through carefully—and analogously—in terms of the Trinity, we can take our next step. For we just saw that the structure of love demands that the Word must breathe with the Father in the Father's self-love. We see now that the Word can only breathe in the Father's self-love if He loves, with the Father, whatever the Father loves in His self-love. Yet what the Father loves in His self-love is the divine goodness *as fatherly*. In the Father's self-love, therefore, Love can only proceed from a Word if that Word loves the divine goodness as fatherly. And, because love cannot proceed *at all* unless it proceeds from a word, Love can only proceed in the Father's self-love if, in that self-love, the Word loves the divine goodness as fatherly.[30]

---

28 *ST* I q. 37, a. 1.

29 *ST* I q. 37, a. 1. See also *SCG* IV 19§4; and *Comp. Theo.* I, ch. 45.

30 To say that self-love in the Father is love for the divine goodness as fatherly (or to say, as we will say shortly, that self-love in the Son is love for the divine goodness as sonly) is not to deny that there is one essential divine goodness that all three Persons love. It is merely to clarify that this essential goodness is no fourth thing stacked alongside the Persons. Instead, it only ever exists as fatherly, as sonly, and as proceeding. Just so, I have spoken of "the Father's self-love," and I will speak of the Word's self-love. I do not, however, mean that the Father has one act of self-love and the Son another. I mean that there is one act of self-love that They share perfectly, but that They possess in different ways (see *ST* I q. 37, a. 1, ad 4; and *de 108 art.*, q. 27).

In the Father's self-love, then, the Word must love the Father. Indeed, He must love the Father as a Person distinct from Himself. Again, He loves not merely the divine goodness but the divine goodness as fatherly. Even more, He loves the Father in the Father's self-love not merely because He is really identical to the Father's act of essential love but also because He is the Word of the Father. When He loves the Father in the Father's own self-love, He does so as a Person distinct from the Father. Finally, because to love notionally is simply to breathe forth love, and because love proceeds from a lover's word no less than from the lover himself, the Word loves the Father in the Father's self-love just as basically as the Father loves Himself. The Word, therefore, enters into the foundation of the Father's self-love not only insofar as, from the beginning, He loves *with* the Father; He does so insofar as, from the beginning, *He loves the Father Himself*. In the Father, self-love is not only loving *with* another; it is just as basically being loved *by* another.

All the same points would hold, though differently, for the Word. First of all, if a lover cannot breathe forth love alone, then neither can a word. Love proceeds neither from a lover alone nor from a word alone; it proceeds from a lover and his word together. In notional love, therefore, the Word cannot love Himself alone. If He did, then His Love-impression would proceed from a word alone, which is impossible. He can only breathe forth Love in loving Himself if He breathes with His Speaker. The Father, therefore—as the Speaker of a Word, and so as a Person distinct from the Word—enters into the inmost architecture of self-love as it exists in the Word. He loves with His Word as His Word loves Himself.

Finally, as was the case with the Father, the Word cannot love a generic divine goodness. Instead, when He loves Himself, He must love the one divine goodness as sonly. The Father, however, can only breathe with the Word in the Word's self-love if the Father Himself loves what the Word loves. The Word, therefore, cannot love Himself notionally unless the Father loves the divine goodness as sonly, and unless He loves this goodness-as-sonly just as basically as the Son Himself does. The Word can only love Himself if, in His self-love, He is just as basically loved by the Father.

For both the Father and the Son, then, to love oneself is to be loved by another Person. In the one divine act of notional love, each loves the other in the other's self-love, and each is loved by the other in His own self-love. Each, moreover, loves and is loved insofar as He is distinct from the other. Just so, neither loves the other as a function of loving Himself, and neither loves the other in a moment logically subsequent to loving Himself. Instead, because the two Persons are a Word and His Speaker, each is loved by another just as basically as He loves Himself. Finally, this otherness is not juxtaposed to self-love. Instead, in Thomas's psychological analogy, it is *in self-love itself* that each Person must be loved by another. Because love can only proceed if it proceeds from a word, there can be no self-love in God that is not just as basically mutual love.

At the same time, mutual love in God is just as basically self-love: the Father loves *Himself* when He loves with His Word and is loved by His Word, and His Word loves *Himself* when He loves with the Father and is loved by the Father. In the procession of the Holy Spirit as Love, self-love is just as basically mutual love and mutual love is just as basically self-love.

A Second Tier?

With these points in mind, we can return to the readings of Thomas with which we began this chapter. First of all, what we have seen goes beyond Penido. For we have established that interpersonal love in God is no mere metaphor: it really is interpersonal. Penido, in other words, is right that each divine Person loves nothing but His own goodness in loving another Person. Yet he misses the fact that this goodness only ever exists as fatherly, as sonly, and as proceeding—and so he misses the fact that each Person really loves *another Person* when He loves His own goodness in another Person. Just so, Penido recognizes one respect in which self-love includes otherness: he recognizes that, insofar as each Person is identical to the same goodness, each loves the others in loving His own goodness. Yet he misses any respect in which each enters into the other's self-love insofar as They are distinct: he forgets that one Person is a Word and the other is a Speaker, and he forgets that love cannot proceed at all unless it proceeds from a lover and from his word. Thus, ironically, Penido is as fierce a partisan as one is likely to find for a psychological Trinity over against an interpersonal Trinity.

Yet he misses certain interpersonal dimensions of Thomas's Trinity because his analysis is inadequately psychological. He pays insufficient attention to the role of a word in love, and he considers the Father and the Son only insofar as They are both God, not insofar as one is a Speaker and the other is a Word. And he therefore ends with an ersatz interpersonal love that is merely self-love in disguise.

What we have seen can take us not only beyond Penido but beyond Emery and Bourassa as well. Beyond Emery, mutual love would not stand as a "second tier" atop the logical foundation of self-love. Instead, mutual love goes to the foundation of self-love itself. Finally, beyond Bourassa, the Holy Spirit does not proceed as self-love *and* proceed just as basically as mutual love; He proceeds as mutual love *in* proceeding as self-love. It is self-love itself that is mutual all the way down.

SELF-LOVE AS MUTUAL LOVE
The Good as Apprehended

Our conclusions to this point have required that we massage Thomas's principles a good deal, and they have taken us beyond any claims Thomas explicitly registers. One might certainly challenge some of the details in those conclusions. One point, however, seems undeniable: it is absolutely bedrock to Thomas's psychological analogy that love can only proceed from a word. Whatever the precise role of the Word in the Father's self-love, therefore, it is indisputable that the Word enters *somehow* into the Father's self-love, at least insofar as "love" is taken notionally. It also seems plain that He does so as a Word, and so as distinct from the Father. Finally, because love only proceeds at all insofar as it proceeds from a word, it seems hard to deny that the Word enters into the Father's self-love from its first logical foundation.

To clarify things, we might distinguish interpersonal love, which is love that involves more than one person, from mutual love, in which two or more people love each other. When my friend and I together love theology, for example, that love is interpersonal—more than one person is involved in it—but it is not mutual: the theology we love does not love us back. My love for my friend himself, in contrast, is mutual: I love him and he loves me. We can conclude with confidence that, in

Thomas's psychological analogy, self-love is interpersonal: both in the Speaker and in His Word, to love oneself is to love with another. We can propose more gingerly that self-love is also mutual love: it seems that, in Their self-love, Speaker and Word can only love *with* each other if They love *each other*. Drawing this second conclusion requires that we connect a good deal of dots that Thomas leaves unconnected. But those dots are there, and they are ready to be connected. We can therefore at least suggest that when each Person loves Himself, He is just as basically loved by another.

Bracketing mutual love for a moment, our conclusions regarding interpersonal love are firmer, and they are already enough to take us beyond Penido, Bourassa, and Emery. For if we have shown only that the nature of a love-impression demands that interpersonal otherness enter into divine self-love, then we will already have seen that Thomas's psychological analogy is a good deal more interpersonal than is generally acknowledged. Yet we should remain a moment longer with mutual love, in part because readers of Thomas have paid so much attention to it, and in part because it is intrinsically interesting and important. We can only do so, however, if we proceed even more tentatively. For our next set of conclusions will be built almost entirely on a principle that runs all through Thomas's corpus, but whose implications—at least in this regard—Thomas never draws out. Indeed, I should admit that this principle might point only vaguely in the direction in which I will develop it. Still, it seems suggestive enough to warrant our at least taking a few steps gingerly down this path.

In short, Thomas teaches that "the proper object of love is the good."[31] Yet he also clarifies that the object of love is not merely goodness, but goodness as *apprehended*.[32] As he puts it, "good is the cause of love, as being its object. But good is not the object of the appetite,

---

[31] *ST* II-II q. 23, a. 4.

[32] For the different shapes such apprehensions can take in different natures, see *ST* I-II q. 26, a. 1.

except as apprehended."[33] Whenever a lover loves anything, he loves goodness-as-apprehended.[34]

Yet to say that a lover loves goodness-as-apprehended may be to say—or at least to open the door towards the suggestion—that whenever a lover loves anything, he loves his *word* of the beloved thing. First of all, within his Trinitarian theology, Thomas links goodness-as-apprehended to the lover's word of the good thing. In the *Summa*, he writes that "nothing can be loved by the will unless it is conceived in the intellect."[35] A lover not only loves goodness as apprehended; he loves goodness as *conceived* in a word. Thomas continues several questions later that "we do not love anything unless we *apprehend* it by a mental *conception*."[36] If we love goodness as apprehended, then we love it as apprehended by a word. Outside of his Trinitarian theology, he writes that "since the understood good is the object of the will, the will can will anything *conceived by the intellect* in which the nature of the good is present."[37] Again, will and love are directed not merely towards the good as apprehended, but towards the good as *conceived*: an agent wills that which he conceives in his word. Finally, back in his Trinitarian theology, Thomas seems to identify the apprehended good with the word: "the presence of the beloved object in the lover is brought about by ... the intelligible object as *apprehended*, which is the *word* conceived about the lovable object."[38] The intelligible object is not only apprehended *in* a word; it is apprehended *as* a word.

Thomas offers his most developed articulation of this point in the first appearance of his mature theology of the Word:

---

[33] *ST* I-II q. 27, a. 2.

[34] For an impressive array of texts to this effect (which generally speak of "will" instead of "love"), see Michael Sherwin, *By Knowledge and by Love: Charity and Knowledge in the Moral Theology of St. Thomas Aquinas* (Washington, DC: The Catholic University of America Press, 2005), 21n12. Sherwin also treats of a host of issues—the relationship between speculative and practical intellect, between love of concupiscence and love of friendship, between specification and exercise, and so on—which we will not address here, but which are helpful to have in the background.

[35] *ST* I q. 27, a. 3, ad 3.

[36] *ST* I q. 36, a. 2.

[37] *SCG* I 81§3.

[38] *Comp. Theo.* I, 49.

> everything that is understood, insofar as it is understood, must be in him who understands, for the very act of intellect signifies the *apprehension* of that which is understood by the intellect; hence, even our intellect understanding itself is within itself, not only as identified by essence, but also as *apprehended* by itself in the act of understanding. God, therefore, must be in Himself as the thing understood in him who understands. But the thing understood in him who understands is the *intention understood* and the *word*. There is, therefore, in God understanding Himself the Word of God.[39]

To understand is to apprehend by intellect. In one who understands, therefore, the presence of the thing *apprehended* is the presence of the thing *understood*. Yet the presence of "the thing understood in him who understands" is, by definition, an inner word.[40] Shifting to love and goodness, when I apprehend goodness, this goodness exists in my intellect as apprehended. Yet Thomas suggests here that the goodness-as-apprehended that exists in my intellect is my *word* of that goodness. If the object of love, therefore, is goodness-as-apprehended, then it may be that the object of intelligent love is a lover's word of a good thing.

These texts where Thomas connects the word to goodness-as-apprehended, moreover, give voice to principles we sketched at length in our last chapter. Again, if the object of love in general is goodness-as-apprehended, then the object of love in an intellectual nature is goodness-as-understood. Yet we saw all through our last chapter that to understand anything is to understand it in one's word of that thing. If, therefore, the object of intelligent love is goodness-as-understood, then the object of intelligent love must be goodness-as-understood-*in-a-word*.

At the very least, then, these principles seem to suggest that a word is bound up with the object of love. And, given that the object of love is that which a lover loves when he loves, these principles suggest that love passes somehow through a word, that love happens somehow in a

---

39 *SCG* IV 11§9.
40 See also *ST* I q. 37, a. 1.

word, or that love at least touches somehow on a word. These principles, that is, might suggest some respect in which the word *itself* is somehow loved—albeit perhaps indirectly—whenever anyone loves anything.

To say as much, of course, is not to deny that when a lover loves something, he really loves that thing in itself. Nor is it to deny that whereas the act of understanding terminates within the mind, the act of love terminates in the beloved thing.[41] Instead, it is simply to think through Thomas's claim that intelligent agents never love anything except insofar as those things are understood. We saw in our last chapter that intellect does not know its word instead of knowing the thing in itself; it knows the thing itself *in* knowing its word. Again, our words are transparent windows that put us in contact with things-in-themselves. We may see something similar here. For it seems that a lover need not set his words aside in order to love things-in-themselves. Instead, a lover only ever loves anything at all if he loves it as understood, and he only ever understands anything if he understands it in his word.

"Nor Is It Only the Knowledge of the Beloved That Is Loved"

Again, we can only propose these points tentatively. Thomas, however, might at least point in the direction we are headed in two texts from his Trinitarian theology. In the first, he writes that "because the Son is in the Father *as His Word*, the Father could not have perfect joy *in Himself* except in the Son. In the same way, a man does not delight in himself except through the concept he has of himself."[42] Neither in this passage itself nor in its larger context does Thomas speak directly to the role of a word in joy. He also does not explain why the Father could have no joy except in His Word.[43] He seems instead to take for granted, first, that we can only take joy in ourselves through our words of ourselves, and, second, that the Father likewise can only take

---

41 See *De Ver.*, q. 1, a. 2.

42 *De Pot.*, q. 9, a. 5, ad 24. See also *in Matt.*, #302: the Father "is not totally pleased except in the Son."

43 In the corpus of this article, however, he gives some clues as to why joy might be linked to a word. For more here, see my "Does Goodness Require Another?"

joy in Himself in His Word. Joy and love, of course, are not simply synonymous. Yet they are closely related. Thomas teaches elsewhere that love finds its "completion and end" in joy, which suggests that love cannot be perfect apart from joy.[44] God's love, for its part, cannot exist at all except as complete, and so God's love for His own goodness must be joy in His own goodness.[45] To say, therefore, that the Father cannot take joy in Himself except in His Word may be to say that the Father cannot *love* Himself except in His Word. Because of Thomas's psychological categories—"because the Son is in the Father *as His Word*"—the Father's self-love must be in another Person.

A second passage is more complicated, but also more suggestive. Thomas writes that

> a thing's being in the will as a beloved in a lover bears a certain order to the conception by which the intellect conceives the thing, and to the thing itself whose intellectual conception is called a word. For it would not be loved unless it were somehow known; nor is it *only* the knowledge of the beloved that is loved, but the beloved as good in itself [*nec solum amati cognitio amatur, sed secundum quod in se bonum est*]. Necessarily, therefore, does the Love by which God is in the divine will as a beloved in a lover proceed both from the Word of God and from the God Whose Word He is.[46]

Thomas is keen to insist that a lover does not love his word—or his "knowledge"—of the thing instead of the thing itself. Yet he does not deny that a lover loves his word of the beloved thing: to say that a lover does not love "*only* the knowledge of the beloved thing" seems to imply that he does, in fact, love this knowledge. He does not love it exclusively, but he still loves it.[47] Indeed, Thomas's whole burden here

---

44 *ST* I-II q. 25, a. 4. For Thomas's earlier distinction between perfect and imperfect love, see H. D. Simonin, "Autour de la solution," 183–84.

45 See *SCG* I, ch. 90 and 91§7.

46 *SCG* IV 19§8.

47 Usually, when Thomas wants to refer not only to one thing but also to a second, he will use the formula *nec solum . . . sed etiam*. Here, he omits the *etiam*. This might seem to suggest that the thing-in-itself is loved *instead* of the thing-as-known. Elsewhere, however, Thomas uses the formula he does here (*nec solum . . . sed*, without an *etiam*) to

is to establish that the divine Love proceeds both from the Father Who loves Himself and from His Word. And the logic seems to run that, if both the word of the thing and the thing itself were not loved, then love would not proceed from both. To insist that the beloved thing itself is loved *instead of* our knowledge or word of it, therefore, would be to undermine Thomas's purpose here.[48]

That said, these texts, at most, point only loosely towards the conclusion we have suggested here. Even more, they only carry any real weight if they give expression to an implication that follows from Thomas's teaching that goodness-as-apprehended is the object of love. Yet, returning to this teaching in light of these texts, we can gingerly propose our main conclusion. If the Father loves His own goodness, then He only loves that goodness as understood. Yet He only understands it *in* His Word, and the presence of His goodness-as-understood within Him *is* His Word. It may be, therefore, that the Father's love for His own goodness passes somehow through His Word, happens somehow in His Word, touches somehow on His Word, or even is directed somehow towards His Word—which suggests that the Father might somehow love His Word, as a Person distinct from Himself, in loving Himself.

---

indicate *two* things that are *both* true. The second thing generally goes somehow beyond the first, but the first remains true: see *in Iob*, c. 7, l. 3; *contra impugnantes* I; *in de anima* #257; twice in *in Eph.*, c. 4, l. 5; *in Heb.*, #122; *ST* I q. 10, a. 2, and q. 29, a. 2, ad 3, and q. 74, a. 4, s.c.; and III q. 41, a. 4, ad 3. I know of no contrary instance in which *nec solum . . . sed* without *etiam* is used to indicate a second thing *instead of* the first.

48 Thomas's reasoning might pick up on a dynamic that surfaces elsewhere in his teaching on love. As he puts it, "the cause of love must be love's object" (*ST* I-II q. 27, a. 1). To be the cause of love is to be the object of love. This point can perhaps make sense of our current passage, where Thomas reasons that love proceeds both from a word and from the beloved thing (they are both the cause of love) because both the word and the beloved thing are loved (they are both the object of love). Thomas elsewhere applies this logic to goodness-as-apprehended: "the apprehended good moves the will as its object" (*SCG* III 73§3; see also *SCG* III 26§21; *ST* I-II q. 9, a. 1; *De Malo* 6; and *in Ioan.*, #1742), and that goodness-as-understood moves the will as its *final* cause (see *ST* I q. 82, a. 4 and *SCG* I 72§7; for a lengthy discussion of this point, see Simonin, "Autour de la solution," 199–245). The apprehended good *causes* the will and love because it is will*ed* and lov*ed*: to cause love is to be loved. Much more would need to be said here, and I propose this point only tentatively, but it may be that whenever Thomas teaches that love proceeds from a word (or that a word is the cause of love), he gives further grounds for suggesting that the word itself is somehow loved.

He would not, however, love Himself or His own goodness any less directly for loving it in another Person. Again, a word only exists in order to manifest, and to put its speaker in contact with, the thing-in-itself that is understood. If, therefore, the Father loves Himself in His Word, then he really loves *Himself* in His Word. He loves another in loving Himself, and He loves Himself in loving another.[49]

Again, in the end, it may be that these principles can only suggest—without establishing unambiguously—that mutual love is just as basic as self-love. Yet they are hopefully enough, at the very least, to reinforce the conclusions on self-love and interpersonal love that we drew less tentatively earlier in this chapter. Be that as it may, we will return to mutual love and interpersonal love at the end of this chapter. For now, we can cease being so tentative. For Thomas points much more directly to the conclusions we will draw in our next two sections, and these conclusions will take us deeper into the marriage of the interpersonal and the intrapersonal in the procession of divine Love.

SELF-LOVE AS INTERPERSONAL LOVE AS INTERPERSONAL COMMUNION AS INTERPERSONAL SELF-GIVING
To Another with Another

The next point should by now be familiar, at least in part. We saw at length in chapter four that, in a simple nature, to speak a word or to breathe Love is to give the whole of oneself to one's Word or Love. We saw in our last chapter that this self-giving enters into the fabric of divine self-knowledge. We will see the same thing now with self-love: the Father can only love Himself notionally if He breathes forth Love, and He can only breathe forth Love if He gives the whole of Himself

---

[49] Something similar perhaps holds for the Son. First, the Son too can only love the divine goodness as apprehended in a word. Yet the Son *is* the Word in which this goodness is understood. He must love this goodness, therefore, as apprehended in Himself. Yet, as we saw in our last chapter, the good thing that the Word manifests is not a generic or impersonal divine goodness; it is the Father. If, therefore, to love a word is to love the thing-in-itself that is manifested in that word, then the Son would love the Father (as the thing manifested in the Word, and so as distinct from Himself) in loving Himself.

to His Love—His Love Who subsists as a distinct Person. In notional love, to love oneself is to give oneself.

The self-giving required by Love, however, goes beyond anything we saw in the Word. For a word proceeds from a speaker alone. In the conception of the divine Word, therefore, only one Person gives Himself to another. Love, however, proceeds both from a lover and from his word. In the procession of divine Love, therefore, two Persons give Themselves to a third. Because Love proceeds both from a lover and from his word, to breathe forth Love in God is not merely to give oneself to another; it is to give oneself *to* another *with* another. Divine love is a matter not only of self-love, of interpersonal love, and of interpersonal self-giving; it is a matter of self-love, of interpersonal love, and of *joint* interpersonal self-giving. It is a shared giving in which a Speaker and His Word, together, give Themselves to a third Person.

Indeed, it is a matter of joint self-giving that is *itself* given and received. Because the Word can possess nothing unless He receives it from His Speaker, the Word must receive even this power to give Himself from His Speaker.[50] As Thomas puts it, "the power to breathe is given to the Son by the Father."[51] Even more, this giving shapes the way in which each Person breathes: "The Son is the source of the Holy Spirit in another way than the Father is, insofar as the Son has this sourcing from another, and the Father does not."[52] Each Person breathes in a distinct way: the Word breathes as receiving this breathing from the Father, and the Father breathes as giving this breathing to His Word.[53] This self-giving, then, is interpersonal not only insofar as

---

[50] See *SCG* IV 14§5, which we studied in chapter four.

[51] *De Pot.*, q. 10, a. 4, ad 18.

[52] *De 108 art.*, q. 27.

[53] This point answers Penido's claim (which is important for his overall argument) that "The notionality of love concerns in no way the mutual relations between the first two Persons; it concerns their relation with the third": for Penido, this breathing is "strictly common" to the Father and the Son, and Their distinction from each other therefore has nothing to do with it ("Gloses sur la procession," 59–60). We see now, however, that it is common to Them in distinct ways, and that Their "mutual relations" (that is, the fact that one gives and the other receives) *do* therefore enter into Their relationship to the Holy Spirit. For more ways in which the distinction of the Father and the Son enters into this common giving, see Emile Bailleux, "Le personnalisme de saint Thomas

two Persons give Themselves to a third Person. It is interpersonal also insofar as this giving *itself* is given by a first Person to a second Person as They both give Themselves to a third Person.

To Bind and to Loose

We saw in the beginning of this chapter that in God, self-love is never closed in on itself: to love oneself is to love oneself with another Person. We now see enough to point towards a deeper conclusion: not even interpersonal love is closed in on itself. In notional love, a Speaker and His Word can only love with each other if They give Themselves together to a third Person. Thomas puts the matter strongly in terms of mutual love: "from the fact that the Father and the Son mutually love one another, it must be that this mutual Love, the Holy Spirit, proceeds from both."[54] In God, mutual love is not a private affair. Instead, from the very fact that two lovers love each other, They must open up beyond each other: They must together give existence—and hence give Themselves—to a third Person Who proceeds from Them.[55]

Thomas goes deeper into this point later in the same passage. This passage as a whole is prompted by the objection that the Holy Spirit cannot be Love, for love is a bond, and "a bond is a medium between what it joins together, not something proceeding from them."[56] Thomas responds, "As regards origin, the Holy Spirit is not the medium, but the third Person in the Trinity; whereas as regards [His status as mutual Love], He is the bond between the two Persons, as proceeding from both."[57] The Holy Spirit is the Love-bond Who stands "between" the

---

en théologie trinitaire," *Revue Thomiste* 61 (1961): 36–38. For some basic background on this shared giving, see Emery, *TTTA*, 289–94.

54 *ST* I q. 37, a. 1, ad 3.

55 I will use this language of "open up" and "beyond" in what follows. This language is, of course, inexact. By "open up," I mean simply that because of the Holy Spirit, the Father and the Son are in relation not only to each other but to a third Person as well. By "beyond," I mean that the Holy Spirit really is a third distinct Person, not in any way reducible to the first two.

56 *ST* I q. 37, a. 1, arg. 3.

57 *ST* I q. 37, a. 1, ad 3.

Father and the Son. Yet He is also a third divine Person Who, because He proceeds from Them as subsistent, stands beyond the Father and the Son.[58]

These two aspects of the Holy Spirit, moreover, are not merely juxtaposed. The Spirit is not merely between the Father and the Son *and* beyond the Father and the Son; He is between Them *as* beyond Them and beyond Them *as* between Them. To begin with the second half of this paradox, we saw above that "from the fact that the Father and the Son mutually love one another, it must be that *this mutual Love*, the Holy Spirit, proceeds from both."[59] That which proceeds from the Father and the Son as a third Person—the third Person, that is, to Whom They jointly give Themselves—is nothing but Their mutual Love itself. In opening up beyond His Beloved to this third Person, therefore, each lover turns to the Love that binds Him to his beloved. Putting the matter crassly and anthropomorphically, neither the Father nor the Son needs to turn His gaze away from His beloved in order to give Himself, with His beloved, to a third Person. Instead, in giving beyond His beloved, each is turned towards the very Love that binds Him to His beloved.

Thomas had put the matter more succinctly in the previous question: the Holy Spirit "proceeds from the Father and the Son *as* the unitive love

---

[58] For Thomas, of course, the Trinitarian *taxis* is inviolable: the Father is the first Person, the Son the second, and the Spirit the third. Yet the fact that Thomas can allow for one sense in which the Holy Spirit is "between" the Father and the Son and another in which He is "the third Person" might suggest a certain flexibility in his *taxis*. This flexibility-within-an-inviolable-order might build on—and ultimately ground—the flexible hierarchy in creation we mentioned in chapter three. It might also allow Thomas to dialogue with some contemporary thinkers who have played with—while retaining—the traditional taxis. For more on such thinkers, see Matthew Lewis Sutton, "A Compelling Trinitarian Taxonomy: Hans Urs von Balthasar's Theology of the Trinitarian Inversion and Reversion," *International Journal of Systematic Theology* 14, no. 2 (2012): 161–75.
Remaining with this language of "between," Levering judges that talk of the Holy Spirit as "between" the Father and the Son "falls into anthropomorphism" (*Engaging*, 42n115. Levering is responding to David Coffey, but he seems to take issue with any talk of the Holy Spirit as "between"). Levering does not cite Thomas in criticizing this language, and he is not claiming to speak in Thomas's name. Yet his study as a whole is devoted to expositing Thomas on the Holy Spirit, and he never mentions that Thomas himself speaks of the Holy Spirit as "between" the Father and the Son.

[59] *ST* I q. 37, a. 1, ad 3.

of both," and He "proceeds *as* the bond of both."[60] Elsewhere, Thomas repeats that the Holy Spirit "proceeds *as* the bond of both,"[61] and, in the most detail, he speaks of "the Holy Spirit Who proceeds *as* the love, the communion, and the bond of Father and Son."[62] Indeed, in this last passage, Thomas even specifies that the Holy Spirit's "procession . . . is not *logically* prior to communion." Even logically speaking, the Holy Spirit does not first proceed from the Father and the Son and only subsequently begin to bind Them together. He proceeds *as* Their bond and *as* Their communion. They do not first give Themselves to Him and only subsequently find Themselves bound together by Him; They are *already* bound together by Him *as* They give Themselves to Him.[63]

Thomas also points in the opposite direction. Early in his career, he writes that "the Holy Spirit is the union itself [of Father and Son] . . . insofar as He proceeds from Them."[64] We just saw that the Holy Spirit only proceeds from the Father and the Son insofar as He already binds Them together. We see now that He only binds Them together insofar as He already proceeds from Them. Thomas puts matters more strongly in the *Summa*: "if the Holy Spirit, Who is the bond of the two, were to be excluded, then the unity of connection between Father and Son could not be understood."[65] The bond between two divine Person cannot exist at all—it cannot even be *understood* to exist—unless it exists *as* a third Person to Whom the first two jointly give Themselves. If the Father and the Son were closed up in a merely mutual intimacy, then that intimacy itself would dissolve: there would be no "unity of connection" between Them. Even logically speaking, the Father and the Son do not first unite Themselves to each other and only subsequently begin to open up beyond each other by giving Themselves to a third

---

60 *ST* I q. 36, a. 4, ad 1.

61 *De 108 art.*, q. 25.

62 *De Pot.*, q. 10, a. 5, ad 11.

63 For more on intra-divine communion in Aquinas, see Emery, "Qu'est-ce que la 'communion trinitaire'?" *Nova et Vetera* French edition 96 (2014): 258–83.

64 I *Sent.*, d. 32, q. 1, a. 1, ad 4.

65 *ST* I q. 39, a. 8.

Person. Instead, the bond that unites Them *is* a third Person to Whom They have *already* given the whole of Themselves.

The Holy Spirit, then, does not merely bind and loose; He binds as He looses and He looses as He binds.[66]

Most basically, we saw above that in the procession of the Holy Spirit, mutual love is just as logically basic as self-love. We see now that self-giving is just as logically basic as both. Speaker and Word give Themselves to a third Person as already bound together in mutual love, and They are bound together as already giving Themselves. We also see that the communion of the Speaker and His Word is just as logically basic as this self-giving: again, procession "is not *logically* prior to communion."[67] Yet, because communion is just as logically basic as procession, and because procession is just as logically basic as self-love and mutual love, communion itself must be just as logically basic as self-love and mutual love. In the immanent procession of a divine Love-impression, self-love, mutual love, interpersonal communion, and interpersonal self-giving all kiss, and each is just as logically basic as all the others.

---

[66] Emery, citing the same passages we have given here, sums matters up: "The communion of Father and Son and the procession of the Holy Spirit are so wholly caught up with one another that the communion is inconceivable without the procession of the Holy Spirit as mutual love and bond . . . The inverse is equally true" ("Communion trinitaire," 274. See also *TTTA*, 241; and Torrell, *Spiritual Master*, 187–88). In a very different idiom, E. E. Cummings perhaps points to this marriage of binding and loosing in human love:

> your slightest look easily will unclose me
> though i have closed myself as fingers,
> you open always petal by petal myself as Spring opens
> (touching skilfully,mysteriously)her first rose
> or if your wish be to close me,i and

> my life will shut very beautifully,suddenly,
> as when the heart of this flower imagines
> the snow carefully everywhere descending . . .

> nobody,not even the rain,has such small hands.

For Cummings, to love is both to open and the close. For Thomas, this dynamic might ultimately be rooted in the procession of divine Love. More basically, and building on Cummings, we should also note at least in passing that a set of very rich resonances with human life and love (regarding, for example, the relationship between an intimate friendship and the broader community, or regarding the inseparability of the unitive and procreative meaning of the conjugal act) could likely be drawn out here.

[67] *De Pot.*, q. 10, a. 5, ad 11.

SELF-LOVE AS INTERPERSONAL LOVE AS INTERPERSONAL COMMUNION AS INTERPERSONAL SELF-GIVING AS INTERPERSONAL BEING-GIVEN

One more dimension of notional love is worth exploring before we turn to essential love:

> The Holy Spirit is said to proceed *from the Father to the Son* inasmuch as He is the love whereby the Father loves the Son; and in the same way it may be said that the Holy Spirit proceeds *from the Son to the Father* inasmuch as He is the love whereby the Son loves the Father. He may be understood, however, to proceed *from the Father to the Son* inasmuch as the Son receives from the Father the power to breathe forth the Holy Spirit, and in this sense He cannot be said to proceed from the Son to the Father, seeing that the Father receives nothing from the Son.[68]

We just saw that the Holy Spirit proceeds from the Father *and* the Son insofar as He is the mutual love of both. We see now that, for the same reason, He proceeds from the Father *to* the Son and from the Son *to* the Father. His procession is interpersonal not only insofar as He proceeds *from* two Persons; it is interpersonal also insofar as He proceeds *between* two Persons.

Yet He proceeds from the Father to the Son not only insofar as the Father loves the Son. He does so also insofar as "the Son receives from the Father the power to breathe forth the Holy Spirit." Talk of the Holy Spirit as proceeding from the Son to the Father never appears after the *De Potentia*. Yet Thomas continues developing the claim that the Holy Spirit proceeds from the Father to the Son—and he uses language that is even more relevant to us—through the end of his career. In his commentary on John, when he comes to John 3:34, "He gives the Spirit without measure," Thomas writes that

---

[68] *De Pot.*, q. 10, a. 4, ad 10.

both as God and as man, Christ has the Holy Spirit beyond measure. For God the Father is said to give the Holy Spirit without measure to Christ *as God*, because He gives to Christ the power and might to breathe forth the Holy Spirit, *Who*, since He is infinite, *was infinitely given to Him by the Father*. For the Father gives Him just as He Himself has Him, so that the Holy Spirit proceeds from Son as much as from the Father. And He gave Him this by an everlasting generation.[69]

In the *De Potentia*, the Holy Spirit had proceeded from the Father to the Son; now He is *given* by the Father to the Son. The meaning is doubtless very similar, if not the same. Yet Thomas's final and most developed articulation of this dynamic foregrounds the language of interpersonal giving: it makes explicit that in giving the Son the power to breathe forth the Holy Spirit, the Father gives the Holy Spirit Himself to the Son.

Elsewhere, Thomas lays out the principles that stand behind this language, and which suggest that it must be taken seriously. In the *Summa*, when Thomas asks whether "gift" is a personal name in God, he tells us that "a gift would not be given by anyone unless it belonged to him."[70] He then outlines three senses in which something can belong to someone: first, by identity, as one is one's own; second, "as a possession or a slave"; and, third, "through origin only. And it is in this last sense that the Son belongs to the Father, and the Holy Spirit to both."[71] The Holy Spirit does not belong to the Father and the Son as a slave, and He is not a thing They possess. He belongs to Them only by origin. Yet He really does *belong to Them* by origin. Indeed, Thomas suggests elsewhere that because the Holy Spirit proceeds from the Son, He belongs to the Son "absolutely [*absolute*]," and not merely "in a certain sense [*secundum quid*]."[72] More basically, if the Holy Spirit did not really belong to the Father and the Son, then They

---

69 *In Ioan.*, #543.

70 *ST* I q. 38, a. 1.

71 *ST* I q. 38, a. 1, ad 1.

72 *De Pot.*, q. 10, a. 4.

could not give Him to us. Yet, because They do give Him to us, He must belong to Them, and He can only belong to Them insofar as He proceeds from Them.[73]

Thus, returning to our current passage, Thomas writes that the Father eternally gives the Holy Spirit to the Son insofar as He gives the Son the power to breathe forth the Spirit. Yet we see now that, because the Father gives to the Son the power to breathe forth the Holy Spirit, the Father *really does* eternally give the Person of the Holy Spirit to the Person of the Son. Again, the Holy Spirit only belongs to the Son insofar as the Son breathes Him, and the Son only breathes the Holy Spirit insofar as the Father gives this breathing to the Son—which means that the Father gives the Holy Spirit Himself to the Son in giving this breathing to the Son. The procession of the Holy Spirit, then, is a matter of interpersonal giving not only insofar as the Father and the Son give Themselves to the Holy Spirit; it is a matter of interpersonal giving also insofar as the Holy Spirit Himself is given by the Father to the Son. Divine love is a matter not only of giving oneself to another Person but of being-given by another Person to still another Person.[74]

Thomas, of course, does not use his psychological terms in this passage. Yet, if we think through his psychological terms, we can see that they demand this conclusion. For Love cannot proceed in God unless both the Father and His Word breathe Love forth as a third Person. Yet the Word cannot breathe forth Love unless He has the power to breathe forth Love. A word can possess nothing, however, that it does not receive from its speaker.[75] The divine Word therefore cannot have

---

[73] Thomas reiterates this link between proceeding-from-another and belonging-to-another with reference to the Scripture language of "the Spirit of the Son": see *Contra Errores Greacorum* II, 11; *SCG* IV 24§2; *De Pot.*, q. 10, a. 5; *in Gal.*, #213; *ST* I q. 36, a. 2; and *in Ioan.*, #2065.

[74] For some deep reflections on the importance in human life not merely of our giving ourselves, but of our being given by another (of saying "God has given you to me" and "God has given me to you"), see John Paul II, "Meditation on Givenness," *Communio: International Catholic Review* 41, no. 4 (2014): 871–83. See also *Man and Woman He Created Them*, 196–97. David L. Schindler has drawn out some of the metaphysical and anthropological implications that ripple out from this point: see "Being, Gift, Self-Gift." For our part, we can add that when we find ourselves given to another, we are perhaps living an echo of the pattern of perfect love that is eternally present in the Trinity.

[75] See *SCG* IV 14§5.

this power to breathe unless His Speaker gives it to Him. Yet we just saw that in giving this power to breathe Love, the Speaker gives the Love Himself Who is breathed. Because of the role of a word in love, therefore—and because divine Love belongs to Whoever breathes Him forth—a Love-impression can only proceed within the divine nature if a Speaker gives His subsistent Love to His subsistent Word. Thomas's psychological categories, then, demand that the immanent procession of Love be a matter not only of two Persons' giving Themselves to a third as They love each other but also of one Person's giving a third Person to a second as They love each other.

ESSENTIAL LOVE
"From the Fact that Anyone Loves Anything"

For all that, it may still seem as though the interpersonal goes less deep into God's love than it does into His knowledge. In our last chapter, it was not only the conception of the divine Word that was bound up with interpersonal knowledge and self-giving; it was God's essential act of understanding as well. To this point, however, we have said nothing of the essential act of divine love. We have instead focused on notional and personal love. Yet notional and personal love do not correspond to the divine act of understanding. They correspond, respectively, to the act of conceiving the Word and to the Word Himself. Indeed, especially at the beginning of this chapter, we focused on a dimension of notional love that does not hold in essential love: it was because, in notional love, the Father loves Himself "by the Holy Spirit," that interpersonal love entered into the fabric of self-love. Yet Thomas is clear that "when love is taken essentially, it means that the Father and the Son love each other not by the Holy Spirit, but by Their essence."[76] It seems, therefore, that none of the interpersonal dimensions we have drawn out of notional love hold in essential love: so far as essential love goes, self-love seems first of all to be a matter of self-love alone.

We will respond to this charge on several levels. First, and most superficially, we should recall that our concern here is with Thomas's

---

76 *ST* I q. 37, a. 2.

psychological analogy for the Trinity. Yet we have already mentioned that Thomas's psychological Trinity is a matter not merely of the bare act of essential love but of the Love-impression Who proceeds in that love. Because, therefore, the procession of this Love-impression is awash in our interpersonal elements, we can already say that Thomas's psychological analogy is awash in the interpersonal. Our main burden, therefore, can be secured even without engaging directly with essential love.

This point is certainly valid. Yet it concedes too much: it concedes that there is a dimension of self-love in God that is not shot through with the interpersonal. We can go a step deeper—but only a step—by reflecting on a point on which there is no disagreement: for Thomas, nothing can be willed or loved unless it is already known.[77] In God, of course, understanding, will, and love are really identical. Insofar as they are logically distinct, however, understanding comes first. Yet we saw in our last chapter that the conception of the divine Word is just as logically basic as the divine act of understanding. We see now that understanding is more logically basic even than God's *essential* will and *essential* act of love—which means that the conception of the divine Word must be more logically basic than God's essential act of love.[78] The Father, then, cannot love Himself notionally unless He breathes forth His Love with His Word. Yet He cannot even love Himself *essentially* unless, logically speaking, His Word is already present to Him as He loves Himself. Even insofar as love is taken essentially, another Person is present from the foundation of the Father's self-love.

If we were to leave things there, however, we still would not go far enough. For, on such a reading, another Person would be present to the Father's act of self-love. Yet the Father alone would be actively involved in this self-love. The Father would not love Himself with another Person in His self-love, and He would not be loved by another Person in His self-love. Or, better, He would love with another and be

---

[77] This point picks up on a long tradition stemming from Augustine: see Sherwin, *By Knowledge and by Love*, xvii.

[78] This is not to deny that non-Christians can discover (essential) love to be present in God without knowing of the divine Word. It is rather to say that when Revelation comes, and when we think it through, we see that, in fact, the conception of a personal Word (which can only be known if it is revealed) is more logically basic than essential love (which reason can discover).

loved by another only insofar as that other is really identical to His act of love and to His goodness. This other Person would not love with the Father, and He would not love the Father, insofar as He is distinct from the Father.

We can only adequately respond to this objection if we sort through the relationship between essential love, notional love, and personal love in God. For we have seen that notional and personal love are a matter of interpersonal love, of interpersonal communion, of interpersonal self-giving, and of interpersonal being-given. If, therefore, essential love is bound up with notional love, then essential love itself—by virtue of its association with notional and personal love—will be bound up with this array of interpersonal elements.

We can start with a more modest point: notional and personal love are logically distinct from essential love, but they are not logically sealed off from essential love. As Thomas puts it in the *Summa*,

> just as, from the fact that anyone understands anything, there comes forth in the one who understands a conception of the object understood, which conception we call word, so *from the fact that anyone loves anything*, there comes forth a certain impression, so to speak, of the beloved thing in the affection of the lover, according to which the beloved is said to be in the lover, just as the thing understood is said to be in the one understanding.[79]

We saw last chapter that the Father does not understand *and* speak His Word; He understands *in* His Word and He speaks His Word *in* understanding. Thomas draws a parallel here between the word vis-à-vis understanding and a love-impression vis-à-vis love. Just as a word comes forth "from the fact that anyone understands anything," so a love-impression comes forth—that is, a lover breathes forth love—"from the fact that anyone loves anything." Thomas repeats this point a few sentences later: a lover breathes forth love "from the fact that he loves." We do not merely love things *and* breathe forth impressions of those things. We breathe "from the fact" that we love things: our breathing

---

[79] *ST* I q. 37, a. 1.

follows organically on, and it is therefore bound organically up with, our acts of love.

Thomas, moreover, lays out this pattern in order to illustrate the relationship between essential love, notional love, and personal love in God. In God, there is not merely essential love *and* notional *and* personal love: the three are not logically stacked alongside each other. Instead, even insofar as these modes of love are logically distinct, the Father and the Son love notionally *in* loving essentially, and the Holy Spirit proceeds as personal love *in* essential love. It is in the one essential divine act of love, and it is "from the fact that" God loves His own goodness, that the Father and His Word breathe Their Love-impression.

At the very least, therefore, we can say that essential love, even insofar as it is logically distinct from notional and personal love, is intimately interwoven with notional and personal love—which means that essential love is intimately interwoven with interpersonal love, communion, self-giving, and being-given.[80]

THREE PATHS

We still, however, have not said enough. For we have seen that all of these interpersonal notes are present in essential love. Yet, if a love-impression proceeds "from the fact that anyone loves anything," it may seem as though the procession of a love-impression arises from—and is therefore less logically basic than—the act of love. Notional love, that is, might seem less logically basic than essential love. Yet it is through notional love that all of our interpersonal elements enter into divine love. If breathing forth a love-impression, therefore, is less logically basic than the act of loving things, then interpersonal love will be less logically basic than self-love in Thomas's Trinity. So far as essential love goes, the interpersonal would be a sort of "second tier" erected atop self-love.[81]

---

[80] Though the details differ from text to text, the (essential) act of love is similarly interwoven with the (notional and personal) procession of a love-impression—again with reference to the relationship between a word and understanding—in *SCG* IV 19§4 and *Comp. Theo.* I, 45.

[81] Quoted from Emery, *TTTA*, 236

By the same token, however, if we can show that breathing forth a love-impression is just as logically basic as the act of loving, then we will have shown that notional love is just as logically basic as essential love—and we will therefore have shown that all of our interpersonal elements, all of which go to the foundation of notional love, are just as basic as self-love, even insofar as self-love is taken essentially.[82]

Before beginning, we should admit that Thomas never speaks directly to the logical priority of essential love versus notional love. Even more, the limited and indirect indications he gives are not as clear as those we saw him give regarding the word in relation to understanding. We will not, therefore, be able to draw this conclusion as cleanly with love as we did with knowledge. Yet we will at least be able to point out three paths that Thomas opens up that might lead in a fruitful direction.

We have already seen the rudiments of the first path. We just saw that when Thomas speaks of the procession of love, he admits that he lacks the range of language required to speak clearly. Yet he often compensates for this lack by drawing a strong parallel between word and love: just as a word—for which we *do* have adequate language—proceeds in the act of understanding, so a love-impression proceeds in the act of love.[83] If, therefore, we want to know what the procession of divine Love looks like—and if we want to put our finger on its precise relationship to the essential act of love—then we might look to the procession of the divine Word in relation to the essential act of understanding. We saw in our last chapter, however, that the conception of the divine Word is just as logically basic as the essential act of understanding. These parallels between word and love, then, might already suggest that just as the conception of a word goes to the logical foundation of

---

[82] As we saw in note 10 above, notional love *is* less logically basic than essential love in the sense that, historically speaking, thinkers operating with natural reason could have discovered essential divine love before the Revelation of notional love (that is, the procession of the Holy Spirit had been revealed). Yet we will ask whether, once the Trinity is revealed, the notional love that is *chronologically* revealed later can be seen to be, in fact, just as *logically* basic as the essential love that, chronologically, could have been discovered first.

[83] This point is most evident through the corpus of *ST* I q. 37, a. 1. It also emerges in q. 37, a. 1, ad 4, and q. 37, a. 2. See also *SCG* IV 19§4; and *Comp. Theo.* I, 45.

the act of understanding, so the breathing of love goes to the logical foundation of the act of love.

The second path goes deeper, and it recalls another point we explored in our last chapter. When treating of the Holy Spirit as Love, Thomas raises the objection that because every lover breathes forth love, the Holy Spirit should breathe forth His own Love-impression, and a fourth Person should therefore proceed in God. Thomas responds:

> Although the Son understands, it does not belong to Him to produce a word: for it belongs to Him to understand as the Word proceeding. In the same way, although the Holy Spirit loves, taking love as an essential term, still it does not belong to Him to breathe forth love, which is to take love as a notional term; because *He loves essentially as Love proceeding*, but not as the one from Whom Love proceeds.[84]

As we saw in our last chapter, there is no such thing as an impersonal or generic essential act of understanding. Instead, understanding exists in the Father "as producing a Word" and in the Son "as the Word proceeding."[85] Thomas here draws a parallel between understanding and love. Like understanding, essential love can be no fourth thing juxtaposed to the divine Persons. Nor, therefore, can it be juxtaposed to those Persons' acts of breathing and being-breathed. Instead, essential love exists as breathing in the Father and the Son and as breathed in the Holy Spirit. The Holy Spirit "loves essentially as Love proceeding," and the Father and the Son—so the logic runs—love essentially "as the one from Whom Love proceeds."

This point bears at least indirectly on our current question. We saw in our last chapter that the Father does not understand Himself and *then* conceive a Word; He understands Himself *as* conceiving a Word. Just so, the Father and the Son do not love Themselves essentially and *then* breathe forth Love; They love Themselves essentially *as* breathing forth Love. Their breathing is not an afterthought appended to essential love; it is the *way* in which They love essentially. *Even insofar as love*

---

[84] *ST* I q. 37, a. 1, ad 4.
[85] *ST* I q. 34, a. 2, ad 4.

is taken essentially, the Father and the Son only ever love Themselves as breathing forth a Love-impression—which means that They only ever love Themselves as loving with each other, as bound together in communion, as giving Themselves together to a third Person, and as giving and receiving that third Person Himself. Just so, the Holy Spirit only ever loves essentially "as Love proceeding"—which means that He only ever loves Himself as binding two lovers together in communion, as receiving the whole of Himself from those lovers, and as being given from one lover to another. Again, these interpersonal elements are not layered atop a more basic act of essential self-love; they are the ways in which essential love eternally exists. Indeed, they are the *only* ways in which essential love *ever* exists. And they therefore seem to go all the way to the logical foundation of essential love.

The third and final route is the least certain, and we will probe it most gingerly. Outside of his Trinitarian theology, in his more direct treatments of love, Thomas sometimes draws a link between the impression that proceeds in the affection of the lover and the lover's *complacentia* in the beloved object.[86] First, he writes that "the object loved is said to be in the lover inasmuch as it is in his affections by a kind of complacency."[87] In his Trinitarian theology, Thomas identifies this presence of the beloved in the affections of the lover with a love-impression.[88] Thomas is more direct later in the same article: "the beloved is contained in the lover insofar as it is *impressed* in his affections through a sort of complacency."[89] Also relevant is Thomas's claim, while commenting on Genesis 1, that "the Person of the Father is indicated by God that speaks, and the Person of the Son by the Word in which He speaks, and the Person of the Holy Spirit by the *complacentia* with which God saw that what was made was good."[90] It seems safe to say,

---

[86] For more on *complacentia* in Thomas's mature teaching on love, see H. D. Simonin, "Autour de la solution," 191–97; Sherwin, *By Knowledge and by Love*, 70–71, 76–78; and Fredrick E. Crowe, "Complacency and Concern," *Theological Studies* 20 (1959): 1–39, 198–230, and 343–95.

[87] *ST* I-II q. 28, a. 2.

[88] See *ST* I q. 37, a. 1; and *Comp. Theo.* I, ch. 52.

[89] *ST* I-II q. 28, a. 2, ad 1.

[90] *ST* I q. 74, a. 3, ad 4.

therefore, that a love-impression is bound up with complacency. Indeed, some scholars have argued that the impression that proceeds in love *is* the lover's complacency in the beloved object.[91] We cannot assess their arguments here, which is why I introduce this third path more tentatively. What seems clear, however, is that, in Thomas's mature thought, there is nothing in love so logically basic as this *complacentia*.[92] If, therefore, the Holy Spirit proceeds as this *complacentia*—that is, if these scholars' arguments ultimately hold up—then it follows that there is nothing in God's love so logically basic as the act by which the Father and the Son breathe Love forth.

Again, we can only scratch the surface of these points. Yet, taking these three paths together, even these brief forays should be enough to suggest that, logically speaking, the Father and the Son might not first love Themselves essentially and only then breathe forth Love. Instead, They might only love Themselves essentially as already, and as just as basically, breathing forth Love. If these paths prove fruitful, that is, then notional love would go to the deepest logical bottom of essential love. Yet, because interpersonal love, mutual love, interpersonal communion, interpersonal self-giving, and interpersonal being-given all go to the deepest logical bottom of notional love, these interpersonal notes would *themselves* go to the deepest logical bottom of essential love. Because of the role of a word and a love-impression in the act of love—that is, because of Thomas's particular rendering of his psychological categories—there would be no divine self-love, on any level or in any respect,

---

[91] See Crowe, "Complacency and Concern," especially 18, 198, 223–24, and 346. For a detailed account of Crowe's argument, see Michael Eades, *And in Our Hearts Take up Thy Rest: The Trinitarian Pneumatology of Fredrick Crowe, SJ* (Toronto: University of Toronto Press, 2019), 49–53. William Rossner does not use the language of *complacentia*, but he argues that the love-impression (which he calls a "pondus") is, like complacency, the most logically deep dimension of love, prior to any act of love: see "The Procession of Human Intellectual Love, Or Spirating a Pondus," *The Thomist* 36, no. 1 (1972): 39–74.

[92] See *ST* I-II q. 26, a. 2, and q. 28, a. 2. Sherwin describes the lover's *complacentia* as "love's primary act" (*By Knowledge and by Love*, 95). This point is evident throughout his analysis on 70–71 and 76–78. Elsewhere, Sherwin writes that acts of love, in which we will some good to someone, "flow from" complacency (see "Aquinas, Augustine, and the Medieval Scholastic Crisis concerning Charity," in *Aquinas the Augustinian*, 196–98; quoted on 198). Crowe and Rossner argue for the same point in the articles just cited.

which is not just as basically interpersonal. Be it essential, notional, or personal, self-love would be interpersonal all the way down.

Challenges might be posed around this question of logical priority. Again, we have had to venture quite a bit beyond any conclusions Thomas explicitly draws in order to suggest this final point. I hope, however, that our most basic burden has been established beyond any real doubt. For, again, Thomas's psychological analogy for the Trinity concerns not essential love but the immanent procession of a divine Love-impression. If this procession turns out to be less logically basic than essential love, then our conclusions will not be quite so strong. Yet they will not be put asunder. Whatever the ultimate logical relationship between essential love and notional or personal love, there is no doubt that notional and personal love are intimately bound up with essential love. More deeply, there is no doubt that when the Father breathes forth His Love-impression in loving Himself, His Word breathes with Him. There is no doubt that Their joint breathing is Their joint giving of Themselves to a third Person. There is no doubt that the Father and the Son are bound in communion and mutual love as They give Themselves to this third Person, for this third Person *is* Their communion and mutual love. Finally, there is no doubt that the Father gives this Person-Love to His Word as They breathe Him forth. It is precisely the immanent procession of a Love-impression—and so it is Thomas's psychological analogy for the Trinity—which includes and requires—and *is*—this outpouring of the interpersonal. It is in this immanent procession that we find a kaleidoscopic coincidence of self-love, self-giving, interpersonal love, interpersonal communion, and interpersonal being-given.[93]

---

93 Returning for a final time to the readings of Thomas we mentioned in note 9 in chapter three, we can point one step further. For it may be that, given the meaning of understanding and of will, there could be no perfect act of understanding or will *at all* without this marriage of the interpersonal and the intrapersonal. First, we saw that according to these readings, the very meaning of understanding demands that there could be no understanding in a simple nature without the procession of a personal Word. One could also argue that the meaning of will demands that there could be no will in a simple nature without the procession of a personal Love-impression (see, for example, the language of *"necesse est"* in *SCG* IV 19§7). Finally, given that a perfect act of understanding and of will can only exist within a simple nature, it may be that, *because of the meaning of understanding and will*, neither perfect understanding nor perfect will could possibly exist without the processions of distinct divine Persons—which, in turn,

CONCLUSION

Taking a step back, we can conclude with a basic point. For Thomas, the Holy Spirit proceeds in an act of self-love: He proceeds as God loves His own goodness. Just so, the Son proceeds as God knows His own essence. Thomas affirms as much all through his corpus, and we need not shoo away these texts—of which there are so many—in order to affirm that Thomas's Trinity is superabundantly interpersonal. Nor need we complement these texts from the outside with other texts—of which there are also many—where Thomas speaks of the relations between the divine Person in more obviously interpersonal terms. Instead, we have seen that these processions by way of self-knowledge and self-love are *themselves* saturated with interpersonal knowledge, with interpersonal love, with interpersonal communion, with interpersonal self-giving, and with a first Person's giving a third Person to still a second Person. All of these interpersonal upwellings dwell within self-knowledge and self-love, and none can exist independently of self-knowledge or self-love. Indeed, all of them are just another way of talking about self-knowledge and self-love. Yet none of them can be reduced unilaterally to self-knowledge or self-love. These interpersonal superabundances are entirely a matter of self-knowledge and self-love; yet self-knowledge and self-love are no less entirely a matter of these interpersonal superabundances. Indeed, self-knowledge and self-love are just another way of talking about all of these interpersonal overflowings—all of which are really interpersonal. It is not self *or* other, inward *or* outward, social *or* psychological, interpersonal *or* intrapersonal. Instead, Thomas's psychological categories arrange a marriage in which all are bound together and all are equally basic.

And this marriage matters for us. Having spent this whole study focused on God, we can end by asking what everything we have seen here might have to do with our understanding, with our willing and loving, and with our perfection as human beings.

---

would mean that they could not possibly exist without the marriage of the interpersonal and the intrapersonal we have sketched here. If these readings are valid, therefore, the pattern we have sketched in the last two chapters would not merely be the form that perfect understanding and love happen to take. It would be the form that perfect understanding and love, by their own logic, must necessarily take.

7

THE IMAGE OF GOD

Thomas's psychological analogy was criticized not only for what it did to God, but for what it did to us: having given us an isolated and self-centered God, it allegedly gave us an isolated and self-centered image of God. Indeed, for some social Trinitarians, herein lay Thomas's chief offense. For a number of them were interested in Trinitarian theology not as a contemplative exercise, but as an engine for social and political renewal: they saw a social God as an antidote to contemporary individualism, and they found in the Trinity a blueprint for a more communal society, politics, and economy.[1] Yet they accused Thomas's psychological analogy of short-circuiting this social transformation and of underwriting the very individualism they were trying to overthrow.[2]

---

[1] For a critical assessment of this move, see Karen Kilby, "Trinity, Tradition, and Politics," in *Recent Developments in Trinitarian Theology: An International Symposium*, ed. Christophe Chalamet and Marc Vial, 73–86 (Minneapolis: Fortress Press, 2014); and "Perichoresis and Projection." Kilby is certainly right that there is much to challenge in the particulars of these proposals. Yet some version of this move seems to have entered into recent Catholic social teaching: see Pope Benedict XVI, Encyclical Letter *Caritas in Veritate* (June 29, 2009), 53–55; and Pope Francis, Encyclical Letter *Laudato Si'* (May 24, 2015), 238–40.

[2] See Gunton, *The Promise of Trinitarian Theology*, 102–3; and Moltmann, *The Trinity and the Kingdom*, 198–99.

We cannot answer this charge in full. Others have suggested that Thomas's political and economic vision can actually help us to move beyond the individualism, consumerism, and exploitation against which social Trinitarians inveighed.[3] For our part, we can limit ourselves to Thomas's teaching on the *imago Dei*. Yet we cannot even offer a full account of this teaching.[4] Instead, we will ask whether the marriage of the interpersonal and the intrapersonal we have uncovered in Thomas's psychological Trinity might find echoes in his psychological *imago Trinitatis*.[5]

Before doing so, however, we should note that Thomas's social critics are right: just as Thomas gives us a psychological Trinity, so he gives us a psychological image of the Trinity. He writes that "as the uncreated Trinity is distinguished by the procession of the Word from the Speaker and of Love from both of these, so we may say that, in rational creatures wherein we find a procession of the word in the intellect and a procession of the love in the will, there exists an image of the uncreated Trinity."[6] We image God by the words and loves that remain within our minds. We have seen, however, that the

---

[3] See, for example, Mary Hirschfeld, *Aquinas and the Market: Toward a Humane Economy* (Cambridge, MA: Harvard University Press, 2018). In a different vein, see Gregory H. Speltz, *The Importance of the Rural Life According to the Philosophy of St. Thomas Aquinas: A Study in Economic Philosophy* (Lexington, KY: St. Pius X Press, 2011).

[4] For a broader treatment, see Merriel D. Juvenal, *To the Image of the Trinity: A Study in the Development of Aquinas' Teaching* (Toronto: Pontifical Institute of Medieval Studies, 1990); and van Nieuvenhove, "In the image of God." We also cannot speak to those passages where Thomas seems to distance himself from a more social *imago Dei* (I speak to two of the most important such passages—*ST* I q. 36, a. 3, ad 1 and q. 93, a. 6, ad 2—in "The Family as an Image of the Trinity").

[5] The points we will explore here pick up on a pattern that is already present in Augustine, whose "psychological" *imago Dei* is a matter not first of remembering, knowing, and loving oneself, but of remembering, knowing, and loving God. Indeed, we will see Thomas cite Augustine at a crucial juncture in *ST* I q. 93, a. 8. For this point in Augustine, see Rowan Williams, "*Sapientia* and the Trinity: Reflections on the *De Trinitate*," *Augustiniana* 40 (1990): 317–32. For a further dimension, see Lewis Ayres, "The Christological Context of Augustine's *De trinitate* XIII: Toward Relocating Books VIII-XV," *Augustinian Studies* 29, no. 1 (1998): 111–39. Again, my aim here is not to exonerate or rehabilitate "the" psychological analogy in general. Yet we can at least note that, in the texts we will study here, Thomas may be faithfully carrying forward an insight he received from the figure in the tradition to whom his psychological categories are most indebted.

[6] *ST* I q. 93, a. 6. Thomas makes this point throughout aa. 6–8. See also *ST* I q. 45, a. 7.

processions of the divine Word and Love are a matter of more than mere self-regard. Instead, these immanent processions themselves are already fully social. We will now ask whether something similar holds in us when we image God.[7]

KNOWING AND LOVING ANOTHER IN KNOWING AND LOVING ONESELF

We can begin with a claim that Thomas registers explicitly, prominently, and repeatedly.[8] This point comes out when he asks whether we image God every time we conceive a word and breathe love, or whether we do so only when we know and love certain things. Thomas begins right where we might expect him to begin: with self-knowledge and self-love. He writes that "the Word of God is born of God by the knowledge of Himself; and Love proceeds from God according as He loves Himself."[9] We might expect Thomas to extend this frame of self-regard into the *imago Dei*: we might expect him to conclude that, just as the divine Persons proceed in God's self-knowledge and self-love, so we image God in our self-knowledge and self-love. Yet he does not. Instead, he argues that "we refer the divine image in man to the verbal concept born of the knowledge *of God*, and to the love derived from it. Thus the image of God is found in the soul according as the soul turns *to God*, or possesses a nature which enables it to turn *to God*."[10] I do not image God insofar as, like God, my knowledge and love is directed towards myself; I image God insofar as, like God, my knowledge and love is directed towards God. Unlike the divine Persons, however, I am not God—which means that *I image God by knowing and loving*

---

[7] I hope that our conclusions here will not only extend those of our previous chapters but also reinforce them. For, if Thomas's *imago Dei* conforms to the pattern we have drawn out of his psychological Trinity, then it seems all the more reasonable to conclude that this pattern really does hold in his psychological Trinity.

[8] Emery recognizes this first point in *TTTA*, 398.

[9] *ST* I q. 93, a. 8.

[10] *ST* I q. 93, a. 8. In q. 93, a. 4. Thomas begins that our mind "imitates God chiefly in this, that God understands and loves Himself." But he spends the rest of the article discussing our knowledge and love not of ourselves but of God. See also *De Ver.*, q. 10, a. 7; and *De Pot.*, q. 9, a. 9.

Another. Indeed, Thomas so strongly privileges other-directedness over self-directedness that he ends this corpus by recalling Augustine's formulation: "The image of God exists in the mind, *not* because it remembers itself, loves itself, and understands itself, *but* because it can also remember, understand, and love the God by Whom it was made."[11] Our imaging God is so emphatically a matter of our turning towards Another that, for Thomas, we do not image God insofar as we merely know and love ourselves.

Taking a step back, we have already seen that Thomas's psychological Trinity is itself an interpersonal Trinity. We see now that, just so, his psychological *imago* is itself an interpersonal *imago*. I image God by the words and loves that remain within me, but I do so only when I know and love three divine Persons Who are distinct from me.

If we were to leave things there, however, we might risk reinforcing the same opposition between the interpersonal and the intrapersonal that we have been fighting since the first page of this study. Earlier in the same corpus, Thomas had added a helpful nuance:

> Now, the mind may turn towards an object in two ways: directly and immediately, or indirectly and mediately; as, for instance, when anyone sees a man reflected in a mirror, he may be said to be turned towards that man. So Augustine says, "the mind remembers itself, understands itself, and loves itself. If we perceive this, we perceive a trinity; not, indeed, God, but, nevertheless, rightly called the image of God." But this is due to the fact, not that the mind reflects on itself absolutely, but that *by reflecting on itself it can furthermore turn to God.*[12]

I do not need to turn away from myself in order to image God. Instead, I see a trinity, and I therefore image the Trinity, when I look inwards. Yet I only image God through self-reflection because the self on which I reflect is *itself* a mirror reflecting God. Just as in the Trinity, it is not self-knowledge and self-love versus interpersonal knowledge and

---

11 *ST* I q. 93, a. 8, *s.c.* Thomas refers back to this passage in the final words of this corpus.
12 *ST* I q. 93, a. 8.

interpersonal love. Instead, it is self *and* other—to the point that self-knowledge and self-love *themselves* turn me towards Another.

They turn me towards Another, finally, Who is turned towards me. For the God Whom I know and love already knows me and loves me. Indeed, I only exist at all insofar as God knows me and loves me,[13] and I am therefore known and loved before I know or love anything. If, therefore, I image God in knowing and loving God, then this knowledge and love is not only interpersonal; it is reciprocal. I know and love as I am known and loved.

INTIMATE INDWELLING, INFINITE DISTANCE, INTERPERSONAL GIVING

Again, this emphasis on interpersonal knowledge and love is already evident on the surface of the *Summa*'s direct treatment of the *imago Dei*. We can go deeper, however, if we put Thomas's claims here in dialogue with conclusions he embraces elsewhere.

First of all, we just saw that our very selves—and so our self-knowledge and self-love—turn us towards God. We can stress now that even insofar as God is distinct from us, He dwells *within* us. As Thomas puts it, "God is in all things, and innermostly."[14] In turning to ourselves, we are turned to Another; yet the other to Whom we turn dwells within our selves. Indeed, He dwells in us in the most intimate way possible. Even insofar as God is other than us, therefore, we need not merely abandon ourselves in order to find Him. Instead, we find Him within all things, including ourselves. More basically, just as the divine Persons remain perfectly within each other as They know and love each other, so God dwells innermostly within us as we know and love Him.

God, however, not only dwells intimately within us. He also stands at an infinite—though nonspatial—distance from us. Thomas articulates this point with reference to angels: "an angel's intellect and essence are infinitely distant [*in infinitum distant*] from God,"

---

13 See *ST* I q. 14, a. 8, and q. 19, a. 4.
14 *ST* I q. 8, a. 1.

and "God is infinitely distant from the angel."[15] Thomas also extends this point beyond the angels: "the creature is infinitely distant from God," and this infinite distance "will remain even in heaven."[16] All creatures—including us—are infinitely distant from God, and we will remain infinitely distant from Him even when we are perfectly united to Him in heaven.[17] This distance, therefore, is not that of sin; it is the distance between creature and Creator: it holds between God and the blessed angles who never sin, and it will hold between God and us when we are freed from sin in glory. There would be much to say here, but we can limit ourselves to a single point: God both resides intimately within us and stands at an infinite distance from us. Remaining-within and standing-outside, therefore, coincide not only in the relationships between the divine Persons; they also coincide in the relationship between God and creation. Zeroing in on our current question, we saw all through part two that the Persons Whom we image know and love each other, and we saw all through part one that They do so both as perfectly within each other and as standing somehow "outside" of each other. We see now that we image God by knowing and loving the God Who both resides perfectly within us and stands infinitely distant from us. Thomas's *imago Trinitatis* contains an echo of the same paradox we saw in Thomas's Trinity.

We can take our next step by remaining with indwelling. In brief, it is only because God gives us our existence that He dwells within us. As Thomas writes, "God is in all places as *giving* it being, power, and operation"; He is in all places because "He *gives* existence to the things that fill all places."[18] God is interior to me because He gives me everything I have. Thus, in his direct treatment of the *imago Dei*, Thomas teaches expressly that I only image God when I know and love God. Yet, elsewhere in his thought, he makes clear that, when I know and love God, I know and love Another Who dwells innermostly

---

15 *ST* I q. 56, a. 3, ad 2.

16 *ST* II-II q. 19, a. 11, ad 3.

17 Indeed, there is even a sense in which we become *more* distant from God (or, at least, we more fully recognize and respect the infinite distance between us and God) the *more* united we are to Him (see my "The More We Wonder").

18 *ST* I q. 8, a. 2.

within me, Who stands infinitely distant from me, Who gives me my existence, and from Whom I receive all that I have. Thomas's *imago Dei*, therefore, is a marriage of self-knowledge, self-love, interpersonal knowledge, interpersonal love, intimate interpersonal indwelling, infinite interpersonal distance, and interpersonal giving and receiving.[19]

SELF-GIVING

Indeed, it is a marriage of all these notes with interpersonal *self*-giving. For all human beings image God insofar as we are naturally able to know and to love Him. Yet we image God more when we know and love Him by grace, and we image Him most of all only when we know and love Him perfectly in glory.[20] We enjoy these gifts of grace and glory, however, only insofar as the divine Persons *give Themselves* to us. Thomas puts the matter succinctly: "in giving eternal life, God gives Himself."[21] God not only gives us to ourselves; He also gives Himself to us. Thomas puts the same point in Trinitarian terms: he writes that, when the Father dwells within us in grace and glory, "the Father gives Himself, as freely communicating Himself to be enjoyed by the creature."[22] Regarding the Son, he writes that "the greatest thing a person can do for a friend is to give himself for that friend. This is what Christ did."[23] Regarding the Holy Spirit, "The Holy Spirit gives Himself" to us in giving us grace.[24] Indeed, Thomas argues that the

---

19 This point regarding giving also suggests that God does not dwell intimately within us *despite* standing at an infinite distance from us. Instead, He dwells most intimately within us *because* of the mode in which He stands infinitely distant. For He stands at an infinite distance because we are created and He creates us (see *ST* II-II q. 19, a. 11, ad 3). Yet He dwells in us innermostly because, in creating us, He gives us existence. He is infinitely other than us and He is innermostly interior to us, therefore, for one and the same reason: because He creates us. As we saw in chapter three, perfect interiority and radical distinction are not opposed; they stand or fall together.

20 See *ST* I q. 93, a. 4; and *De Pot.*, q. 9, a. 9.

21 *In Ioan.*, #480. See also I *Sent.*, d. 15, q. 1, a. 1; IV *Sent.*, d. 10, q. 1, a. 1; and *SCG* IV 23§11.

22 *ST* I q. 43, a. 4, ad 1.

23 *In Ioan.*, #1838.

24 *ST* I q. 38, a. 1, ad 1.

Holy Spirit's principal gift is nothing but Himself, and that all other gifts He gives follow on this foundational self-giving.[25]

Indeed, Thomas's *imago Dei* includes a dimension of self-giving that goes beyond anything we saw in his Trinitarian theology. For he writes that "the purpose of charity is that a man give the whole of himself to God."[26] In glory, when our charity achieves its purpose—and when we will finally image God perfectly—we will give ourselves totally to God. Thus, when God creates us, He gives us all we have; when He redeems us, He gives Himself to us; and, when we are made perfect, we give the whole of ourselves back to Him. We image God most fully, therefore, not only in self-giving, but in reciprocal self-giving: we give ourselves to the God Who has already given Himself to us.

Finally, remaining with God's gift to us, God's self-giving has everything to do with our knowing and loving Him. His gift of Himself to us has everything to do, that is, with the knowledge and love of God in which Thomas's *imago* principally consists. Because the Son is a Word, His self-giving brings about "the illumination of the mind" in our knowledge of God; because the Holy Spirit is Love, His self-giving brings about "the enkindling of the affections" in our love for God.[27] God's gift of Himself to us does not bypass these "psychological" acts of knowing and loving. Nor does it bypass Thomas's psychological Trinity. This self-giving is not a departure from the Son's status as Word or from the Spirit's status as a Love-impression. Instead, the Son gives Himself *as* the Word and the Holy Spirit gives Himself *as* Love, and Their self-giving brings our knowledge and love of God to perfection. More deeply, we saw in chapter four that the Father eternally gives Himself to the Son and to the Holy Spirit by way of intellect and will. We might say now that the Son and the Holy Spirit give Themselves to us in the same way: They give Themselves by way of intellect and will. The most basic point, however, is that the psychological need not be cleared away in order to make room for the interpersonal. Instead, interpersonal

---

25 See Emery, *TTTA*, 254–55.

26 *De virtutibus* q. 2, a. 12, ad 9. See also *Quodl.* III, q. 5, a. 3; *contra impugnantes* II, ch. 5, ad 23; *de decem praeceptis*, a. 1; *de perfectione*, ch. 4; *in II Cor.*, #289; and *in Heb.*, #645.

27 *ST* I q. 43, a. 5, ad 3. See Emery, *TTTA*, 388–90.

self-giving is inextricable from the psychological acts of knowing and loving. Thomas's psychological *imago* itself is entirely interpersonal, and his interpersonal *imago* remains entirely psychological.

"GIVEN TO US BY THE FATHER AND THE SON"

We can draw one more wrinkle out of God's self-giving. For the divine Persons do not merely give Themselves to us. Instead, the Son and the Holy Spirit are also *given* to us by another. This point comes out most fully in Thomas's teaching on the divine missions, where he teaches that the Father sends the Son to us and that the Father and the Son send the Holy Spirit to us.[28] Yet Thomas also writes that, in this sending, the Son is *given* to us by the Father, and the Holy Spirit is *given* to us by the Father and the Son.[29] With reference to the Son, Thomas writes that "the Son is given out of the Father's love."[30] Because the Father loves us, He gives the Son to us. Thomas develops this point at greater length with the Holy Spirit:

> The Holy Spirit has it from the Father and the Son that, by the love which He causes in us, He is in us and He is possessed by us. Fittingly, therefore, He is said to be *given to us by the Father and the Son*. Yet . . . He is said also to be given us *even by Himself* in that He causes in us the love by which He dwells in us together with the Father and the Son.[31]

The Holy Spirit does not give Himself to us instead of being given to us by another. Nor is He given by another instead of giving Himself. Instead, He is both giving and given: He gives Himself as He is given by the Father and the Son.

---

[28] For background information on the missions, see Emery, *TTTA*, 360–412.
[29] See *ST* I q. 43, a. 3, ad 1; and Emery, *TTTA*, 384.
[30] *ST* I q. 38, a. 2, ad 1.
[31] *SCG* IV 23§11. See also *in Ioan.*, #577.

Summing up, our imaging God is a matter of our knowing and loving three divine Persons as we know and love ourselves. These divine Persons, moreover, already know and love us, and They both dwell intimately within us and stand at an infinite distance from us. Even more, those Persons give us to ourselves in creating us, and our imaging God most fully is a matter of those Persons' giving Themselves to us, of our giving ourselves to Them in return, of the first divine Person's giving the second Person to us, and of the first and second Persons' giving the third Person to us. We saw all through part one that Thomas's psychological analogy for the Trinity arranges a marriage between perfect interiority and radical distinction. We have seen all through part two that it arranges a similar marriage of self-knowledge, self-love, interpersonal knowledge, interpersonal love, interpersonal self-giving, and interpersonal being-given. We see now that, in Thomas's psychological image of the Trinity—and therefore in his account of human perfection—we are invited into a created echo of this same marriage.

Of course, only a few of these interpersonal notes enter directly into our imaging God. Yet even our opening points on self-love as interpersonal love—all of which Thomas explicitly registers when he treats of the image of God—are enough to ensure the rudiments of my claim here. For to say that we image God by knowing and loving God is already enough to show that Thomas's psychological *imago* is itself an interpersonal *imago*. Just so, to say that we know and love God in knowing and loving ourselves is already enough to show that this *imago* integrates the interpersonal and the intrapersonal. More deeply, however, all of the additional elements we have drawn out—self-giving, being-given, and so on—really do enter into the *imago Dei*. Indeed, they enter so intimately into it that this image would cease to exist in its fullness if any one of them were removed. If, for example, God did not give Himself to us, then we would not receive His grace and glory, and we therefore could not image Him as perfectly as possible. None of these elements enter directly or explicitly into Thomas's account of our imaging God. Yet we could not image God most fully if even one of them were absent.

"ALL FELLOW MEN"

A final point is just as important. For many social Trinitarians might welcome an *imago Dei* cast in terms of interpersonal intimacy and self-giving between us and God. Yet others might demand that we go further. For central to many social Trinitarian projects is the claim that we image God in our relationships with other human beings. Yet, in the telling of some, it might be theoretically possible for me to enjoy a personal relationship with God that is mine and mine alone and that bears no necessary reference to human intimacy, community, or solidarity.[32] To fully meet their concerns, therefore, we would need to image God not only in our relationship with God, but also in our relationships with each other.

Happily, Thomas can open up a path in this direction. As he puts it succinctly, "it is necessary that whoever loves God should love his neighbor."[33] In more detail, he writes that "charity loves God for His own sake; and because of Him, it loves all others according as they are ordered to God. Thus, in a way, charity loves God in all fellow men."[34] We saw above that I image God to a certain extent in my natural love, but that I only image God most fully in supernatural charity. We see now that, when I love God with this charity, I cannot love God alone. Nor can I merely love God *and* others. Instead, in charity, I love God and I *therefore* love others. Indeed, I love God *in* others, and I love others *in* God: my love of God itself opens up and includes others. Indeed, my love of God opens up and includes "*all* others": I only love with charity if I love "all fellow men"—and I only image God most fully if I love with charity.

Thus, once more, my love for my wife, for my family, for my friends, for the Church—or, for that matter, for my enemies or for "all others"—is not foregrounded when Thomas discusses the *imago Dei*. Yet the elements Thomas *does* highlight carry these social dimensions

---

[32] For an example of such an individualistic spirituality, see Henri de Lubac, *Catholicism: Christ and the Common Destiny of Man*, trans. Lancelot C. Sheppard and Elizabeth Englund (San Francisco: Ignatius, 1988), 13.

[33] *In Ioan.*, #2007. See also *in Rom.*, #1049.

[34] *De virtutibus* q. 2, a. 4.

in its wake. My love for my friends or for strangers is not an optional addendum to an individualistic *imago Dei*. Instead, my love for my fellow men follows organically and necessarily on the knowledge and love of God in which that *imago* principally consists. Thomas's psychological *imago Dei*, then, is social not only in that it entails my knowing and loving God; it is social also in that, in loving God, I love others, and I give myself to the upbuilding of the sort of human community in which so many social Trinitarians are interested.

CONCLUSION

God is Love.

God is three Persons, each of Whom loves the others, each of Whom knows the others, each of Whom shares all He has with the others, and each of Whom gives Himself to or receives Himself from the others.

That's what a lot of Trinitarian theologians have said recently. It's also what Thomas Aquinas said eight hundred years ago. There are, of course, immense differences between Thomas and many—if not all—social Trinitarians. Thomas's psychological analogy will never yield the social Trinity of a Moltmann or a Balthasar. Yet neither does it yield a supreme and solitary solipsist, sunk in endless empty self-regard. Instead, for Thomas too, God is the superabundant fullness of interpersonal intimacy and of interpersonal communion, of interpersonal distinction and of interpersonal encounter, of reciprocal knowledge and of reciprocal love, and of giving the whole of oneself to another and of welcoming the whole of another into the depths of one's heart. Yet God is all of these things because a Word and Love eternally proceed within the unity of the divine nature.

BIBLIOGRAPHY

WORKS BY THOMAS AQUINAS

Catena aurea in quatuor Evangelia Expositio in Matthaeum. Edited by A. Guarenti. Turin and Rome: Marietti, 1953.

Collationes in decem praeceptis. In J. P. Torrell. *Recherches thomasiennes. Études revues et augmentées.* Paris: J. Vrin, 2000.

Compendium theologiae seu Brevis compilatio theologiae ad fratrem Raynaldum. In *Opuscula Theologica*, vol. 1. Edited by Raymundi A. Verardo. Turin: Marietti, 1954.

Contra errores Graecorum ad Urbanum papam. In *Sancti Thomae de Aquino opera omnia*, vol. 40 A. Leonine Edition. Rome: Ad Sanctae Sabinae, 1967.

De perfectione spiritualis vitae. In *Sancti Thomae de Aquino opera omnia*, vol. 41 B. Leonine Edition. Rome: Ad Sanctae Sabinae, 1969.

De potentia Dei. Edited by P. M. Pession. In *Quaestiones disputatae*, vol. 2. Turin and Rome: Marietti, 1965.

De rationibus fidei ad Cantorem Antiochenum. In *Sancti Thomae de Aquino opera omnia*, vol. 40 B. Leonine Edition. Rome: Editori di San Tommaso, 1968.

De veritate. In *Sancti Thomae de Aquino opera omnia*, vol. 22. Leonine Edition. Rome: Editori di San Tommaso, 1975–76.

Expositio super Iob ad litteram. In *Sancti Thomae de Aquino opera omnia*, vol. 26. Leonine Edition. Rome: Ad Sanctae Sabinae, 1965.

Expositio super primam et secundam Decretalem ad archidiaconum Tudertinum. In *Sancti Thomae de Aquino opera omnia*, vol. 40 E. Leonine Edition. Rome: Editori di San Tommaso, 1968.

In duodecim libros Metaphysicorum Aristotelis expositio. Edited by M. R. Cathala and R. M. Spiazzi. Turin and Rome: Marietti, 1971.

In psalmos Davidis exposition. In *Opera omnia*, vol. 14. Parma: Typis Petri Fiaccadori, 1863.

In Symbolum Apostolorum, scilicet "Credo in Deum" exposition. In *Opuscula theologica*, vol. 2. Edited by R. M. Spiazzi. Turin and Rome: Marietti, 1953.

Lectura romana in primum Sententiarum Petri Lombardi. Edited by L. E. Boyle and J. F. Boyle. Toronto: Pontifical Institute of Medieval Studies, 2006.

Liber contra impugnantes Dei cultum et religionem. In *Sancti Thomae de Aquino opera omnia*, vol. 41. Leonine Edition. Rome: Editori di San Tommaso, 1970.

Liber de veritate catholicae Fidei contra errores infidelium seu Summa contra Gentiles. Edited by P. Marc, C. Pera, and P. Caramello. Turin and Rome: Marietti, 1961.

Quaestiones de quolibet. In *Sancti Thomae de Aquino opera omnia*, vol. 25/2. Leonine Edition. Rome and Paris: Cerf, 1996.

Quaestiones disputatae de anima. In *Sancti Thomae de Aquino opera omnia*, vol. 24/1. Leonine Edition. Rome and Paris: Cerf, 1996.

Quaestiones disputatae de malo. In *Sancti Thomae de Aquino opera omnia*, vol. 23. Leonine Edition. Rome: Editori di San Tommaso, 1982.

Quaestiones disputatae de virtutibus. In *Quaestiones disputatae.* Vol 2, *Quaestio disputata de caritate.* Edited by E. Odetto. Turin and Rome: Marietti, 1965.

Responsio ad magistrum Ioannem de Vercellis de 108 articulis. In *Sancti Thomae de Aquino opera omnia*, vol. 42. Leonine Edition. Rome: Editori di San Tommaso, 1979.

Scriptum super libros Sententiarum magistri Petri Lombardi episcopi Parisiensis. Vols 1–2, edited by P. Mandonnet. Paris: P. Lethielleux, 1929. Vols 3–4, edited by M. F. Moos. Paris: P. Lethielleux, 1933–47.

Sentencia libri De sensu et sensato cuius secundus tractatus est De memoria et reminiscencia. In *Sancti Thomae de Aquino opera omnia*, vol. 45/2. Leonine Edition. Rome and Paris: J. Vrin, 1984.

Summa theologiae. In *Sancti Thomae de Aquino opera omnia*, vols. 4–12. Leonine Edition. Rome, Ex Typographia Polyglotta S. C. de Propaganda Fide, 1888–1906.

Super Boetium De Trinitate. In *Sancti Thomae de Aquino opera omnia*, vol. 50. Leonine Edition. Rome and Paris: Cerf, 1992.

Super Epistolam S. Pauli ad Colossenses lectura. In *Super Epistolas S. Pauli lectura*, vol. 2. Edited by R. Cai. Turin and Rome: Marietti, 1953.

Super Epistolam S. Pauli ad Ephesios lectura. In *Super Epistolas S. Pauli lectura*, vol. 2. Edited by R. Cai. Turin and Rome: Marietti, 1953.

Super Epistolam S. Pauli ad Galatas lectura. In *Super Epistolas S. Pauli lectura*, vol. 1. Edited by R. Cai. Turin and Rome: Marietti, 1953.

Super Epistolam S. Pauli ad Hebraeos lectura. In *Super Epistolas S. Pauli lectura*, vol. 2. Edited by R. Cai. Turin and Rome: Marietti, 1953.

Super Epistolam ad Romanos lectura. In *Super Epistolas S. Pauli lectura*, vol. 1. Edited by R. Cai. Turin and Rome: Marietti, 1953.

Super Evangelium S. Ioannis lectura. Edited by R. Cai. Turin and Rome: Marietti, 1972.

Super Evangelium S. Matthaei lectura. Edited by R. Cai. Turin and Rome: Marietti, 1951.

Super Librum Dionysii De divini nominibus. Edited by C. Pera, P. Caramello, and C. Mazzantini. Turin and Rome: Marietti, 1950.

Super primam Epistolam S. Pauli ad Corinthios lectura. In *Super Epistolas S. Pauli lectura*, vol. 1. Edited by R. Cai. Turin and Rome: Marietti, 1953.

Super secundam Epistolam S. Pauli ad Corinthios lectura. In *Super Epistolas S. Pauli lectura*, vol. 1. Edited by R. Cai. Turin and Rome: Marietti, 1953.

TRANSLATIONS OF WORKS BY THOMAS AQUINAS

The Academic Sermons. Translated Mark-Robin Hoogland. Washington, DC: The Catholic University of America Press, 2010.

Commentary on the Gospel of John. Translated by Fabian R. Larcher. Lander, WY: The Aquinas Institute, 2013.

Commentary on the Gospel of Matthew. Translated by Jeremy Holmes. Lander, WY: Aquinas Institute, 2013.

Commentary on the Letters of Saint Paul to the Galatians and Ephesians. Translated by Fabian R. Larcher. Lander, WY: The Aquinas Institute, 2012.

Commentary on the Letter of Saint Paul to the Hebrews. Translated by Fabian R. Larcher. Lander, WY: The Aquinas Institute, 2012.

Commentary on the Metaphysics of Aristotle. Translated by John P. Rowan. Chicago: Regnery, 1961.

Compendium of Theology. Cyril Vollert. St. Louis and London: B. Herder, 1947.

On the Power of God. Translated by the English Dominican Fathers. Westminster, MD: The Newman Press, 1952.

Summa contra Gentiles I. Translated by Anton C. Pegis. Garden City, NY: Doubleday, 1955.

Summa contra Gentiles II. Translated by James F. Anderson. Garden City, NY: Doubleday, 1956.

Summa contra Gentiles III. Translated by Vernon J. Bourke. Garden City, NY: Doubleday, 1956.

Summa contra Gentiles IV. Translated by Charles J. O'Neil. Garden City, NY: Doubleday, 1956.

Summa Theologica. Translated by the English Dominican Province. New York: Benzinger Brothers, 1947.

Truth. Vol 1. Translated by W. Mulligan. Chicago: Regnery, 1952.

Truth. Vol 2. Translated by James V. McGlynn. Chicago: Regnery, 1953.

Truth. Vol 3. Translated by Robert W. Schmidt. Chicago: Regnery, 1954.

OTHER WORKS

Ables, Travis. "A Pneumatology of Christian Knowledge: The Holy Spirit and the Performance of the Mystery of God in Augustine and Barth." PhD diss., Vanderbilt University, 2010.

——. *Incarnational Realism: Trinity and the Spirit in Augustine and Barth.* London: Bloomsbury T&T Clark, 2013.

Allen, Prudence. "Integral Sex Complementarity and Theology of Communion." *Communio: International Catholic Review* 17, no. 4 (1990): 523–44.

Augustine, *De Trinitate*. Translated by Edmund Hill. Hyde Park, NY: New City Press, 1991.

Ayres, Lewis. *Augustine and the Trinity*. Cambridge: Cambridge University Press, 2010.

———. "The Christological Context of Augustine's *De trinitate* XIII: Toward Relocating Books VIII-XV." *Augustinian Studies* 29, no. 1 (1998): 111–39.

Bailleux, Emile. "Le personnalisme de saint Thomas en théologie trinitaire." *Revue Thomiste* 61 (1961): 25–42.

Balthasar, Hans Urs von. *Explorations in Theology III*. Translated by Brian McNeil. San Francisco: Ignatius, 1993.

———. *Explorations in Theology IV*. Translated by Edward T. Oakes, SJ. San Francisco: Ignatius, 1995.

———. *Theo-Drama II*. Translated by Graham Harrison. San Francisco: Ignatius, 1990.

———. *Theo-Drama III*. Translated by Graham Harrison. San Francisco: Ignatius, 1992.

———. *Theo-logic II*. Translated by Adrian J. Walker. San Francisco: Ignatius, 2004.

Barth, Karl. *Church Dogmatics*. Vol. 2/1, *The Doctrine of God*. Translated by G. W. Bromiley. Edinburgh: T&T Clark, 1964.

Benedict XVI. *Caritas in Veritate*. Encyclical Letter. June 29, 2009.

Blankenhorn, Bernhard-Thomas. "The Good as Self-Diffusive in Thomas Aquinas." *Angelicum* 79, no. 4 (2002): 803–37.

Blair, George. "On *Esse* and Relation." *Communio: International Catholic Review* 21, no. 1 (1994): 162–64.

Boff, Leonardo. *Trinity and Society*. Translated by Paul Burns. Maryknoll, NY: Orbis Books, 1988.

Bourassa, François. "Dans la communion de l'Esprit Saint." Pts. 1–3. *Science et Esprit* 34, no. 1 (1982): 31–56; 34, no. 2 (1982): 135–49; 34, no. 3 (1982): 239–68.

———. "Personne et conscience en théologie trinitaire." Pts. 1 and 2. *Gregorianum* 55, no. 3 (1974): 471–93; 55, no. 4 (1974): 677–720.

———. "Sur la Propriéte de l'Esprit, Questions Disputées." Pts. 1 and 2. *Science et Esprit* 28, no. 3 (1976): 243–64; 29, no. 1 (1977): 23–43.

———. "Le Saint-Esprit. 'Communion du Père et du Fils.'" Pts. 1 and 2. *Science et Esprit* 29, no. 4 (1977): 251–81; 30, no. 1 (1978): 5–37.

———. "Le Saint-Esprit unite d'amour du Père et du Fils." *Science et Esprit* 14 (1962): 375–415.

Brink, Gijsbert van den. "Social Trinitarianism: A Discussion of Some Recently Theological Criticisms." *The International Journal of Systematic Theology* 16, no. 3 (2014): 331–50.

Brock, Stephen L. "Intentional Being, Natural Being, and the First-Person Perspective in Thomas Aquinas." *The Thomist* 77, no. 1 (2013): 103–33.

Buber, Martin. *I and Thou*. Translated by Ronald Gregor Smith. New York: Scribner, 1958.

Bulgakov, Sergei. *The Comforter*. Translated by Boris Jakim. Grand Rapids, MI: Eerdmans, 2004.

Butner, Glenn D. "For and Against de Régnon: Trinitarianism East and West." *International Journal of Systematic Theology* 17, no. 4 (2015): 399–412.

Carl, Brian. "Action, Supposit, and Subject: Interpreting *Actiones sunt Suppositorum*." *Nova et Vetera* English edition 17, no. 2 (2019): 545–65.

Clarke, Norris. *Person and Being*. Milwaukee: Marquette University Press, 1993.

Coakley, Sarah. "Afterword: 'Relational Ontology,' Trinity, and Science." In *The Trinity and an Entangled World*, edited by John Polkinghorne, 184–99. Grand Rapids, MI: Eerdmans, 2010.

Coleman, Rachel M. "Thinking the 'Nothing' of Being: Ferdinand Ulrich on Transnihilation." *Communio: International Catholic Review* 46, no. 1 (2019): 182–98.

Cordovilla Pérez, Angel. "The Trinitarian Concept of Person." In *Rethinking Trinitarian Theology*, 105–45.

Cory, Therese Scarpelli. *Aquinas on Human Self-Knowledge*. Cambridge: Cambridge University Press, 2014.

Craig, William Lane. "Toward a Tenable Social Trinitarianism." In *Philosophical and Theological Essays on the Trinity*, 89–99.

Cross, Richard. *Duns Scotus on God*. London: Routledge, 2005.

Crowe, Fredrick E. "Complacency and Concern." Pts. 1–3. *Theological Studies* 20, no. 1 (1959): 1–39; 20, no. 2 (1959): 198–230; 20, no. 3 (1959): 343–95.

Darley, Alan Philip. "Predication or Participation? What is the Nature of Aquinas's Doctrine of Analogy?" *The Heythrop Journal* 57, no. 1 (2016): 312–24.

Dauphinais, Barry David, and Matthew Levering, eds. *Aquinas the Augustinian*. Washington, DC: The Catholic University of America Press, 2007.

Deferrari, Roy J. *A Latin-English Dictionary of St. Thomas Aquinas*. Boston: St. Paul Editions, 1960.

De Lubac, Henri. *Catholicism: Christ and the Common Destiny of Man*. Translated by Lancelot C. Sheppard and Elizabeth Englund. San Francisco: Ignatius, 1988.

De Maio, Andrea. *Il concetto de communicazione: Saggio de lessicografia filosofica e teologica sul tema di 'communicare' in Thommaso d'Aquino*. Rome: Pontificia Università Gregoriana, 1998.

D'Ettore, Domenic. *Analogy after Aquinas: Logical Problems, Thomistic Answers*. Washington, DC: The Catholic University of America Press, 2018.

Doig, James C. "O'Callaghan on *Verbum Mentis* in Aquinas." *American Catholic Philosophical Quarterly* 77, no. 2 (2003): 233–55.

Dolezal, James E. "Trinity, Simplicity and the Status of God's Personal Relations." *International Journal of Systematic Theology* 16, no. 1 (2014): 79–98.

Drilling, Peter. "The Psychological Analogy of the Trinity: Augustine, Aquinas, and Lonergan." *The Irish Theological Quarterly* 71, no. 3–4 (2006): 320–37.

Durand, Emmanuel. *La Périchorèse des personnes divines*. Paris: Cerf, 2005.

———. "Theology of God the Father." In *The Oxford Handbook of Trinitarian Theology*, 371–86.

Durand, Emmanuel, and Vincent Holzer, eds. *Les sources du renouveau de la théologie trinitarie au XXe siècle*. Paris: Cerf, 2008.

———. *Les realizations du renouveau de la théologie trinitarie au XXe siècle*. Paris: Cerf, 2010.

Eades Michael. *And in Our Hearts Take Up Thy Rest: The Trinitarian Pneumatology of Fredrick Crowe, SJ*. Toronto: University of Toronto Press, 2019.

Emery, Gilles. "*Ad aliquid*: Relation in the Thought of St. Thomas Aquinas." In *Theology Needs Philosophy: Acting against Reason Is Contrary to the Nature of God*, edited by Matthew L. Lamb, 175–201. Washington, DC: The Catholic University Press of America, 2016.

———. "Central Aristotelian Themes in Aquinas's Trinitarian Theology." In *Aristotle in Aquinas's Theology*, edited by Gilles Emery and Matthew Levering, 1–28. Oxford: Oxford University Press, 2015.

———. "On the Dignity of Being a Substance: Person, Subsistence, Nature." *Nova et Vetera* English edition 9, no. 4 (2011): 991–1001.

———. "Qu'est-ce que la 'communion trinitaire'?" *Nova et Vetera* French edition 96 (2014): 258–83.

———. Review of *Personarum Trinitatis: De trinitarishe Gottesjehre des heiligen Thomas von Aquin*, by H. C. Schmidbaur. *Revue Thomiste* 96 (1996): 690–93.

———. "Trinitarian Theology as Spiritual Exercise in Augustine and Aquinas." In *Aquinas the Augustinian*, 1–40.

———. *The Trinitarian Theology of St. Thomas Aquinas*. Translated by Francesca Murphy. Oxford: Oxford University Press, 2007.

———. *Trinity in Aquinas*. Ypsilanti, MI: Sapienta Press of Ave Maria University, 2003.

———. *Trinity, Church, and the Human Person: Thomistic Essays*. Naples, FL: Sapientia Press of Ave Maria University, 2007.

Emery, Gilles, and Matthew Levering, eds. *Oxford Handbook of Trinitarian Theology*. Oxford: Oxford University Press, 2012.

Folch Gomes, Cirilo. "La Réciprocité psychologique des personnes divines selon la théologie de St. Thomas d'Aquin." *Studi tomistici* 13 (1981): 153–71.

Francis. *Laudato Si'*. Encyclical Letter. May 24, 2015.

Friedman, Russell L. *Intellectual Traditions at the Medieval University: The Use of Philosophical Psychology in Trinitarian Theology among the Franciscans and Dominicans, 1250–1350*. Leiden: Brill, 2013.

Gauthier, R. A. Introduction to *Saint Thomas d'Aquin, Somme contre les gentils*, edited by Henri Hude. Paris: Vrin, 1993.

Geiger, L.-B. "Les Rédactions Successives de *Contra Gentiles* I, 53 d'aprés l'Autographe." In *Saint Thomas d'Aquin Aujourd'hui*, 221–40. Paris: Desclée de Brouwer, 1963.

González Alió, José Luis. "El entender como posesión: La función gnoselógica del verbo mental." Pts. 1 and 2. *Sapientia* 43 (1988): 243–68; 43 (1988): 332–68.

———. "La santisima Trinidad, comunión de personas." *Scripta Theologica* 18, no. 1 (1986): 11–115.

———. "La visión beatífica como realidad trinitaria." *Scripta Theologica* 19, no. 3 (1987): 597–631.

Goris, Harm. "Theology and Theory of the Word in Aquinas: Understanding Augustine by Innovating Aristotle." In *Aquinas the Augustinian*, 62–78.

Greshake, Gisbert. *Der dreieine Gott: Eine trinitarische Theologie*. Basel: Herder, 1997.

Gunton, A. F. von. "*In principio erat verbum*. Une evolution de saint Thomas en théologie trinitaire." In *Ordo Sapienta et Amoris*, 119–41. Fribourg: Éditions Universitaires Fribourg Suisse, 1993.

Gunton, Colin. *The Promise of Trinitarian Theology*. Edinburgh: T&T Clark, 1997.

Hankey, Wayne. *God in Himself*. Oxford: Oxford University Press, 1987.

Hasker, William. *Metaphysics and the Tri-Personal God*. Oxford: Oxford University Press, 2013.

Higgins, Michael Joseph. "Aquinas on the Role of Another in Perfect Self-Knowledge." *Modern Theology* 38, no. 1 (2022): 19–35.

———. "Does Goodness Require Another? On an Unexplored Corner of Aquinas's Trinitarian Theology." *Communio: International Catholic Review* 47, no. 2 (2020): 368–98.

———. "The Family as an Image of the Trinity in Aquinas." *Communio: International Catholic Review* 49, no. 2 (2022): 299–330.

———. " 'A Mark of Perfection': Receiving and Perfection in Aquinas's Trinitarian Theology." *The International Journal of Systematic Theology* 25, no. 3 (2023): 435–55.

———. " 'The More We Wonder': Union with God, Distance from God, and the Vexing Question of 'Necessary Reasons' in Aquinas's Trinitarian Theology." *Irish Theological Quarterly* 86, no. 2 (2021): 147–16.

———. "On the Open Question of «Necessary Reasons» in Aquinas's Trinitarian Theology." *Angelicum* 97, no. 2 (2020): 177–212.

———. "Perfection and the Necessity of the Trinity in Aquinas." *New Blackfriars* 102, no. 1097 (2021): 75–95.

———. "A Second Tier? Aquinas on Mutual Love in the Procession of the Holy Spirit." Forthcoming in *Nova et Vetera*.

———. "The Reach of Reason and The Eyes of Faith: Pierre Rousselot and the Question of «Necessary Reasons» in Aquinas's Trinitarian Theology." *Gregorianum* 100, no. 3 (2019): 559–83.

Hirschfeld, Mary. *Aquinas and the Market: Toward a Humane Economy.* Cambridge, MA: Harvard University Press, 2018.

Hochschild, Joshua P. "Aquinas's Two Concepts of Analogy and a Complex Semantics for Naming the Simple God." *The Thomist* 83, no. 2 (2019): 155–84.

———. "Proportionality and Divine Naming: Did St. Thomas Change His Mind about Analogy?" *The Thomist* 77, no. 4 (2013): 531–58.

———. *The Semantics of Analogy: Reading Cajetan's* De Nominum Analogia. Notre Dame, IN: University of Notre Dame Press, 2010.

Holmes, Stephen R. "Architectonics Matter: Some Advantages of Treating the Unicity of God in Advance of the Trinity of Persons, in Dialogue with Thomas Aquinas." *International Journal of Systematic Theology* 19, no. 2 (2017): 130–43.

———. *The Quest for the Trinity.* Downers Grove, IL: InterVarsity Press, 2012.

Holtz, Dominic. "Divine Personhood and the Critique of Substance Metaphysics." *Nova et Vetera* English edition 12, no. 4 (2014): 1191–213.

Hunt, Anne. "Psychological Analogy and Paschal Mystery in Trinitarian Theology." *Theological Studies* 59, no. 2 (1998): 197–218.

———. "The Trinity Through Paschal Eyes." In *Rethinking Trinitarian Theology*, 472–89.

Izquierdo, Cesar. "La teología del Verbo en la 'Summa Contra Gentiles.'" *Scripta Theologica* 14, no. 2 (1982): 551–80.

John Paul II. *Man and Woman He Created Them: A Theology of the Body.* Translated by Michael Waldstein. Boston: Pauline Books and Media, 2006.

———. "Meditation on Givenness." *Communio: International Catholic Review* 41, no. 4 (2014): 871–83.

Johnson, Elizabeth. *She Who Is: The Mystery of God in Feminist Theological Discourse.* New York: Crossroad, 1992.

Juvenal, Merriel D. *To the Image of the Trinity: A Study in the Development of Aquinas' Teaching.* Toronto: Pontifical Institute of Medieval Studies, 1990.

Kasper, Walter. *The God of Jesus Christ.* New York: Continuum, 2012.

Keaty, Anthony. "The Holy Spirit Proceeding as Mutual Love: An Interpretation of Aquinas' *Summa Theologiae* I.37." *Angelicum* 77, no. 3/4 (2000): 533–57.

Kelly, Anthony. *The Trinity of Love.* Wilmington, DE: Michael Glazier, 1989.

Kilby, Karen. "Aquinas, the Trinity and the Limits of Understanding." *The International Journal of Systematic Theology* 7, no. 4 (2005): 414–27.

———. "Perichoresis and Projection." *New Blackfriars* 81 (2000): 432–45.

———. "Trinity, Tradition, and Politics." In *Recent Developments in Trinitarian Theology: An International Symposium*, edited by Christophe Chalamet and Marc Vial, 73–86. Minneapolis: Fortress Press, 2014.

Ku, John Baptist. *God the Father in Theology of St. Thomas Aquinas.* New York: P. Lang, 2013.

———. "St. Thomas Aquinas's Treatment of the Name 'Father' in ST I, q. 33, a. 2." *Nova et Vetera* English edition 9, no. 2 (2011): 433–78.

Lafont, Ghislain. *Peut-on Connatire Dieu Jesus-Christ?* Paris: Cerf, 1969.

Legge, Dominic. *The Trinitarian Christology of St Thomas Aquinas.* Oxford: Oxford University Press, 2016.

Levering, Matthew. *Engaging the Doctrine of the Holy Spirit: Love and Gift in the Trinity and the Church.* Grand Rapids, MI: Baker Publishing Group, 2016.

———. *Scripture and Metaphysics.* Oxford: Blackwell, 2004.

Liberto, David. "Person, Being, and Receptivity: W. Norris Clarke's Retrieval and Completion of Thomas's Thought." In *Aquinas as Authority: A Collection of Studies Presented at the Second Conference of the Thomas Instituut te Utrecht, December 14–16, 2000*, 201–11. Leusden-Zuid: Thomas Instituut te Utrecht, 2002.

Long, D. Stephen. *The Perfectly Simple Triune God: Aquinas and His Legacy.* Minneapolis: Fortress, 2016.

Long, Steven A. *Analogia Entis: On the Analogy of Being, Metaphysics, and the Act of Faith.* Notre Dame, IN: University of Notre Dame Press, 2011.

———. "Divine and Creaturely 'Receptivity': The Search for a Middle Term." *Communio: International Catholic Review* 21, no. 1 (1994): 151–61.

———. "Personal Receptivity and Pure Act: A Thomistic Critique." *The Thomist* 61, no. 1 (1997): 1–31.

———. "Thoughts on Analogy and Relation." *Quaestiones Disputatae* 6, no. 1 (2015): 73–89.

Lonergan, Bernard. *The Collected Works of Bernard Lonergan.* Vol. 2, *Verbum: Word and Idea in Aquinas*, edited by Fredrick E. Crowe and Robert M. Doran. Toronto: University of Toronto Press, 1997.

———. *The Collected Works of Bernard Lonergan.* Vol. 12, *The Triune God: Systematics*, edited by Robert M. Doran and H. Daniel Monsour. Toronto: University of Toronto Press, 2009.

Loyer, Kenneth M. *God's Love through the Spirit: The Holy Spirit in Thomas Aquinas and John Wesley.* Washington, DC: The Catholic University of America Press, 2014.

Malloy, Christopher J. "The 'I-Thou' Argument for the Trinity: Wherefore Art Thou?" *Nova et Vetera* English edition 15, no. 1 (2016): 113–59.

Maspero, Giulio, and Robert J. Wozniak, eds. *Rethinking Trinitarian Theology.* New York: Continuum, 2012.

McCabe, Herbert. "Aquinas on the Trinity." *New Blackfriars* 80 (1999): 268–83.

McCall, Thomas H. *Which Trinity? Whose Monotheism? Philosophical and Systematic Theologians on the Metaphysics of Trinitarian Theology.* Grand Rapids, MI: Eerdmans, 2010.

McCall, Thomas, and Michael C. Rea. Introduction to *Philosophical and Theological Essays on the Trinity*, 1–18.

———, eds. *Philosophical and Theological Essays on the Trinity.* Oxford: Oxford University Press, 2009.

McDermott, John D. "Is the Blessed Trinity Naturally Knowable? St. Thomas on Reason, Faith, Nature, Grace, and Person." *Gregorianum* 93, no. 1 (2012): 113–49.

McNall, Joshua. *A Free Corrector: Colin Gunton and the Legacy of Augustine.* Minneapolis: Fortress Press, 2015.

Milbank, John. "Truth and Vision." In *The Radical Orthodoxy Reader*, edited by John Milbank and Simon Oliver, 19–59. New York: Routledge, 2009.

Moltmann, Jürgen. *The Trinity and the Kingdom of God.* Translated by Margaret Kohl. Minneapolis: Fortress, 1993.

Nedoncelle, Maurice. "L'intersubjectivité humaine est-elle pour saint Augustin une image de la Trinité?" In *Augustinus Magister* I, 595–602. Paris, 1954.

Nieuwenhove, Rik van. "In the Image of God: The Trinitarian Anthropology of St Bonaventure, St Thomas Aquinas, and the Blessed Jan Van Ruusbroec." *Irish Theological Quarterly* 66, no. 2 (2001): 109–23.

O'Callaghan, John. "*Verbum Mentis*: Philosophical or Theological Doctrine in Aquinas?" *ACPA Proceedings* 74 (2000): 103–19.

Ormerod, Neil. "The Psychological Analogy for the Trinity: At Odds with Modernity." *Pacifica* 14, no. 3 (2001): 281–94.

Oster, Stephan. "Becoming a Person and the Trinity." In *Rethinking Trinitarian Theology*, 346–67.

Ouellet, Marc. *Divine Likeness: Toward a Trinitarian Anthropology of the Family*. Grand Rapids, MI: Eerdmans, 2006.

Paissac, Hyacinthe. *Théologie du Verbe. Saint Augustin et saint Thomas*. Paris: Cerf, 1951.

Pannenberg, Wolfhart. *Systematic Theology*. Vol. I. Translated by Geoffrey W. Bromiley. Grand Rapids, MI: Eerdmans, 1991.

Penido, M. T. L. "Gloses sur la procession d'amour dans la Trinité." *Ephemerides theologicae lovanienses* 14 (1937): 33–68.

———. "A Propos de la procession d'amour en Dieu." *Ephemerides theologicae lovanienses* 15 (1938): 338–44.

Phan, Peter C. "Systematic Issues in Trinitarian Theology." In *The Cambridge Companion to the Trinity*, edited by Peter C. Phan, 13–30. Cambridge: Cambridge University Press, 2011.

Pieper, Joseph. *Living the Truth*. Translated by Lothar Krauth. San Francisco: Ignatius, 1989.

———. *The Silence of St. Thomas*. Translated by John Murray and Daniel O'Connor. South Bend, IN: St. Augustine's Press, 1999.

Plantinga, Cornelius. "Social Trinity and Tritheism." In *Trinity, Incarnation, and Atonement: Philosophical and Theological Essays*, edited by Ronald J. Feenstra and Cornelius Plantinga, 21–47. South Bend, IN: University of Notre Dame, 1989.

Porro, Pasquale. *Thomas Aquinas: A Historical and Philosophical Profile*. Translated by Joseph G. Trabbic and Roger W. Nutt. Washington, DC: The Catholic University of America Press, 2016.

Rahner, Karl. *The Trinity*. Translated by Joseph Doncell. New York: Herder and Herder, 2010.

Ratzinger, Joseph. "Concerning the Notion of Person in Theology." *Communio: International Catholic Review* 17, no. 3 (1990): 439–54.

———. *Introduction to Christianity*. Translated by J. R. Foster. San Francisco: Ignatius, 2004.

Richard, R. L. *The Problem of an Apologetical Perspective in the Trinitarian Theology of St. Thomas Aquinas*. Rome: Gregorian University Press, 1963.

Rodríguez, Luis Fernández. "El Concepto en santo Tomás." *Anuario Filosófico* 7, no. 1 (1974): 125–90.

Rossner, William. "The Procession of Human Intellectual Love, or Spirating a Pondus." *The Thomist* 36, no. 1 (1972): 39–74.

Rousselot, Pierre. *The Eyes of Faith*. Translated by Avery Dulles. New York: Fordham University Press, 1990.

Schindler, D. C. *The Catholicity of Reason*. Grand Rapids, MI: Eerdmans, 2013.

———. "The Crisis of Marriage as a Crisis of Meaning: On the Sterility of the Modern Will." *Communio: International Catholic Review* 41, no. 2 (2014): 331–71.

———. *Hans Urs von Balthasar and the Dramatic Structure of Truth*. New York: Fordham University Press, 2004.

———. *The Politics of the Real*. Steubenville, OH: New Polity Press, 2021.

———. "The Word as the Center of Man's Onto-Dramatic Task." *Communio: International Catholic Review* 46, no. 1 (2019): 73–85.

Schindler, David L. "Being, Gift, Self-Gift (Part Two)." *Communio: International Catholic Review* 43, no. 3 (2016): 409–83.

———. "Norris Clarke on Person, Being, and St. Thomas." *Communio: International Catholic Review* 20, no. 3 (1993): 580–92.

———. "The Person: Philosophy, Theology, and Receptivity." *Communio: International Catholic Review* 21, no. 1 (1994): 172–90.

Schmaus, Michael. *De Psychologische Trinitätslehre des Heiligen Auginstinus*. Munster: Aschendorffsche Verlagsbuchhandlung, 1927.

Schmitz, Kenneth L. "Created Receptivity and the Philosophy of the Concrete." *The Thomist* 61, no. 3 (1997): 339–76.

Schumacher, Lydia. "The Trinity and Christian Life: A Broadly Thomistic Account of Participation." *New Blackfriars* 96 (2015): 645–57.

Scola, Angelo. *The Nuptial Mystery*. Translated by Michelle K. Boras. Grand Rapids, MI: Eerdmans, 2005.

Sexton, Jason S, ed. *Two Views on the Doctrine of the Trinity*. Grand Rapids, MI: Zondervan, 2014.

Sherwin, Michael. "Aquinas, Augustine, and the Medieval Scholastic Crisis concerning Charity." In *Aquinas the Augustinian*, 181–204.

———. *By Knowledge and by Love: Charity and Knowledge in the Moral Theology of St. Thomas Aquinas*. Washington, DC: The Catholic University of America Press, 2005.

Simonin, H. D. "Autour de la solution Thomiste de problème de l'amour." *Archives d'histoire et littéraire de Moyen Age* 6 (1931): 174–276.

Slotemaker, John T. "Peter Lombard and the *imago Trinitatis*." In *A Companion to Medieval Christian Humanism*, edited by John P. Bequette, 168–88. Leiden: Brill, 2016.

Smith, Timothy L. *Thomas Aquinas's Trinitarian Theology: A Study in Theological Method*. Washington, DC: The Catholic University of America Press, 2003.

Speltz, Gregory H. *The Importance of the Rural Life According to the Philosophy of St. Thomas Aquinas: A Study in Economic Philosophy*. Lexington, KY: St. Pius X Press, 2011.

Speyr, Adrienne von. *The World of Prayer*. Translated by Graham Harrison. San Francisco: Ignatius, 1985.

Sutton, Matthew Lewis. "A Compelling Trinitarian Taxonomy: Hans Urs von Balthasar's Theology of the Trinitarian Inversion and Reversion." *International Journal of Systematic Theology* 14, no. 2 (2012): 161–75.

Tanner, Kathryn. "Social Trinitarianism and Its Critics." In *Rethinking Trinitarian Theology*, 368–86.

Te Velde, Rudi. "The Divine Person(s): Trinity, Person, and Analogous Naming." In *The Oxford Handbook of the Trinity*, 359–70.

Torrell, Jean-Pierre. *St. Thomas Aquinas: Spiritual Master*. Translated by Robert Royal. Washington, DC: The Catholic University of America Press, 2003.

———. *St. Thomas Aquinas: The Person and His Work*. 3rd edition. Translated by Matthew K. Minerd and Robert Royal. Washington, DC: The Catholic University of America Press, 2023.

Ulrich, Ferdinand. *Homo Abyssus: The Drama of the Question of Being*. Translated by D. C. Schindler. Washington, DC: Humanum Academic Press, 2018.

Vagaggini, Cyprian. "La hantise des *rationes necessariae* de saint Anselme dans la théologie des processions trinitaires de saint Thomas." In *Specilegium Beccense. Congrès International de ixe centenaire de l'arrivée d'Anselm au Bec*, 103–39. Paris: Vrin, 1959.

Vanier, Paul. *Théologie Trinitaire chez Saint Thomas d'Aquin. Evolution du Concept d'Action Notionelle*. Montreal: Institut d'Etudes Medievales, 1953.

Waldstein, Michael. *The Glory of the Logos in the Flesh: St. John Paul II's Theology of the Body*. Ave Maria, FL: Sapientia Press of Ave Maria University, 2021.

———. "John Paul II and St. Thomas on Love and the Trinity." *Anthropotes* 18, no. 1 (2002): 113–38.

———. "John Paul II and St. Thomas on Love and the Trinity." *Anthropotes* 18, no. 2 (2002): 269–86.

Waldstein, Susan. "Reading Natural Hierarchy in a Trinitarian Key." *Communio: International Catholic Review* 42, no. 4 (2015): 652–92.

Walker, Adrian J. "Personal Singularity and the *Communio Personarum*: A Creative Development of Thomas Aquinas' Doctrine of *Esse Commune*." *Communio: International Catholic Review* 31, no. 3 (2004): 457–79.

Weinandy, Thomas. *The Father's Spirit of Sonship*. New York: T&T Clark, 1995.

White, Thomas Joseph. "Divine Simplicity and the Holy Trinity." *International Journal of Systematic Theology* 18, no. 1 (2016): 66–93.

———. *The Trinity: On the Nature and Mystery of the One God*. Washington, DC: The Catholic University of America Press, 2022.

Wilkins, Jeremy Daniel. "*Emanatio Intellibilis in Deo*: A Study of the Horizon and Development of Thomas Aquinas's Trinitarian Theology." PhD diss., Boston College, 2004.

———. "Method, Order, and Analogy in Trinitarian Theology: Karl Rahner's Critique of the 'Psychological' Approach." *The Thomist* 74, no. 4 (2010): 563–92.

Williams, A. N. *The Ground of Union*. Oxford: Oxford University Press, 1999.

Williams, Rowan. "*Sapientia* and the Trinity: Reflections on the *De Trinitate*." *Augustiniana* 40 (1990), 317–32.

———. "What Does Love Know? St. Thomas on the Trinity." *New Blackfriars* 82 (2001): 260–72.

Williams, Scott M. "Augustine, Thomas Aquinas, Henry of Ghent and John Duns Scotus: On Theology of the Father's Intellectual Generation of the Word." *Recherches de Théologie et Philosophie médiévales* 77, no. 1 (2010): 35–81.

Wippel, John F. *Metaphysical Themes in Thomas Aquinas*. Washington, DC: The Catholic University of America Press, 1984.

Yin Yam, Cheuk, and Dupont, Anthony. "A Mind-Centered Approach of the *'Imago Dei'*: A Dynamic Construction in Augustine's *'De Trinitate* XIV." *Augustiniana* 62 (2012): 7–43.

Zizioulas, John. *Being as Communion*. New York: St. Vladimir's Seminary Press, 1985.

———. *Communion and Otherness: Further Studies in Personhood and the Church*. Edited by Paul McPartlan. New York: Continuum, 2009.

INDEX

A

Ables, Travis, 4n9, 5n18
Allen, Prudence, 26n73
Analogy, 23–25, 38, 68–69, 140–41, 143, 200, 201n60, 205n70. *See also* Psychological analogy
Anselm, 21n54, 22n56, 57n75
Aristotle, 58–62, 64n94, 65–66, 90n71, 197
Augustine, 3, 6–7, 10, 21n55, 22n58, 52, 58n78, 59, 65n95, 68n3, 126, 206n80, 253n77, 264n5, 266
Ayres, Lewis, 21n55, 65n95, 264n5

B

Bailleux, Emile, 244n53
Balthasar, Hans Urs von, 6–9, 13n37, 26, 58n76, 71nn13–14, 85n59, 122n51, 136, 246n58, 275
Barth, Karl, 71n14, 122n51
Benedict XVI, 263n1
Blair, George, 137n6

Blankenhorn, Bernhard-Thomas, 179n110
Boff, Leonardo, 4, 33n6
Bonum Diffusivum sui. *See* Immanent procession
Bourassa, François, 20n49, 50n59, 53n64, 58n78, 139n15, 187n10, 217n103, 224, 226, 236–37
Brink, Gijsbert van den, 1n1, 165n67
Brock, Stephen L., 143n26
Buber, Martin, 18, 20n48
Bulgakov, Sergei, 81n41
Butner, Glenn D., 2n2

C

Carl, Brian, 146n34, 202n62
Clarke, Norris, 19n44, 19n47, 20n49, 139n18, 150n42, 173n88, 183nn1–2, 227n15
Coakley, Sarah, 1n1
Coleman, Rachel M., 90n69

Communion. *See* Interpersonal communion
Complacency, 258–59
Complementarity, 6–7, 8n26, 9, 26, 226n14
Consubstantiality. *See* Subsistence
Cordovilla Pérez, Angel, 5n13
Cory, Therese Scarpelli, 110n19
Craig, William Lane, 13n40, 70n11, 101n96, 213n97
Cross, Richard, 60n82

D

D'Ettore, Domenic, 23n61
Darley, Alan Philip, 23n63
Dauphinais, Michael, 49n59
David, Barry, 49n59
De Lubac, Henri, 273n32
De Maio, Andrea, 137n9
Deferrari, Roy J., 40n28, 43n41, 127n57
Doig, James C., 64n94
Dolezal, James E., 106nn5–6
Drilling, Peter, 10n31, 21n53
Dupont, Anthony, 3n3
Durand, Emmanuel, 1n1, 121n50, 164n63, 215n101, 225

E

Eades, Michael, 259n91
Emanation, 41–43, 108–12, 125n53, 156–57, 160
Emery, Gilles, 14n41, 31–32, 38, 49n57, 73n21, 88, 198, 224n7, 225–26, 236–37, 247n63; "Central Aristotelian Themes," 59nn80–81, 60n84, 146n34, 202n62; *The Trinitarian Theology of St. Thomas Aquinas*, 19n45, 20nn51–52, 21n54, 31n3, 32nn4–5, 35n10, 36n14, 38n19, 39n25, 50nn58–59, 53n61, 53n64, 55n68, 55n70, 56nn71–72, 56n74, 57n75, 59n79, 59n81, 68n4, 69n8, 86n60, 87n61, 88n63, 89n68, 91n72, 93n77, 95n83, 164n61, 183n3, 198nn51–53, 202n64, 223n1, 225n8, 226n13, 228n16, 229n18, 230n20, 230n22, 245n53, 248n66, 255n81, 265n8, 270n25, 270n27, 271nn28–29; *Trinity, Church, and the Human Person*, 38n20, 83n51, 97n88, 146n36, 190n18; *Trinity in Aquinas*, 17n42, 31n2, 32n5, 35n12, 59n79, 59n81, 82n49, 112n25, 116n39, 169n82, 194n33, 217n105
Essential love, 228–30, 252–60; as interpersonal love, 256–60

F

Face-to-face encounter, 6, 69n9, 71n13, 85n59, 101, 121–22
Faith and reason, 61–65, 107n9. *See also* Revelation
Family. *See* Image of God
Folch Gomes, Cirilo, 20n49, 139n15, 187n10, 217n103
Francis, 263n1
Friedman, Russell L., 194n.33
Fruitfulness, 59–61

G

Gauthier, R. A., 63n90
Geiger, L. B., 62n89, 63n90

INDEX

Generation, 31, 40n33, 111–12, 115–19, 125n53, 137n9, 147n37, 148–59, 164, 166–69, 171n86, 190–91, 203, 206, 250

González Alió, José Luis, 187n10, 195n44, 202n63, 207n81

Goodness as self-communicative, 171–81

Goris, Harm, 50n59, 51n60, 53n61, 55n68, 59n81, 62n87

Greshake, Gisbert, 87n62

Gunton, A. F. von, 50n59

Gunton, Colin, 4, 26, 32, 67, 136n2, 211n92, 263n2

H

Hankey, Wayne, 107n9, 217n103

Hasker, William, 3n7

Hierarchy, 109, 111–12, 125n53, 154, 156–60, 246n58

Hirschfeld, Mary, 264n3

Hochschild, Joshua P., 23nn60–65

Holmes, Stephen R., 1n1, 32n15, 59n79, 80n37

Holtz, Dominic, 69n70

Holy Spirit. *See* Love; Love-impression

Holzer, Vincent, 1n1

Hunt, Anne, 3n5, 17n42

I

Image of God, 263–74

Immanent operation, 59–61

Immanent procession, 14–15, 33–34, 36, 49, 60, 69, 74, 87, 95, 114, 118, 137–38, 140–41, 171n86, 215, 226–27, 231, 248, 252, 260, 265; as interpersonal self-giving, 143–45, 148–53, 155–62, 181–82; as paradox, 33, 39–46, 76–78, 100–101; receptivity and, 145–47; as the self-communication of goodness, 176–81

Individualism, 4, 22, 41n39, 100–101, 263–64, 274

Inner word. *See* Word

Intellect, 42, 114; active, 38, 50; act of, 36, 107n9, 239; Aristotle and, 59–63; angelic/demonic, 110, 111n22, 124, 267; divine, 55n67, 62, 105, 112, 152, 158–60, 164n63, 184n4, 199–203, 217, 221n108, 229; human, 63, 110, 142, 193n32; and understanding/word, 34–35, 51–53, 71–72, 149–52, 158–59, 167, 179, 186, 188–98, 239–41; and will, 20–21, 25, 36, 65n15, 172, 177–78, 181, 183, 209, 238, 264, 270. *See also* Interpersonal Knowledge; Self-Knowledge; Understanding; Word

Interpersonal communion, 1, 247–48, 275

Interpersonal Knowledge, 1, 11–12, 26–27, 275; as self-giving, 218–20; as self-knowledge, 184–85, 212–14, 261

Interpersonal Love, 1, 11–12, 26–27, 275; as interpersonal communion, 245–48; as self-giving, 243–48; and self-love, 231–37, 242–43, 261, 266–67

Izquierdo, Cesar, 112n25, 120n48

J

John Paul II, 13n37, 140n18, 188n10, 251n74
Johnson, Elizabeth, 33n6, 87n62
Juvenal, Merriel D., 264n4

K

Kasper, Walter, 20n48
Keaty, Anthony, 223n1, 224nn5–6
Kelly, Anthony, 136–37
Kilby, Karen, 40n30, 41n39, 46n50, 49n57, 80n37, 263n1
Knowledge. *See* Interpersonal knowledge; Self-knowledge
Ku, John Baptist, 164n61, 164n63, 168n73, 225

L

Lafont, Ghislain, 90n70
Legge, Dominic, 14n41, 164n61, 217n103
Levering, Matthew, 8–9, 14n41, 17n42, 20n50, 34n8, 49n57, 59n80, 80n37, 137n7, 139nn16–17, 169n82, 225, 246n58
Liberto, David, 227n15
Lonergan, Bernard, 10, 20n49, 139n15, 188n13, 190n18, 193n30, 194n34, 196n45, 197n45, 198n52
Long, D. Stephen, 107n9, 180n113
Long, Steven A., 23n65, 69n7, 140n19
Love, 1–3, 5–7, 11–16, 20, 22, 24–27, 31, 33–37, 41, 47–49, 55–56, 59, 66–71, 73–79, 81–87, 92n76, 95, 99–100, 103–5, 108n10, 131, 135, 137, 138n10, 140–45, 171, 177–80, 183–84, 185n8, 213n97, 215n102, 221n108, 223–61, 264–75. *See also* Essential love; Interpersonal love; Love-impression; Notional love; Personal love; Self-love
Love-impression, 35–36, 38n18, 39, 49, 66, 68, 104–6, 140–42, 144, 215n102, 226–31, 233–34, 237, 248, 252–60, 270; development of Thomas's teaching regarding, 56–57; as distinct from the lover, 56–57, 66; as proceeding from a word, 229–30. *See also* Immanent procession
Loyer, Kenneth M., 225, 226n13

M

Malloy, Christopher J., 20n50
Maspero, Giulio, 1n1
McCabe, Herbert, 20n50, 139n16
McCall, Thomas H, 1n1, 12n36, 13n40, 19n46
McDermott, John D., 213n97
McNall, Joshua, 3n4, 4n9, 67n1
Milbank, John, 107n9
Moltmann, Jürgen, 4, 13n40, 27n70, 32, 58n76, 58n77, 100, 101n96, 136n2, 211n92, 263n2, 275

N

Nedoncelle, Maurice, 6n19, 8n26
Neo-Platonism, 176n98
Nieuwenhove, Rik van, 171n85, 264n4
Notional action, 92n76
Notional love, 228–32, 234, 249, 252–56, 259

INDEX

O

O'Callaghan, John, 63, 64n94
Ormerod, Neil, 3n4
Oster, Stephan, 135n1, 183n2, 230n19
Ouellet, Marc, 6n19, 7n20, 163n59, 164n64, 165n67

P

Paissac, Hyacinthe, 38, 50n59, 54nn66–67, 55n69, 63n90, 91n72, 112n25, 197n49
Pannenberg, Wolfhart, 4–5, 33n7, 41n39, 67, 70nn10–11, 107n9, 136n2, 211n92
Penido, M. T. L., 22n52, 56n74, 171n86, 185n8, 224, 226, 235–37, 244n53
Personal love, 228–31, 252–55, 260
Person. *See* Subsistence; Personhood
Personhood, 19–21, 67–70, 74, 120n48; of divine Love, 67–69; of the divine Word, 67–69; as subsistent relation, 10–11, 20n52, 81n41, 86–87. *See also* Subsistence; Subsistent relation
Phan, Peter C., 4
Pieper, Josef, 18n43, 197n50
Plantinga, Cornelius, 13n40, 101n96
Political, 194, 263–64
Porro, Pasquale, 154n46
Psychological analogy: Balthasar's olive branch to, 6; contemporary Thomist, 7–11; modern rejection of, 4–5, 12, 14, 100; not the same in every theologian, 21–23, 264n5; Thomas's, 12, 14–16, 19–27, 32–33, 41n39, 49n57, 50, 57–58, 68–71, 74, 78, 85–87, 92, 95–96, 99, 101, 103, 107, 125–26, 130–31, 136–37, 140–43, 163n58, 164–67, 184, 187, 203, 216, 220, 226–28, 235–37, 253, 260, 271–72

R

Rahner, Karl, 5–6, 25n69, 69n9, 213n97
Ratzinger, Joseph, 3n7, 13n39, 107n9, 150n42
Rea, Michael C., 12n36, 13n40, 19n46
Receptivity, 139–40; and the Word, 145–47. *See also* Immanent procession
Relation: *esse* and *ratio*, 87–92; relative opposition, 93–95. *See also* Subsistent relation
Revelation, 17n42, 36, 45n48, 57–66, 104, 112–14, 123, 126–27, 166, 169n82, 251n73, 193n32, 125n53, 253n78, 256n82
Richard, R. L., 32n5
Rodríguez, Luis Fernández, 194n34
Rossner, William, 259nn91–92
Rousselot, Pierre, 26n73, 108n9

S

Schindler, D. C., 13nn37–38, 26n73, 69n94, 78n34, 135n1, 183n2, 194n33, 230n19
Schindler, David L., 139n18, 150n42, 251n74
Schmaus, Michael, 22n59
Schmitz, Kenneth L., 139n18, 150n42
Schumacher, Lydia, 107n9
Scola, Angelo, 163nn59–60
Scripture. *See* Revelation

Self-communication. *See* Goodness as self-communicative; Immanent procession; Self-giving

Self-giving, 135–45, 148–53, 155–62, 275; and simplicity, 142–45. *See also* Immanent procession; Interpersonal Knowledge; Interpersonal Love; Self-Knowledge; Self-Love

Self-Knowledge, 2, 11–12, 26–27; as interpersonal knowledge, 184–85, 201–8, 212–18, 261, 266–67; as self-giving, 218–20

Self-Love, 2, 11–12, 26–27, 261; as interpersonal communion, 245–48; as interpersonal love, 231–37, 242–43, 261, 266–67; as self-giving, 243–48

Self-possession, 2

Sexton, Jason S., 87n62

Sherwin, Michael, 238n34, 253n77, 258n86, 259n92

Simonin, H. D., 55n70, 107n9, 241n44, 243n48, 258n86

Simplicity. *See* Self-giving; Subsistence

Slotemaker, John T., 3n3, 21n53, 22n59

Smith, Timothy L., 5n16, 20n48, 32n5

Social Trinitarianism, 1–6, 11–13, 14n41, 21–22, 25, 187n62, 100–101, 104–6, 125–45, 163, 165, 263–64, 273–75

Son. *See* Word

Speaker, 35n12, 37–39, 46n49, 55, 93n76, 121, 142, 145, 149, 189, 204, 207, 228–29, 231–32, 243–45, 251, 254, 258, 264n12;

divine Speaker, 42n39, 46n49, 72–74, 85, 96, 104, 108, 114–25, 132, 140, 144, 146, 150, 159–60, 162, 165, 183–84, 189n13, 200, 201n60, 204, 207, 210, 212n93, 213n97, 215, 218, 221n108, 227, 234–37, 244–45, 247–48, 252, 264

Speltz, George H, 264n3

Speyr, Adrienne von, 13n39, 25n72

Subsistence (Subsist/Subsistent), 15, 20, 61n85, 68–71, 92nn75–76, 94–96, 98–99, 114, 124, 142, 145–47, 151–53, 166, 177, 183, 210, 212, 213n97, 227, 246, 252; and action, 201–3; and consubstantiality, 106–8, 123–31; of the divine Love, 67–69; of the divine Word, 67–69; and simplicity, 71–74, 104–8, 113, 123–25; as radical distinction, 85; as standing-outside, 70, 75–85, 120–22

Subsistent relation, 4, 10–11, 20n52, 70n10, 81n41, 86, 87n62, 96, 226. *See also* Personhood; Subsistence

Sutton, Matthew Lewis, 246n58

S

Tanner, Kathryn, 1n1

Te Veldi, Rudi, 20n50, 139n16

Torrell, Jean-Pierre, 14n41, 34n8, 62n87, 63n90, 64n94, 153n46, 225, 248n66

Trinitarian Revivals, 1, 5, 14n41, 59n79. *See also* Social Trinitarianism

INDEX

T

Ulrich, Ferdinand, 19n44, 46n50, 90n69, 154n47
Understanding (Understand), 15, 20, 33–37, 39, 46n49, 51–54, 57n75, 60–61, 63, 64n94, 65–66, 71–73, 105, 110–14, 145–46, 148, 151–53, 158, 160, 177–79, 181–84, 186, 188–209, 211–15, 217–20, 221n108, 228–29, 239–40, 242, 252–54, 255n80, 256–57, 260n93, 261, 266. *See also* Interpersonal Knowledge; Self-Knowledge; Word

V

Vagaggini, Cyprian, 107n9
Vanier, Paul, 137n6, 171n86, 178n104

W

Waldstein, Michael, 7–8, 13n37, 137n7, 154n47
Waldstein, Susan, 108n11
Walker, Adrian J., 6n19, 10, 19n44
Weinandy, Thomas, 227n15
White, Thomas Joseph, 10–11, 22n59, 75n29, 91n72, 137n8, 150n42, 198n53, 200n57, 201n60, 217n103
Wilkins, Jeremy Daniel, 5n17, 137n6, 171, 172n87, 175n95, 176, 177n100, 178n104, 180n112, 188n13

Williams, A. N., 53n64
Williams, Rowan, 187n10, 264n5
Williams, Scott M., 21n54, 60, 213n97
Wippel, John, 43n42
Word: development of Thomas's teaching regarding, 50–55; as distinct from its speaker, 47–50, 53–54, 66; as divine Son, 115–17, 151–53, 158–61, 164–70; as the foundation of the act of understanding, 188–93; as illuminating paradox of an immanent procession, 47–50; as loved in the act of love, 238–42; as receptive, 145–47, 149–50; as revealed, 57–66; as that in which intellect understands, 197–201; as understood in the act of understanding, 194–201
Wozniak, Robert J., 1n1

Y

Yin Yam, Cheuk, 3n3

Z

Zizioulas, John, 4, 20n48, 58n76